Woolf Studies Annual

Volume 17, 2011

Pace University Press • New York

Pace University Press
41 Park Row, Rm. 1510
New York, NY 10038

Printed in the United States of America

ISSN 1080-9317
ISBN 978-1-935625-05-6 (pbk: alk.ppr.)

Member

Council of Editors of Learned Journals

Paper used in this publication meets the minimum requirements of
American National Standard for Information
Sciences–Permanence of Paper for Printed Library Materials,
ANSI Z39.48–1984

Many thanks to readers for volume 17: Andrea Adolph (Kent SU); Stephen Barber (U of Rhode Island); David Bradshaw (Oxford U); Mary Ann Caws (Graduate Ctr, CUNY); Rita Charon (Columbia U); Patrick Collier (Ball SU); Emily Dalgarno (Boston U); Jeanne Dubino (Appalachian SU); David Eberly (Independent Scholar); Penny Farfan (U of Calgary); Christine Froula (Northwestern U); Evelyn Haller (Doane C); Emily Hinnov (Southern New Hampshire U); Molly Hite (Cornell U); Erica Johnson (Wagner C); Georgia Johnston (St. Louis U); Michael Lackey (U of Minnesota); Phyllis Lassner (Northwestern U); Merry Pawlowski (California SU Bakersfield); Anna Snaith (Kings C London); Janet Winston (Humboldt SU); Marilyn Zucker (Stony Brook U).

Woolf Studies Annual is indexed in *Humanities International Complete, ABELL* and the *MLA Bibliography.*

Contents

Woolf Studies Annual

Volume 17, 2011

Abbreviations

AHH	*A Haunted House*
AROO	*A Room of One's Own*
BP	*Books and Portraits*
BTA	*Between the Acts*
CDB	*The Captain's Death Bed and Other Essays*
CE	*Collected Essays* (4 vols.)
CR1	*The Common Reader*
CR2	*The Common Reader, Second Series*
CSF	*The Complete Shorter Fiction*
D	*The Diary of Virginia Woolf* (5 vols.)
DM	*The Death of the Moth and Other Essays*
E	*The Essays of Virginia Woolf* (6 Vols.)
F	*Flush*
FR	*Freshwater*
GR	*Granite & Rainbow: Essays*
JR	*Jacob's Room*
L	*The Letters of Virginia Woolf* (6 Vols.)
M	*The Moment and Other Essays*
MEL	*Melymbrosia*
MOB	*Moments of Being*
MT	*Monday or Tuesday*
MD	*Mrs. Dalloway*
ND	*Night and Day*
O	*Orlando*
PA	*A Passionate Apprentice*
RF	*Roger Fry: A Biography*
TG	*Three Guineas*
TTL	*To the Lighthouse*
TW	*The Waves*
TY	*The Years*
VO	*The Voyage Out*

"With Anger and Emphasis": The Proof Copy of *A Room of One's Own*

Isaac Gewirtz

Probably no other work by Virginia Woolf except for *To the Lighthouse* has influenced the world of letters more than the extended essay which she published in October 1929 as *A Room of One's Own*.[1] Concepts and terminology that are now common in learned and even popular parlance in the fields of literary criticism, aesthetics, gender studies, psychology, and political theory can trace their emergence (if not their origin) to this exploration of the topic of women and literature, often brilliantly woven into the fabric of a semi-fictional narrative. Consequently, students of Virginia Woolf and of English literary modernism have reason to be pleased that the proof copy of *A Room of One's Own*, never having been the subject of a published, systematic study, is now available to scholars and researchers for study, following its purchase in July 2007 by the New York Public Library's Henry W. and Albert A. Berg Collection of English and American Literature.[2]

The book originated in two lectures that Woolf delivered in October 1928 at, respectively, Girton and Newnham Colleges, which at the time were Cambridge University's and Britain's only women's residential colleges.[3] In February 1928, Woolf had accepted the invitation of Newnham's Arts Society to speak in May on "Women and Fiction"; Girton's ODTAA [One damn thing after another] Society invited her for the same purpose, perhaps at the same time or very soon after she

[1] Three editions were published in 1929. The first was printed by Robert S. Josephy and published in New York by the Fountain Press on October 21, 1929 (almost a year to the day after delivering the Newnham lecture), and in London by Woolf's own Hogarth Press on October 24. The press run comprised 492 numbered copies, of which 450 were for sale, each copy signed by Woolf, and the first 100 reserved for sale in Great Britain. The second edition, with title page showing that it was published solely by the Hogarth Press, was issued on October 24, and is the first exclusively British edition, in effect a trade edition, printed in 3040 copies, and reprinted in the second through fifth impressions in November-December 1929, with the fifth appearing in March 1930 (each of these impressions being printed in approximately the same number of copies as the first). The third edition constitutes the first American trade edition and was published in New York by Harcourt, Brace and Co. on October 24 1929 in 4000 copies. See B. J. Kirkpatrick, *A Bibliography of Virginia Woolf, Third Edition* (Oxford: Clarendon Press, 1980) which contains a complete and detailed account of the book's printing history.

[2] To see the record in the NYPL catalog (http://catalog.nypl.org/), the most straightforward option is to search by title.

[3] Girton was co-founded in 1869 by the suffragist Sarah Emily Davies and by the artist and women's rights activist Barbara Bodichon; Newnham was co-founded in 1871 by the suffragist Millicent Garrett Fawcett and the Cambridge philosopher Henry Sidgwick.

delivered the Newnham lecture.[4] But illness and the need to complete the novel *Orlando* delayed her Newnham appearance until the evening of October 20th, when she arrived an hour late for the dinner given in her honor, accompanied by Vanessa Bell and Bell's daughter Angelica, as well as by an unexpected guest, Virginia's husband, Leonard, whose presence upset the seating arrangements.[5] In *A Room of One's Own*, she would lampoon and lament the meal's mediocrity, which she saw as a telling, though apparently mundane, case in point that typified the shameful neglect shown by women of means toward the two impoverished bastions of women's higher education.[6] Of course, one of the chief points of *A Room* is that what we commonly regard as the mundane circumstances of a writer's or would-be writer's life—that is, the extent of their financial means and the independence, privacy, and leisure thereby made possible or impossible—actually play a crucial role in their potential creative success or failure. Our usual unwillingness to recognize this fact, Woolf argued, reflects a romantic and sentimental understanding of creative endeavor and accomplishment. Such sentimentalizing, she noticed, has been especially attractive to male critics when they contemplate the relative scarcity of women writers, since most of them, angry at women for reasons that Woolf painfully and painstakingly discovers and pitilessly dissects, believe that women are incapable of significant literary or artistic achievement.

On October 26th, accompanied by Vita Sackville-West, Woolf returned to Cambridge to deliver what was probably a somewhat different lecture on the same topic, before Girton's ODTAA. The manuscripts containing the texts of the lectures have yet to be discovered and probably do not survive, but Woolf's wording of her introductory notice in the first edition of *A Room* (in the proof copy, it appears as a footnote to the book's title that heads the first page of text) regarding the genesis of the book leads one to believe that the lectures differed from each other to some degree. Woolf informs us, "This essay is based upon two papers read to the Arts Society at Newnham and the ODTAA at Girton in October 1928. The papers were too long to be read in full, and have since been altered and expanded." If she had delivered the same paper at each venue, would not a more accurate wording of the events have read, "This essay is based on *a paper* read to" etc.? But perhaps she wished only to give the impression that she had written two different papers, or perhaps she was merely imprecise in her wording. Regardless, we can gather

[4] I have not been able to find a reference in Woolf's diaries or letters to the date when she received the Girton invitation.

[5] From the account of lecture attendee Elsie Elizabeth Phare (b. 1908), a Newnham student, and in 1928 the secretary of the Arts Society, as cited by S. P. Rosenbaum (xv).

[6] In the narrative portion of the essay, the two colleges are conflated into a single institution, Fernham, mirroring her conflation of Cambridge and Oxford into "Oxbridge." She wished to be clear that what she had to say about her experience at Cambridge should be understood as typifying the attitudes of Britain's educational and cultural establishment.

little definite information about the content of the two papers even from her diary, which does not mention the Newnham lecture's content, nor of her impression of the Newnham event (except for an evaluation of the Newnham students), nor of the lecture's reception.

Woolf does provide some information in her diary about the Girton lecture, though her remarks (in her entry for Saturday, October 27th) are confined largely to her impression of the students, to what she perceived as their casual irreverence toward her (which she does not seem to mind), and to the energizing effect on her of the entire experience. But the reference to the lecture's content is very brief. Here is the Girton portion of the entry in its entirety: "Thank God, my long toil at the women's lecture is this moment ended. I am back from speaking at Girton in floods of rain. Starved but valiant young women—that's my impression. Intelligent, eager, poor; & destined to become schoolmistresses in shoals. I blandly told them to drink wine & have a room of their own. Why should all the splendour, all the luxury of life be lavished on the Julians [she had visited her nephew Julian Bell at King's College just prior to the Girton lecture] & the Francises, & none on the Phares & the Thomases? [for Phare see note 5; Margaret Thomas was one of the ODTAA members who had invited Woolf to Girton.] There's Julian not much relishing it, perhaps. [...][7] I felt elderly & mature. And nobody respected me. They were very eager, egotistical, or rather not much impressed by age & repute. Very little reverence or that sort of thing about" (*D*3 200-01).

Woolf's "bland" and absurdly reductive diary summary of the content of her talk was clearly intended in a spirit of humorous self-deprecation. The diary summary is amusing precisely because it is both an utterly inadequate recapitulation of her complex cultural, historical, and literary argument, and because it is accurate, or, if one prefers, not *in*accurate. Undeniably, embedded in Woolf's seemingly off-hand synopsis is one of her work's essential propositions—that being able to afford a room of one's own, a (good) glass of wine, and the other creature comforts that these amenities represent are the material circumstances without which gifted women cannot hope to write at all, and certainly not express freely whatever literary gift they may possess. Even Shakespeare could not have thrived under such conditions. His plays, Woolf says at the beginning of Chapter 3, are like spider webs that "seem to hang there complete in themselves," unattached to life. But she is acutely aware "that these webs are not spun in mid-air by incorporeal creatures,

[7] The elided portion of the entry reads: "I fancy sometimes the world changes. I think I see reason spreading, but I should have liked closer & thicker knowledge of life. I should have liked to deal with real things sometimes. I get such a sense of tingling & vitality from an evening talk like that; one's angularities & obscurities are smoothed & lit. How little one counts, I think: how little anyone counts; how fast & furious & masterly life is; & how all these thousands are swimming for dear life."

but are the work of suffering human beings and are attached to grossly material things, like health and money and the houses we live in" (58 [41-42]).[8]

The Newnham student E. E. Phare's testimony regarding Woolf's Newnham lecture, cited by Rosenbaum (xv), in fact refers to Woolf talking about the legal and customary limitations which so severely restricted women's financial independence, one of the results of which was that they were unable to write anywhere but in their parlors. This and more, Woolf says, accounts for the relative paucity of women authors through the centuries. Rosenbaum gathers from Woolf's summary of her Girton talk (young women should "drink wine and have a room of their own") that "This does not sound quite like her Newnham paper" (Rosenbaum xvii). But it seems to me that there is every reason to believe (as I have tried to make clear above) that Woolf's views regarding the effect of a would-be writer's material circumstances on the would-be writer's prospects for success was presented not only at Girton but at Newnham.

Though we do not know exactly how the lectures evolved into the early drafts of the book that we know as *A Room of One's Own*, we can now see how Woolf, on the eve of the book's publication, made numerous, substantive changes to her text. Generally, the discovery of a proof copy of a well-known work does not excite great interest. By the time a work is out of galleys, most substantive changes have been incorporated into the text, and by the time a proof copy has been printed, only the correction of typographical and orthographic errors or the occasional, minor alteration of word order should be expected. However, the proof copy of *A Room* contains scores of passages (see the Appendix below) which differ substantively from those which appear in the text of the first and subsequent editions of the work.[9] In view of the importance of this literary artifact and because it is difficult to anticipate the ways in which the physical description of a volume may be used to advance our understanding of the text contained between its covers, an illustrated description follows.

The volume is bound in green printed papers decorated with yellow dots and black crescent shadows pasted on binder's boards, and with the title and author's name gilt tooled within gilt borders on a green calfskin rectangle affixed to the top board (see Figure 1). The title page bears the Hogarth Press imprint (Figure 2), and the book was printed in Edinburgh by R. & R. Clark, Limited, according to the statement on the title page verso. The blue, oval Clark stamp, in the center of

[8] Page references are to the first (Fountain) edition unless otherwise noted. In brackets following this reference is the page number of the corresponding passage in the 2005 Harcourt paperback edition.

[9] The lecture from which this article grew, delivered at the New York Public Library's Stephen A. Schwarzman Building, Celeste Bartos South Court Auditorium in the Fall of 2010, was titled "When Is a Book As Good As a Manuscript?: The Proof Copy of *A Room of One's Own*," to reflect the presence of these numerous differences.

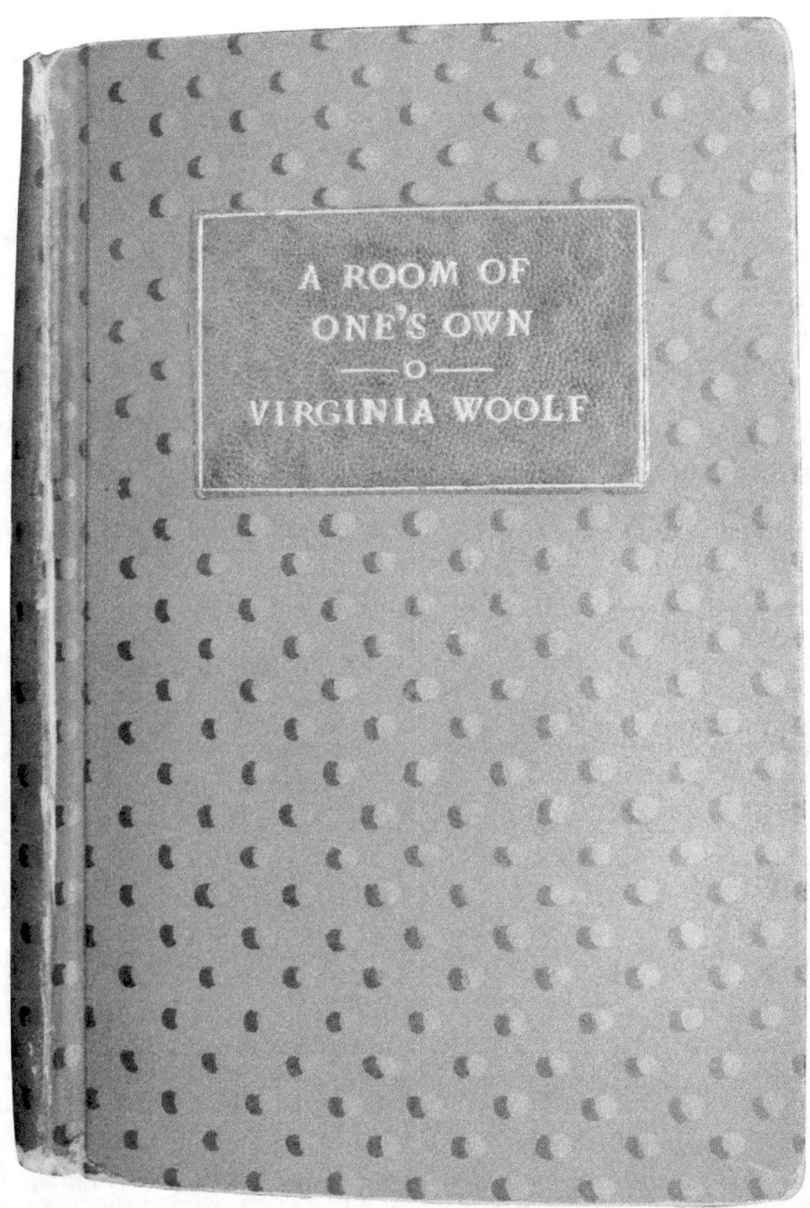

Figure 1: Cover of A Room of One's Own *proof copy*

A ROOM OF ONE'S OWN

BY

VIRGINIA WOOLF

Published by Leonard and Virginia Woolf at the Hogarth Press, 52 Tavistock Square, London, W.C.

1929

Figure 2: Title page from A Room of One's Own *proof copy*

which is the date, beginning 10-JUL-1929 on the half-title page and ending with 22-JUL-1929 on p.161, indicating the date of printing, appears at the bottom of several pages, accompanied by the stamp "FIRST PROOF" at the top of the page (see the half-title page, Figure 3). The papers covering the binding boards have the simple, almost rustic appearance of those that were sometimes used at Hogarth, and the volume may have been bound by Woolf, probably after she revised it. The proof copy's type imposition; the order of its preliminaries, including the half-title page, the list of works by Woolf, and the title page; the text beginning on p. 5—all of this is identical to what is printed in the Hogarth Press edition, according to Kirkpatrick, except that the latter paginates the fourth page (whereas no page number for this page appears in the proof copy), and the text ends on page 172 instead of the proof copy's page 176, a consequence of Woolf's deleting more text from the proof copy than she added to it. As for manuscript evidence of revision within the proof text, no *words* in Woolf's or anyone else's hand are present. But the revision or deletion of lengthy passages are usually accompanied by a light pencil line in the outer and, occasionally, inner margins. (A handful of small, penned and penciled checks appear in the text, but these do not appear beside any passages that were revised or deleted.)[10]

That the proof copy text of *A Room* was so heavily revised should draw the eager attention of anyone who has studied the book's complicated textual evolution and has read Woolf's diary entries about her struggles with the text. The most comprehensive investigation into this process has been undertaken by S. P. Rosenbaum, who realized that what had been thought to be a single Woolf manuscript (housed at the Fitzwilliam Museum) of five chapters titled "Women & Fiction" actually comprises two manuscripts, and who transcribed the texts of those manuscripts, as well as of manuscript pages that are part of the Monks House Papers at the University of Sussex, most of which form a section that links the two groups of Fitzwilliam drafts. In his introduction, Rosenbaum lucidly traces the complex relationships of the Fitzwilliam and Monks House manuscripts and also advances a convincing hypothesis regarding the work's emergence from the two lectures.[11] He also helpfully cites earlier and later talks and publications by Woolf on aspects of topics explored in *A Room*, most notably Woolf's 1929 article "Women and Fiction" published in *The Forum*,[12] which he also transcribes.

10 See, for instance, p. 18, which may be an "x," with the check made in pen, and the diagonal cross line (making the "x") in pencil; and p. 20, which also contains what looks like an indecipherable word, but which may be a check mark over which a squiggle has been inscribed in black pen.

11 Assuming that, as seems likely, the lectures differed at least somewhat from each other.

12 *The Forum* (New York, March 1929, p. 179-183).

Figure 3: Half-title page from A Room of One's Own *proof copy*

In addition, Rosenbaum provides a transcription of selected passages from Woolf's typescript of *A Room* (housed among the Monk's House Papers at Sussex), which, as he notes, Woolf sent to Harcourt Brace in May or June 1929. Rosenbaum based his selection on what he regarded as "The most important differences between the typescript and the first editions" (176). But when different readers examine any complex literary text, it is almost inevitable that they will arrive at different conclusions regarding which passages are "most important." The "most important" or at least highly significant differences that I have discovered in the course of a line-by-line comparison of the proof copy text and the text of the first edition are far more numerous than those indicated in Rosenbaum's selective transcriptions from the Monks House typescript. Some of them will be discussed in this article; the rest will await analysis in this or other forums. The Appendix that I have provided below comprises a transcription of those passages in which the proof copy text differs from the text of the first edition. In compiling this list I have not imposed my judgment on what is or is not important, and have noted every textual change, however insignificant (others may find significance where I do not), including any alteration in word order or tense, typographical errors (few), orthographic differences (again, rare), grammatical errors (even rarer), and punctuation changes,[13] including those reflecting differences between British and American usage in punctuation marks that are adjacent to closed quotation marks. In two instances, I have provided a word in brackets, the absence of which makes the phrase ungrammatical. In those two instances, Woolf changed the passages in the first edition in a manner that omitted the ungrammatical words. If I did not supply the brackets, the reader might falsely suspect that the grammatical error was made by me in transcription.[14]

[13] But the placement of even a comma, as we know, can alter meaning, as in this example:
Proof copy: p. 141-142: "half forgotten perhaps, quite trivial things"
First ed: p. 130: "half forgotten, perhaps quite trivial things"
Consider also the replacement of a conjunction by a colon:
Proof Copy, p. 36: "of the admirable smoke and drink and the deep arm-chairs and the pleasant carpets **and of** the urbanity, the geniality, the dignity which are the offspring of luxury and privacy and space."
First ed., p. 32: "of the admirable smoke and drink and the deep arm-chairs and the pleasant carpets**:** the urbanity, the geniality, the dignity which are the offspring of luxury and privacy and space."
The colon helps emphasize that good tobacco and drink, and deep arm-chairs, i.e., the physical goods that wealth affords, are signifiers of the presence of urbanity, geniality, and dignity, which are born of luxury, privacy and space.

[14] At this point, I would be negligent if I did not thank Mark Hussey, the Editor of *Woolf Studies Annual*, whose efforts, over and above those usually afforded by an editor, greatly enhanced the accuracy and completeness of the Appendix. His checking of the emendations listed in the Appendix against the proof copy, as well as against the Hogarth edition of October 24 and the Harcourt, Brace edition of the same date, allowed him to correct my errors and omissions.

An examination of Rosenbaum's selected transcriptions from the Monks House typescript, i.e., those in which the typescript differs from the first edition in what he identified as "very important" ways, reveals that some of the typescript passages were revised before passing into the proof copy, meaning, no doubt, that a second typescript was prepared bearing these revisions, and that, then, those proof copy passages were significantly revised again for the first edition, which changes would have been embodied in a third typescript. (Whether separate ribbon copy typescripts or carbons of the third typescript were used for the Hogarth Press and Harcourt Brace editions is not known. In any case, no typescript in either ribbon or carbon copy is known to survive.) Because I have not yet seen the Monks House typescript or a facsimile of it, I have not been able to compare it with the proof copy and, therefore, cannot say which of the other differences between the proof copy and the first edition that I have noted were already present in the typescript. I must assume that many are not, since they seem to me so important that I doubt that Rosenbaum would have omitted them from his selection of "very important" differences.[15]

Before commencing our analysis of the most important variants between the proof copy and first edition texts, we should acknowledge the importance of identifying even those passages that Woolf transcribed into the proof text verbatim (or nearly so) from the Monks House typescript and which she changed only upon rereading the proof. One might think that for such passages, since they do not differ from the Monks House typescript, the proof copy would be irrelevant. Not so. That these passages survived Woolf's scrutiny until the very last moment is itself significant, revealing how strongly she felt about what they stated or implied, to the extent that she felt compelled to shift and, in some cases, reverse their sense. Accordingly, I have included the more remarkable of these changes (limited by what I could compile from Rosenbaum's selective transcriptions) among my analyses and interpretations of the changes that Woolf, in preparing the first edition text, had made to proof copy passages that themselves bear no change made to the Monks House typescript text.

As an introduction to our comparison of the proof copy and the first edition, it will be useful to examine the initial footnote that appears in the proof copy and which appears in the first edition printed in italic on the recto of the leaf following

[15] This uncertainty makes it important that the Monks House typescript be digitized and fully transcribed, and that the differences between the typescript and the first edition be identified and published. At the very least, I hope that my Appendix will be annotated by a careful scholar who has access to the typescript, and that s/he will indicate which of the proof text passages that I have identified as differing from the first edition reflect a revision of the typescript, and which of the proof text passages that I have identified as differing from the first edition passed into the proof copy unchanged. I intend to publish the Appendix on the New York Public Library website so that researchers who do not read *Woolf Studies Annual* may have access to the Appendix, and so that all researchers will benefit from the ease of working with an electronic document.

the title page and preceding the half-title. The note, as we saw above, informs us that in writing the book Woolf expanded the two papers that she read at Newnham and Girton. As the reader soon discovers, a good portion of the expansion is due to the introductory, semi-fictional narrative that Woolf creates, in which she conflates the two visits into one, and describes what she did on this visit, what she saw, reacted to, reflected on, and felt. Cambridge has become "Oxbridge"—not the first time the term was used in print (Thackeray was probably the first, in the late 1840s), but its appearance in *A Room of One's Own* is arguably most responsible for its popularity. Its use is significant because the book was intended, in large part, as an exposure of the misogyny of England's patriarchal educational and social elite, whose training grounds were Oxford and Cambridge. In the first edition of *A Room*, about half of the 200 or so emended passages contain changes of word order that do not appreciably affect the sense of what had appeared in the proof text, though they seem to have been intended as stylistic improvements, and may largely be regarded as such. Only two dozen or so passages contain punctuation changes, and the proof contains a mere handful of typos. But more than seventy of the changes alter the sense of the passages significantly.

Many of the changes occur in passages that contain, in Woolf's characteristically allusive, subtle, and often elliptical fashion, references to dense and complex ideas. The alterations to these passages are interesting in themselves—that is, in the shifts, even reversals, of meaning they impart to the text. But they are also interesting *en masse*, in the characteristics that they share. Most of them flatten and chill the tone of passages marked by confessional immediacy, by an anger that crackles with wit and mockery, by vivid metaphor, by dramatic scenes depicting the dynamic of male-female relationships, and by a rhythmic alternation of arguments entertainingly elaborated, explored, and consummated in robust detail, and slyly elliptical musings of the kind we have seen flicker across the minds of Woolf's fictional characters. True, much of the vibrant spirit, subtlety, and, certainly, acute psychological and cultural analysis remains in the published text; the book is an astonishing achievement. But equally certain is that Woolf's editorial surgery, which reshaped her genre-melding essayistic journey into a more traditional and formal polemic bled much of the life out of it, as she exchanged metaphor and colloquialism for abstraction, the particular for the general, the hortatory for the expositive, the contemplative essayist's nuanced and tentative reflection for the partisan's certitude,[16] and imagined scenes rich in drama and psychological insight for well wrought but prosaic declarations of principles.

[16] For instance, when the narrator critiques the novel of a young, contemporary author named "Mary Carmichael," she is more frank and expansive in the proof copy than in the emended first edition text about her inability to say exactly what aspects of an author's writing she likes before she has finished reading one of the author's works (p. 127): "and I

Why did Woolf make so many changes in the proof copy, so late in the editorial day? Many of the changes, as I noted above, are purely stylistic (or as "pure," i.e., free from implications about meaning, as a stylistic change can ever be said to be);[17] they clarify the sense or read more smoothly than the readings that they replace; and some of them correct punctuation and orthography. But what of the others, the changes that significantly affect the meaning? Many of them reflect a desire to soften or reverse the meaning of passages that might be read as stereotypical portrayals of women (as being too angry at men, self-pitying, incapable of intellectual analysis, vague, or uncertain), or which might make women appear as complicit partners in their own oppression. Others, again, have a different origin. This study's title is a phrase taken from a passage that appears toward the end of Chapter 4, as Woolf identifies the fatal flaw in most of the novels written by women in the early nineteenth century: "One has only to skim those old forgotten novels and listen to the tone of voice in which they are written to divine that the writer was meeting criticism; she was saying this by way of aggression, or that by way of conciliation. She was admitting that she was 'only a woman', or protesting that she was 'as good as a man'. She met that criticism as her temperament dictated, with docility and diffidence, or with anger and emphasis. It does not matter which it was; she was thinking of something other than the thing itself" (103 [73]). Woolf herself wrote much of *A Room of One's Own* "with anger and emphasis," and, as we will see below, at the last moment softened or even reversed the meaning of some of her angriest and most emphatic passages, including some of the best. This she did not from "docility and diffidence," but under the influence of a doctrine of literary creativity that regarded the expression of the "personal" as incompatible with the purest expression of artistic truth. Woolf's central proposition, as expressed in her title, is that women must have the financial means to acquire the private and quiet space, the leisure, and, yes, the decent food and drink that will allow

---

was beginning to enjoy some quality in her style—**I know not what—(one must wait till the end to name these things)**; if she has a room to herself, of which I am not quite sure, if she has five hundred a year of her own—" etc. The first edition text omits the bolded phrase (p. 117): "and I was beginning to enjoy some quality in her style; if she has a room to herself, of which I am not quite sure; if she has five hundred a year of her own—" etc.

[17] But we should always be cautious about distinguishing too categorically between style and content, the relationship of which is a subject that has inspired systematic study, rigorous theorizing, and fierce polemics in the West from Cicero to the most formidably learned Renaissance humanists, including Leonardo Bruni, Lefèvre d'Étaples, and Erasmus. Woolf herself alludes in *A Room* to the difficulty of disentangling style from content when she wonders why Thackeray wrote the way he did. Was the style natural to him or was he was striving for an effect?: "But then one would have to decide what is style and what is meaning, a question which—" (9). Here is a characteristic example of Woolf's highly sophisticated wit; a brief phrase that points allusively and elliptically to something profound in a way that illustrates itself.

them to channel their creative energies into their writing. But she does not ignore psychological factors, most of which are linked to the writer's need to transcend her conditioning and personality. Only such transcendence, in Woolf's view, will enable the writer to look upon the "thing in itself," free of resentment and biased judgment, and thereby allow her to express her creativity in its most perfect form.

T. S. Eliot first formulated this theory in his landmark essay on the relationship of poetic creativity to tradition, in "Tradition and the Individual Talent" (1919).[18] According to Eliot, great poetry can be written only if it conforms to (not imitates) the culture's grand poetic tradition (in his and Woolf's case, the Western tradition) and, within that, the poetic tradition of the poet's "own country." Eliot believes that "the historical sense compels" a good poet to write with the feeling that the entirety of European literature (not just the best of it, but the most authentic), including that of his own country, is "in his bones." For Eliot, great poems, the great works of literature in general, exist in "an ideal order," where relationships among the works are modified by each new work that enters the order. In this timeless, ideal realm, the works converse with each other and modify each other's meanings; not only past works influencing those created in the present, but new works influencing the meaning of those created in the past. The most important factor that determines whether or not a poet will succeed in creating a poem that is good or authentic enough to join the ideal order is the "extinction of [his or her] personality," which s/he will accomplish by digesting and transmuting "the passions." Eliot's corollary to this principle is that great poetry owes its greatness not to the intensity of emotion that may have prompted its composition, but to the intensity of the artistic process itself. For Eliot, great poetry is not an expression of emotion and personality, but, as he puts it, an "escape" from them. The great task of the artist is to "transmute" his passion and personality through the intensity of the creative process: "the more perfect the artist, the more completely separate in him will be the man who suffers and the mind which creates; the more perfectly will the mind digest and transmute the passions which are its material." Woolf took this teaching to heart, probably because it conformed to what she already believed or wished to believe.

For Woolf, Shakespeare is the supreme alchemist of transmutation. Her paean to him at the end of Chapter 3 reveals how categorically she excludes the writer's emotional life from her conception of authentic artistic creativity, and concludes with these lines: "The reason perhaps why we know so little of Shakespeare—compared with Donne or Ben Jonson or Milton—is that his grudges and spites and antipathies are hidden from us. [...] All desire to protest, to preach, to proclaim an injury, to pay off a score, to make the world the witness of some hardship or grievance was fired out of him and consumed. Therefore his poetry flows from him

[18] First published in the London literary journal *Egoist* (Sept. 1919),vol. VI, no. 4, 54-55, and later reprinted in Eliot's collection of essays *The Sacred Wood* (London: Methuen,1920).

free and unimpeded. If ever a human being got his work expressed completely, it was Shakespeare. If ever a mind was incandescent, unimpeded, I thought, turning again to the bookcase, it was Shakespeare's mind" (79 [56]).

Defining Shakespeare's genius and artistic success in these terms allows Woolf to pair him with Jane Austen, the sole writer, male or female, to whom Woolf pays this tribute. (Emily Brontë is praised with Austen for daring "to hold fast to the thing as they saw it," but without particulars in Brontë's case.)[19] In Chapter 3, having returned home from Oxbridge, Woolf continues her research into the subject of women and literature, and taking from her bookcase a volume of Shakespeare, reads from *Antony and Cleopatra.* What she will, in Chapter 6 of the proof copy (page 160), call the play's "molten uniformity" (the phrase forms part of a long passage on the play omitted from the first edition) prompts this reflection: "when people compare Shakespeare and Jane Austen, they may mean that the minds of both had consumed all impediments; and for that reason we do not know Jane Austen and we do not know Shakespeare, and for that reason Jane Austen pervades every word that she wrote, and so does Shakespeare" (94 [67]).[20] The extended proof copy passage on *Antony and Cleopatra* (in Chapter 6), just alluded to (most, but not all of which is in the Monks House typescript), was largely omitted from the first edition. The style is a bit rough, as Woolf is still struggling to clarify for herself the mystery of how Shakespeare reconciled the fragments of his tumultuous emotions and thoughts, uniting them in "some marriage of opposites." "Marriage of opposites" is a phrase that Woolf will use and elaborate upon toward the book's conclusion, when she speaks of the need for novelists to be uninhibitedly open, even unconsciously so, to their inherent androgyny.

Woolf theorizes that Austen must have achieved this uninhibited, Shakespearean, probably unconscious, access to her androgynous sensibility. (If Shakespeare had consciously directed his creativity in any way, it would have constituted a form of inhibition. One would not experience a "sense of freedom" after reading *Antony and Cleopatra*, "if Shakespeare had interfered, had checked his mind and forced

[19] "What genius, what integrity it must have required in face of all that criticism, in the midst of that purely patriarchal society, to hold fast to the thing as they saw it without shrinking. Only Jane Austen did it and Emily Brontë" (103).

[20] Mark Hussey's valuable emendation of the Appendix shows that the proof copy passage regarding Austen's state of mind, which follows this comparison to Shakespeare, differs from the first edition passage. The emendation is significant. The first edition (p. 94) reads: "But perhaps **it was the nature of Jane Austen not to want** what she had not." The proof copy (p. 103), however, gives a contrary explanation. It was not nature, but nurture: "But perhaps Jane Austen was **so perfectly adapted that she never wanted** what she had not." Woolf did not want to portray her heroine of impersonal creation, the writer who "had consumed all impediments," as being afflicted with the very weakness which Woolf says women must overcome: the desire to accommodate themselves to the patriarchy's sensibility and strictures.

it to do this and that. Any such consciousness would have chilled the flow of the words that are all melted together and made them harden and fall off separately one by one.") But Austen is exceptional. Much more typical of the early nineteenth-century women novelists, says Woolf, is Charlotte Brontë, whose *Jane Eyre* she compares to Austen's *Pride and Prejudice*, finding the former fatally marred by Brontë's simmering rancor[21] against men, a reaction to the severe limitations on her ability to gain experience of the world, which their misogyny has imposed on her. Brontë's resentment, says Woolf, prevented her from looking freely, uninhibitedly, at the world around her; consequently, she could not fulfill her genius. As an example of the way in which Brontë's wounded psyche afflicted her creativity, Woolf quotes a passage from *Jane Eyre* in which Jane surveys the countryside around her, a description that is jarringly interrupted by Jane's recollection of Grace Poole's harsh laughter. Brontë's breaking into Jane's reverie at that moment is, in Woolf's opinion, a serious artistic error; it is an instance of Brontë's anger deforming her artistic expression. Woolf concedes that Brontë's pages exhibit "more genius" than Austen's; "but if one reads them over and marks that jerk in them, that indignation, one sees that she will never get her genius expressed whole and entire. Her books will be deformed and twisted. She will write in a rage where she should write calmly. She will write foolishly where she should write wisely. She will write of herself where she should write of her characters. She is at war with her lot. How could she help but die young, cramped and thwarted?"(96).

Toward the end of Chapter 4, Woolf explicitly states that women must forge their own literary style, since "The sentence that was current at the beginning of the nineteenth century"[22] would be "a clumsy weapon" in their hands. Such was the case, says Woolf, with Charlotte Brontë, since in her hands that kind of sentence was fashioned by a male sensibility.[23] Woolf is ruthless in her attack on Brontë and her female contemporaries for their inability to transmute their anger, their "impediments," in the fire of creativity and forge a style, a literature, which authentically expressed their experience of the world. Of Brontë's writing she says: "Now, in the

[21] Woolf writes that in Brontë's portrait of Rochester and throughout *Jane Eyre* "we constantly feel an acidity which is the result of oppression, buried suffering smouldering beneath her passion, **a rancour** which contracts those books [...]" (102 [72]). But Mark Hussey notes that the proof copy (p. 111) does not contain the words "a rancour." The addition does not redirect Woolf's intent, but it does intensify it, reflecting perhaps Woolf's wish to emphasize the presence in Brontë of the disfiguring anger for which Woolf so harshly criticizes her.

[22] First ed., p. 106.The sentence reads: "'The grandeur of their works was an argument with them, not to stop short, but to proceed. They could have no higher excitement or satisfaction than in the exercise of their art and endless generations of truth and beauty. Success prompts to exertion; and habit facilitates success.'"

[23] Woolf's advocacy for what might be called a woman's style is not nullified by her argument in Chapter 5 that good literature can be created only by a mind that is androgynous, since in the woman the female sensibility predominates, and in the androgynous man, the male.

passages I have quoted from *Jane Eyre*, it is clear that anger was tampering with the integrity of Charlotte Brontë the novelist. She left her story, to which her entire devotion was due, to attend to some personal grievance" (101 [72]). The irony of Brontë's predicament, and that of her female peers, is that they had to imitate the unsuitable style of the male writers of their time because their hostility toward men prevented them from creating a style of their own.

Yet a similar irony characterizes Woolf's predicament. Her most significant emendations, in which she recasts her characteristically supple, allusive, and intense style into the "clumsy weapon" of masculine polemic, is a form of self-censorship for which she had attacked Brontë et al., and against which she was warning her own contemporaries. The irony is compounded, because much of this kind of emendatory surgery was performed with the intention of presenting to us the ideal visage of the transmuted, "impersonal" artist. When we say that Woolf judges Austen to be the solitary example of a woman writer whose mind has "consumed all impediments," including her anger at having to pursue her literary vocation surreptitiously, subject to numerous interruptions in the parlor, we need to add to the word "solitary" the qualifying phrase, "except for Woolf herself." The proof copy is rife with examples of Woolf attempting to erase from the text any evidence of her untransmuted anger, or of what might be called an aggrieved sensibility.[24]

In the very passage in which Woolf praises Austen for having been able to write despite the interruptions endemic to a parlor, the proof copy version reads: "If a woman wrote, she would have to write in the common sitting-room. And **though it must always be difficult to write in the common sitting-room with people going in and out,** still it would be easier to write prose and fiction there than to write poetry or a play. Less concentration is required. **One would not lose one's temper so violently if interrupted.** Jane Austen wrote like that to the end of her days" (Proof, 100-101).[25] Woolf cannot know that Austen would have lost her temper violently had she written poetry instead of fiction. Note that Woolf says "so violently," implying that Austen must have lost her temper at least a little when she was writing her novels. But Woolf cannot know this either. In fact, in the very next line, she quotes Austen's nephew expressing his surprise at his aunt's equa-

[24] The passage on Brontë's "awkward break" has been discussed a great deal in Woolf criticism. See, for example, Cora Kaplan, "Pandora's Box" Subjectivity, Class and Sexuality in Socialist-Feminist Criticism." *British Feminist Thought*, ed. Terry Lovell. (Cambridge, UK: Blackwell, 1990): 345-66; Jane Marcus, "Daughters of Anger/Material Girls: Con/textualizing Feminist Criticism." *Women's Studies* 15 (1988): 281-308; Adrienne Rich, "When We Dead Awaken: Writing as Re-Vision." *On Lies, Secrets and Silence. Selected Prose 1966-1978* (NY: W. W. Norton, 1979): 33-49.

[25] Differences between the proof copy and first edition texts, in both the Appendix and in the body of this article, are indicated in bold.

nimity and success in the face of such interruptions.[26] Clearly Woolf is imagining how she (or probably any of us) would have felt if compelled to write under similar circumstances. It is an honest, dramatic, effective passage. The phrase "with people going in and out" shows that the writer has keenly imagined what it would be like to try and write anything, poetry or a novel, in a parlor. But in the first edition, Woolf omitted the reference to losing one's temper or to "people going in and out" and added a quote from Florence Nightingale,[27] so that the passage now reads: "If a woman wrote, she would have to write in the common sitting-room. **And, as Miss Nightingale was so vehemently to complain, — 'women never have an half hour ... that they can call their own'—she was always interrupted.** Still it would be easier to write prose and fiction there than to write poetry or a play. Less concentration is required. Jane Austen wrote like that to the end of her days" (92 [66]). Woolf did not wish to have others see her, or Austen for that matter, as anything less than an exemplar of the impersonal creator whose anger and resentment had been consumed in the fires of her creativity.

Related to this editorial program are Woolf's moderation and deletion of proof copy passages proclaiming or describing the pathetic situation of women, as well as of passages which imply that women are complicit with men in the virilization of English letters and, more generally, of Western culture and politics, all of which will propel Europe into another major war. Even Woolf's apparently simple, declarative statement near the beginning of the book, about the impossibility of arriving at a definitive conclusion that would address the permutations of the subject encompassed by "women and fiction," has been changed significantly from the proof copy. The proof text reads: "I have shirked the duty of coming to a conclusion upon these two questions—women and fiction remain, so far as I am concerned, **mysterious, unknown**" (Proof, 6) This phrase Woolf emended to read in the first edition thus: "I have shirked the duty of coming to a conclusion upon these two questions—women and fiction remain, so far as I am concerned, **unsolved problems**" (4 [4]). The prosaic "unsolved problems," a typical phrase

26 "'How she was able to effect all this', her nephew writes in his Memoir, 'is surprising, for she had no separate study to repair to, and most of the work must have been done in the general sitting-room, subject to all kinds of casual interruptions. She was careful that her occupation should not be suspected by servants or visitors or any persons beyond her own family party.'"

27 The Monks House typescript contains a lengthy passage (Rosenbaum, 183-185) on the Crimean War and Florence Nightingale which Woolf omitted completely from the proof copy. She reintroduced Nightingale here, in the first edition, as a brief aside, and again alluded to the Crimean War and Nightingale in Chapter 6: "However, thanks to the toils of those obscure women in the past, of whom I wish we knew more, thanks, curiously enough to two wars, the Crimean which let Florence Nightingale out of her drawing-room, and the European War which opened the doors to the average woman some sixty years later, these evils are in the way to be bettered" (151).

in any standard expository essay, has replaced the more metaphysical and poetic "mysterious, unknown." Why did Woolf emend the passage in this way? Read in the context of the book's main themes and in concert with other similar changes she made to the proof text, some of which we will analyze below, one can conclude only that she feared that the proof copy phrase might help male critics to perpetuate a stereotype of women as embodiments of "mystery," the corollary of which would be that this essential quality of their natures limits their understanding of whatever subject they are supposedly investigating. Ideas presented by a woman who commences her examination of the subject(s) of women and fiction by calling them mysteries and unknowns (implying "unknowable") would fit too easily into stereotypical male conceptions of women's "essential nature." Woolf, understandably, feared exposing herself to accusations of being a "typical woman," dependent on intuition and unable to analyze the subjects about which she writes. The phrase "unsolved problems," however, denotes analysis, allegedly the male domain.[28] "I can argue with (and *like*) the best of you," Woolf implicitly asserts in such changes. But in excising "mysterious, unknown"—in submitting to male judgment—Woolf was denying an essential feature of her approach to literature and was committing the very sin of which she found Charlotte Brontë guilty.

A vast expanse of consciousness divides those who see the world only as a set of problems which can or cannot be solved, and those who see the world as containing not only problems to be solved, but mysteries and phenomena which are essentially unknowable and which require us to move through life guided by intuitive sympathy and humility as much as by reason. Woolf's novels, short-stories, and essays reveal a mind capacious enough to encompass both ways of apprehending the world and its recreation in art. Her innovations in fiction, beginning most obviously with *Jacob's Room* (1922), show her attempting to find a means of imaginatively representing the human organism—mind and body—in its moment-to-moment reactions to the world, to its memories, and to the interactions of past and present. The identity of the narrative voice itself, whether it belongs to an omniscient narrator or to some part of a character's consciousness, is often intentionally unclear, as is the boundary between the outside world and its interpretation through the perceptions of that character. Her most audacious narrative style is akin to interior monologue (not quite stream of consciousness), distinguished by the eloquently unfinished thought or observation, allowing the reader to see motivations that are obscure to the character herself. Hints of this approach are displayed effectively

[28] Woolf's concern for the way in which she has portrayed her own mental processes is revealed in even apparently minor emendations. In Chapter 5, objecting to the ways in which women's relationships have been described by male poets, playwrights, and novelists, she reviews them in her mind, "rapidly recalling the splendid gallery of fictitious women" (114). In the proof copy, she had written "vaguely recalling." But no "vague" woman she.

and sometimes with brilliant wit in *A Room*, especially in its narrative portions, and though much of this remains in the published text, much of it was omitted. The difficulty for Woolf was that the "uninhibited" quality of her writing in *A Room*, whether it took the form of allusion and indirection or of vehement sarcasm and irony, conflicted with her conscious attempt to present herself as the authentic, "impersonal" artist who has resolved all "impediments."

In the book's opening, narrative portion, two representatives of Oxbridge officialdom shake her artist's equanimity by forcing on her the awareness that she—as a woman—is an alien, unwanted presence in the university. In Chapter 1, an officious Oxbridge Beadle shoos her off of a plot of grass (which, having been rolled for centuries into a dense lushness, is as characteristic of Oxbridge tradition as the magnificent buildings), his face expressing "horror and indignation" (7 [6]). Though the incident is a representative example of the kind of exclusionary prejudice that she will explore in *A Room*, the Beadle's arm-waving fury does not seem to have aroused in her an anger to match his, though her dryly ironic recapitulation of the event barely hides her irritation. But she does admit to having been overcome with anger during her next encounter with male officialdom at Oxbridge, when she is refused entry into a college library (she wished to examine the manuscript of Milton's "Lycidas") because she is a "lady." In this instance, the official is, in his manner, inoffensive, "a deprecating, silvery, kindly gentleman, who regretted in a low voice" (9 [7-8]) that he could not permit her to enter the library except in the company of a College Fellow or with a letter of introduction. But his kindly manner does not alter the fact that she has been injured and insulted by Oxbridge's institutional misogyny, and after cursing the library, she leaves it "in anger" (10 [8]).

Obviously, Woolf is ready to admit that she gets angry when she is wronged. What she will not concede is that the emotion can dominate her for very long, for a writer who has not transmuted her anger is incapable of producing great literature. Toward the end of the first chapter, as she strolls back to her inn at nightfall, she recalls her treatment at the hands of the Beadle and library guardian, and also reflects on the grand manner in which an ancient tradition of reverence for literature, rigorous intellectual inquiry, and scholarship has manifested itself in nobly designed, luxuriously appointed buildings, libraries, and dining halls supplied with well-stocked larders and wine cellars. A prodigious amount of wealth, labor, and skill has been carefully organized over the centuries for the improvement and enjoyment of a select group of men. Unlike Eliot, Woolf is not reluctant to bear witness to the ways in which "grossly material things," and not just familiarity with the great literary works of the "ideal order," may promote the nurturing of great writers. She understands that the functions of body, mind, and emotions are inseparable from each other. As she puts it, "One cannot think well, love well, sleep well, if one has not dined well" (25 [18]).

Yet at the conclusion of that first night in Oxbridge, having been treated as an interloper in the sacred grove of higher learning, and "thinking of the safety and prosperity of the one sex and of the poverty and insecurity of the other and of the effect of tradition and of the lack of tradition upon the mind of a writer," she is ready, but with suspicious ease, "to roll up the crumpled skin of the day, with its arguments and its impressions and its anger and its laughter, and cast it into the hedge" (33 [24]). Anger and laughter alike are briskly discarded, for, after all, isn't the ability to transcend the personal, especially anger, one of the distinguishing marks of a great writer? For Woolf, the presence of anger in women is a pitiable sign that they yet regard themselves as victims, as in the case of Charlotte Brontë and almost all other women novelists of the early nineteenth century. This attitude accounts, in part, for her emendation of proof copy passages that might be read as indictments of women in general for this sin.

Such a passage is the one just quoted. In the proof copy, the passage reads "and, thinking of the safety and prosperity of the one sex and **of [the] poverty and insecurity of the other** and of their effect upon the mind of a writer," (Proof, 37). To the first edition text of this passage Woolf added a phrase, so that the passage reads: "thinking of the safety and prosperity of the one sex and of **the** poverty and insecurity of the other and **of the effect of tradition and of the lack of tradition** upon the mind of a writer," (33 [24]). The addition emphasizes that enormous financial resources are necessary for the preservation and cultivation of a literary tradition. But the added phrase also ensures that the passage does not read as an indictment of the Fernham students as stereotypical female victims, impoverished and afraid. By drawing the reader's attention to the disparity between the female and male students' material circumstances in the larger historical context of women's restricted access to culture and wealth, Woolf reminds us that Fernham's relative poverty is not a consequence of women's inherent weakness, but of centuries of male oppression. Similarly, the revised passage implies, women's relatively meager representation in the tradition (or as Eliot might say, in the "ideal order") is attributable to having been deprived of the means, material as well as intellectual, to enter it.

Having confronted and reflected on the painfully wide disparity between the resources available to men and to women, and the relationship of this disparity to literary creativity, Woolf seeks to discover what the historians, scientists, and great writers have said on the subject.[29] The obvious place to begin such an inquiry is the British Museum Library, where she is overwhelmed, first, by the staggering number of books written by men about women, and then by the jumble of contradictory opinions that these books express. Women are said to have certain capabilities either

29 "Why did men drink wine and women water? Why was one sex so prosperous and the other so poor? What effect has poverty on fiction? What conditions are necessary for the creation of works of art?" (34).

in abundance (usually, forms of idealization) or to lack them entirely. The confusion of opinions and competing authorities distresses, bewilders, and humiliates her: "Truth had run through my fingers. Every drop had escaped" (41 [30]). In the proof copy, however, she had confessed simply, "It made me wish more than ever that I had been educated at Oxbridge" (Proof, 45).[30] The first edition change is certainly a masterly use of metaphor, perfectly matched to sense, and one can plausibly argue that it enhances the argument's progress. The metaphorical image vividly and tersely conveys how unsuitable the source material was for her purposes; the confused writings of angry men cannot contain the slightest truth about women. As readers, we know that we are in the presence of a writer whose wit and intelligence are equal to anything found in the writings of Oxbridge men. The advantages of this phrase over the phrase in the proof copy are obvious. But the appealingly innocent, confessional quality of the proof text passage has been lost. No doubt, Woolf did not wish to be seen as envying too keenly the Oxbridge which had educated so many of the men whose asinine remarks about women she is about to quote. A female polemicist who argues that women are at least as capable as men does not need to complicate her task by expressing a yearning to have attended Oxbridge, thereby giving her opponents the opportunity to call into question her confidence in those very capabilities which she asserts are equal to a man's.

In the course of her research into the causes of women's subservient status, Woolf is shocked by the numerous assertions of men—educated, wealthy, powerful men—about women's alleged intellectual inferiority and weakness of character, and by their failing to provide any supporting evidence. Their assertions of so-called fact are no more than angry screeds. This anger she finds puzzling, since these men and others like them in her day held and continued to hold the levers of power and privilege. Accordingly, Woolf's curiosity is drawn to the question, Why are privileged men so angry at women? Her ironic descriptions of the shrill, absurd, misogynistic arguments of the male scholars and writers that she quotes and paraphrases as she conducts her investigation are corrosive, and her sarcasm shriveling. The most hateful figure in the rogue's gallery that she assembles is the fictional (but, in Woolf's view, representative) Professor von X, the author of the idiotic treatise, "The Mental, Moral, and Physical Inferiority of the Female Sex." Her encounter with his writings and the pain and anger with which she reacts to it, reveal to her the nature of male anger, and anger in general, even her own. Her

[30] Near the book's conclusion, Woolf reviews what she has written and prescribed for women with humility. The proof copy reads: "How to justify this instinct or belief I do not know, for, **not having** been educated at a university, **I am incapable of using scientific words correctly**" (169). But this must have seemed to her a bit too humble, because the first edition text reads: "How to justify this instinct or belief I do not know, for **philosophic words, if one has not** been educated at a university, **are apt to play one false**" (153).

reaction will also prove to be the perfect occasion to share the experience of her own transmutation.

Professor von X, as Woolf says she imagined him as she read his book in the British Museum, has been warped by his anger; he is ugly in body and soul. She attempts to discover the source of his hostility to women. But as she reads his ignorant assertions about women, she finds, to her chagrin, that she herself has become very angry, if only in reaction to the misogyny of this learned ignoramus. A causal chain of hostile thoughts and feelings unspools in her psyche, until the chain is suddenly broken, she says, by the realization that a subconscious stream of sadness flows beneath the angry surface of the theories of Professor von X and of other ever-acquisitive, powerful men.[31] She sees that "the patriarchs, the professors," the men who wield power and wealth, are tortured by a self-generated suffering, which is the obsession to acquire ever more power and wealth. As she considers these men's subconscious wretchedness, "by degrees fear and bitterness modified themselves into pity and toleration," which "in a year or two" was transformed into a "freedom to think of things in themselves," i.e., without the distorting effects of anger, or, presumably, any other conditioned "personal" response. Having now presented herself as an embodiment of transcendence or transmutation (to use Eliot's term), naturally she would be distressed on rereading the proof copy by passages that contained evidence to the contrary. The impulse to deflect the original intention of these passages would have been overwhelming, even at the eleventh editorial hour.

What may surprise the reader of the proof copy is that the hostility that is expressed in the proof text and which was modified or omitted from the first edition, is directed against women as well as men. The starkest example of this appears mid-way through Chapter 2, in the aftermath of the narrator (whether we call her Virginia Woolf, or Mary Beton, Mary Seton, or Mary Carmichael) sharing her revelation that members of the patriarchy may be "admiring, devoted, exemplary in the relations of private life";[32] they are not so much concerned with maintaining the inferiority of others, she now sees, as they are with maintaining their own superiority. (Whether or not this is mere sophism, a distinction without a difference, is beside the point for our purposes.) Feeding this sense of superiority is the human need for confidence, however illusory, without which we could not survive the struggle that is life. One example of this phenomenon present in both the proof

[31] See the passage beginning "He was heavily built" and ending "not anger pure and simple" (42-44 [30-31]).

[32] This passage comprises a relatively minor example of Woolf attempting to efface the personal element from her text. The first edition passage reads : "Possibly they were not 'angry' at all; often, indeed, they were admiring, devoted, exemplary **in the relations of private life**" (47). The proof copy passage reads: "Possibly they were not 'angry' at all; often, indeed, they were admiring, devoted exemplary **fathers and husbands** in private life" (52).

copy and the first edition is found in Chapter 2, as Woolf, seated in restaurant, considers how the eyes of women have for centuries served as a kind of magnifying mirror for their mates, reflecting "the figure of man at twice its natural size." But the passages which immediately follow this insight differ greatly in the proof copy and in the first edition. The first edition reads: "**Without that power probably the earth would still be swamp and jungle. The glories of all our wars would be unknown. We should still be scratching the outlines of deer on the remains of mutton bones and bartering flints for sheepskins or whatever simple ornament took our unsophisticated taste.** Supermen **and** Fingers of Destiny **would never have existed.** The Czar **and** the Kaiser **would never have worn their crowns or lost them. Whatever may be their use in civilized societies,** mirrors are essential to **all violent and heroic action**" (49 [35]). The proof copy passage differs from this dramatically: "**The Czar looks into the eyes of the Czarina; the Kaiser looks into the eyes of the Kaiserin; in both they see themselves reflected far bigger than they appear elsewhere. Thus they begin bragging and boasting; they imagine themselves** Supermen or Fingers of Destiny **or whatever the phrase may be; and we are plunged in all the glories of a European war.** Mirrors are essential to **men of action in particular, I thought**" (Proof, 53-54).

In the proof copy text, Woolf sketches the lineaments of a dramatic scene, in which each monarch looks into his wife's eyes and sees himself magnified. Woolf thereby links the dynamic of male-female intimacy with the "glories," that is, the horrors, of the First World War. The worship that is enforced or seduced in the royal drawing room or bedroom, she is saying, unleashes a paroxysm of male violence on the battlefield. Though the first edition text implicates women as complicit agents of their mates' narcissism, since "Women have served all these centuries as looking-glasses," that complicity is passive and only implied. The proof copy passage, however, extends the mirror metaphor and explicitly implicates the wives as enablers of their husbands' narcissism, thereby increasing their share of the blame for the ensuing carnage. In rereading the proof copy, Woolf chose to delete entirely the depiction of the royal couples staring into each other's eyes, and replace it with an ironic reprise of a common nineteenth-century rationalization of warfare as an evil which is necessary for the formation and maintenance of human society. She implies, in the first edition passage, that humanity might have been better off remaining a race of relatively peaceful cave-dwellers, if the price of so-called civilization is periodic mass slaughter. This is effective, passionate polemic. Sacrificed to it, however, is the psychological insight and complexity of the scene delineated in the proof copy passage, resonant with the echo of Greek myth and tragic drama—of the psychological dynamic of royal couplings which inexorably drag kingdoms into war, doom innocents to slaughter, and leave civilizations in smoking ruin. In the proof passage, the culpability for the consequences of the Czar's and Kaiser's narcissistic warrior fantasies is shared by their enabling consorts. But the moral ambiguity of such a passage blurs the clear lines of Woolf's polemical argument against a patriarchal culture. The gazing-into-the-eyes passage had to go.[33]

But just as Woolf does not wish the complex nuances of her ideas about women's culpability for men's transgressions, as found in the proof copy, to be caricatured or otherwise misused by male critics (for which reason she emended the proof copy passages), so she is also wary about being taken for an angry women's rights agitator. In the proof copy, as she looks out of the restaurant window at the throngs of purposefully striding men, energized by their wives' magnifying, reflecting gaze, she realizes that the looking-glass theory of male-female relationship also explains why men are driven to limit women's possibilities, despite the fact that enabling them to cultivate and employ their talents would improve society. Men are hopelessly addicted to the idea that they are superior to women because it is the only way that they can get through the day. So addicted are they to this illusion, that (Woolf fantasizes) if documentary proof were discovered of the literary and scientific superiority of a heretofore unknown tribe of women in Central Asia, the news would so enrage the patriarchs that they would either steal the documents or put a man's name on them: "they say to themselves as they go into the room, I am the superior of half the people here, and it is **then** that they speak with that self-confidence, that self-assurance—but the course of these reflections was interrupted. The waiter brought the bill. **¶And the theory of the looking-glass, I thought, as I opened my purse, also serves to explain what otherwise seems irrational and against human interest—the strong wish on the part of one sex that the other shall not bring trophies to the common store surpassing those which he brings**

[33] Other proof copy passages that convey dramatic action, or what might be called novelistic detail, were similarly omitted from the first edition. For instance, in Chapter 5, in Woolf's critique of "Mary Carmichael's" novel, Woolf expresses anxiety about Carmichael's ability to describe the "unrecorded gestures" and "unsaid or half-said words" which women exchange when men are not around, and women's changed behavior when men are present. In men's presence, Woolf writes in the proof copy (128), "women are **so wary,** so suspicious of any interest that has not some obvious motive behind it, [...] that they are off at the flicker of an eye turned observingly in their direction. **Oh yes, he will be in in half an hour, they say, and sit down and talk about the weather.** The only way for you to do it," etc. However, in the first edition (118), the passage reads: "for women are so suspicious of any interest that has not some obvious motive behind it, [...] that they are off at the flicker of an eye turned observingly in their direction. The only way for you to do it," etc. A bit later, when arguing that women's creative expression differs from men's, she writes in the proof copy (133): "But **how different is** this creative power from the creative power of men. [...] it would be a thousand pities if **her creative power** were hindered or wasted," etc. However, in the first edition, the dramatic, hortatory mode is exchanged for prosaic description: "But this creative power **differs greatly** from the creative power of men. [...] it would be a thousand pities if **it** were hindered or wasted," (122).

himself. Were a tribe of women discovered in Central Asia, say, one of whom had written plays better than *Lear*, another made a discovery of greater importance than Einsteins [sic], **the news would be received in London at first with incredulity; later, if it were confirmed, such a rage, such a jealousy would seize upon the rivals that they would steal off at dead of night and make away with these divine works, or write over the Anne or Jane on the title-page an emphatic George or John."**[34]

The first edition passage omits the elaborate thought-experiment entirely, even the introductory repetition of the looking-glass metaphor. Instead of Woolf's ringing mockery and vibrant imagery, we are treated to a small, dry biscuit of a conclusion regarding the consequences of men's sense of superiority over women: "they say to themselves as they go into the room, I am the superior of half the people here, and it is **thus** that they speak with that self-confidence, that self-assurance, **which have had such profound consequences in public life and lead to such curious notes in the margin of the private mind**" (50 [36]). This relatively arid generalization[35] pales in comparison to the proof copy, and continues Woolf's editorial program of muffling the attack on men's narcissism that we saw in the Czar and Kaiser passage.

The "profound public consequences" of the patriarchy's sense of superiority, dramatized so vividly in the proof copy's deleted "tribe of women" passage, is a subject to which Woolf returns forcefully in the book's final chapter. Looking out of her window at the London streets, she is struck by how isolated and indifferent everyone seems to each other, and certainly to *Antony and Cleopatra*, which Woolf regarded as Shakespeare's supreme expression of the androgynous creativity, of which he was master. But when a young man and woman and a taxi happen to converge, and the man and woman share the taxi and ride off, Woolf is cheered: "For certainly when I saw the couple get into the taxicab the mind felt as if, after being divided, it had come together again in a natural fusion" (135-36 [96]).[36]

[34] Proof, 55. The Monks House typescript passage differs only incidentally from the proof copy. It begins: "<Perhaps> I thought, as I opened my purse, the looking glass theory" etc. (Rosenbaum 181).

[35] The phrase "margin of the private mind" creates a vivid image that embodies one of the chief innovations of Woolf's fiction—drawing the reader's attention as if by the way of a fragment of a thought or half remembered scene, the significance of which ripens as the novel unfolds. But the phrase alone does not match the powder of the descriptive passage it has replaced.

[36] This transformation of London from a confluence of indifferent, mechanized male energies, to a magical river alive with spontaneously formed eddies in which women and men are drawn together in natural sympathy, contrasts with an emendation that Woolf made to the proof text at the end of Chapter 2. Returning in the evening to her home, she is elated by London's transformation since the morning, when the city had appeared to her like an indifferent soulless machine. But now, with the lamps lit, it seems to her that the day's labor

Unfortunately, such moments are exceptional. Woolf realizes that the mind seems inherently riven by competing desires, a fragmenting process that alienates people from themselves and each other.

Though the work of certain writers, like Coleridge, possesses an androgynous sensibility that heals and unifies the mind, the work of contemporary male writers reflects the hyper-masculinization of English culture. Woolf cites the example of "Mr. A,"[37] whose talents she admires, but the explicit sexuality of whose writing she finds boringly representative of the "self-assertive virility" that she had said was beginning to contaminate British literature (he is "in the prime of life," she dryly observes). But, typically, Woolf backs away from the proof copy's mocking, ironic attack on male presumption. These passages were incorporated into the proof text largely as they appear in the Monks House typescript, but Woolf's willingness to stand by them until the very last moment shows how concerned she was by how they might be exploited by her critics. The first of the important passages about Mr. A to be emended reads: "But why was I bored? Partly because of the dominance of the letter 'I' and the aridity, which, like the giant beech tree, it casts within its shade. Nothing will grow there. **That, however, is all Lady Bessborough's fault. Lady Bessborough with her passion for politics always pretended that the Napoleonic wars were not half so important as Lord Granville's maiden speech. Naturally, he believed her, and when he comes to write (for Mr. A descends from Lord Granville, just as Mary Carmichael descends from Lady Winchilsea) his pen forms the letter 'I' by instinct. And then, of course, he descends from Oscar Browning, who found the stupidest man more intelligent than the cleverest woman; so that when he comes to write about women he has nothing of great interest to say about them; but simplifies them and cannot put a bone in their bodies.** And **then I continued,** remembering the lunch party at Oxbridge" (Proof, 152).[38]

---

had produced "a few yards of something very exciting and beautiful—a fiery fabric flashing with red eyes, **a tawny monster roaring with hot breath**. Even the wind seemed flung like a flag as it lashed the houses and rattled the hoardings" (54). But Woolf had originally used a much more feminine image to indicate the city's transformation, one which had the added advantage of maintaining the textile metaphor: "It was as if the great machine after labouring all day had made with our help a few yards of something very exciting and beautiful—a fiery fabric flashing with red eyes, **flaunting in the breeze**. Even the wind seemed flung like a flag as it lashed the houses and rattled the hoardings" (Proof, 60). Note also the alliterative harmony maintained by the feminine "flaunting."

[37] Probably D. H. Lawrence, as many scholars have noted.

[38] The proof copy passage that Woolf omitted is nearly identical to the passage in the Monks House typescript, with these exceptions: in the Monks House typescript "I said" succeeds "That, however,"; "for Mr. A is the spiritual descendant of Lord Granville" is changed in the proof text to "Mr. A descends from Lord Granville"; and the Monks House "And then, I continued, he descends too from Oscar Browning," etc. is emended in the proof text to:

Just as Woolf ironically blamed the reformers "Miss Davies and Miss Clough" for the hostility of Britain's nineteenth-century patriarchy, she now ironically blames the devoted, supremely capable, self-effacing Lady Bessborough, not only for her husband Lord Granville's narcissism, but for the strutting egotism of Mr. A, who is, after all, the "descendant" of the narcissistic Lord Granville and the misogynist Cambridge educator Oscar Browning. Perhaps, too, Woolf may have felt that, indeed, Lady Bessborough at least enabled (as we would say today) her husband's narcissism by deferring so abjectly to him, and that such deference by bright, talented women like Lady Bessborough contributed to the flourishing of the British patriarchy's self-regard. But the passage's irony reads as the more dominant meaning, especially considering the sentiment she ascribes to Oscar Browning, "who found the stupidest man more intelligent than the cleverest woman." Woolf, accordingly, not wishing to be caricatured as a feminist harridan, uprooted yet another nettle bush of mockery and replaced it with a skillfully trimmed topiary: "But why was I bored? Partly because of the dominance of the letter 'I' and the aridity, which, like the giant beech tree, it casts within its shade. Nothing will grow there. **And partly for some obscure reason. There seemed to be some obstacle, some impediment in Mr. A's mind which blocked the fountain of creative energy and shored it within narrow limits.** And remembering the lunch party at Oxbridge" (139-40 [99]).

Woolf continues her ironic taunting of the patriarchy in the proof text, as she focuses more explicitly on Mr. A's obsession with sex. She introduces the subject by referring to the tiresome way in which Mr. A repeatedly describes acts of sexual intercourse: "Over and over (I said turning the pages) and over again. And that, I added, aware of the awful nature of the confession, **which proved me cold as ice and old as the hills**, seems somehow dull" (153). The first edition, we are indebted to Mark Hussey for observing, omits the "cold" and "old" phrase. Woolf sacrificed an effective, drily ironic, self-deprecating phrase out of the very fear of attack by hostile, literal-minded critics which the phrase had been created to repulse: that she was a frigid crone whose point of view could be dismissed without consideration. As she delves further, in the proof text, into the subject of male writers' interest in and depictions of sexual acts, she again employs the redoubtable Clough and Davies: "Shakespeare's indecency uproots a thousand other things in one's mind, and is far from being dull. But Shakespeare does it for pleasure; Mr. A, as the nurses say, does it on purpose. But it is not Mr. A's fault, I said, skipping through the rest of the book; it is the fault of Miss Clough and Miss Emily Davies. When Miss Clough and Miss Emily Davies said that girls had brains and must be allowed to use them, Mr. A's grandfather said on the contrary they have but two desires, to serve men and to minister to their needs; and Mr. A (who descends, of course,

---

"And then, of course, he descends from Oscar Browning," etc. (Rosenbaum 186).

from his grandfather) puts his grandfather's teaching very piously into practice. It is partly in protest against Miss Clough and Miss Davies that he does it, again and again, and attaches what would otherwise seem to be disproportionate importance to the physical act which Shakespeare, who had not known Miss Clough and Miss Davies, lumps up together with a thousand other states of mind and makes poetry of.¶ What, then, one must begin to fear, I thought, and glancing at a critic, and then at a biographer, and then at a poet, all well known and young and brilliant, is that virility has now become self-conscious—men, that is to say, are now writing only with the male side of their brains" (Proof, 153-54).[39] The first edition rendition of this highly charged passage is much more circumspect (see Appendix for the heavily emended first edition passage).

Woolf then even goes so far as to criticize by name two of the most beloved English novelists of her day, John Galsworthy and Rudyard Kipling. In the proof copy, she uses the familiar technique of pretending to fault women for the flaw she is about to lament or laugh at in men. In this case, she says it must be women's fault that they cannot appreciate some of Galsworthy's and Kipling's novels. Perhaps she was sincere when she wrote that these novels comprise "some of the finest works of our greatest living writers." But her main point, as she writes in the proof text, is that these novels "fail in suggestive power." The passage reads: "**All this is one's own fault, no doubt, or the fault of one's sex; but it is a thousand pities,** for it means that some of the finest works of our greatest living writers, **the Forsyte Saga and the works of Mr. Kipling, for instance, are not appreciated by women. They fail in suggestive power.** It is not only that they celebrate male virtues, enforce male values and describe the world of men;" (Proof, 155). The first edition passage, however, omits the sarcastic phrase that faults women for not being able to appreciate those novels: "**But whatever the reason may be, it is a fact that one must deplore.** For it means—**here I had come to rows of books by Mr. Galsworthy and Mr. Kipling**—that some of the finest works of our greatest living

[39] The Monks House typescript contains a biographical point omitted from the proof copy portrait of Mr. A's grandfather: he was "the anonymous gentleman who wrote for the Saturday Review." Other changes in the Monks House version of the proof copy passage on Mr. A, Miss Clough, Miss Davies, and Shakespeare are confined to punctuation (in the new paragraph, in the Monks House typescript, a comma follows each of the three adjectives describing the critic, biographer, and poet) and a typographic error ("had not know" for "had not known"), except for the following three instances: instead of the proof copy's "puts his grandfather's teaching very piously into practice" Woolf had earlier typed in the Monks House text "says in much the same manner 'And they can't do this!'"; the Monks House "And it is in protest against Miss Clough" etc. becomes in the proof text the qualified statement "It is partly in protest against Miss Clough" etc.; the new paragraph in the Monks House typescript begins "What, then, I began to fear, I thought, <shutting Mr. A &> glancing at a critic," etc., in the proof copy reads "What, then, one must begin to fear, I thought, and glancing at a critic," etc. (Rosenbaum 187).

writers **fall upon deaf ears. Do what she will a woman cannot find in them that fountain of perpetual life which the critics assure her is there.** It is not only that they celebrate male virtues," (142 [100]). Then, in considering the overwrought, grandiose sympathy as well as the predictability with which Galsworthy constructs the incidents that will culminate in the death of the elder Jolyon (*The Forsyte Saga*), Woolf confesses, in the proof copy, that what so moves men's emotions in this treatment will drive women to laugh among the gooseberry bushes before its culmination: "But one will rush away before that happens and hide in the gooseberry bushes, for the emotion which is so deep, so supple, so symbolical to a man moves a woman to **laughter**" (Proof, 156). But "laughter" implies mockery, and mockery implies anger. Accordingly, Woolf emended the text so that in the first edition "laughter" is replaced by "wonder" (142 [101]), which not only blunts the emotional force of the passage but even mangles its sense. One might run away and hide in the bushes (metaphorically speaking) so that the comical man will not be offended by one's laughter; one need not run away and hide in the bushes to camouflage one's astonishment.

Even as Woolf's argument reaches its culmination against the "unmitigated masculinity" that characterizes British culture and politics her emendation of the proof text reveals her fear of being seen as too harsh a judge of this phenomenon. In the realm of British letters she sees foreshadowed "an age to come of pure, of self-assertive virility," [40] which is already flourishing in Fascist Italy and in its perverse forms of literature. Fascism is a form of social and political organization the spirit of which Woolf would have recognized from her familiarity with

[40] Woolf cites, as an example of hyper-virility, the letters of Sir Walter Alexander Raleigh (1861-1922), the literary critic who held the first Chair of English Literature at Oxford. After his death, his wife edited a selection of his letters, which were published in 1926. Though Woolf does not address the question at length, she does provide an indication of why she, in fact, prefers the writings of men who lived much earlier than Davies and Clough to literature by their male contemporaries and successors. Toward the end of Chapter 4, she writes: "What was Shakespeare's state of mind, for instance, when he wrote *Lear* and *Antony and Cleopatra*? It was certainly the state of mind most favourable to poetry that there has ever existed. But Shakespeare himself said nothing about it. We only know casually and by chance that he 'never blotted a line'. Nothing indeed was ever said by the artist himself about his state of mind until the eighteenth century perhaps. Rousseau perhaps began it. At any rate, by the nineteenth century self-consciousness had developed so far that it was the habit for men of letters to describe their minds in confessions and autobiographies. Their lives also were written, and their letters were printed after their deaths. Thus, though we do not know what Shakespeare went through when he wrote *Lear*, we do know what Carlyle went through when he wrote the *French Revolution*; what Flaubert went through when he wrote *Madame Bovary*; what Keats was going through when he tried to write poetry against the coming death and the indifference of the world" (71). In other words, it was the ability of Shakespeare and others like him to transmute their personalities in the impersonal fires of creativity that allowed them to compose great literature.

Britain's institutionalized misogyny. The first edition passage does condemn the domination of culture by the masculine sensibility: "For one can hardly fail to be impressed in Rome by the sense of unmitigated masculinity; **and whatever the value of unmitigated masculinity upon the state, one may question the effect of it** upon the art of poetry. **At any rate**, according to the newspapers, there is a certain anxiety about fiction in Italy" (143 [101]). But this is a much milder and more narrowly focused condemnation of the masculine spirit animating Italian Fascism than Woolf presents in the proof copy passage. There, she describes in dramatic, mocking detail the sweeping scope of oppressive regulations that have been imposed on even the most benign aspects of daily life and of the adolescent aggression that has taken over the public square.

Fascism, she recognizes, is no more than an extreme expression of the male need to dominate and control, a need which emerges out of the male yearning for security and fear of death. All of this expresses itself in the worship of a god-like, father-figure warrior and in playing soldier. Thus, escapist warrior fantasies and political oppression are transformed into socially acceptable "manly ideals," glorifying so absurd an activity as "grown men in black shirts wheeling and turning in response to the shouts of officers." The entire indictment reads: "For one can hardly fail to be impressed in Rome by the sense of unmitigated masculinity; **by the network of regulations—one must not put one's foot there, one must not take off one's coat here. On every little grocer's shop there is stamped the head of a man whom one is invited to wish to live for ever** [i.e., Mussolini]. **And not a blank wall is without its poster celebrating the triumph of some General; and not a courtyard is without its grown men in black shirts wheeling and turning in response to the shouts of officers. But the military side of it is beyond our purview; what effect has all this drumming and trampling, this trumpeting of manly ideals** upon the art of poetry**? Well,** according to the newspapers, there is a certain anxiety about fiction in Italy. There has been a meeting of academicians" (Proof, 157).[41]

The proof copy passage strongly implies that the inevitable consequence of the hyper-virilization of culture and politics is a police state run by Il Duce or his equivalent. But in the first edition, Woolf omitted the specific examples of the Fascists' pathetically juvenile, rampant masculinity, and her ridiculing of Mussolini's crude attempts at self-aggrandizement. What she has given us instead is much more circumspect, bloodless, and cool: "whatever the value of unmitigated masculinity upon the state, one may question the effect of it upon the art of poetry." These lines

[41] The passage on Fascist Italy and Mussolini's omnipresent visage emerges from a similar passage in the Fitzwilliam manuscript, but the proof passage, virtually suppressed in the first edition, is lengthier, more detailed and more derisive than the Fitzwilliam passage. (See Rosenbaum 160.)

could have been written by one of the supercilious male professors whom Woolf mocks throughout the book. Even the conversational "Well" has been replaced by the more formal "At any rate." Astonishingly, Woolf then says in the first edition, "All this" is at least as much the fault of women—of women reformers in particular—as of men. But, perhaps, it is not so astonishing to the reader who has read only the first edition passage, in which "all this" has been reduced to the relatively tepid abstraction "unmitigated masculinity." The first edition's "blame" passage reads: "The Fascist poem, one may fear, will be a horrid little abortion such as one sees in a glass jar [...] Two heads on one body do not make for length of life. ¶However, the **blame** for all this, **if one is anxious to lay blame, rests no more on one sex than another. All seducers and reformers are responsible; Lady Bessborough when she lied to Lord Granville; Miss Davies when she told the truth to Mr. Greg. All who have brought about a state of sex-consciousness are to blame,** and it is they who drive me, when I want to stretch my faculties on a book, to seek it in that happy age, before Miss Davies and Miss Clough were born, when the writer used both sides of his mind equally" (143-44 [102]).

The proof copy text, however, uses an ironically exaggerated attack on women reformers alone in order to make it clear that, in fact, only men are at fault: "The Fascist poem, one may fear, will be a horrid little abortion such as one sees in a glass jar [...] Two heads on one body **or two bodies without a head** do not make for length of life. ¶ However, the **fault** for all this rests **with women, of course, for had they stayed shut up in their sitting-rooms embroidering bags, or now and again taking a walk on the leads and looking at the view, the other sex would not have had to assert its virility. The blame for all this cock-a-doodling is to be laid, strange though it may seem, to the charge of certain very small demure women, who issued sometime about 1850 from obscure parsonages and middle-class homes in the English provinces: Miss Clough, Miss Leigh Smith, Miss Emily Davies. It is entirely their fault that English literature is infected with cock-a-doodle-dum;** and it is they who drive me, when I want to stretch all my faculties on a book, to seek it in that happy age, before Miss Davies and Miss Clough were born, when the writer used both sides of his mind equally" (Proof, 158).

Woolf has, first of all, omitted from the first edition the second of the two outlandishly gruesome fetus images, metaphors of the misshapen poems that she foresees as Fascism's literary legacy. The omission is in keeping with the strategy behind most of Woolf's emendations, which is to remove or soften the proof text's jagged edges of vehement personal expression, especially anger. In both the proof and first edition passages, the fetus metaphor is followed by Woolf identifying the culprits—those who are responsible for the grotesque "abortions" and for the hyper-masculine culture that has contaminated British letters and dominates Italy. But those whom she identifies in the first edition are different from those identified in the proof copy text. In the first edition, she assigns blame with serene evenhandedness, even sniffily suggesting that she is too high-minded to indulge in blaming at all. But, if she must, "if one is anxious to lay blame," then she will blame men and women alike, since "All seducers and reformers are responsible," "All who have brought about a state of sex-consciousness are to blame." The male gender is not even explicitly mentioned, and the only two "seducers and reformers" whom she mentions by name are women. On reading such a passage, the phrase "blaming the victim" inevitably comes to mind. Should women, one wants to ask Woolf, have refrained from organizing politically and fighting for the right to own property and to vote? It is one thing to say that transcending the personal is essential for the creation of great art, or even that great art cannot be created if an artist's primary intentions are moralistic or didactic; it is another to say that an artist may not as a human being respond politically to injustice.

The proof copy passage, however, faults men alone (Woolf uses the word "fault" instead of the first edition's "blame") for "all this," though with an irony that *pretends* to fault women. Women are at fault for "all this" (which, let us remember, includes Fascism) because they dared to leave their sitting rooms. The sight of unaccompanied women walking about Britain's towns and countryside so enraged the late nineteenth-century patriarchy that it was compelled "to assert its virility." Note also that the irony of this passage is darkened by its juxtaposition with the image of the aborted, monstrous fetuses. Woolf may have intended the extended passage, as it appears in the proof copy, to elicit the specter of rape, which, if resulting in a pregnancy, might have motivated the woman to seek an abortion. In any case, Woolf certainly is blaming, not absolving, the patriarchy for having attacked the "very small demure" women's rights activists and theoreticians Emily Davies (1830-1921) and Anne Jemima Clough (1820-1892).[42] One of the central propositions in *A Room* is that men oppress women because they feel compelled to

[42] In a passage near the book's conclusion, as Woolf conducts a review of "these notes and criticize[s] my own train of thought as I made them," she much more obviously and shockingly retreats from too explicitly identifying men as perpetrators of violence against women. In the proof text, she says that she sees that through this book courses a "conviction" or "instinct" that "good writers, even if they **cheat and lie and beat their husbands and wives**, are still good human beings" (Proof, 168). This passage is obviously an ironic evenhanded condemnation of women and men for infidelity, lying and violence. The extreme rarity of husband-beating, especially in Woolf's day, and Woolf's giving it priority over wife-beating, should make this self-evident. The first edition text reads: "and that good writers, even if they **show every variety of human depravity**, are still good human beings" (152-53). Woolf goes on to urge women to write, because it "will be for your good and for the good of the world at large." In the proof text, this desire is a natural response to the specter of male violence. Women need to write and publish as part of a larger effort to establish their financial, legal, and psychological independence.

maintain their sense of superiority. The "self-assertive virility" that has manifested itself so recently in the works written by British men is merely an instance of this reaction. Davies and Clough, eminently middle-class and unthreatening, were regarded by men as a threat only because they dared to write and organize politically for women's rights. "It is entirely their [Davies and Clough] fault," Woolf ironically concludes, "that English literature is infected with cock-a-doodle-dum," by which she means, of course, that it is not their fault at all.

But Woolf's ironic argument is hedged with complications. For she is sincere when she says that in order to find an uninfected male author she must go back to "that happy age, before Miss Davies and Miss Clough were born, when the writer used both sides of his mind equally." Who are the writers who successfully employed the female as well as the male aspects of their consciousness?: "One must turn back to Shakespeare then, for Shakespeare was androgynous; and so were Keats and Sterne and Cowper and Lamb and Coleridge. Shelley perhaps was sexless. Milton and Ben Jonson had a dash too much of the male in them. So had Wordsworth and Tolstoi. In our time Proust was wholly androgynous, if not perhaps a little too much of a woman [...]" (144 [102]). Here, again, in the continuation of this passage, Woolf altered the proof text in order to soften her condemnation of men and the masculine sensibility. (Her observation about Shelley is also an emendation that she made to the proof copy, which does not mention him.) The first edition reads: "But that failing is too rare for one to complain of it, since without **some mixture of the kind the intellect seems to predominate and the other faculties of the mind harden and become barren**" (ibid.). The intellect, she explicitly states, plays a role in literary composition, only it must be part of "some mixture" with the female aspect of consciousness. However, the proof copy passage reads: "But that failing is too rare for one to complain of it, since without **that quality books are airless and sterile**." The first edition passage subtly, but significantly, shifts Woolf's emphasis. Though the proof copy passage implies that the male aspect of consciousness is important—indeed, Woolf stated this explicitly a little earlier[43] and is about to say it again,[44] prescribing androgyny as the writer's ideal creative state—here, in a passage that follows on the heels of her ironic attack on male "cockle-doodle-dum," she does not explicitly mention the intellect (the so-called masculine domain). In the proof copy, the feminine "quality" is given credit for saving literature from sterility. But in the first edition passage, Woolf takes a more explicitly balanced approach, saying that the artist's consciousness must contain

[43] "Perhaps a mind that is purely masculine cannot create, any more than a mind that is purely feminine, I thought. But it would be well to test what one meant by man-womanly, and conversely by woman-manly, by pausing and looking at a book or two" (137).

[44] "It is fatal to be a man or woman pure and simple; one must be woman-manly or man-womanly" (145).

"some mixture" of the masculine and the feminine. The change, especially read in the context of the proof and first edition passages that preceded it, probably reflects, at least in part, an attempt to ensure that her argument will not be misunderstood, or misrepresented, as a feminist's assertion of female superiority.

This change and others like it also reflect a concern as important to Woolf as women's rights and is linked to it: the proper understanding of what comprises literary creativity. For her, the privacy and quiet of a room of one's own, as well as the freedom to travel near and far, and the financial independence that these entail are important for women writers not just so that they may write at all, but so that they may have a chance to write well.[45] And one of the necessary conditions for writing well, in Woolf's view, for becoming a true artist, is the ability to look at "the thing itself," which is possible only if the writer's vision is not distorted by anger or resentment, however justified. When, in Chapter 5, Woolf critiques a lesbian-themed novel, "*Life's Adventure*," by a young, contemporary writer, "Mary Carmichael," she observes admiringly that in Carmichael "Fear and hatred [of men] were almost gone" (129 [91]). But transcendence of even this impressive measure is insufficient. Woolf insists that the writers' very consciousness of her (or his) gender, at least in the process of writing, must disappear. This is why she considers it most promising that Carmichael "had—I began to think—mastered the first great lesson; she wrote as a woman, but as a woman who has forgotten that she is a woman" (129 [91]). Woolf elaborates on this idea toward the end of the chapter: "It is fatal to be a man or woman pure and simple; one must be woman-manly or man-womanly. It is fatal for a woman to lay the least stress on any grievance; to plead even with justice any cause; in any way to speak consciously as a woman. And fatal is no figure of speech; for anything written with that conscious bias is doomed to death. It ceases to be fertilized" (145 [103]).

As Woolf weighs the strengths and weaknesses of Carmichael's novel, she advises her young contemporary to explore what is uniquely a woman's experience of life, to "illumine your own soul with its profundities and shallows, [...] and what is your relation to the everchanging and turning world of gloves and shoes and stuffs" (125 [88]). Such scenes, Woolf asserts, are as worthy of "the pen" as tales of adventure, and a shop girl's story is at least as interesting as the 150th life of Napoleon or a book on "Keats and his use of Miltonic inversion which old **Thing-em-a-bob** and his like are now inditing" (Proof, 137). But Woolf must

[45] In this regard, we should note a change to the proof text that Woolf made near the book's end, just before commencing her "peroration." Addressing her young women readers, she writes: "So that when I ask you to earn money and have a room of your own, **to try to write a book, even if it is a bad one,** I am asking you to live in the presence of reality, [...]" (Proof, 170). The first edition text (154) omits the bolded phrase, perhaps because Woolf thought that it might sound defeatist to some (male) ears.

have worried that she had gone too far in her mockery of the academic patriarchy because the first edition passage reads: "Keats and his use of Miltonic inversion which old **Professor Z** and his like are now inditing" (126 [89]).

Woolf similarly pulls back from an acerbic criticism of men in one of the most famous passages in *A Room*. In Woolf's view, what Carmichael must learn to do above all, is "to learn to laugh, without bitterness, at the vanities—say rather at the peculiarities, for it is a less offensive word—of the other sex. For there is a spot the size of a shilling at the back of the head which one can never see for oneself. It is one of the good offices that sex can discharge for sex—to describe that spot the size of a shilling at the back of the head. Think how much women have profited by the comments of Juvenal; by the criticism of Strindberg. Think with what humanity and brilliancy men, from the earliest ages, have pointed out to **women that dark place at the back of the head**!" (126 [89]). Any male reader attempting to grab this bouquet of conciliation will find that he has pierced his hand on a skillfully placed thorn. Woolf is serious when she speaks of the service that one gender can perform for another. The metaphor of a spot at the back of the head that can be seen only by a person of the other gender harmonizes with the culmination of Woolf's androgyny argument. But Woolf pointedly reminds her readers that men have *not* been women's helpmates, by citing the example of the misogynistic Juvenal[46] and Strindberg.

In the context of *A Room* as a whole it would have been clear enough that Woolf's reference to the "humanity and brilliancy" demonstrated by men in showing women their blind spots is acidly ironic. But this is all the more stingingly evident in the wake of these references. The proof copy passage, however, bears yet another thorn, which Woolf clipped off before transferring the passage into the first edition. The unemended portion of the proof passage reads: "Think **how** with what humanity and brilliancy men, from the earliest ages, have pointed out to women **their faults**!" (Proof, 137). Here, Woolf momentarily forsakes irony in regard to men's aims and does not even try to pretend that they have fulfilled their role as helpmates to women. Pointing out to a friend or spouse a fault that he or she *may* have (and since Juvenal and Strindberg are identified as the typical men who

[46] See Juvenal's Satire 6, which is devoted to women's perfidy, selfish cunning, vanity, and greed. Here is an example: "The bed that holds a wife is never free from wrangling and mutual bickerings; no sleep is to be got there! It is there that she sets upon her husband, more savage than a tigress that has lost her cubs; conscious of her own secret slips, she affects a grievance, abusing his slaves, or weeping over some imagined mistress. She has an abundant supply of tears always ready in their place, awaiting her command in which fashion they should flow. You, poor dolt, are delighted, believing them to be tears of love, and kiss them away; but what notes, what love-letters would you find if you opened the desk of your green-eyed adulterous wife! If you find her in the arms of a slave or of a knight, [...]." Translated by G. G. Ramsay, *Loeb Classical Library*.

do this for women, Woolf probably thought that most men should say nothing to women about their presumed faults) is very different from helping him or her learn a truth about himself/herself that s/he cannot see unaided. But this harshly honest assessment is present only in the proof text. For the first edition version of the passage, Woolf yet again softened her attack on male presumption and arrogance.

Later in her critique of Carmichael's novel, Woolf praises the young novelist for not being a mere "skimmer of surfaces." In the proof copy, Woolf's evidence for this is that Carmichael "had been scattering her pages with forethought" (Proof, 141). But the first edition reads, "had looked beneath into the depths" (130 [92]). The balance of the passage flows more naturally from the proof copy text, since Woolf is praising Carmichael for summoning to the reader's memory "half forgotten, perhaps quite trivial things in other chapters dropped by the way." Why did Woolf emend the proof copy passage? Though Woolf is not shy about pointing out Carmichael's faults, and even doubts if she has "staying power," she did not want her praise of Carmichael's strengths to be vulnerable to misinterpretation by male critics as stereotypical female traits. The phrase "scattering her pages with forethoughts" calls up an image that an unsympathetic reader might regard as too whimsically feminine and unserious.[47] No one can pretend, however, that looking beneath the depths is not the sign of a serious novelist, regardless of gender.

Woolf's apprehensiveness about possible attacks by hostile male critics on her description of Carmichael's writing recurs only a page later. Woolf chastises Carmichael for breaking up "Jane Austen's sentence," but then tempers her criticism: "Perhaps she had done this unconsciously, merely giving things their natural order, **as they came in her mind,** as a woman would, if she wrote like a woman" (Proof, 138-39). The first edition rendering of the passage, however, omits the phrase "as they came to her mind," so that the phrase reads "merely giving things their natural order, as a woman would, if she wrote like a woman" (127 [90]). The phrase "natural order" could be taken to mean the most commonly assumed, even "reasonable" order, in which the relationship of ideas or observations is most easily understood. However, when the phrase is paired with "as they came in her mind," as in the proof copy, an unsympathetic reader might choose to read this as Woolf

[47] For a similar reason, Woolf emended the passage in which she recounts her reaction to the introductory portions of Carmichael's novel. The proof copy reads: "and I was beginning to enjoy some quality in her style—**I know not what—(one must wait till the end to name these things)**; if she has a room to herself, of which I am not quite sure, if she has five hundred a year of her own—" (Proof, 127). But in the first edition, Woolf omits the reference to her own uncertainty, and to her conviction that when reading a novel one should not be too quick to form an opinion of its merit: "and I was beginning to enjoy some quality in her style; if she has a room to herself, of which I am not quite sure; if she has five hundred a year of her own—" (117). Clearly, Woolf wished to erase any indication that she was what a male critic might have regarded as a vacillating woman, unsure of her own opinion.

admitting that a woman's mind is a hodge-podge of thoughts and emotions, not capable of bringing order to the unruly process of creation.

Woolf's emendation of this passage, however minor it may at first seem, is significant and even poignant, since one of her chief contributions to literary modernism is the artistic depiction of the mind in its moment-to-moment reactions to the world and to its own memories. Her novels and short stories illustrate that, indeed, everyone's mind is a hodge-podge of thoughts and emotions. The proof copy sentence asserts that a woman author would be better able than a man (*pace* James Joyce) to be aware of and acknowledge that we cannot control what happens to us, and certainly not what goes on in our minds, and to incorporate this insight into her fiction. That Woolf would be willing to eviscerate from this passage (perhaps unconsciously, like the fictional Carmichael) what might be considered the heart of her "teaching" shows the extent to which she feared saying what she meant in the way she meant to say it, whether, as in this case, it might be caricatured as vagueness, or as unjustified rancor. The specter of the hostile male critic, tensed and waiting to pounce on even the passing shadow of female sensibility, haunts all of these tamed passages.

Although Woolf's praise and admonition of Mary Carmichael and other young women authors bear the marks of this anxiety, Woolf left intact the semi-fictional narrative structure of the proof text, though not always the passages which themselves so effectively embody the literary insights that the narrator ostensibly discovers as her narrative unfolds. The best of these appear in the first chapter, and include what is probably the book's most famous scene; it also contains one of the few passages in which Woolf emended the proof copy text to enhance, rather than delete or muffle, a novelistic effect. Having lunched sumptuously at one of Oxbridge's wealthy male colleges, Woolf moves to a window seat, lights a cigarette, and, when she needs to knock off the ash, chances to glance out the window into the quadrangle below, where she notices a tailless Manx cat. The odd looking animal arrests her attention and then "changed by some fluke of the subconscious intelligence the emotional light for me" (15 [11]).

It seems to Woolf that the hesitant cat, like herself, "questioned the universe," and she suddenly realizes that an essential quality of these luncheons has changed since the war: "Everything was different." Before the war, the tone of the conversation between men and women was infused with the sensibility of Tennyson's and Christina Rossetti's romantic, idealizing poetry. Their vanished world seems to her so comically romanticized that she laughs, and then must explain her laughter (to a passerby?) by pointing at the cat. She wonders, apparently to herself, "Was he really born so, or had he lost his tail in an accident?" The "truncated animal," so odd looking and out of place on the quadrangle lawn may also remind her of herself, a creature out of place in patriarchal Oxbridge. Perhaps it represents, too, all women (though it is a "he"), an alien presence in the world of art, learning, and power. Regardless, the narrator's reaction to the cat has sparked in her an awareness of the shift in British sensibility from the idealizing world of Tennyson and Rossetti to that of her own day.

The balance of the narrator's remarks about the cat in the first edition reads: "The tailless cat, though some are said to exist in the Isle of Man, is rarer than one thinks. It is a queer animal, quaint, rather than beautiful. **It is strange what a difference a tail makes.** You know, the sort of thing one says as a lunch party breaks up and people are finding their coats and hats" (17 [13]). On reading the last sentence, we realize with a start that the previous lines, which we thought were a continuation of the narrator's internal monologue, were actually spoken aloud by the narrator to a luncheon companion. One of the revolutionary changes that Woolf, along with Joyce and Eliot, brought to literature is the imaginative recreation of an intensified awareness of the mind's contents and of the degree to which the mind creates our experience of the world. This awareness permeates the barrier that we usually suppose divides "interior" from "exterior" and the observing narrator from the observed character. When the reader realizes, in the Manx cat scene, that what s/he thought had been occurring in the mind of the narrator was actually occurring in the "outside" world, as an exchange between the narrator and an interlocutor, s/he realizes that the narrator regards the distinction between inner and outer as a mere psychological convention (the length of time that the narrator has been in conversation is unclear and unimportant), since everything that the narrator experiences is, essentially, the result of an interior process.

The scene is a tour-de-force because Woolf has embodied in her style the very shift in sensibility about which she is writing. She has joined her subject—how she became aware of a change in English sensibility, a change which she now realizes has had a profound effect on her as a writer and on her peers (those whom we call modernists)—to her style, in perfect marriage. What makes the technique of space (and to an extent, time) displacement work so well is Woolf's creation of the illusion that we are reading the narrator's unspoken thoughts until we are jolted into awareness of the contrary by "you know, the sort of thing one says." But without the Sybil-like musing "it is strange what a difference a tail makes," the magical spell could not have been so effectively cast. In fact, the proof copy does not contain this wonderfully allusive phrase. Rather, it reads, "The tailless cat, though some are said to exist in the Isle of Man, is rarer than one thinks. It is a queer animal, quaint, rather than beautiful. You know, the kind of thing one says as a lunch party breaks up and people are finding their coats and hats" (Proof, 20). As the proof copy stood, we would not have been as thoroughly seduced as we are in the first edition into assuming that we are listening to the narrator's internal voice.

Woolf's enhancement of this scene and her shaping of its expression to embody its sense make all the more curious an emendation that she made to a proof copy passage only two pages later, when she explicitly addressed the subject of the differences between nineteenth-century and contemporary poetry. Though Rossetti's and Tennyson's romantic poetry made her laugh when she recalled it at an Oxbridge luncheon, after she has left the college and walks through the campus quadrangles she is overwhelmed with those poets' rapturous power and admits that no poet of her own day could match them. Tennyson's and Rossetti's poetry excites us because "it celebrates some feeling that one used to have," and, because of this familiarity, one accepts it "without troubling to check the feeling or compare it with any that one has now. But the living poets express a feeling that is actually being made and torn out of us at this very moment." The proof copy text continues: "One does not recognize it in the first place; often for some reason one fears it; **that** one watches it with keenness and compares it jealously and suspiciously with **what is being born in one at the moment**. Hence the difficulty of modern poetry" (Proof, 22).

The use of "that" syntactically implies the following expanded reading: we so fear the feeling, or state of being, that contemporary poetry ascribes to us *that* we watch it suspiciously and compare it with our moment-to-moment psychological states. That is, we jealously wish to hold onto the old sensibility, to the comfort of the known, by suspiciously trying to detect an error in the new poetry's representation of ourselves. We jealously observe it (jealous, because it will steal our old feeling), hoping that we will find it contradicted as we compare it to "what is being born in one at the moment." But Woolf's extraordinary analysis penetrates into even deeper levels of motivation. The new poets have not just torn out and displayed their "feeling" (their experience of what it means to be human when traditional authorities have been rejected), which we are loath to admit is ours as well. In the act of showing us their raw sensibility, they have "made" it, created it, in us, in the sense that they have forced us to recognize that the feeling that they have torn from themselves, has in fact, been torn from us as well. It had been living in us all along; only we were not aware of it till the "living poets" showed it to us.

But this lapidary passage, so densely packed with psycho-literary insight, has yet another level of complexity encoded in it. The phrase "what is being born in one at the moment," may indeed be read as referring to our moment-to-moment existence; that is, what it is like for us moment by moment to be in relationship with others, with our own consciousness, with the world. Yet the syntax and logic of the sentence in which it appears also allows for a different referent for that phrase. Woolf may have been referring to our moment-to-moment reaction to the new poetry itself. It has awakened in us an awareness that the poet's strange feeling has been torn from our psyche as well as his. But our awareness, our recognition that the feeling that is in him is in us, may be confined to our interaction with the poetry, or more generally, imaginative literature. This would imply an eternal, solipsistic cycle, in which we are continuously reacting to our reactions, racing along the interior of the walls which literature has built around the psyche, unable to break out and touch "the thing itself." These are ideas to which Woolf could have devoted an entire essay, but exploring them was not the purpose of *A Room*. When she had added "it is strange what a difference a tail makes" to her reaction to the sight of the Manx, she indeed complicated and enriched the passage by marrying her subject to her "in the moment" style. But this is a very different kind of enterprise than an intellectual exposition of an argument.

Contemplating the implications of the proof copy's "what is being born in one at the moment" and the abyss of analytical and interpretive complexity that opened before her, Woolf prudently pulled back from the edge and emended the passage. The first edition version of the passage reads: "But the living poets express a feeling that is actually being made and torn out of us at this very moment. One does not recognize it in the first place; often for some reason one fears it; one watches it with keenness and compares it jealously and suspiciously with the old feeling that one knew. Hence the difficulty of modern poetry" (19 [14]). The emendation simplifies Woolf's explication of the cause and effect of our reaction to modern poetry, reducing it to an awareness of the difference between the present and the past. That is, we compare our old sense of what we and the world were (say, Rossetti's and Tennyson's sensibility) to what we feel when we are compelled by contemporary poets (T. S. Eliot, perhaps) to look at ourselves and the world. We are fearful and suspicious because it pains us to give up the comfort and security of familiar feelings. This much was in the proof passage. What Woolf has eliminated is her allusion to an even deeper psychological dynamic in the mind's interaction with contemporary poetry. But confining the analysis of that interplay to a matter of contrasting past and present had the added advantage of reinforcing the essential point that Woolf wished to make in the luncheon scene and its aftermath; the contrast of past and present. England had changed irrevocably. The war, and perhaps other forces, had seen to that. Among their victims was a casualty which we should not lament—the death of the idealizing habit. Even in bastions of male privilege like Oxbridge, the resident men and visiting women can no longer recognize themselves in Rossetti's "My heart is gladder than all these / Because my love is come to me." Inevitably, therefore, contemporary authors and poets had to find a new way to express this new awareness.

Past versus present—a simplification, but hardly simple. The dichotomous rubric, in fact, encompasses most of the topics that Woolf courageously faces throughout the book, which include the construction of socio-cultural attitudes toward gender, literary creativity, higher education, political power, money, and class. All of these forces, she persuasively shows, had an effect on women's fate as writers. She was probably the only writer of her day who could have so honestly (in both the intellectual and emotional sense), forcefully, and elegantly advanced so complex an "argument" (in the most general sense of the word) both through polemical exposition and a pioneering narrative technique borrowed from her fiction. In fact, she did not so much wish to make an argument as to tell a story. In the book's first paragraph, maintaining the illusion that she is speaking to the students of Fernham she observes, "Fiction here is likely to contain more truth than fact. Therefore I propose, making use of all the liberties and licences of a novelist, to tell you the story of the two days that preceded my coming here."

Despite Woolf's repeated exhortations to women that they get a room of their own in which to write, she realized that this message was unintelligible to anyone who had not reflected on the history of women in Britain over the past few centuries, who had not recreated, at least in imagination, some of those women's lives. Woolf, therefore, told these stories of past and present, of herself and others. Inevitably, she did so in a way that expressed her mind's unique combination of powers: preternaturally intelligent and sensitive, aware of even its most subtle movements; delighting in nuanced analysis and in allusive and elliptical narrative; and which from a height could spy the merest twitch of deflected desire or hypocrisy, and descend on it with tearing beak and talons. One of the most satisfying pleasures of the proof copy is the way in which these powers are borne aloft by the vehemence of the narrator's emotions, by her cold fury and hilarity at men's obtuse self-regard, which she transmutes not into "impersonal" observation, but the most corrosive, mocking irony. Linked to this is the book's other great literary pleasure, more a presence in the proof text than the first edition: the embodiment of the content of Woolf's story in her stylistic approach to the narrative and even to analysis and argument.

Woolf does not explicitly link the two psycho-literary aptitudes which she prizes most highly: the ability "to express a feeling that is being made and torn out of us at the moment" and the ability to draw upon both the male and female aspects of consciousness. But implicit in her statements in *A Room* about literary creativity is her recognition that they exist in symbiotic relationship. Therefore, since most men seemed to be dedicated to the virilization of culture, it would be left to women, and to the enlightened male "living poets," to create an authentic literature in Britain. That Woolf's fear of the literary patriarchy compelled her to omit from the first edition, or admit only in modified form, expressions of what she would have identified in another writer as the "womanly" aspects of consciousness is the proof copy's painfully and perhaps frustratingly ironic lesson. Yet, we must also acknowledge that we have benefited from Woolf's emendations of this remarkable text. This is so not only because many of the emendations improve the style or clarify a point, but because even in those many passages which redirect or reverse an intention there pulses the dynamic energy of Woolf's perceptiveness, alive and sympathetic to different, even conflicting, facets of a story or argument. In this sense, the two texts complement each other, and perhaps, in the sympathetic and studious reader's mind, may find a consummation in a marriage of opposites, one of several for which Woolf yearned.

Works Cited

Woolf, Virginia. *The Diary of Virginia Woolf, Vol. 3 1925-1930*. Ed. Anne Olivier Bell, with the assistance of Andrew McNeillie. NY: Harcourt Brace Jovanovich, 1980.

——. *A Room of One's Own*. Proof Copy. 10 – 22 July 1929. R & R Clark for The Hogarth Press. Henry W. and Albert A. Berg Collection of English and American Literature, New York Public Library.

——. *A Room of One's Own*. New York: The Fountain Press, 1929. [Kirkpatrick A12a]

——. *A Room of One's Own*. London: The Hogarth Press, 1929. [Kirkpatrick A12b]

——. *A Room of One's Own*. New York: Harcourt, Brace & Company, 1929. [Kirkpatrick A12c]

——. *A Room of One's Own*. Annotated and with an introduction by Susan Gubar. Orlando: Harcourt, 2005.

——. *Women and Fiction. The Manuscript Versions of* A Room of One's Own. Transcribed and edited by S. P. Rosenbaum. Oxford: Blackwell, 1992.

Appendix of Variants Between the Proof Copy and the First Edition of *A Room of One's Own*

Compiled by Isaac Gewirtz from the Proof Copy Housed in the Henry W. and Albert A. Berg Collection of English and American Literature The New York Public Library, Astor, Lenox and Tilden Foundation

Grateful acknowledgment is made to The Society of Authors as the Literary Representative of the Estate of Virginia Woolf.

Note: Monks House typescript passages have been included where they differ from the proof copy passages listed below, i.e., the proof copy passages that differ from the first edition text. The Monks House passages are provided in a footnote; following Rosenbaum's transcription, words added to the typescript in Woolf's hand are supplied between the symbols < >.

CHAPTER 1

Proof Copy	First Edition
p. 6: I have shirked the duty of coming to a conclusion upon these two questions—women and fiction remain, so far as I am concerned, **mysterious, unknown**.	p. 4. I have shirked the duty of coming to a conclusion upon these two questions—women and fiction remain, so far as I am concerned, **unsolved problems**.
p. 8: That collar I have spoken of, **W**omen and **F**iction, the need of coming to some conclusion,	p. 5: That collar I have spoken of, **w**omen and **f**iction, the need of coming to some conclusion,
p. 8: On the f**a**rther bank **beautiful** willows wept in perpetual lamentation,	p. 6: On the f**u**rther bank **the** willows wept in perpetual lamentation,
p. 9: But however small it was, it had, nevertheless, the mysterious property of its kind—put back into the mind, it became at once very **beautiful**, and important;	p. 6: But however small it was, it had, nevertheless, the mysterious property of its kind—put back into the mind, it became at once very **exciting**, and important;
p. 9: Only the Fellows and Scholars are allowed here; the gravel is the place for me. **To think this was** the work of a moment.	p. 7: Only the Fellows and Scholars are allowed here; the gravel is the place for me. **Such thoughts were** the work of a moment.

Proof Copy	First Edition
p. 10: for if the spirit of peace dwells anywhere, it is **here** in the courts and quadrangles of Oxbridge on a fine October morning.	p. 7: for if the spirit of peace dwells anywhere, it is in the courts and quadrangles of Oxbridge on a fine October morning.
p. 12: The critics often say that *Esmond* is Thackeray's **more** perfect novel.	p. 9: The critics often say that *Esmond* is Thackeray's **most** perfect novel.
p. 12: **only perhaps** the eighteenth-century style was **indeed quite** natural to Thackeray—	p. 9: **unless indeed** the eighteenth-century style was natural to Thackeray—
p. 13: I had no wish to **go in** had I the right,	p. 10: I had no wish to **enter** had I the right,
p. 13: busying themselves at the door like bees at the mouth of a hive.	p. 11: busying themselves at the door **of the Chapel** like bees at the mouth of a hive.
p. 14: the venerable congregation had gone inside. **But** the outside of the chapel remained.	p. 11: the venerable congregation had gone inside. The outside of the chapel remained.
p. 16: as if soup**,** salmon and ducklings	p. 13: as if soup **and** salmon and ducklings
p. 16 of no importance **whatever**,	p. 13: "of no importance **whatsoever**,
p. 17: but the more profound, subtle and subterranean glow, the rich yellow flame of rational intercourse.	p. 14: but the more profound, subtle and subterranean glow, **which is** the rich yellow flame of rational intercourse.
p. 18: padding softly across the quadrangle by some fluke of the sub-conscious intelligence **changed** the emotional light for me.	p. 15: padding softly across the quadrangle **changed** by some fluke of the sub-conscious intelligence the emotional light for me.
p. 18: Certainly, as I watched the manx cat,	p. 15: Certainly, as I watched the **M**anx cat,

Proof Copy	First Edition
p. 20: Was that what women **sang** at luncheon parties before the war?	p. 17: Was that what women **hummed** at luncheon parties before the war?
p. 20: There was something so ludicrous in thinking of people **saying** such things	p. 17: There was something so ludicrous in thinking of people **humming** such things
p. 20: by pointing at the manx cat,	p. 17: by pointing at the **M**anx cat,
p. 20: It is a queer animal, quaint rather than beautiful—you know the sort of things one says as a lunch party breaks up and people are finding their coats and hats.	p. 17: It is a queer animal, quaint rather than beautiful. **It is strange what a difference a tail makes**—you know the sort of things one says as a lunch party breaks up and people are finding their coats and hats.
p. 22: But the living poets express a feeling that is actually being made and torn out of us at this very moment. One does not recognise it in the first place; often for some reason one fears it; **that** one watches it with keenness and compares it jealously and suspiciously with **what is being born in one at the moment**. Hence the difficulty of modern poetry.	p. 19: But the living poets express a feeling that is actually being made and torn out of us at this very moment. One does not recognise it in the first place; often for some reason one fears it; one watches it with keenness and compares it jealously and suspiciously with **the old feeling that one knew**. Hence the difficulty of modern poetry.
p. 23-24: For truth ... those dots mark the spot where, in search of truth, I missed the turning up to Fernham. **The truth**—Which was truth and which was illusion, I asked myself? What **is** the truth about these houses, for example,	p. 20: For truth ... those dots mark the spot where, in search of truth, I missed the turning up to Fernham. **Yes indeed,** which was truth and which was illusion, I asked myself? What **was** the truth about these houses, for example,
p. 25: when for some reason the beauty of the world revealed and yet soon to **pass** [...] the beauty of the world which is so soon to **pass**,	p. 22: when for some reason the beauty of the world revealed and yet soon to **perish** [...] the beauty of the world which is so soon to **perish**,

Proof Copy	First Edition
p. 25: here I pushed into the garden **by an open door,** for, unwisely	p. 22: here I pushed into the garden, for, unwisely
p. 26 could it be **that** famous scholar,	p. 23: could it be **the** famous scholar,
p. 27: That was all. Everybody scraped their chairs back;	p. 24: That was all. **The meal was over.** Everybody scraped their chairs back;
p. 29: In a minute or so we **slipped** freely in and out among all those objects of curiosity and interest	p. 25: In a minute or so we **were slipping** freely in and out among all those objects of curiosity and interest
p. 29: which spring naturally such beginnings.	p. 25: which spring naturally **from** such beginnings.
p. 29: While these things were being said I became shamefacedly aware, **however,** of a current	p. 25: While these things were being said**, however,** I became shamefacedly aware of a current
p. 30: what lies beneath its gallant red **bricks**	p.26: what lies beneath its gallant red **brick**
p. 31: Can anyone persuade the editor of the — to **take** a letter?	p. 27: Can anyone persuade the editor of the — to **print** a letter?
p. 32: Now if she had gone into **business, become** a manufacturer	p. 28: Now if she had gone into **business; had become** a manufacturer
p. 32: if she had left two or three hundred thousand pounds to **this college**,	p. 28: if she had left two or three hundred thousand pounds to **Fernham**,
p. 32: at our ease **to-night**	p. 28: at our ease **tonight**

Proof Copy	**First Edition**
p. 33: we might have dined very tolerably up here alone off a bird and a bottle of wine**, and** have looked forward without undue confidence to a lifetime spent in the shelter of one of the liberally endowed professions.	p. 29: we might have dined very tolerably up here alone off a bird and a bottle of wine; **we might** have looked forward without undue confidence to a lifetime spent in the shelter of one of the liberally endowed professions.
p. 34: For, to endow a college would necessitate the suppression of families altogether. **Thirteen brothers and sisters. No** human being could stand it.	p. 30: For, to endow a college would necessitate the suppression of families altogether. **Making a fortune and bearing** thirteen **children—no** human being could stand it.
p. 35: perhaps to found a scholarship or endow a fellowship	p. 31: perhaps to found a scholarship or **to** endow a fellowship
p. 35: Not a penny could be spared for "amenities"; partridges and wine,	p. 31: Not a penny could be spared for "amenities"; **for** partridges and wine,
p. 36: of the painted windows that would be throwing strange **blues and purples** on the pavement;	p. 32: of the painted windows that would be throwing strange **globes and crescents** on the pavement;
p. 36: of the admirable smoke and drink and the deep arm-chairs and the pleasant carpets **and** of the urbanity, the geniality, the dignity which are the offspring of luxury and privacy and space.	p. 32: of the admirable smoke and drink and the deep arm-chairs and the pleasant carpets**:** the urbanity, the geniality, the dignity which are the offspring of luxury and privacy and space.
p. 37: and I thought how unpleasant it is to be locked out; and **then** I thought how it is worse perhaps to be locked in; and, thinking of the safety and prosperity of the one sex and **of [the] poverty and insecurity of the other** and of their effect upon the mind of a writer,	p. 33: and I thought how unpleasant it is to be locked out; and I thought how it is worse perhaps to be locked in; and, thinking of the safety and prosperity of the one sex and of the poverty and insecurity of the other and **of the effect of tradition and of the lack of tradition** upon the mind of a writer,

CHAPTER 2

Proof Copy	First Edition
p. 39: the learned and the unprejudiced, who **have** removed themselves above the strife of tongue and the confusion of body	p. 35: the learned and the unprejudiced, who **had** removed themselves above the strife of tongue and the confusion of body
p. 39: in Bloomsbury boarding-houses in the winter.	p. 35: in **the** boarding-houses **of Bloomsbury** in the winter.
p. 41: and waited in my stall, among the other seekers**,** for the essential oil of truth.	p. 37: and waited in my stall, among the other **seekers for** the essential oil of truth.
p. 43: Condition **of, in Middle Ages**, In the **Feejee** Islands, Worshipped as goddesses by, **Lacking** in moral sense, Greater conscientiousness of, Age of puberty among South Sea Islanders,	p. 39: Condition **in Middle Ages of**, **Habits** in the **Fiji** Islands **of,** Worshipped as goddesses by, **Weaker in** moral sense **than,** Greater conscientiousness of, **South Sea Islanders, age of puberty among**,
p. 44: Here I drew breath. **I** added, indeed, in the margin,	p. 40: Here I drew breath **and** added, indeed, in the margin, Why
p. 44: but by now somewhat har**r**assed thought, what is so unfortunate is that wise men never **say** the same thing about women.	p. 40: but by now somewhat harassed thought, what is so unfortunate is that wise men never **think** the same thing about women.
p. 44: a direct contradiction **it seems by men** who were contemporary.	p. 40: a direct contradiction **by keen observers** who were contemporary.
p. 44-45: Dr. Johnson thought the **very** opposite.	p. 40: Dr. Johnson thought the opposite.

Proof Copy	First Edition
p. 45: It was distressing, it was bewildering, it was humiliating. **It made me wish more than ever that I had been educated at Oxbridge**.	p. 41: It was distressing, it was bewildering, it was humiliating. **Truth had run through my fingers. Every drop had escaped**.
p. 45 footnote 1: women knowing as much as themselves. . . . In	p. 40: footnote 1: women knowing as much as themselves.' **. . .** In
p. 46: or that the age of puberty among the **Feejee** Islanders is nine,	p. 41: or that the age of puberty among the **South Sea** Islanders is nine,
p. 46: And if I could not grasp the truth about W. [...] in the past, why bother about W. **and** the future?	p. 42: And if I could not grasp the truth about W. [...] in the past, why bother about W. **in** the future?
p. 46: all those gentlemen who specialise in **women** and her effect on whatever it may be**;** politics, children, **ways**, morality, numerous and learned as they are. One might as well leave **them** unopened.	p. 42: all those gentlemen who specialise in **woman** and her effect on whatever it may be—politics, children, **wages**, morality—numerous and learned as they are. One might as well leave **their books** unopened.
p. 48: I looked at the student next me.	p. 43-44: I looked at the student next **to** me.
p. 49: the habits of the **Feejee** Islanders.	p. 44: the habits of the **Fiji** Islanders.
p. 52: Possibly they were not "angry" at all; often, indeed, they were admiring, devoted, exemplary **fathers and husbands** in private life.	p. 47: Possibly they were not "angry" at all; often, indeed, they were admiring, devoted, exemplary **in the relations of** private life.
p. 53: Does it help to explain some of those psychological puzzles that one **meets with so frequently in** daily life?	p. 48: Does it help to explain some of those psychological puzzles that one **notes in the margin of** daily life?

Proof Copy

p. 53-54: Women have served all these centuries as looking-glasses possessing the magic and delicious power of reflecting the figure of man at twice its natural size. **The Czar looks into the eyes of the Czarina; the Kaiser looks into the eyes of the Kaiserin; in both they see themselves reflected far bigger than they appear elsewhere. Thus they begin bragging and boasting; they imagine themselves** Supermen or Fingers of Destiny **or whatever the phrase may be; and we are plunged in all the glories of a European war.** Mirrors are essential to **men of action in particular, I thought**.

p. 54-55: unless he can see himself at breakfast and at dinner at least twice the size he really is? The looking-glass vision, **the superiority complex—if one must drag in such ugly words—has become a necessity to him**. It charges **him with** vitality; it stimulates **his** nervous system. Take it away and **he** may die, like the drug fiend deprived of his cocaine.

First Edition

p. 49: Women have served all these centuries as looking-glasses possessing the magic and delicious power of reflecting the figure of man at twice its natural size. **Without that power probably the earth would still be swamp and jungle. The glories of all our wars would be unknown. We should still be scratching the outlines of deer on the remains of mutton bones and bartering flints for sheepskins or whatever simple ornament took our unsophisticated taste**. Supermen **and** Fingers of Destiny **would never have existed**. The Czar **and** the Kaiser **would never have worn their crowns or lost them. Whatever may be their use in civilized societies,** mirrors are essential to **all violent and heroic action**.

p. 50: unless he can see himself at breakfast and at dinner at least twice the size he really is? **So I reflected, crumbling my bread and stirring my coffee and now and again looking at the people in the street**. The looking-glass vision **is of supreme importance because** it charges **the** vitality; it stimulates **the** nervous system. Take it away and **man** may die, like the drug fiend deprived of his cocaine.

Proof Copy

p. 55: they say to themselves as they go into the room, I am the superior of half the people here, and it is **then** that they speak with that self-confidence, that self-assurance—but the course of these reflections was interrupted. The waiter brought the bill.

And the theory of the looking-glass, I thought, as I opened my purse, also serves to explain what otherwise seems irrational and against human interest—the strong wish on the part of one sex that the other shall not bring trophies to the common store surpassing those which he brings himself. Were a tribe of women discovered in Central Asia, say, one of whom had written plays better than *Lear*, another made a discovery of greater importance than Einsteins [sic], **the news would be received in London at first with incredulity; later, if it were confirmed, such a rage, such a jealousy would seize upon the rivals that they would steal off at dead of night and make away with these divine works, or write over the Anne or Jane on the title-page an emphatic George or John.**

But these contributions to the dangerous and fascinating subject of the psychology of the other sex—it is one, I hope, that you will investigate when you have five hundred a year of your own—**was** interrupted by the necessity of paying the bill.[1]

First Edition

p. 50: they say to themselves as they go into the room, I am the superior of half the people here, and it is **thus** that they speak with that self-confidence, that self-assurance, **which have had such profound consequences in public life and lead to such curious notes in the margin of the private mind.**

But these contributions to the dangerous and fascinating subject of the psychology of the other sex—it is one, I hope, that you will investigate when you have five hundred a year of your own—**were** interrupted by the necessity of paying the bill.

[1] The Monks House typescript is nearly identical to the proof copy, with the exceptional passages confined to word order, punctuation and word division. The Monks House passage begins: <Perhaps> I thought, as I opened my purse, the looking glass theory (Rosenbaum 181).

Proof Copy	**First Edition**
p. 56: pieces of paper which were left me by an aunt, for no other reason that that I share her name.	p. 51: pieces of paper which were left me by an aunt, for no other reason **than** that I share her name.
p. 56: To begin with, always to be doing work that one did not wish to do, and **then** to do it like a slave,	p. 52: To begin with, always to be doing work that one did not wish to do, and to do it like a slave,
p. 57: and the stakes were too great to run **any risk**;	p. 52: and the stakes were too great to run **risks**;
p. 57: perishing and with it **my self**, my soul,	p. 52: perishing and with it **myself**, my soul,
p. 57-58: and whenever I change a ten-shilling note a little of that rust and corrosion is rubbed off **by those silver shillings,** and fear and bitterness go.	p. 52: and whenever I change a ten-shilling note a little of that rust and corrosion is rubbed off**;** fear and bitterness go.
p. 58: Indeed, I thought, slipping the **change** into my purse,	p. 52: Indeed, I thought, slipping the **silver** into my purse,
p. 58: I need not flatter any man; he **had** nothing to give me.	p. 52: I need not flatter any man; he **has** nothing to give me.
p. 58: It was absurd to blame any sex or any class, **I thought,** as a whole.	p. 52: It was absurd to blame any sex or any class, as a whole.
p. 58: had endless difficulties, **terrific** drawbacks to contend with.	p. 53: had endless difficulties, **terrible** drawbacks to contend with.
p. 59: to make **barriers** and flags;	p. 53: to make **frontiers** and flags;
p. 60: So **in** thinking **and** speculating I found my way back to my house by the river.	p. 54: So thinking**, so** speculating, I found my way back to my house by the river.

Proof Copy	**First Edition**
p. 60: It was as if the great machine after labouring all day had made with our help a few yards of something very exciting and beautiful—a fiery fabric flashing with red eyes, **flaunting in the breeze**.	p. 54: It was as if the great machine after labouring all day had made with our help a few yards of something very exciting and beautiful—a fiery fabric flashing with red eyes, **a tawny monster roaring with hot breath**.
p. 61: is the charwoman who has brought up eight children **less valuable**	p. 55: is the charwoman who has brought up eight children **of** less **value**
p. 62: upon the subject of my paper, **which is** Women and Fiction?	p. 56: upon the subject of my paper, Women and Fiction?

CHAPTER 3

Proof Copy	**First Edition**
p. 63: **It would be better to narrow the enquiry.** It would be better to draw the curtains; *to shut out* ***all*** *distractions*; to light the lamp; to **go to the bookcase** and to ask the historian, who records not opinions but facts, to describe under what conditions women lived, not throughout the ages, but in England, say in the time of Elizabeth.	p. 57: It would be better to draw the curtains; to shut out distractions; to light the lamp; **to narrow the enquiry** and to ask the historian, who records not opinions but facts, to describe under what conditions women lived, not throughout the ages, but in England, say in the time of Elizabeth.
p. 65: the Duchess of Malfi, **to begin with** among the dramatists;	p. 59: the Duchess of Malfi, among the dramatists;
p. 66, note 1: Cassandra Atossa	p. 60, note 1: Cassandra**,** Atossa

Proof Copy	First Edition
p. 67-68: What one must do to bring her to life, **to make an ordinary human being of her,** was to think poetically and prosaically at one and the same moment, thus keeping in touch with fact—that she is Mrs. Martin dressed in blue, wearing a black hat and brown shoes; but not losing sight of fiction either—that she is a vessel **of** all sorts of spirits and forces, coursing and flashing perpetually **through her veins**.	p. 61: What one must do to bring her to life was to think poetically and prosaically at one and the same moment, thus keeping in touch with fact—that she is Mrs. Martin, **aged thirty-six,** dressed in blue, wearing a black hat and brown shoes; but not losing sight of fiction either—that she is a vessel **in which** all sorts of spirits and forces **are** coursing and flashing perpetually.
p. 68: to see what history meant to him, **and** I found	p. 61: to see what history meant to him**.** I found
p. 68: **History did not mean women:** occasionally an individual woman is mentioned, an Elizabeth, **a** Mary;	p. 62: Occasionally an individual woman is mentioned, an Elizabeth, **or a** Mary;
p. 69: presumably in parish registers	p. 62: presumably**,** in parish registers
p. 71: How the borders of ignorance shrank at their approach!	p. 64: How the borders of ignorance shrank **back** at their approach!
p. 71: it would have been impossible, **utterly** and entirely, for any woman to have written the plays of Shakespeare in the age of Shakespeare.	p. 64: it would have been impossible, **completely** and entirely, for any woman to have written the plays of Shakespeare in the age of Shakespeare.
p. 72: Very soon he got work in the theatre, became a **hard-working** actor,	p. 65: Very soon he got work in the theatre, became a **successful** actor,
p. 77: which if not implanted by the other sex was liberally encouraged by them**. T**he chief glory of a woman is not to be talked of, said Pericles, himself a much talked-of man—that publicity in women is detestable.	p. 70: which if not implanted by the other sex was liberally encouraged by them **(**the chief glory of a woman is not to be talked of, said Pericles, himself a much talked-of man**),** that publicity in women is detestable.

Proof Copy	First Edition
p. 77: will pass a tombstone or a signpost without feeling **any** irresistible desire to cut their names on it,	p. 70: will pass a tombstone or a signpost without feeling **an** irresistible desire to cut their names on it,
p. 78: What was Shakespeare's state of mind when he wrote *Lear* and *Antony and Cleopatra*, **I wondered**?	p. 71: What was Shakespeare's state of mind, **for instance,** when he wrote *Lear* and *Antony and Cleopatra*?
p. 78: the state of mind most favourable to poetry that there has ever **been**.	p. 71: the state of mind most favourable to poetry that there has ever **existed**.
p. 79: "Mighty poets in their misery dead"**,** that is the burden of their song.	p. 72: "Mighty poets in their misery dead"—that is the burden of their song.
p. 80: was not in her case indifference but hostility.	p. 73: was **in her case not** indifference but hostility.
p. 81: I will quote, **I thought, going to the bookcase**, Mr. Oscar Browning,	p. 74: I will quote, **however**, Mr. Oscar Browning,
p. 82: And happily in this age of biography the two pictures **are often available**,	p. 74: And happily in this age of biography the two pictures **often do complete each other**,
p. 83: said Mr. Greg, "are that *they are supported by, and they minister to, men*"—	p. 83 said Mr. Greg **emphatically**, "are that *they are supported by, and they minister to, men*"—
p. 84: On the contrary, she was snubbed **and** slapped, lectured and exhorted.	p. 76: On the contrary, she was snubbed**,** slapped, lectured and exhorted.
p. 84: Her mind must have been strained and **harassed with** the need of opposing this **or** disproving that. For here again we come within range of that very interesting and obscure masculine complex—**as I suppose one must call it**; that deep-seated desire,	p. 76: Her mind must have been strained and **her vitality lowered by** the need of opposing this**, of** disproving that. For here again we come within range of that very interesting and obscure masculine complex **which has had so much influence upon the woman's movement**; that deep-seated desire,

First Edition	Proof Copy
p. 84: "[…] all my violence in politi**k**s"	p. 77: "[…] all my violence in politi**c**s"
p. 85: The spectacle is certainly a strange one, I thought. An amusing book might be made of it if some young student at Girton or Newnham would collect examples and **anecdotes and sayings**,—but she would need thick gloves on her hands, and bars to protect her of solid gold.	p. 77: The spectacle is certainly a strange one, I thought. **The history of men's opposition to women's emancipation is more interesting perhaps than the story of that emancipation itself.** An amusing book might be made of it if some young student at Girton or Newnham would collect examples and **deduce a theory**,—but she would need thick gloves on her hands, and bars to protect her of solid gold.
p. 85, note 1: by **Ray** Strachey.	p. 78, note 1: by **R.** Strachey.
p. 86: Think of Tennyson**——**think—but I need hardly multiply instances	p. 78: Think of Tennyson**;** think—but I need hardly multiply instances
p. 86: who have minded beyond reason the **opinion** of others.	p. 78: who have minded beyond reason the **opinions** of others.
p. 87: to make the world the witness of some hardship or **injury** was fired out of him and consumed.	p. 79: to make the world the witness of some hardship or **grievance** was fired out of him and consumed.
p. 87: If ever a human being got his work expressed completely, it was Shakespeare. **His** mind **was** incandescent, unimpeded, I thought, turning again to the bookcase.	p. 79: If ever a human being got his work expressed completely, it was Shakespeare. **If ever a** mind was incandescent, unimpeded, I thought, turning again to the bookcase, **it was Shakespeare's mind**.

CHAPTER 4

First Edition	Proof Copy
p. 89: The human race is split up for her into two **parts**.	p. 81: The human race is split up for her into two **parties**.

Proof Copy	**First Edition**
p. 91: "must have**",**	p. 83: "must have**,"**
p. 92: and so, putting her back **ont he** shelf,	p. 84: and so, putting her back **on the** shelf,
p. 93: What a vision of loneliness and riot the thought of Margaret Cavendish brings to mind! **It is as** if some giant cucumber had spread itself over all the roses and carnations in the garden and choked them to death.	p. 85: What a vision of loneliness and riot the thought of Margaret Cavendish brings to mind! **as** if some giant cucumber had spread itself over all the roses and carnations in the garden and choked them to death.
p. 95: and then I a**n** gon.	p. 86: and then I a**m** gon.
p. 96: a middle-class woman with all the plebeian virtues of humour, **candour,** vitality and courage;	p. 88: a middle-class woman with all the plebeian virtues of humour, vitality and courage;
p. 96: "Martyrs I have made**",**	p. 88: "Martyrs I have made**,"**
p. 97: Lord Dudley, *The Times* said when Lady Dudley died the other day, "a man of cultivated **cultured** taste and many accomplishments was benevolent and bountiful,	p. 88-89: Lord Dudley, *The Times* said when Lady Dudley died the other day, 'a man of cultivated taste and many accomplishments**,** was benevolent and bountiful,
p. 97: Then Lord Dudley had a stroke and she nursed him and ruled the estates with supreme competence for ever after. That was in the nineteenth century too.	p. 89: Then Lord Dudley had a stroke and she nursed him and ruled **his** estates with supreme competence for ever after. That **whimsical despotism** was in the nineteenth century too.
p. 100: Both in France and in England the **poetesses** precede the **prose writers**.	p. 91: Both in France and in England the **women poets** precede the **women novelists**.

Proof Copy	First Edition
p. 100-101: If a woman wrote, she would have to write in the common sitting-room. And **though it must always be difficult to write in the common sitting-room with people going in and out,** still it would be easier to write prose and fiction there than to write poetry or a play. Less concentration is required. **One would not lose one's temper so violently if interrupted.** Jane Austen wrote like that to the end of her days.	p. 92: If a woman wrote, she would have to write in the common sitting-room. **And, as Miss Nightingale was so vehemently to complain, — "women never have an half hour ... that they can call their own"—she was always interrupted.** Still it would be easier to write prose and fiction there than to write poetry or a play. Less concentration is required. Jane Austen wrote like that to the end of her days.
p. 102: the overflow of George Eliot's capacious mind should have spread itself upon history or biography when the creative impulse was spent.	p. 93: the overflow of George Eliot's capacious mind should have spread itself **when the creative impulse was spent** upon history or biography.
p. 103: But perhaps Jane Austen **was so perfectly adapted that she never wanted** what she had not.	p. 94: But perhaps **it was the nature of** Jane Austen **not to want** what she had not.
p. 103: and my eye was caught by the phrase "Anybody may blame"	p. 94, and my eye was caught by the phrase**,** "Anybody may blame"
p. 103-104: and it was this that they blamed her **for**	p. 95: and it was **for** this that they blamed her
p. 105: That is an awkward break, I thought**, the continuity is disturbed**. It is upsetting to come upon Grace Poole all of a sudden.	p. 96: That is an awkward break, I thought. It is upsetting to come upon Grace Poole all of a sudden.
p. 108-109: The whole structure, **it seems to me**, thinking back on any famous novel, is one of infinite complexity;	p. 99: The whole structure, **it is obvious**, thinking back on any famous novel, is one of infinite complexity,

Proof Copy	First Edition
p. 109: Or perhaps it is rather, **I thought, trying to match my own emotions more exactly**, that Nature, **very queerly and for no reason that I can see,** has traced in invisible ink on the walls of the mind a premonition which these great geniuses confirm;	p. 100: Or perhaps it is rather that Nature, **in her most irrational mood**, has traced in invisible ink on the walls of the mind a premonition which these great geniuses confirm;
p. 110: but there they stop**;**	p. 101: but there they stop**:**
p. 110: in their development**;**	p. 101: in their development**:**
p.110: to go on with **this** vast labour	p. 101: to go on with **the** vast labour
p. 111: a buried suffering smouldering beneath her passion, which contracts those books,	p. 102: a buried suffering smouldering beneath her passion, **a rancour** which contracts those books,
p. 112: everywhere and much more subtly the difference persists.	p. 102: everywhere and much more subtly the difference **of value** persists.
p. 112: with docility and diffidence, with anger and emphasis.	p. 103: with docility and diffidence, **or** with anger and emphasis.
p. 113: like some too conscientious governess, **nagging at them,** adjuring them,	p. 104: like some too conscientious governess, adjuring them,
p. 114, note 2: by courageously acknowledging the limitations of their sex, Jane Austen, **and, in our own time, Mrs. Virginia Woolf have** [has] demonstrated how gracefully this gesture can be accomplished)**....**[2]	p. 104, note 2: by courageously acknowledging the limitations of their sex, **(**Jane Austen [has] demonstrated how gracefully this gesture can be accomplished**)**.

[2] The Monks House typescript and the proof copy give identical readings (except for the placement of the parentheses). The passage is not included among the Monks House selected typescript passages, but Rosenbaum cites it in his introduction, p. xxx.

Proof Copy	First Edition
p. 114: that this sentence was written **in August 1928 and not in August 1828**,	p. 104: that this sentence was written **not in August 1828 but in August 1928**,
p. 115: when they came to set their thoughts on paper**, and** that is	p. 105: when they came to set their thoughts on paper**—**that is
p. 116: **which has taken** their own tint without ceasing to be common property.	p. 106: **taking** their own tint without ceasing to be common property.
p. 116: ran something like this**: P**erhaps the grandeur of their works […] and habit facilitates success. That is a man's sentence;	p. 106: ran something like this **perhaps: "T**he grandeur of their works […] and habit facilitates success.**"** That is a man's sentence;
p. 116-117: for her own use and never departed from it. **She examined their employments, looked at their work and advised them to do it differently; found fault with the arrangement of the furniture, or detected the housemaid in negligence; and if she accepted any refreshment, seemed to do it only for the sake of finding out that Mrs. Collins' joints of meat were too large for her family.** Thus, with less genius for writing than Charlotte Brontë,[3]	p. 107: for her own use and never departed from it. Thus, with less genius for writing than Charlotte Brontë,
p. 117: Indeed, since freedom and fullness of expression **is** of the essence of **writing**,	p. 107: Indeed, since freedom and fullness of expression **are** of the essence of **the art**,

[3] The passage omitted from the first edition text was added in Woolf's hand to the Monks House typescript with only a single difference between typescript and proof copy—a word present in the typescript that is absent in the proof copy. The typescript reads: "She examined **into** their employments" (Rosenbaum 182).

Proof Copy	First Edition
p. 117: And this shape too has been made by men **and cut by** their own **need** for their own uses.[4]	p. 107: And this shape too has been made by men **out of** their own **needs** for their own uses.
p. 117: my sense of the words inadequacy	p. 107: my sense of the words' inadequacy
p. 118: And I went on to ponder how a woman would write a poetic tragedy in five acts **nowadays—not in verse, I think.**	p. 107-108: And I went on to ponder how a woman **nowadays** would write a poetic tragedy in five acts—**would she use verse—would she not use prose rather?**
p. 119: but something different, and what that difference **should be**?	p. 108-109: but something **that is** different; and what **should** that difference **be**?
p. 119: If **they** are not going to be allowed to practise medicine—[5]	p. 109: If **through their incapacity to play football women** are not going to be allowed to practise medicine—

CHAPTER 5

Proof Copy	First Edition
p. 120: There **is** Jane Harrison's **book** on Greek archaeology; Vernon Lee's **book** on aesthetics; Gertrude Bell's **book** on Persia.[6]	p. 110: There **are** Jane Harrison's **books** on Greek archaeology; Vernon Lee's **books** on aesthetics; Gertrude Bell's **books** on Persia.
p. 121: and was published this October.	p. 111: and was published **in** this **very month of** October.
p. 121: in a fairly long series**;** continuing all those other books,	p. 111: in a fairly long series**,** continuing all those other books,

[4] The passage in the Monks House typescript reads: "And this shape too **is also largely traditional,** <&> **handed down to men by the men who made them**" (Rosenbaum 182).

[5] The proof copy passage is identical to that in the Monks House typescript (Rosenbaum 183).

[6] The Vernon Lee reference is not present in the Monks House typescript. (Rosenbaum 183).

Proof Copy	First Edition
p. 122: For while Jane Austen breaks from melody to melody, to read this writing was like being out at sea on an open boat.	p. 112: For while Jane Austen breaks from melody to melody **as Mozart from song to song**, to read this writing was like being out at sea on an open boat.
p. 122: might mean that she **is** afraid of something;	p. 112: might mean that she **was** afraid of something;
p. 123: I give her every liberty, I said,	p. 113: I **will** give her every liberty, I said,
p. 125: **vaguely** recalling the splendid gallery of fictitious women,	p. 114: **rapidly** recalling the splendid gallery of fictitious women,
p. 126: even in Proust,	p. 115: even in **the writing of** Proust,
p. 127: and I was beginning to enjoy some quality in her style—**I know not what—(one must wait till the end to name these things)**; if she has a room to herself, of which I am not quite sure**,** if she has five hundred a year of her own—	p. 117: and I was beginning to enjoy some quality in her style; if she has a room to herself, of which I am not quite sure**;** if she has five hundred a year of her own—
p. 127: like those **Serpentine** Caves	p. 117: like those **serpentine** Caves
p. 128: for women are **so wary,** so suspicious of any interest that has not some obvious motive behind it, […] that they are off at the flicker of an eye turned observingly in their direction. **Oh yes, he will be in in half an hour, they say, and sit down and talk about the weather.**" The only way for you to do it,	p. 118: for women are so suspicious of any interest that has not some obvious motive behind it, […] that they are off at the flicker of an eye turned observingly in their direction. The only way for you to do it,

Proof Copy	First Edition
p. 129: so as to absorb **it into the rest** without disturbing the infinitely intricate and elaborate balance of the whole.	p. 118: so as to absorb **the new into the old** without disturbing the infinitely intricate and elaborate balance of the whole.
p. 129: One **cannot** go to the map and say Columbus discovered America and Columbus was a woman;	p. 118-119: One **could not** go to the map and say Columbus discovered America and Columbus was a woman;
p. 130: and has received a certain number of degrees, offices, medals and other distinctions.	p. 119: and has received a certain number of degrees, offices, medals and other distinctions **by which his merits are stamped upon him indelibly**.
p. 130: "infinitely intricate" of women,	p. 119: "infinitely intricate**,**" of women,
p. 130-131: And I began thinking of all those great men who have for one reason or another sought out, lived with, confided in, made love to, written of, **admired**, trusted in, and shown what can only be described as some need of and dependence upon certain persons of the opposite sex.	p. 120: And I began thinking of all those great men who have for one reason or another **admired**, sought out, lived with, confided in, made love to, written of, trusted in, and shown what can only be described as some need of and dependence upon certain persons of the opposite sex.
p. 132: hard as horsehair or soft as feathers—	p. 122: **are** hard as horsehair or soft as feathers—
p. 133: But **how different is** this creative power from the creative power of men. [...] it would be a thousand pities if **her creative power** were hindered or wasted,	p. 122: But this creative power **differs greatly** from the creative power of men. [...] it would be a thousand pities if **it** were hindered or wasted,
p. 137: of Keats and his use of Miltonic inversion which old **Thing-em-a-bob** and his like are now inditing.	p. 126: of Keats and his use of Miltonic inversion which old **Professor Z** and his like are now inditing.

Proof Copy	First Edition
p. 137: Think **how** with what humanity and brilliancy men, from the earliest ages, have pointed out to women **their faults**!	p. 126: Think with what humanity and brilliancy men, from the earliest ages, have pointed out to women **that dark place at the back of the head**!
p. 138: to see what in fact Mary Carmichael **was writing**.	p. 127: to see what in fact Mary Carmichael **did write**.
p. 138-139: merely giving things their natural order, **as they came in her mind,** as a woman would, if she wrote like a woman.	127: merely giving things their natural order, as a woman would, if she wrote like a woman.
p. 141: that she was not a skimmer of surfaces merely, **but had been scattering her pages with forethought**.	p. 130: that she was not a skimmer of surfaces merely, **but had looked beneath into the depths**.
p. 141-142: half forgotten perhaps, quite trivial things	p. 130: half forgotten, perhaps quite trivial things
p. 142: while **some one** sewed	p. 130: while **someone** sewed
p. 142: But there was fence beyond that and a fence beyond that.	p. 131: But there was **a** fence beyond that and a fence beyond that.
p. 143: give her a room of her own and **an adequate income**,	p. 131: give her a room of her own and **five hundred a year**,

CHAPTER 6

Proof Copy	First Edition
p. 144: and see what London was doing on the morning of the **26th** of October 1928.	p. 132: and see what London was doing on the morning of the **twenty-sixth** of October 1928.
p. 144: for the future of fiction, the death of poetry or the development by the average woman of a style completely expressive of her mind.	p. 132: for the future of fiction, the death of poetry or the development by the average woman of a **prose** style completely expressive of her mind.

Proof Copy	First Edition
p. 147 "the unity of the mind", I pondered,	p. 134-135: "the unity of the mind," I pondered,
p. 148: that the union of man and woman makes for the greatest **possible** satisfaction **and** happiness.	p. 136: that the union of man and woman makes for the greatest satisfaction**, the most complete** happiness.
p. 149: But it would be well to test what one meant by **an androgynous**, conversely by a **gynandros mind**, by looking at a book or two.	p. 137: But it would be well to test what one meant by **man-womanly**, **and** conversely by **woman-manly**, by **pausing and** looking at a book or two.
p. 150: how much harder it is to attain that condition now than ever before, **I thought, coming** to the books by living writers, and there **pausing** and **wondering** if this fact were not at the root of something that had long **been puzzling** me.	p. 137: how much harder it is to attain that condition now than ever before. **Here I came** to the books by living writers, and there **paused** and **wondered** if this fact were not at the root of something that had long **puzzled** me.
p. 150: a new novel by Mr. A who is in the prime of life	p. 138: a new novel by Mr. A**,** who is in the prime of life
p. 151: something like the letter "I"**.** One began dodging	p. 138: something like the letter "I." One began dodging
p. 151: hailed to the letter "I"**.** One began to be tired of "I"**.** Not but what	p. 139: hailed to the letter "I." One began to be tired of "I." Not but what
p. 152: One cannot go on saying "But"**.** One must finish	p. 139: One cannot go on saying "But." One must finish

Proof Copy

p. 152: But why was I bored? Partly because of the dominance of the letter "I" and the aridity, which, like the giant beech tree, it casts within its shade. Nothing will grow there. **That, however, is all Lady Bessborough's fault. Lady Bessborough with her passion for politics always pretended that the Napoleonic wars were not half so important as Lord Granville's maiden speech. Naturally, he believed her, and when he comes to write (for Mr. A descends from Lord Granville, just as Mary Carmichael descends from Lady Winchilsea) his pen forms the letter "I" by instinct. And then, of course, he descends from Oscar Browning, who found the stupidest man more intelligent than the cleverest woman; so that when he comes to write about women he has nothing of great interest to say about them; but simplifies them and cannot put a bone in their bodies.** And **then I continued,** remembering the lunch party at Oxbridge, and the cigarette ash and the Manx cat and Tennyson and Christina Rossetti all in a bunch," as he no longer hums under his breath, 'There has fallen a splendid tear from the passion-flower at the gate', when Phoebe crosses the beach, and she no longer replies, "My heart is like a singing bird whose nest is in a water'd shoot", when **he** approaches what can he do?[7]

First Edition

p. 139-140: like the giant beech tree, it casts within its shade. Nothing will grow there. **And partly for some obscure reason. There seemed to be some obstacle, some impediment in Mr. A's mind which blocked the fountain of creative energy and shored it within narrow limits.** And remembering the lunch party at Oxbridge, and the cigarette ash and the Manx cat and Tennyson and Christina Rossetti all in a bunch, **it seemed possible that the impediment lay there. A**s he no longer hums under his breath, "There has fallen a splendid tear from the passion-flower at the gate," when Phoebe crosses the beach, and she no longer replies, "My heart is like a singing bird whose nest is in a water'd shoot," when **Alan** approaches what can he do?

[7] The proof copy passage that Woolf omitted is nearly identical to the passage in the Monks House typescript, with these exceptions: in the Monks House typescript "I said" succeeds "That, however,"; "for Mr. A is the spiritual descendant of Lord Granville" is changed in

Proof Copy	**First Edition**
p. 153: aware of the awful nature of the confession, **which proved me cold as ice and old as the hills,** seems somehow dull.	p. 140: aware of the awful nature of the confession, seems somehow dull.
p. 153-154: But Shakespeare does it for pleasure; Mr. A, as the nurses say, does it on purpose. **But it is not Mr. A's fault, I said, skipping through the rest of the book; it is the fault of Miss Clough and Miss Emily Davies. When Miss Clough and Miss Emily Davies said that girls had brains and must be allowed to use them, Mr. A's grandfather said on the contrary they have but two desires, to serve men and [p. 154] to minister to their needs; and Mr. A (who descends, of course, from his grandfather) puts his grandfather's teaching very piously into practice. It is partly in protest against Miss Clough and Miss Davies that he does it, again and again, and attaches what would otherwise seem to be disproportionate importance to the physical act which Shakespeare, who had not known Miss Clough and Miss Davies, lumps up together with a thousand other states of mind and makes poetry of.** What, then, **one must begin to fear, I thought, and glancing at a critic, and then at a biographer, and then at a poet, all well known and young and brilliant,** is that virility has now become self-conscious—men, that is to	p. 140: But Shakespeare does it for pleasure; Mr. A, as the nurses say, does it on purpose. **He does it in protest. He is protesting against the equality of the other sex by asserting his own superiority. He is therefore impeded and inhibited and self-conscious as Shakespeare might have been if he too had known** Miss Clough and Miss Davies. **Doubtless Elizabethan literature would have been very different from what it is if the woman's movement** [p. 141] **had begun in the sixteenth century and not in the nineteenth.** What, then, **it amounts to, if this theory of the two sides of the mind holds good,** is that virility has now become self-conscious—men, that is to say, are now writing only with the male side of their brains.

the proof text to "Mr. A descends from Lord Granville"; and the Monks House "And then, I continued, he descends too from Oscar Browning," is emended in the proof text to: "And then, of course, he descends from Oscar Browning," (Rosenbaum 186).

say, are now writing only with the male side side of their brains.[8]

Proof Copy

p. 154: but the trouble **is, it seems,** that his feelings no longer **communicate**; his mind **is separated** into different chambers; not a sound **carries** from one to the other.

[In this instance, the Monks House typescript differences have been integrated into the proof copy passage for ease of transcription and comprehension.]

p. 155: but when one takes a sentence of Coleridge into the mind, it explodes and gives birth to all kinds of other ideas, and that is the only sort of writing of which one can say that it has the secret of perpetual life.

But of course this is a purely subjective test and may very well

First Edition

p. 141: but the trouble **was**, that his feelings no longer **communicated**; his mind **seemed separated** into different chambers; not a sound **carried** from one to the other.

p. 141-142: but when one takes a sentence of Coleridge into the mind, it explodes and gives birth to all kinds of other ideas, and that is the only sort of writing of which one can say that it has the secret of perpetual life.

But whatever the reason may be, it is a fact that one must deplore. For it means—**here I had come to rows of books by Mr. Galsworthy and Mr. Kipling**—that some of the finest works of our greatest living writers **fall upon deaf ears. Do what she will a woman**

[8] The Monks House typescript contains a biographical point omitted from the proof copy portrait of Mr. A's grandfather: he was "the anonymous gentleman who wrote for the Saturday Review." Other changes in the Monks House version of the proof copy passage on Mr. A, Miss Clough, Miss Davies, and Shakespeare are confined to punctuation (in the new paragraph, in the Monks House typescript, a comma follows each of the three adjectives describing the critic, biographer, and poet) and a typographic error ("had not know" for "had not known"), except for the following three instances: instead of the proof copy's "puts his grandfather's teaching very piously into practice" Woolf had earlier typed in the Monks House text "says in much the same manner 'And they can't do this!'"; the Monks House "And it is in protest against Miss Clough" etc. becomes in the proof text the qualified statement "It is partly in protest against Miss Clough" etc.; the new paragraph in the Monks House typescript begins "What, then, I began to fear, I thought, <shutting Mr. A &> glancing at a critic," in the proof copy reads "What, then, one must begin to fear, I thought, and glancing at a critic," (Rosenbaum 187)."puts his grandfather's teaching very piously into practice" Woolf had earlier typed in the Monks House text "says in much the same manner 'And they can't do this!'"; the Monks House "And it is in protest against Miss Clough" etc. becomes in the proof text the qualified statement "It is partly in protest against Miss Clough" etc.; the new paragraph in the Monks House typescript begins "What, then, I began to fear, I thought, <shutting Mr. A &> glancing at a critic," in the proof copy reads "What, then, one must begin to fear, I thought, and glancing at a critic," (Rosenbaum 187).

prove only my limitations as a reader, not Mr. B's as a critic. It is also my fault, I cannot doubt, that when I read those eloquent passages by Mr. C. which seem to blossom in purple and red, I feel as if the gilt arm-chair [arm chair] **were spouting to the mahogany sideboard** [side board] **in the dusk. And when I see his metaphors approaching slowly over the horizon they look like the stuffed ravens in the Götterdämmerung, and one is anxious lest they should topple over in mid-air** <in mid-career> **and fly out again upside-down** [up side down] **among the laughter of the audience.** [From "Everything seems <to be> at least ten sizes too big for a living person," continuing for about 1000 words, containing the critique of Kipling and Galsworthy is omitted from the proof copy, with the exception of the two lines below, until the reminiscence of fascist Italy] **All this is one's own fault, no doubt, or the fault of one's sex; but it is a thousand pities,** for it means that some of the finest works of our greatest living writers, **the *Forsyte Saga* and the works of Mr. Kipling, for instance, are not appreciated by women. They fail in suggestive power.** It is not only that they celebrate male virtues, enforce male values and describe the world of men;

cannot find in them that fountain of perpetual life which the critics assure her is there. It is not only that they celebrate male virtues,

Proof Copy

p.156: But one will rush away before that happens and hide in the gooseberry bushes, for the emotion which is so deep, so supple, so symbolical to a man moves a woman to **laughter**.

First Edition

p. 142: But one will rush away before that happens and hide in the gooseberry bushes, for the emotion which is so deep, so supple, so symbolical to a man moves a woman to **wonder**.

Proof Copy

p. 156: **To women, therefore, books which are said to be the finest of our time remain dusty monuments, cabinets to which men alone have the key.**

First Edition

p. 142: **Thus all their qualities seem to a woman, if one may generalise, crude and immature. They lack suggestive power. And when a book lacks suggestive power, however hard it hits the surface of the mind it cannot penetrate within**.

p. 157: For one can hardly fail to be impressed in Rome by the sense of unmitigated masculinity; **by the network of regulations—one must not put one's foot there, one must not take off one's coat here. On every little grocer's shop there is stamped the head of a man whom one is invited to wish to live for ever. And not a blank wall is without its poster celebrating the triumph of some General; and not a courtyard is without its grown men in black shirts wheeling and turning in response to the shouts of officers. But the military side of it is beyond our purview; what effect has all this drumming and trampling, this trumpeting of manly ideals** upon the art of poetry**? Well,** according to the newspapers, there is a certain anxiety about fiction in Italy. There has been a meeting of academicians

p. 143: For one can hardly fail to be impressed in Rome by the sense of unmitigated masculinity; **and whatever the value of unmitigated masculinity upon the state, one may question the effect of it** upon the art of poetry. **At any rate**, according to the newspapers, there is a certain anxiety about fiction in Italy.

Proof Copy

p. 158: The Fascist poem, one may fear, will be a horrid little abortion such as one sees in a glass jar [...] Two heads on one body **or two bodies without a head** do not make for length of life.

However, the **fault** for all this rests **with women, of course, for had they stayed shut up in their sitting-rooms embroidering bags, or now and again taking a walk on the leads and looking at the view, the other sex would not have had to assert its virility. The blame for all this cock-a-doodling is to be laid, strange though it may seem, to the charge of certain very small demure women, who issued sometime about 1850 from obscure parsonages and middle-class homes in the English provinces: Miss Clough, Miss Leigh Smith, Miss Emily Davies. It is entirely their fault that English literature is infected with cock-a-doodle-dum;** and it is they who drive me, when I want to stretch all my faculties on a book, to seek it in that happy age, before Miss Davies and Miss Clough were born, when the writer used both sides of his mind equally.

First Edition

p. 143-144: The Fascist poem, one may fear, will be a horrid little abortion such as one sees in a glass jar [...] Two heads on one body do not make for length of life.

However, the **blame** for all this, **if one is anxious to lay blame, rests no more upon one sex than upon the other. All seducers and reformers are responsible, Lady Bessborough when she lied to Lord Granville; Miss Davies when she told the truth to Mr. Greg. All who have brought about a state of sex-consciousness are to blame,** and it is they who drive me, when I want to stretch my faculties on a book, to seek it in that happy age, before Miss Davies and Miss Clough were born, when the writer used both sides of his mind equally. One must turn back to Shakespeare then,

Proof Copy

p. 158-159: One must turn back to Shakespeare then, for Shakespeare was androgynous; and so was Keats and Sterne and Cowper and Lamb and Coleridge. Milton and Ben Jonson had a dash too much of the male in them. So had Wordsworth and Tolstoi. In our time Proust was wholly androgynous, if not perhaps a little too much of a woman. But that failing is too rare for one to complain of it, since without **that quality books are airless and sterile.**

First Edition

p. 144: One must turn back to Shakespeare then, for Shakespeare was androgynous; and so was Keats and Sterne and Cowper and Lamb and Coleridge. **Shelley perhaps was sexless**. Milton and Ben Jonson had a dash too much of the male in them. So had Wordsworth and Tolstoi. In our time Proust was wholly androgynous, if not perhaps a little too much of a woman. But that failing is too rare for one to complain of it, since without **some mixture of the kind the intellect seems to predominate and the other faculties of the mind harden and become barren**. However, I consoled myself with the reflection

Proof Copy

p. 160-161: Some collaboration has to take place in the mind between the woman and the man before the **art** of creation can be accomplished. **What this collaboration is, how it takes place or has in the past taken place no critic or psychologist can tell us. With *Antony and Cleopatra* to guide us, one may say that the prelude to creation is an experience of such width and variety that one must take the sea and sky for likeness if one seeks one. The experience was agitated, broken, tempestuous; the mind was taken and thrown against the rocks and shattered in a thousand fragments. But there must have then here been some reconciliation;** some marriage of opposites **must have taken place to produce that sense of**

First Edition

p. 145: Some collaboration has to take place in the mind between the woman and the man before the **act** of creation can be accomplished. **Some marriage of opposites has to be consummated**. The whole of the mind must lie wide open if we are to get the sense that the writer is communicating his experience with perfect fullness.

freedom that remains with one when one has read the play. One would not have had that feeling if Shakespeare had interfered, had checked his mind and forced it to do this and that. Any such consciousness would have chilled the flow of the words that are all melted together and made them harden and fall off separately one by one. "Daffodils that come before the swallow dares" must have been written at a stroke; whole scenes have that molten uniformity. It is presumptuous, it may be, even to hazard a guess at what went on in that particular brain. But whatever was Shakespeare's state of mind, one may perhaps arrive at the general statement that the whole of the mind must lie wide open if **it is to work freely, if this marriage is to take place between opposites,** if we are to get the sense that the writer is communicating his experience with perfect fullness.[9]

Proof Copy	**First Edition**
p. 161: that tremendous stream. Here, then,	p. 145: that tremendous stream. Here, then,
p. 162 She [Mary Beaton] has asked you to follow her flying into the arms of a Beadle, lunching **at a men's college**, dining **at a woman's**, drawing pictures in the British Museum,	p. 146: She [Mary Beaton] has asked you to follow her flying into the arms of a Beadle, lunching **here**, dining **there**, drawing pictures in the British Museum,

[9] The Monks House typescript differs from the proof copy in the following passages: "**One might hazard a guess from reading** *Antony and Cleopatra* that the prelude to creation [...] **And** the experience was agitated [...] One would not have had that feeling if Shakespeare had **been interfering and checking and forcing his mind back**. [...] it is presumptuous, it may be, even to **make an image of** what went on in that particular brain (Rosenbaum 192).

Proof Copy	First Edition
p. 162: While she has been doing all these things, **I hope that** you have been contradicting her and making whatever additions and deductions seem good to you. **Many things are visible to you that are not visible to her. Much that she thinks plain will seem to you questionable.** That is all as it should be,[10]	p. 146: "While she has been doing all these things, you **no doubt have been observing her failings and foibles and deciding what effect they have had on her opinions**. You have been contradicting her and making whatever additions and deductions seem good to you. That is all as it should be,
p. 162: No opinion has been expressed, you may say, upon the comparative merits of the sexes even as writers. That was done purposely, **not from cowardice or evasiveness, but** because, even if the time had come for such a valuation, I do not believe that gifts, whether of mind or character, can be weighed like sugar or butter, not even in Cambridge,	p. 147: No opinion has been expressed, you may say, upon the comparative merits of the sexes even as writers. That was done purposely, because, even if the time had come for such a valuation—**and it is far more important at the moment to know how much money women had and how many rooms than to theorise about their capacities—even if the time had come** I do not believe that gifts, whether of mind or character, can be weighed like sugar or butter, not even in Cambridge,
p. 163: that a Commander of the Bath will ultimately walk **into** dinner behind a Master in Lunacy.	p. 147: that a Commander of the Bath will ultimately walk **in to** dinner behind a Master in Lunacy.
p. 163: where there are "sides**"**, and it is necessary	p. 147: where there are "sides,**"** and it is necessary

[10] The Monks House typescript differs from the proof copy in the following passages: While **I have been talking** I hope that you have been contradicting—making whatever additions and **inferences** <**seemed** good to you.> Many things are visible to you that are not visible to **me and much** that **I think** plain will seem to you questionable.

Proof Copy	First Edition
p. 163: Are not reviews of current literature a **source** of perpetual **amusement**? "This great book"—"this worthless book"—the same book is called by both names.	p. 148: Are not reviews of current literature a perpetual **illustration** of **the difficulty of judgment**? "This great book," "this worthless book," the same book is called by both names.
p. 164: Even allowing a generous margin for symbolism, **allowing** that five hundred a year stands for the power to contemplate, **and** that a lock on the door means the power to think for oneself	p. 148: Even allowing a generous margin for symbolism, that five hundred a year stands for the power to contemplate, that a lock on the door means the power to think for oneself
p. 166: of which great writing are born.	p. 150: of which great writings are born.
p. 167: **Speaking selfishly**, I hope that you will possess yourselves of money enough to travel and to idle,	p. 151: **By hook or by crook**, I hope that you will possess yourselves of money enough to travel and to idle,
p. 167-168: let the line of thoughts dip deep into the stream.	p. 152: let the line of thought dip deep into the stream.
p. 168: you will find that she is an inheritor as well as an originator, and has come into existence because women **for some time previously had had** the habit of writing;	p. 152: you will find that she is an inheritor as well as an originator, and has come into existence because women **have come to have** the habit of writing **naturally**;
p. 168: and that good writers, even if they **cheat and lie and beat their husbands and wives**, are still good human beings.	p. 152-153: and that good writers, even if they **show every variety of human depravity**, are still good human beings.
p. 169: How to justify this instinct or belief I do not know, for**, not having** been educated at a university, **I am incapable of using scientific words correctly**.	p. 153: How to justify this instinct or belief I do not know, for **philosophic words, if one has not** been educated at a university, **are apt to play one false**.

Proof Copy	First Edition
p. 169: What do I mean by "reality"? **I wonder.** It would seem to be	p. 153: What **is meant** by "reality"? It would seem to be
p. 170: the world seems bared, its covering **rolled off it**. Those are the enviable people who live at enmity with unreality. Those are the pitiable who are knocked on the head	p. 154: the world seems bared **of** its covering **and given an intenser life**. Those are the enviable people who live at enmity with unreality**; and those** are the pitiable who are knocked on the head
p. 170: So that when I ask you to earn money and have a room of your own, **to try to write a book, even if it is a bad one,** I am asking you to live in the presence of reality,	p. 154: So that when I ask you to earn money and have a room of your own, I am asking you to live in the presence of reality,
p. 170: But those exhortations can safely, I think, be left to the other sex, who will put them, **I feel sure,** with far greater eloquence than I can.	p. 154: So that when I ask you to earn money and have a room of your own, I am asking you to live in the presence of reality,
p. 171: The truth is, I often like women. **I often find them very interesting.** I like their unconventionality.	p. 154: The truth is, I often like women. I like their unconventionality.
p. 172: from Mr. John Langdon Davies.[1] **He** warns women"	p. 156: "from Mr. John Langdon Davies.[1] **Mr. John Langdon Davies** warns women"
p. 172: "women cease to be altogether necessary**".**	p. 156: "women cease to be altogether necessary**.**"
p. 173: We**—or our mothers—**have borne and bred and washed, and taught,	p. 156: We have borne and bred and washed, and taught,
p. 173: at present in existence, and that, allowing that some had **nurses to** help **them**, takes time.	p. 157: at present in existence, and that, allowing that some had help, takes time.

Bloomsbury at Play

Elizabeth Wright

The authors have sent me, and asked me to say
They beg all your pardons for writing this play,
And hope none of our audience consider us rude
Either those we've no time for, or those we include.
So please don't object to the tales we have told
For they're all of them true and they're most of them old.
Besides, before blaming us, think of the pain
Which we might have inflicted, and yet we refrain.

—Julian Bell, 'Epilogue' to unidentified play, King's/JHB/1/12

An evening's entertainment in Bloomsbury could range from Shakespeare to can-can dancing; from ballet to bawdy music-hall ditties; it could be meticulously planned or entirely spontaneous; topical or historical; serious, but generally silly. The participants in and subjects of these dramas often included Leonard and Virginia Woolf; Vanessa, Clive, Julian, Quentin and Angelica Bell; Adrian, Ann and Judith Stephen; Lydia Lopokova and John Maynard Keynes; Desmond and Molly MacCarthy; Duncan Grant, Roger Fry, Jane Bussy and David Garnett, though the theatrical evenings often widened their cast to include any visitor (in one instance a German refugee was asked to give a parody of Hitler [Bell 21]). One of the large variety of theatrical pieces performed in Bloomsbury was *Freshwater: A Comedy*, the only piece of theatre exclusively written by Virginia Woolf.[1] To date critics

[1] The following plays are accessible: "A Hundred Years After or Ladies and Gentlemen" (British Library Archives, BL 4016C/ADD 83330); "The Conspirators" (BL 4016C/ADD 83331.1); "Chinoiseries or Grizzle's Successor: A Sequel to 'The Conspirators'" (BL 4016C/ADD 83331.2); "Country Life" (BL 4016C/ADD 83331.3); "Don't Be Frightened or Pippington Park" (King's College Cambridge Archives, King's/LLK/2/7 and King's/JMK/PP/15); "Leonard into Wolf or The Press Gang" (King's/GHWR/4/4); "A Present For a Princess: A Sentimental Comedy in One Act, to be performed by children" (King's/JHB/1/12); an untitled play in French (King's/LLK/2/6); "African Love: A Comedy from the French of Mérimée" (King's/LLK/2/5/1); "Chant Credule" (King's/JHB/1/12); "Henry and Emma" (King's/JHB/1/12); "Vulcan" (King's/JHB/1/12); "It's a Long Worm that has no Turning" (King's/JHB/1/12; MS at BL 4016C/ADD 30331.3); "Mad Misery" (King's/JHB/1/12); "A Masque" (King's/JHB/1/12); "Love and Liberty" (Trinity College Library/Bell/1/16); various plays and programs by Lytton and Marjorie Strachey (BL 81887 A. Strachey Papers [Additional]).

The play entitled "A Quiet Morning in Whistler Studios" is likely to be the untitled, unfinished play in Vanessa Bell's handwriting held at the British Library (BL 4016C/ADD 83330); a program cover design by Angelica Bell is held at King's College, Cambridge (Kings/AG/2/4). Sadly, I have been unable to trace "The Last Days of Old Pompeii," although photographs of the production can be found in Vanessa Bell's family albums held at Tate Britain; nor the adaptations of Thackeray's "The Rose and the Ring" and Carroll's

have scarcely considered the significance of private theatre in Bloomsbury and yet it performed a number of interesting tasks, while masquerading as comic family entertainment—revealing secrets, lampooning embarrassing idiosyncrasies, flattering, criticizing, resolving disputes and soothing hurts.

The theatricals exposed as much about the participants' attitudes and opinions as many of their letters, diaries and autobiographies. Plays written and privately performed by the group of friends revolved around their sexual and social relationships; their political and artistic stances and their response to their Victorian upbringing, all of which were explored through a miasma of allusion, parody and satire. The primary function of this form of entertainment was to allow the authors and performers to bring the impermissible into the open. This could be to comment on a friend's folly; to explore the latest scandal; launch an attack on the social, moral, political and artistic structures of their parents' generation; or to criticize the current hierarchy. In *Performance Theory*, Richard Schechner describes this process of theatricalization as

> a reflection of, or mediation among [...] interactions, freed as they are by theatrical convention from being "really real." Instead, actions are segregated "in the theatre" where through exaggeration, repetition, and metaphorisation they can be displayed and handled. (Schechner 243)

The relationships between the group of friends, family and acquaintances, and their reactions to the world at large, were often dramatized in comic skits which, as Schechner avers, allowed disagreements or sensitive subjects to be "displayed and handled," explored and occasionally resolved in a safe environment. The safety of this theatrical environment was largely secured through the use of jokes and the creation of comedic situations, which, as Simon Critchley points out in *On Humour*, act as "small anthropological essays [...]defamiliarising the familiar, demythologising the exotic [and, one might add, the taboo] and inverting the world of common sense" (Critchley 65). Critchley argues that by setting up this fictional frame colored by comedy, humor reveals the hidden, and forces both audience and performer to confront their reality with the aim of either celebrating it or altering it. As the private productions written by members of the group took inspiration from the group itself, comedy, which as Henri Bergson notes is "situated on the borderline between art and life" (Bergson 150), was the most suitable tone to strike. Thus humor, combined with the performance frame, allowed for the safe exploration of difficult subjects, not only in the therapeutic sense propounded by Alexander Bain and Herbert Spencer, whose work on humor considered the comic

---

"Through the Looking Glass."

to provide a physical feeling of relief,[2] but also in a Freudian sense, whereby rebellion against others and their ideas was made safe by the comic performance,[3] as well as in a Bergsonian disciplinary sense, whereby laughter contains "an unavowed intention to humiliate, and consequently to correct our neighbour" (Bergson 136). However, humor in these private theatricals served numerous other functions, particularly in terms of helping to create group cohesion; as Bergson notes, laughter "is always the laughter of a group," it "appears to stand in need of an echo" (Bergson 6 and 5).[4] Certainly, the comic elements of these private productions were not all for critique and control, relief or rebellion, but to create a sense of group worth and identity in the manner of the Bakhtinian carnival, which evoked a form of transgressive humor resulting in the cohesion of the community. However, these productions did not simply evoke the ring of a "laughter [which] only unites" (Bakhtin 135), but also set up boundaries between those who were within the close-knit society of artists and intellectuals and those who were not.

Certainly these personal comedies present the critic with a series of paradoxes that cannot be explained by reference to one theory of humor alone. As Michael Billig avers we should not "seek to reduce laughter to a single cause [...] humour is not to be considered as a unitary entity" (Billig 175). Billig argues that humor is both "universal and particular," "social and anti-social," and is both "mysterious and resistant to analysis, but [...] also understandable and analyzable" (Billig 176). In this exploration of private comedies written for performance in Bloomsbury, these paradoxes will be explored, but there must be (and this is the "mysterious" aspect of the study) an element of speculation in the realm of reaction; for less is known about the manner in which these skits were received. How hard did Virginia and Leonard Woolf laugh at "Leonard into Wolf"? Did Vanessa Bell enjoy her place in the satire "Pippington Park"? The letters and diaries of the participants are only partly illuminating. Nevertheless, one must admit that if these pieces were not received positively (even with their darker subtexts) then few would have been written and performed.

The private theatricals enjoyed in Bloomsbury were born out of the interest in amateur dramatics prevalent in the drawing rooms of their Victorian youth. Throughout the nineteenth century, charades, tableaux and dramas were privately performed, largely for recreational purposes. As Henry James noted with disgust in 1876 after his move to London: "If you go to an evening party, nothing is more

[2] See Alexander Bain. *The Emotions and the Will.* 2nd Ed. London: Longman, Green and Co., 1865, and Herbert Spencer, "The Physiology of Laughter" in *Essays Scientific, Political and Speculative* (Second Series). New York: D. Appleton, 1864.

[3] See Freud, *Jokes*.

[4] This sentiment is echoed in turn by contemporary anthropological theorists such as G. A. Fine in his chapter "Sociological Approaches to the Study of Humour" in P. E. McGee and J. H. Goldstein, eds., *Handbook of Humour Research*, Vol. 1, New York: Springer, 1983.

probable than that all of a sudden a young lady or a young gentleman will jump up and strike an attitude and begin to recite a poem or speech."[5] Sara Hudston, Pamela Cobrin and Nina Auerbach examine these pastimes in detail, demonstrating how they were designed for more than mere entertainment and often contained controversial socio-political critiques, as well as offering women, in particular, "the chance to experiment with subversive ideas and radical identities" (Cobrin 386).[6] These subversive elements of parlor dramatics were a partial response to the censorship of the stage by the Lord Chamberlain's Office, which checked plays, intended for public consumption, to ensure that they were scrupulously moral and pro-establishment. However, the performances that can be traced through the childhood drawing rooms of "Old Bloomsbury"[7] were generally mirrors of the more conventional literature read at the time, and were designed for the approval of an adult audience comprised of family and servants, such as "Her Long Lost Brother" by the young Stracheys, or "Clementina's Lovers" by the Stephen children.[8] Indeed, the manuscripts of Lytton Strachey held in the British Library contain several amusing juvenile theatrical experiments, while Quentin Bell describes in his biography of Virginia Woolf how the Stephen children regularly wrote and performed plays for the family and servants of Hyde Park Gate. "Such performances," he states, "were always advertised by means of a handbill which began thus: DENIZENS OF THE KITCHEN/ COME IN YOUR THOUSANDS!!" (Bell 50). In her early journals, Virginia Stephen recorded the performance of "Clementina's Lovers":

> After tea we gave a most striking representation of the tragedy "Clementinas Lovers" by J. T[hoby] S[tephen] in which *everyone* is killed. The servants — Pauline (who thought we were acting Aladdin) Elizabeth and Florrie, pronounced it most excellent. (*PA* 7)

Though an imitation tragedy, Thoby Stephen appears to have had a sophisticated grasp of what is to be expected in such pieces; sophisticated enough to mock the general trend for a large body-count at their conclusion. Such dramatic enterprises at home were coupled with regular theater trips selected as much for their morally

[5] Henry James quoted in Hudston (11). Such drawing room dramas were immortalised in the literature of the nineteenth century: the tableaux formed at Rochester's party in *Jane Eyre* (1847); Becky Sharpe's charades in *Vanity Fair* (1848); or Gwendolen's dramatic pretensions in *Daniel Deronda* (1876) suggest themselves in this connection.

[6] See also Auerbach, and Hudston.

[7] "Old Bloomsbury," according to Leonard Woolf, consisted of Virginia and Leonard Woolf, Adrian Stephen, Clive and Vanessa Bell, Lytton Strachey, Saxon Sydney-Turner, Desmond and Molly MacCarthy, John Maynard Keynes, Duncan Grant, E. M. Forster and Roger Fry.

[8] "Her Long Lost Brother" can be found in The British Library (81887 A. STRACHEY PAPERS (ADDITIONAL). Vol. III A (ff. 4-20), "Clementina's Lovers" is untraced.

instructive qualities as for their entertainment value. Virginia Stephen's early journals mention various trips to see insipid dramas and musical comedies, such as *The Gay Parisienne* (*PA* 14), *The White Elephant* (*PA* 17), *The White Silk Dress* (*PA* 12-13), *The French Maid* (*PA* 88) and *Talk of the Town* (*PA* 234), many of which were examples from the *pièce bien faite* and musical comedy traditions, "silly but amusing" (*PA* 234), and containing "much the same kind of thing" (*PA* 14). It is unsurprising that the Stephen children, considering their background, were shepherded to plays propounding conservative social and moral sentiments that reinforced the roles to which they were supposed to be confined. The "correspondent" reviewing an early pantomime in *The Hyde Park Gate News* notices that Santa Claus made "several moral remarks in a burly tone," while a performance of *The Swiss Express* is an extravaganza of clowns, explosions and "a supernaturally large horse," culminating in "everyone [...] arriv[ing] safe at the 'Black Bear Inn' at Chamonix in the end" (Woolf, *Hyde Park* 167 and 26). As a young woman of eighteen, still in the clutches of 22 Hyde Park Gate, Woolf recalls how she was taken (by accident) to see an "immoral" French play, and the subsequent reaction of her conservative companions:

> Lady Carnarvon, Mrs Popham of Littlecote and George Duckworth rose simultaneously. Not a word was said. Out we filed. And as our procession made its way down the stalls I saw Arthur Cane leap up in his seat like a jack-in-the-box, amazed and considerably amused that George Duckworth and Lady Carnarvon of all people had taken a girl of eighteen to see the French actors copulate upon the stage. (*MOB* 174-5)

The theatre was clearly a place to socialize and be seen, provided, of course, that it was the "right kind" of play. After all, this was an era in which many believed that "a mind ready to explode will only be made more inflammable by the shows of the stage" (Pollock 613).

As the older generation died away or lost their power over their now adult offspring, the plays seen and read by the members of "Old Bloomsbury" became much more experimental and risqué, thus offering a tacit challenge to the prohibitions of their parents. One of the first forays into the performance of drama made by "Old Bloomsbury" as young adults, was The Play Reading Society, which enabled the group of friends to experiment with drama without the need for actual performance. The selection of plays that were read at these evenings consisted mainly of bloody Renaissance tragedies or bawdy Restoration comedies with a dash of Ibsen (*Rosmersholm* on 14 February 1908) and Schnitzler (*Anatole* on 2 December 1914). The choice of Vanburgh's "saucy" comedy *The Relapse* as the society's opening piece signified the changing views and the increasing freedom of sexual self-expression desired by the fledgling circle of friends.[9] Quentin Bell describes *The Relapse* as "hardly the kind of play that Sir Leslie would have cared to have heard his daughters reading aloud in the company of young men" (Bell 124), which was, of course, the very reason for selecting it. Indeed, many of the comic plays written, read and performed by Bloomsbury were deliberately chosen as opportunities to assert a new sense of self in the face of Victorian censorship and were naturally much more challenging (intellectually, aesthetically and morally) than those selected for them by their parents' generation, or written for the entertainment of that generation. These plays were a form of rebellious humor in which the reader, writer, audience and performers stood at odds with conventional manners and morals. As James Sully averred in his *Essay on Laughter* (1902): "the laughter at what is lawless, and still more at the indecent and the profane, certainly derives a part of its gusto from a sense of the relief from restraint, which is a main ingredient in the enjoyment of all license" (Sully 118). There is certainly a sense of this "license" being taken in the selection of plays seen and read by the group at this time.

The theater also increasingly became a means to earn a living. Some members of the mature group eventually had their own dramas professionally performed, such as Lytton Strachey whose "Son of Heaven" was produced at The Scala in July 1925, while T. S. Eliot's poetic enterprises were increasingly fêted from *Sweeney Agonistes* (first performed, 1934) to *The Elder Statesman* (first performed, 1958). However, many of the group's serious dramatic pretensions were largely unsuccessful as they generally harked back to the poetic Renaissance dramas which, as Woolf claimed in "Poetry, Fiction and the Future," was "the one form which seems dead beyond all possibility of resurrection today" (*CE*2 219).[10] From 1906 Desmond MacCarthy made his name as a theatrical reviewer, and others, such as, Leonard and Virginia Woolf, T. S. Eliot and J. M. Keynes all sporadically wrote dramatic critiques. Woolf also wrote on the actress Ellen Terry (*CE*4 67-72); reviewed Francis Gribble's biography of Rachel Félix (*E*1 351-54), Sarah Bernhardt's memoirs (*BP* 201-207), and Elizabeth Robins' *A Dark Lantern* (*E*1 42-43) and *The Mills of the Gods and Other Stories* (*E*3 228-29); while the Hogarth Press published Robins' *Ibsen and the Actress* (1928). Woolf also read and commented on the manuscripts of Robins' autobiographies, *Both Sides of the Curtain* (1940) and *Raymond and I* (1956). These essays and reviews were, as Penny Farfan highlights, redolent with discussion about reality and identity, which she carried into her representation of

[9] Saxon Sydney-Turner's minutes for Friday 27th December 1907 read: "We regaled ourselves (in my opinion) with a saucy play" (King's/CHA/5/1).

[10] Woolf lampooned Lytton Strachey's efforts to write poetic plays in her first two novels where he appears as the highly intelligent, but obtuse, St. John Hirst and as William Rodney, both of whom are scribbling mock-Renaissance poetic dramas.

Ellen Terry in the play *Freshwater* (Farfan 49-64). The wider circle of acquaintances and friends also included aspiring, amateur and professional actors, directors, theatre owners and set designers.[11] In 1922, Vanessa Bell and Duncan Grant advertised themselves as "decorators domestic, ecclesiastical, theatrical, 8 Fitzroy St, W1." and were employed in all three categories.[12] Duncan Grant's passionate interest in great actresses also led him into theatrical portraiture; he painted and sketched, variously, Eleonora Duse, Madame Réjane and Marie-Hélène Dasté. This interest in production, performance and performer thus increasingly became both an amateur and professional preoccupation. Though this examination of archival material will focus on the private theatricals, rather than the group's professional connections, the professional skills developed helped to turn ordinary amateur dramatics into quite complex and lavish productions as Vanessa Bell's family albums attest.[13]

The penchant for amateur dramatics cultivated in their childhoods continued throughout their lives and it was usual for the plays written or performed privately to contain a plethora of in-jokes, which were focused on the correction of wrongs and the criticism of unpleasant characteristics, while, conversely, celebrating amusing idiosyncrasies. The comedy of such plays as "Don't Be Frightened or Pippington Park," "The Conspirators," "Chinoiseries or Grizzle's Successor," "A Hundred Years Hence or Ladies and Gentlemen," "Leonard Into Wolf," "A Quiet Morning in Whistler Studios" and "Truth Will Out or The Unfortunate Lovers" relies on a thorough knowledge of some of the central figures within and connected to Bloomsbury. Certainly Bergson, in his philosophical enquiry into the function of laughter, is clear that humor is only possible in a social environment where the performer and the audience have common ground and argues convincingly that

[11] Such acquaintances included: G. B. Shaw, W. B. Yeats, Arnold Bennett, J. B. Priestley, Noel Coward, Christopher Isherwood, W. H. Auden, Stephen Spender, Louis MacNeice, Beatrice Mayor, Max Beerbohm, Elizabeth Robins, Lydia Lopokova, Betty Potter, Virginia Isham, Ethel Smyth, Edward Sackville-West, James Strachey and Edith Craig.

[12] Quoted in *Duncan Grant & Vanessa Bell: Design and Decoration 1910-1960 Exhibition Catalogue* (London: Spink, 1991): 2. Vanessa Bell painted the scenery for the ballets, *High Yellow* (1932), *Pomona* (1933) and *Fête Galante* (1934), while Duncan Grant designed the scenery for Jacques Copeau's ballet *Twelfth Night* at the Théatre du Vieux Colombier (1914), *Pelléas et Mèlisande* (1918), *Togo or The Noble Savage* for the Stoll Review at Covent Garden (1923), Strachey's *Son of Heaven* (1925) at the Scala, "The Postman" pas de deux at The Coliseum (1925) and *Le Lac des Cygnes* and *The Enchanted Grove* for the Camargo Society at The Savoy and Old Vic (1932) and began, though failed to complete, designs for Harley Granville Barker's *Macbeth* (1912) and Copeau's *Saul* (1921). An analysis of Grant as set designer has been made by Asya Chorley in her essay "Duncan Grant as Stage Designer" in *A Cézanne in the Hedge and Other Memories of Charleston and Bloomsbury*, ed. Hugh Lee (London: Collins and Brown Ltd, 1992): 27-31. Grant also designed the costumes for Copeau's *Twelfth Night* (1914), while Bell designed those for *Pelléas et Mèlisande* (1918).

[13] The Tate Britain holds ten volumes of Vanessa Bell's family photographs from which the private photographs in this article are taken (TGA 9020).

it functions primarily as a corrective to anti-social behavior. Bergson claims that "society holds suspended over each individual member, if not the threat of correction, at all events the prospect of a snubbing, which, although it is slight, is none the less dreaded," thus comedy (and ridicule in particular) "pursues a utilitarian aim of general improvement" (Bergson 135 and 20). The private theatricals performed in Bloomsbury certainly bear out elements of Bergson's arguments. Humor, combined with the fictional frame of the stage, allowed the writers and performers to create "safe make-believe precincts" in which "actions [could] be carried to extremes" both for fun and to impart more serious messages (Schechner xix). Thus, having been "freed […] from being 'really real,'" the plays allowed the impermissible to be "displayed and handled" (Schechner 243), while their humor, if we take Bergson's line, functioned to keep the participants toeing the line. One skit, written by Dadie Rylands entitled "Leonard into Wolf or The Press Gang" (the title a play on David Garnett's novel *Lady into Fox*), does just this.[14] The play was performed at the Keynes's party at Gordon Square in 1925 and is a hilarious satire on Leonard's draconian management of the Hogarth Press and the numerous assistants that he hired and fired. The audience is invited to laugh at the depiction of Leonard Woolf's style of management, but many, including Ralph Partridge, Dadie Rylands, Richard Mortimer, Angus Davidson and John Lehmann, were to experience it at first hand. As well as lampooning Leonard and suggesting, through its comedy, that he consider amending his ways, the sketch also satirizes Ralph Partridge's intractability ("I won't clean the foul machine"); Marjorie Joad's various illnesses ("My temperature was 103 this morning") and Dadie Rylands's foppery ("I danced till four last night. [yawns]"). Virginia Woolf is most comprehensively ridiculed in this production: she is lampooned for her absent-mindedness, a trait which, to Bergson, "is always comical" (Bergson 146) ("[Enter Virginia, rather vague, like a visitor in a strange house]"); her inability to manage her servants ("I would ask you all to come and have a cup of tea but Nelly has forbidden us to have tea in today"); her creativity ("I saw an old woman selling heather on a little hand-cart […] She was a most curious old lady with green eyes and a feather in her bonnet"), and the results of her many indiscretions:

> Dadie — Virginia, Raymond has heard what you said about his shirts. Is it true that he gave you a pair of flowered pyjamas?
>
> Virginia — What did I say? I never say anything against any one. Mr. Mortimer is a very talented young man – of course it is very unfortunate that his – (Re-enter Leonard)[15]

[14] King's/PP/GHWR/4/4.

[15] King's/PP/GHWR/4/4.

Such self-aware performances were designed to instruct as well as entertain, as Bergson and, more recently, Michael Billig suggest. The audience is being asked to "become aware of itself" (Schechner 14) in a comic frame that defuses tension and avoids insult (though not necessarily embarrassment) at the same time that it criticizes and reforms.

In "Don't Be Frightened or Pippington Park," written by Maynard and Lydia Keynes, the ridicule of Vanessa Bell's character is hidden not only behind the play's comic tone, but also beneath a "topical cause célèbre."[16] A sordid affair, recently reported in the press, was used to disguise and "make safe" what could otherwise, more simply, be termed a satire on Bloomsbury. David Garnett gives the background to the tale in his memoirs:

> Mr Hayley Morris, a wealthy gentleman who had retired from the trade with China, and lived at Pippingford Park near Uckfield, had received unwelcome notoriety in the gutter press while being convicted for an offence against *les moeurs* involving a young woman under the age of consent. He also kept a number of large dogs which featured in the case. "Georgeston" is of course Charleston; Clarissa, Vanessa Bell who was impersonated by Molly MacCarthy who could not have looked less like, a fact which added to the audience's amusement. Before the performance Molly wrote to Vanessa asking whether she minded her playing the part. Vanessa grimly replied: "How can I possibly tell until I have seen it" (Garnett 3: 64)

In this play, Vanessa Bell (under the alias Clarissa Dell) is seduced by Mr. Hayley Morris (under the alias Mr. Maley Horace). Horace tempts Clarissa by offering her the chance to redesign his house and to examine his paintings in return for her living at Pippington Park.[17] The comedy of the skit relies on a thorough knowledge of Vanessa's character: her well-known dislike of visitors and dogs; her artistic preferences; her devotion to her children; her common-sense and her mixed proverbs ("Of course there's a dark horse in every cupboard in the place–

[16] Frances Partridge, "Bloomsbury House," in Hugh Lee, ed., *A Cézanne in the Hedge and Other Memories of Charleston and Bloomsbury* (London: Collins and Brown Ltd, 1992): 131.
[17] In the MS version, Maley Horace is called Hailey Morris, and the other characters keep their real-life names. The manuscript is incomplete, but is entitled "Bloomsbury Burlesque" (MS King's/JMK/PP/15/1-8). The earlier typescript, found among Lopokova's papers, is not titled and is incomplete (TS King's/LLK/2/7). The second typescript found, among Keynes's papers, appears to be complete and is probably the version used for the production (TS King's/JMK/PP/15/9-18). In this version Vanessa becomes Clarissa Dell, Roger become Codger Spry (though David Garnett remembers it as Scrodger Pry) and Clive Bell is replaced by Walter Sickert.

but after all every skeleton has a silver lining").[18] Having been seduced by Horace/Morris, Vanessa/Clarissa moves to Pippingford/ton Park and becomes Horace/Morris's "kennel maid" (an amusingly unlikely scenario considering Vanessa's antipathy toward dogs). Vanessa/Clarissa is eventually rescued by her ex-lover, her husband and her current lover: Roger Fry, Clive Bell and Duncan Grant, respectively, who are disguised as dogs. The alteration of Clive to Walter Sickert in a later version was arguably made in order to unify her rescuers as painters of the London Group; to appeal to Sickert who may have been part of the audience; or because the three men's sexual connections with Vanessa may have caused, even for Bloomsbury, an unpleasant level of discomfort in the audience. Despite ostensibly being written about the case at Pippingford Park the play is really about Bloomsbury's artistic tastes; the idiosyncrasies of the inhabitants and their sexual relationships. "Pippington Park" is an excellent example of deliberately self-referential Bloomsbury theatricals—the comedy stemming from the audience's familiarity with the characters being portrayed (even if thinly disguised). That Vanessa replied "grimly" (according to Garnett) to Molly MacCarthy's enquiry suggests her awareness of the, sometimes uncomfortable, gap between the comic style and the critical message.

Virginia Woolf was undoubtedly one of the favourite targets at these theatricals, as a letter from Vanessa Bell to her husband suggests: "then came Angelica with a most ambitious entertainment à la Ruth Draper [...] several rather good hits at Virginia were got in."[19] Woolf's quirks were also lampooned in "The Conspirators"; "Chinoiseries or Grizzle's Successor"; the manuscript in Vanessa Bell's hand, probably, though untitled, "A Quiet Morning in Whistler Studios"; and "A Hundred Years Hence." David Garnett recalls how Julian Bell's plays in particular were "largely aimed at making fun of Virginia" (Garnett 3: 63). In a letter to Julian, Vanessa Bell colludes in her son's skit on her sister and youngest son by advising him to approach Clive before the performance, and later encourages him to keep it a secret:

> She [Virginia] was very inquisitive about your play & she & Quentin hob-nobbed a good deal [...] He walked over to see her the day after, so I think they have got a grand revenge on hand. I wouldn't let her see the play as I think it will be much more effective read out when we're all there & I daresay it won't lose too much of its sting by keeping.[20]

That there is a "sting" in the play's tale is a detail which suggests these productions were, at least partly, intended to wound; firstly, as a means to reform their subject,

[18] King's/JMK/PP/15/9-18.
[19] Tate/Bell/ 9311/58.
[20] King's/CHA/1/59/2/17 and 30.

but perhaps also as a form of defense, as the prefatory note to "The Conspirators" suggests: "This work is intended as a reply to the series of libels and caricatures with which Charlestonians have been overwhelmed during the last two years."[21] Another private skit forced Vanessa to send warning to her sister that the production was perhaps more malicious than intended:

> I must warn you that an almost too painful reprisal has been prepared for you. I really don't know how either you or Leonard will take it. I will say that its most painful points were sharpened innocently.[22]

The gap between teasing and maliciousness was clearly not meant to be crossed—a pinch rather than a stab, seems to have been the objective—with the functional aims of criticism, correction and self-defense, in addition to general amusement.

There is also a significant amount of comedy surrounding the intellectual preoccupations of the group, particularly Woolf's writing. An interesting addendum to the play "Chinoiseries or Grizzle's Successor," for example, provides a perceptive, if lengthy, parody of Woolf's literary style in which the author (either Julian or Quentin Bell) demonstrates his own acute understanding of Woolf's fiction while amusing his audience at her expense:

> But then things were like that, she thought. The children had just run upstairs with the scuffle of a pack of hounds, and her freed mind floated gently, like a goldfish basking in the autumn sunshine among the pale, star-like blooms of the water lilies (They must get a new refrigerator, she thought). She looked at the muscular Christian, as the children called him. He was a disagreeable character, she thought. Yet he skinned eels to perfection, yet he always upset the coffee. Yet he amused the children. Yet he brightened the pigs at the farm, with that face of his. It was all very mysterious this life.[23]

The author certainly captures and lampoons the poetic quality of Woolf's prose; the dreamlike observations of the "freed mind" (not unlike Woolf's "lonely mind" of *The Waves* [*D*3 251]); and also appears to parody the parenthetical asides to be found in the central section of *To the Lighthouse*. This literary conversation between Woolf and her nephews continued to be carried out publicly in other

[21] BL 4016C/ ADD 83331.1.

[22] Letter from Vanessa Bell to Virginia Woolf, 27th December 1926 (Berg/Reel 21/ Folder 60). None of the plays extant are as malicious as this letter implies; it is therefore likely that the skit Vanessa is referring to has been lost.

[23] BL 4016C/ADD 83331.2.

spoofs, such as Julian Bell's short untitled play held in the Monks House Papers, in which he lampoons both Woolf and himself for their, sometimes difficult, relationship as writers:

> Grace Please Mr Julian, Mrs Woolf is downstairs and says would you stop making that noise.
>
> Julian Tell her I'm not making a noise. I'm writing poetry in the manner of Gerard Hopkins.
>
> Grace Oh well she says the sound is so hideous she cant get on with her novel.
>
> Julian God bless the woman – tell her words have no sound; they've only got sense.
>
> Seepy, creaking, sweeping, with a creaking kind of beating of the penultimate dorsal jutting out femoral tail the siskin whisking round the peeled off mouldy bottle green pear tree rivers.
>
> Well I flatter myself that's a pretty good poem – all true to an inch. Anyhow nobody could say that was written by Virginia Woolf.
>
> Grace Mrs Woolf says couldn't you try putting it all in one image. You'd find it shorter.[24]

Both of these parodies examine the author's relationship with his famous aunt by mocking their own and their aunt's predilections in terms of their literary art. That Julian, Quentin and Angelica Bell used the pen and performance to turn the mockery of the adults back on themselves is unsurprising, and this childish precocity was, to E. M. Forster at least, "terrifyingly sophisticated" (*D*3 158). As Billig points out: "Children can turn around the lessons that they learn in order to take their revenge against their parents. They can mock the parents' attempts to impose rules. They can even wait years to enjoy the opportunity" (Billig 205). Their spoofs on the behavior of the older generation are a form of rebellious humor, designed to set up their own sense of identity outside the shadow of their (in)famous parents.

Though Woolf was a favorite target, most figures found themselves immortalized in some form in all of these productions, as Vanessa states of a skit by Julian in a letter to Clive Bell: the play was "amusing and successful, and gave everyone in Bloomsbury smart raps."[25] An epilogue to an unidentified play among Julian's

[24] Sussex/MHP/ A18.

[25] 23 January 1931[?] (Tate/CHA/ 8010/2/229).

papers perhaps best summarizes the cheeky, rather than malicious, attacks on one another that such theatrical entertainments allowed:

> Besides, before blaming us, think of the pain
> Which we might have inflicted, and yet we refrain
> Not a word of our father's diminishing hair,
> Not a word of the Keynes' financial affairs.[26]
> If we've Frankie's old clothes, we've escaped Raymond's new
> And Lytton has squeaked and then vanished from view.
> As for Vita and Dotty[,] I hope you have noted
> Though they're both of them poets, their verses weren't quoted,
> And having good hearts, we don't tell what we know
> Of the oddness of Bunny, the queerness of Bo,[27]
> While it seemed to us kinder, as well as much shorter
> To omit Tommy's wife and poor Oliver's daughter,[28]
> While endless odd characters hidden away
> Down there in the audience, are not in the play,
> Though as curious and silly and mad and absurd
> As those on the stage, I will give you my word,
> Now my dear Aunt has told me – I'm sure she must know –
> "Don't write till you're aged about 60 or so, ["]
> And she'll probably think that we've made matters worse,
> By adding an Epilogue written in verse,
> Which we hope is not mystic, obscene or confusing,
> Like her or Tom Eliot, who are much more amusing.
> Well, as Nessa says, what you can't make or mend
> You must sleep in yourself – and so that is the end.[29]

This epilogue ridicules most of the notable figures in the Bloomsbury milieu; it ranges from personal comments on appearance to veiled criticism of writers and their style—no-one appears to be safe from the satirist's whip. The ribaldry in this epilogue weaves together a tissue of personal allusions which are critical of the audience, without being malicious. Though Bergson argues that humor acts as a corrective, and must therefore "make a painful impression on the person

[26] Here Julian is referring to the money that was unsuccessfully invested on behalf of Vanessa Bell by John Maynard Keynes.
[27] Bunny is David Garnett and Bo is probably Beatrice Mayor, though why they are described as odd and queer is more to do with rhyme and metre than fact.
[28] Tommy's (Stephen Tomlin's) wife and Oliver's daughter are the same person.
[29] King's/JHB/1/12.

against whom it is directed," it is difficult to admit this to be the case in this particular instance (Bergson 197). Though, admittedly, as Michael Billig points out, the targets may not have been able to reveal their displeasure out of fear that "they risk the accusation that they lack a sense of humour" (Billig 155). In these instances, the criticisms and observations of individuals, are not aggressive enough to cause serious offence. Therefore, rather than viewing the performance and the jokes as the means to keep the victim toeing the line, which Bergson and Billig suggest is the central premise of humor, these comic skits also *celebrate* the individual's eccentricities, egging them on to cultivate more that will serve as future amusement.

Though the author of the epilogue apologizes for missing people out, which may have been a relief for some, there is the sense that to have been overlooked was a slight. A reference no matter how small or impertinent was a considerable accolade—after all Woolf did write to Ethel Smyth: "being abused is a compliment" (*L6* 65). Simon Critchley rephrases this sentiment: "we smile and find ourselves ridiculous. Our wretchedness is our greatness" (Critchley 111). In her view, Woolf is suggesting that "any press is good press"; in other words, that being ridiculed renders her the center of attention and that this somehow validates her as a notable presence in Bloomsbury. Such self-interest helped to create and perpetuate the myth that developed in the 1920s and 30s of an exclusive and closed community of intellectual and aesthetic narcissists. The productions cultivated a Hobbesian sense of superiority; a form of humor, as Critchley suggests, akin to "sharing a secret code" (Critchley 68).[30] Though they laugh at themselves in these theatrical pieces, this laughter is exclusive, it reminds the uninitiated that they are not able to laugh because they are not part of the group. There is a difference between the comedy aimed at the audience who was invited to laugh at itself and the character assassination of those whose position was outside or on the periphery of the group. Figures such as Ottoline Morrell and Sybil Colefax were not meant to see or to read their representation in these comedies. For instance, Lady Ottoline was not supposed to witness the version of herself, performed by the younger generation of Bloomsbury for the amusement of their adult audience, at a 1917 production: "We had great fun last night with the children who acted a play, entirely their own invention. Rachel [MacCarthy] as Ottoline, [?] 'Morrell', Julian 'Keynes' and Quentin a lunatic. Rachel was amazing, accepting first Morrell and then Keynes. I can't think how they got hold of it all."[31] Nor were these great ladies meant to ap-

[30] Although Billig points out that Hobbes's argument ignores the communal aspects of humor, the sense that the Bloomsbury theatricals cultivated a feeling of superiority over the uninitiated is too compelling to ignore.

[31] Letter from Vanessa Bell to Virginia Stephen, 19th September 1917 (Berg/Reel 20/Folder 46). David Garnett also recalls: "Molly MacCarthy brought her children to stay and one

preciate "The Conspirators," in which they both appear imprisoned in a lavatory; or the party at which Vanessa herself dressed up and imitated Ottoline's "drawl."[32] It is not difficult to imagine the "unlaughter"[33] with which these skits would have been received by Lady Ottoline had she been present; for every tendentious joke, as Freud averred, "calls for three people: in addition to the one who makes the joke, there must be a second who is taken as the object of the hostile or sexual aggressiveness, and a third in whom the joke's aim of producing pleasure is fulfilled" (Freud, *Jokes* 143). Sadly for them, Morrell and Colefax were taken as the "objects" by their satirists who aimed to produce pleasure in themselves and their co-conspirators in the audience.

The theatricals establish a sense of the group's understanding of their self-worth; none more so than Quentin Bell's "A Hundred Years After or Ladies and Gentlemen," which was performed to great acclaim at Charleston on August 30, 1936.[34] The cast included Jane Bussy as Madame de Canquaillotte, a French tourist; Quentin Bell as Miss Helena B. Conker, an American tourist; and Christopher Strachey as the tour guide. It is not clear who played the part of Nancy Bugge, Madame de Canquaillotte's English niece, possibly Angelica Bell or Eve Younger who were both present on the evening. The plot was very simply based on a futuristic tour of Charleston Museum in the year 2036.

The play complimented its audience by suggesting that their fame would continue into the future—even if the truth has been somewhat distorted by the passing of the years. Lydia Lopokova becomes a "soviet parachutist"; Virginia

---

evening they announced that they had got up a play for our benefit. The little wretches had been listening to conversation at table and the central figure was Ottoline, involved in some emotional entanglement and played by Rachel MacCarthy. The enchanting little girl, as lively and innocent as a squirrel, was not cut out by nature for the part. But Julian, as producer, had coached her carefully from memory, and her imitation, at second-hand, of Lady Ottoline's menacing growl and drawling whine, and the airs of aristocratic majesty which she put on, sent us into fits of laughter, though Molly, I think, was wondering what might not be coming next" (Garnett 2: 178-79).

[32] For Vanessa's performance see her letter to Julian Bell, 5th September 1935 (Tate/ Bell/9311/58).

[33] A term coined by Michael Billig to denote the reaction of the audience to an aggressive or uncomfortable joke. Unlaughter is the opposite reaction to the one intended by the teller, i.e. whatever stands in place of the laughter that was anticipated. Billig discusses this term at length in his chapter "Laughter and Unlaughter" (Billig 175-199).

[34] BL 4016C ADD/ 83330. Woolf wrote to her sister following the production: "Congratulations to all the actors last night. We thought it the most brilliant of all the performances"(*L6* 69). In a letter to Julian Bell, 5th September 1936, Vanessa gave a lengthy account of the play and the other highlights of the evening which involved a song by Eve Younger, a recitation by Jane Bussy, an "ambitious entertainment à la Ruth Draper" by Angelica Bell, a "turn" by Lydia Lopokova, a Spanish dance in the costume of a semi-naked woman by Duncan Grant and a cameo of Ottoline played by Vanessa herself (see Tate/ Bell/ 9311/ 58).

Fig. 1. *Jane Bussy and Quentin Bell in "A Hundred Years After or Ladies and Gentlemen" (Tate/TGA.9020/F22). Further photographs can be found in TGA/9020/Album 8. ©Tate, London, 2011 and ©Estate of Vanessa Bell courtesy of Henrietta Garnett.*

Woolf transforms into "Virginia Sackville-West" wife of "Sir Clive Bell the famous sportsman and wit"; John Maynard Keynes's *Economic Consequences of the Peace* is equated with *Das Kapital*; photographs of pictures by Vanessa Bell are signed Duncan Grant "owing to the illiberal prejudices of the 20th Century against women painters"; and the tourists are asked to "notice the significant form" of the pictures, which comically over-simplifies Roger Fry's artistic theory. Even the audience was co-opted into this play as pieces of furniture:

> Guide (pointing to Lydia) This charming occasional table is an excellent specimen of Russian workmanship a product of the old imperial school, very highly polished. (pointing to Maynard) This monumental grandfather clock was designed by Sir Isaac Newton.
>
> Madam C Tiens elle retarde cette pendule.
>
> Guide Now the ladies will be interested in this Louis XV escritoire (pointing to Clive) can we not imagine the fair ladies of yore penning their billet doux on its richly inlaid surface.

This "device," as Quentin and Angelica observe, was "rather successful as a means of ensuring audience participation" (Vanessa Bell 126).[35] In this production, the confidence in their fame and their work, though comically distorted, is clear. Indeed, the prediction that Charleston would, one day, become a museum to the group has been fulfilled. "100 Years After" exemplifies the self-congratulatory nature of Bloomsbury, highlighting their self-confidence, as well as their sense of segregation and celebration of their difference from the world at large.

Thus far it is clear that these private theatricals were designed to criticize, include, exclude and admire (albeit in a backhanded manner), as well as simply to entertain their audience who were often their subjects. However, as suggested by the selection of plays read, written, performed and attended in the early years of the twentieth century, there was a further undercurrent running beneath these theatricals. Private comic theater also offered a way of processing and explaining

[35] It is important to bear in mind the many differences among the recollections of such performances. In Angelica's recollections Clive is an eighteenth-century chair, not a Louis XV escritoire; Keynes is a safe, not a "monumental grandfather clock […] designed by Sir Isaac Newton"; Lopokova remains a "charming occasional table," but unnamed audience members, absent from the play script, are recalled as an oak table and Venetian mirror; there is no mention of Angelica's recollection of "Virginia as a tall writing desk"; Quentin Bell's description for *A Cézanne in the Hedge* has Leonard and Virginia as bookcases labelled fact and fiction, but again, this is not in the script held at the British Library. These anomalies suggest that there may have been a later typescript than the one currently held at the British Library.

Fig. 2. *Illustration of Lopokova as Queen Victoria by Quentin Bell from* The New Bulletin, *3 September 1927 [?] (c) British Library Board. All Rights Reserved. BL 4016B/ ADD 83320.*

the repressive elements of their youth—an aspect of humor that Freud explored in *Jokes and their Relation to the Unconscious*, first published in 1905. In this work, Freud posited the idea that the "tendentious" joke "will evade restrictions and open sources of pleasure that have become inaccessible," thus the joke allows what has been repressed (Freud suggests these things to be connected to hostility and sexuality) to become "accessible" (Freud 147). The private theatricals were an opportunity to criticize and reframe their present, but they also offered the chance to publicly criticize and process the repressive elements of their past.

Thus, the favorite characters, images and themes at parties and plays included Victorian figures of authority and their repressive essentialist sexual morality, which polarized men and women into immutable gender roles and swept discussion of sex and sexuality under the proverbial carpet. In reaction to the taboos which governed their youth, Bloomsbury plays were frivolous, often sexually provocative and thoroughly disrespectful of hierarchy. *The New Bulletin* article of September 3rd 1927[?], for example, reports a dance performed by Lydia Lopokova, the Russian ballerina and divorcée, in the character of Queen Victoria, the epitome of British national identity and the ideal of womanliness. Such a representation would have been considered an impertinence in the days of the circle's nineteenth century youth, but in Bloomsbury it was enjoyed for its delightful irreverence. Other symbols of authority, such as the police force and the aristocracy, are similarly ridiculed, particularly in "The Conspirators," "Chinoiseries," and "A Quiet Morning in Whistler Studio" in which the police force is portrayed as bumbling and inefficient, and the aristocracy, in the forms of Lady Ottoline Morrell and Lady Sybil Colefax, are represented as interfering and ignorant. This lampooning of the elements of hierarchy revered by the Victorian age continued into the village pageant which appears in Woolf's final novel, *Between the Acts*. Here she represents the age with a comical policeman and a melodramatic engagement (symbols of law and patrilineal order):

> *Go to Church on Sunday; on Monday, nine sharp, catch the City Bus. On Tuesday it may be, attend a meeting at the Mansion House for the redemption of the sinner; at dinner on Wednesday attend another—turtle soup. Some bother it may be in Ireland; Famine. Fenians. What not. On Thursday it's the natives of Peru require protection and correction; we give 'em what's due. But mark you, our rule don't end there. It's a Christian country, our Empire; under the White Queen Victoria. Over thought and religion; drink; dress; manners; marriage too, I wield my truncheon. Prosperity and respectability always go, as we know, 'and in 'and.* (*BA* 162)[36]

[36] The village pageant in Woolf's *Between the Acts* deserves further analysis than I have time to give it here; Penny Farfan gives it thorough attention in her chapter "Writing/performing:

However, the attack on rigid gender boundaries and desire for freedom of sexual self-expression was at the heart of these productions and deliberately lay in contrast to the strictures preached in the Victorian pulpit. At one event Vanessa Bell performed a dance during which she lost half of her clothing; at another J. T. Sheppard impersonated the great soprano Madam Alemita Galli-Curci; Lytton Strachey's transvestite play, "The Unfortunate Lovers or Truth Will Out," written in 1913, caused a stir when it represented Bloomsbury's partner-swapping antics; as did Woolf's incestuous casting of *Freshwater*.[37] In a letter to Julian, Vanessa Bell described Duncan Grant's "obscene" performance as a Spanish senorita for Quentin's twenty-sixth birthday:

> I had to be dressing or undressing Duncan in his obscene cardboard figure, tying it to him by tapes and arranging his mask, comb and mantilla—(I hope to have photos to sent you) [...] I'm rather uncertain how or where to get the ones of Duncan developed they're so indecent, or should be) [...] Duncan went on properly equipped and pirouetted about and was generally admitted to be the last word in obscenity.[38]

If a professionally written play was performed it was selected as much for its dissident qualities as for its literary merit. These included: *Salome*, the banned play by Oscar Wilde, which was presented as a shadow play, "featur[ing] a protruding severed head made by Duncan Grant out of cardboard and oozing red gelatine" (Ruotolo vii); Milton's *Comus*, which revolves around an attempted rape; and Schnitzler's *La Ronde* in which simulated sexual intercourse by Ralph Partridge made even the permissive Bloomsbury audience feel very uncomfortable. As Vanessa Bell writes to Roger Fry: "It seemed to me pointless & rather painful, as they acted very realistically & rather slowly & the audience felt simply as if a real copulation were going on in the room & tried to talk to drown the very realistic groans made by Partridge!"[39] *La Ronde* and *Salome* were highly controversial in their time, and both deal with an amoral or frankly sadistic element in human sexuality. The transvestism, homosexuality, gender confusion, and sexual and feminist themes explored through such entertainments, whether professionally or privately written, were designed to challenge and deconstruct the rigid precepts surrounding

---

Virginia Woolf between the acts" (89-101).

[37] The play saw Angelica take the part of the young Ellen Terry partnered by her brother Julian as Lieutenant John Craig (the lover) and her father Duncan Grant as George Frederick Watts (the husband), while Vanessa, as Julia Margaret Cameron, was the wife of Leonard as Charles Hay Cameron. This casting was, as Hermione Lee argues, "good for knowing laughs" (Lee 661).

[38] 5 September 1936 (Tate/Bell/9311/58).

[39] 22nd June 1924 (King's/CHA/1/59/4/15).

Fig. 3. *Duncan Grant as a Spanish dancer. Courtesy of Tate Britain (Tate/TGA/9020/AA43). Further photographs can be found in TGA/9020/Album 8. ©Tate, London, 2011 and ©Estate of Vanessa Bell, courtesy of Henrietta Garnett.*

gender identity and gender roles preached to them in their youth. Though speaking of writing more generally, E. M. Forster made it clear that he desired aesthetes in repressed England to "write freely about sex" and wanted "it recognized that sex is a subject for serious treatment and also for comic treatment," the latter of which was the aim of some, if not all, of Bloomsbury's privately written plays and costume parties (Forster 81).

While exploring the themes of homosexuality, transvestism and promiscuity, many of the plays undermined the stable and romantic Victorian notion of marriage as symbolized for Virginia Woolf by Leslie and Julia Stephen and Stella and Jack Hills (*MB* 196). "Love and Liberty: A Farcical Comedy in Three Acts" (c. 1924) written by Clive Bell after the style of Oscar Wilde and the eighteenth century comedy of manners, reflects some of the group's views regarding the institution of marriage, though the Bells' permissive relationship was not the only (or ideal) view of marriage held by the circle of family and friends.[40] In Bell's play, the Wildean Sir Isaac suggests that wedlock should be treated as a "business association" in which love has no place:

> Sir Isaac: (meditative) The beauty of marriage is that it makes love possible—for the lovers I mean. As Gretton justly points out, marriage is a business association between a man and a woman. Love has nothing to do with business, and, what is more, business destroys love. Keep them apart. Lovers who attempt to share the common round, the daily task, will very soon cease to be lovers. A man must never be anything but a lover to the woman he adores, and she must never be anything but his mistress. Every woman needs a comrade, a work-day, business companion—and a lover. If women were to live with their lovers, love would vanish from the face of the earth. Happily, they have husbands. Marriage is the safeguard of love.[41]

After the idealized vision of marriage and fidelity propounded by their parents' generation, Bell attempts a form of theater in a style recognized by that generation, but containing deliberately sexually subversive sentiments. By ridiculing his parents' perception of marriage using the framework of the comedy of manners, Bell is exercising a form of rebellion. In this play, his is a Freudian tendentious humor that mocks the old hierarchies by addressing subjects that they ruled out as taboo, in this instance any questioning of the sanctity of marriage. Of course such an overt challenge to the establishment could only really be voiced in such private pieces which would never see the censor's red pen.

[40] Clive Bell, "Love and Liberty" (Trinity College Library/Bell/1/16).
[41] Trinity College Library/BELL/1/16.

In *Freshwater*, Woolf offers a more feminist view of the institution. Woolf's play depicts the teenage actress Ellen Terry leaving her aged artist husband, George Frederick Watts, refusing his name and casting her wedding ring into the sea:

Nell Oh but what about this? [She takes her wedding ring off.]
John Did the old gentleman with a white beard really give you that?
Nell Yes. It was dug out of a tomb. Beatrice's. No, Laura's! Lady Raven Mount Temple gave it him on the top of the Acropolis at dawn. It symbolises—let me see, what does this wedding ring symbolise? With this ring I thee wed; with this brush I thee worship—It symbolises Signor's marriage to his art.
John He's committed bigamy. I thought so! (*FR* 27-28)

The wedding ring, having been decided as a symbol of Watts's union with his art, rather than with his wife, is then disrespectfully cast into the sea and swallowed by a porpoise. Thus, Ellen Terry escapes from a loveless and lifeless marriage to the ideal Victorian "great man" (George Frederick Watts) and into the arms of the modern man (Lieutenant John Craig). With Ellen's last act of self-assertion, Woolf discards the definitive symbol of the Victorian marriage, the wedding ring, an emblem of a union which in Ellen's case consolidated patriarchal order, erased her individuality and forced her into childlike dependency. It is no coincidence that in Woolf's earlier work the nineteenth century makes Orlando's finger begin to itch for a ring, as "couples trudge and plod in the middle of the road indissolubly linked together" (*O* 166).

Ellen's marriage to Watts has not only removed her freedom, but more sinisterly her identity. Just as the ring symbolizes Ellen's slavery to Watts, the eradication of her own name in favor of his, or of an abstract concept chosen by him, symbolizes the loss of her individuality:

Nell And my name is Mrs George Frederick Watts.
John But haven't you got another?
Ellen Oh plenty! Sometimes I'm Modesty. Sometimes I'm Poetry. Sometimes I'm Chastity. Sometimes, generally before breakfast, I'm merely Nell.
John I like Nell best. (*FR* 23-24)

Eventually and significantly, Ellen reclaims her identity by re-establishing her own name, as well as her freedom, by casting her ring into the sea. In order to achieve emancipation Ellen must leave the confines of life as a wife, "angel in the house" and artistic muse in order to seek a "real" life in Bloomsbury involving "beef steaks; beer; standing under an umbrella in the rain; waiting to go into a theatre; crowds of people; hot chestnuts; omnibuses" (*FR* 26). Therefore, Nicola Shaughnessy argues in her 1995 thesis, "the character of Terry herself could be read as a parodic reconstruction of the New Woman role" (Shaughnessy 36-7). Ellen's elopement certainly represents the age of the "new woman" who takes control of her own destiny eschewing the prescriptions of the older generation who seek to confine her to a stereotype. As Penny Farfan notes in *Women, Modernism and Performance*, the early drafts of the play focus less on Terry and more on Woolf's great aunt, Julia Margaret Cameron; but in the lapse of over ten years it is Terry, not Cameron, who is transformed into "the 'central' character" (Farfan 49) and the focus shifts towards questions of female identity, rather than ancestry. On the other hand, Shaughnessy asserts that *Freshwater* should be read as a "self-reflexive exploration of gender representation" and as "codedly autobiographical" in terms of its lesbian subtext (Shaughnessy 6). Shaughnessy makes a convincing case for the play's questioning of a lesbian identity, arguing that Ellen's cross-dressing, cut out in the performed version of *Freshwater*, was also employed in reality by lesbians such as Vita Sackville-West, Radclyffe Hall and Christopher St John. Shaughnessy claims that the original casting of Ann Stephen as Craig and her representation of the male characters, who suggest a "subtle disavowal of heterosexuality" because of their a-sexuality, impotence or lustfulness, help to contribute to the play's Sapphic undertones (Shaughnessy 40 and 183-84). Thus, the play not only opens up questions of female identity, but also of the fluidity of gender identity more generally—both of these readings set the play in clear opposition to the biological essentialism of her childhood.

The dense tissue of quotations and artistic allusions that Woolf weaves through the play also serve her feminist cause by demonstrating how women's language has been requisitioned by their male counterparts. Replacing her own language with the words of others, and more specifically with the words of such "great men" as Keats, Tennyson and Watts, Ellen unwittingly illustrates how women's voices have been commandeered by the Victorian patriarchal establishment. In *Freshwater*, Ellen's various misquotations and her haphazard list of allusions to the work of great male writers is comically lost on Craig:

> Nell — And beauty is truth; truth beauty; that is all we know and all we ought to ask. Be good, sweet maid, and let who will be clever. Oh, and the utmost for the highest, I was forgetting that.
>
> John — It's worse than shooting the sun with a sextant. (*FR* 25)

That Ellen jumbles a misquotation from Keats's "Ode on a Grecian Urn" and a chauvinist phrase from Charles Kingsley's poem "A Farewell" with her husband's catchphrase suggests a lack of both understanding and an affinity with the language of patriarchy. Ellen has mimicked the sound, but has no concept of the sense. Craig openly mocks Ellen's adoption of the language of the great Victorian male:

> John I'm a lieutenant in the Royal Navy. That's my ship over there. Can't you see it?
>
> [Nell *looks*.]
>
> Nell That? That's a real ship. That's not the kind of ship that sinks with all we love below the verge.
>
> John My dear girl. I don't know what you're talking about. Of course it's a real ship. The *Iron Duke*. Thirty-two guns. Captain Andrew Hatch. My name's Craig. Lieutenant John Craig of Her Majesty's Navy. (*FR* 23)

In response to Ellen's romantic and tragic quotation from Tennyson's "The Princess," Craig lists the very prosaic facts of his ship—that it is real; that it is called *The Iron Duke*; that it has thirty-two guns; and that the captain is one Andrew Hatch. Here, Craig's mundane response comically diffuses the tension set up by Ellen's quotation. *Freshwater* uses intertextuality to highlight the egotism of the archetypal Victorian "great man" who coins phrases and recites his own poetry expecting his female acolytes to use this language in lieu of their own mode of self-expression. However, Ellen finds her voice because she elopes with a "new man," someone who does not understand (or expect her) to use the language that she has been assigned at Freshwater.

Woolf clearly and systematically makes fun of the Victorian view of gender identity and its attendant layers of hypocrisy in *Freshwater*, but the play also deconstructs the unconditional hero-worship of "great men" and the Victorian penchant for moral art. In *Freshwater*, while appreciating that Watts and Tennyson are great artists in their respective forms, Woolf deliberately presents them as slightly ridiculous, self-obsessed old men. She portrays Tennyson with soft skin talking of wet dreams (*FR* 14) and reciting "Maud" to an unappreciative audience, while Watts mistakenly paints the Egyptian symbol of fertility on the veil of Modesty:

> Watts Horror! Horror! I have been most cruelly deceived! Listen: [He reads.] "The Milky Way among the ancients was the universal token of fertility. It symbolised the spawn of fish, the innumerable progeny of the sea, and the fertility of the marriage bed." Horror! Oh Horror! I who have always lived

> for the Utmost for the Highest have made Modesty symbolise the fertility of fish! (*FR* 18)

Watts's desire to impart a moral message to his viewers is comically defused by his mistake. His claim "it shall never be said that George Frederick Watts painted a single hair that did not tend directly—or indirectly—to the spiritual and moral elevation of the British Public" (*FR* 65) is ludicrous in the light of his error and in the loss of his wife/muse to a naval lieutenant. The incontrovertibility of Victorian artistic symbolism was "hateful" to Woolf, who stated in a letter to Roger Fry: "I can't manage Symbolism except in this vague, generalised way" (*L*3 385). To Woolf, symbols were fluid, offering a variety of meanings to different individuals, whether written or painted. In her earlier draft, Woolf demonstrates more clearly her antipathy for such imagery. Watts's sham symbolism which, for expediency's sake, transforms Modesty into Maternity, is laughable (*FR* 66), particularly because he then transposes a letter arguing against "spiritous liquors" onto the figures of Mammon and Maternity, concluding that:

> Mammon typifies British love of beer. Maternity, two million horse marines [...] Thus the picture will serve I hope a very high and holy purpose. I shall call it Mammon trampling on Maternity, or the Prosperity of the British Empire being endangered. (*FR* 67)

Watts's self-righteousness and self-serving concept of symbolism is, Woolf makes clear in *Freshwater*, abhorrent. The Victorian desire to create a strict symbolic code in art and literature was in direct opposition to this view and she aired her opinions overtly— the privacy of such a piece daring her to more obviously critical observations than she would ever allow herself in her fiction.

While enjoying the paraphernalia of the age—"masses of Cameron photographs, shawls, cameos, peg-top trousers, laurel trees, laureates and all the rest" (*L*3 73) and particularly her aunt's eccentricities—there is no doubt that Woolf holds the Victorians responsible for a number of wider reaching sins in this play, including nationalism and empire building, aesthetic conservatism and the cult of the "great man." Though Woolf disclaimed the piece prior to production as "spirited fun" (*D*2 251); "a farce —for a joke" (*D*4 264-65) and "donkeys work" (*D*4 273); and afterwards claimed it "was to amuse my sisters' children" (*L*5 365; see also *L*5 454) and "a family joke [...] a mere Christmas scrap, and not actable in a serious sense" (*L*5 454), it was a piece of writing that had taken over ten years to complete, while the opinions of those present at the performance were dissected seriously and at length in her diary (*D*4 274-75). Nor, as Farfan rightly argues, was the play "simply 'a joke' entirely without connection to her other work" (Farfan

49), for many of the topics represented in this light-hearted piece were linked to Woolf's social, sexual and political outlooks. Like many of the other Bloomsbury theatricals which challenged the Victorian world with their sexual amorality and moral ambiguity, *Freshwater* similarly ridicules the patriarchal establishment upheld by her father and mother's generation. Victorian rules of etiquette; their sexual morality; their belief in strictly segregated gender roles; their love of law, order and social stability; their worship of the cult of great men and their didactic codification of aesthetics, were all subjects to come under the satirist's knives. In *Freshwater*, Woolf takes the opportunity to highlight, deride and thereby reject some of these repressive elements for an audience, many of whom would have experienced them all. Woolf's *Freshwater* is more than just "a joke"; it was another chance to negotiate between her modernist present and Victorian past. Woolf, and the group's, preoccupation with "the sins of their fathers" caused them continually to communicate with and criticize the Victorian age throughout their private theatricals and their public work, whether consciously or not.[42]

However, *Freshwater* is more than a simple skit on Victorian manners and morals; it shows Woolf testing out an unfamiliar medium, which, though always read, seen and considered, had not been properly written by her. Though "a joke," the piece offered Woolf the opportunity to experiment with drama, which in her literary manifesto "Poetry, Fiction and the Future" (1927), plays a central role in her creation of the novel of the future: "It will have something of the exaltation of poetry, but much of the ordinariness of prose. It will be dramatic, and yet not a play. It will be read, not acted" (*E*4 435). In this essay, drama must combine with prose and poetry in order to express and interest the "modern mind" (*E*4 433). *Between the Acts*, of all her novels, arguably moves the closest towards achieving this aim, a point which Mark Hussey and Anne Yanko Wilkinson (54) have considered. Hussey argues that *Between the Acts* was written to the vision outlined in this essay "in so precise a way that it seems almost as if Woolf wrote the book with the essay of 1927 before her" (144). Ann Yanko Wilkinson prefigures this statement in her 1966 essay: "*Between the Acts* is 'the novel to come' (arriving on schedule in 1941) that Virginia Woolf wrote of in 1927 [...] it seems almost as if the writer had her own fifteen-year-old prescription in front of her as she wrote" (54-56). Following the success of *Freshwater*, the desire to write another play surfaced in a diary entry dated 19 January 1935 (the night after the performance): "I have an idea for a 'play' Summers night [sic]. Someone on a seat. And voices speaking from the flowers" (*D*4 275). However, the inverted commas around the word "play" suggest that this is not quite what Woolf means; perhaps this thought is the first inkling of the novel of the future, *Between the Acts*?

[42] It is important to bear in mind that, though Woolf criticized the age, she also had some respect and affection for it, as Steve Ellis demonstrates.

Woolf certainly envisaged *Between the Acts* as "becom[ing] in the end a play" (*D5* 139) and in the first typescript sectioned the novel into titled scenes, included a list of characters in the style of dramatis personae and added the title "The Second Act" to the beginning of the section of the novel containing the second act of the pageant, though the actual second act of the pageant does not begin until a number of pages later.[43] It is also important to note that the pageant in Woolf's typescript was not italicized, which suggests that it was not to be seen as separate from the audience sections, unlike the interludes of *The Waves*.[44] Upon completion, Woolf described her novel as "the Pageant: the Play—finally *Between the Acts*" (*D5* 356). However, the result was not a straightforward performable play like *Freshwater*; after all, she was clear in her definition of the novel of the future that "it will be dramatic, and yet not a play" (*E4* 435). *Between the Acts* is novel, poem and play. Though it keeps the general form of a third person narrative novel, the text is interspersed with the script of the pageant, extracts of poetry, and is rich with theatrical metaphor. *Freshwater* certainly demonstrated Woolf's ability to turn her hand to playwriting and it is no coincidence that the germ for *Between the Acts* appeared in Woolf's diary the day after the performance. *Freshwater* is one of the many prefigurations of the pageant in *Between the Acts*; other sources include the penchant for patriotic pageants of the time by figures such as E. M. Forster and T. S. Eliot; the village plays in Rodmell in 1940 (*L6* 400); the production of *Gammer Gurton's Needle* performed by Angelica Bell in 1938; Leonard Woolf's play *The Hotel*, written during the novel's inception; and the sense of the building war as a theatrical production (*D5* 343; 202; 231). In *Freshwater*, we are given a piece of theater which arguably helped to inspire and inform her final novel or "pageant" as she termed it upon finishing the draft (*D5* 340).

Nevertheless, the significance of *Freshwater* to Woolf's serious creative work should not be overstated. Ultimately, Woolf's play was one of the many comic pieces performed privately in Bloomsbury, which are as revealing of the participants' opinions and relationships as their letters, diaries and memoirs. They enlighten idiosyncrasies, rivalries, loves, hates, follies and foibles, which were brought safely into the open within their comic theatrical frames. They also served to reinforce the myth of exclusivity and intellectual vanity with which Bloomsbury came to be linked. On occasion they betray the circle's socio-political views; but more often, when not aiming hits at one another, cast light on their aesthetic and sexual philosophies, which were deliberately at odds with both their parents'

[43] See the Earlier Typescript, Draft 1, Scenes 1 and 25, pp. 5-6 and p. 155 in *Virginia Woolf Pointz Hall: The Earlier and Later Typescripts of* Between the Acts. Ed. Mitchell A. Leaska. New York: University Publications, 1983: 36 and 128.

[44] A case for this is made by Mark Hussey in his edition of *Between the Acts* (Cambridge UP, 2011)

and their own generations. Woolf's *Freshwater* is one of the most accomplished pieces that looked more widely at these topics, though this may partly be linked to the pressure of a large audience of approximately eighty guests for which it was performed, as well as to Woolf's own desire for acclaim. The piece also, and more significantly, helped to focus the use of drama in fiction, as it opened for Woolf the potential of the pageant in *Between the Acts*, the piece which Woolf referred to throughout her diary as her "play." Most importantly, the theatricals were not simply a moment of physiological relaxation achieved through the release of laughter, as Victorian relief theorists Bain and Spenser argue. The pieces are not saying, to use Freud's words: "Look! Here is the world, which seems so dangerous! It is nothing but a game for children, just worth making a jest about" ("Humour" 166). Though this laughter does "unite" in a Bakhtinian sense, it is also, and simultaneously, "repressive" and "contestive" (Holmes 159-85), "disciplinary" and "rebellious."[45] The skits form a complex web of references revealing sometimes more than they necessarily intended about the relationships between the players, audience and their social context, as well as, particularly in Woolf's case, their creative projects, and for these reasons they should be viewed as very serious jokes.

Works Cited

Auerbach, Nina. *Private Theatricals: The Lives of the Victorians*. Cambridge, MA: Harvard UP, 1990. Print.

Bakhtin, Mikhail. *Speech Genres and Other Late Essays*. Austin: U of Texas P, 1986. Print.

Bell, Quentin. *Virginia Woolf*. London: Hogarth P, 1990. Print.

Bell, Vanessa. *Vanessa Bell's Family Album*. Eds. Angelica Garnett and Quentin Bell. London: J. Norman and Hobhouse, 1981. Print.

Bergson, Henri. *Laughter: An Essay on the Meaning of the Comic*. London: Macmillan & Co., 1911. Print.

Billig, Michael. *Laughter and Ridicule: Towards a Social Critique of Humour*. London: Sage, 2005. Print.

Berg. *Virginia Woolf Manuscripts from the Berg Collection at the New York Public Library*. 21 Reels. NY: Primary Source Microfilm, 1993.

Cobrin, Pamela. "Dangerous Flirtations: Politics, the Parlour, and the Nineteenth Century Victorian Amateur Actress." *Women and Performance: A Journal of Feminist Theory* 16: 3 (November 2006): 385-402. Print.

Critchley, Simon. *On Humour*. Abingdon: Routledge, 2002. Print.

[45] Disciplinary humor is the aspect of humor that forms Bergson's focus, while its rebellious aspects are centred on by Freud.

Ellis, Steve. *Virginia Woolf and The Victorians*. Cambridge: Cambridge UP, 2007. Print.

Farfan, Penny. *Women, Modernism and Performance*. Cambridge: Cambridge UP, 2004. Print.

Forster, E.M. "Liberty in England." *Abinger Harvest* (1936). Harmondsworth: Penguin, 1967. Print.

Freud, Sigmund. *Jokes and their Relation to the Unconscious* [1905], Vol. 6. London: Penguin Freud Library, 1991. Print.

——. "Humour" (1927). *The Standard Edition of the Complete Works of Freud: The Future of an Illusion, Civilisation and its Discontents, and Other Works*, Vol. XXI, London: Hogarth Press, 1961: 161-66. Print.

Garnett, David. *The Golden Echo*. Vols. 1-3. London: Chatto & Windus, 1955. Print.

Holmes, Janet. "Politeness, Power and Provocation: How Humour Functions in the Work-place." *Discourse Studies* 2 (2000): 159-85. Print.

Hudston, Sara. *Victorian Theatricals: From Menageries to Melodrama*. London: Methuen, 2000. Print.

Hussey, Mark. "'"I" Rejected; "We" Substituted:' Self and Society in *Between the Acts*." *Reading and Writing Women's Lives: A Study of the Novel of Manners*. Ed. Bege K. Bowers and Barbara Brothers. Ann Arbor: UMI Research Press, 1990: 141-52. Print.

Lee, Hermione. *Virginia Woolf*. London: Vintage, 1997. Print.

Lee, Hugh, ed. *A Cézanne in the Hedge and Other Memories of Charleston and Bloomsbury*. London: Collins and Brown Ltd, 1992. Print.

Noble, Joan Russell, ed. *Recollections of Virginia Woolf*. London: Peter Owen, 1972. Print.

Pollock, Judith. "For and Against the Play: A Dialogue." *Nineteenth Century: A Monthly Review*. Vol. I, June 1877. London: Henry S. King and Co., 1877. Print.

Schechner, Richard. *Performance Theory*. London: Routledge, 2003. Print.

Shaughnessy, Nicola. "The Dramatic Writings of Gertrude Stein, Virginia Woolf and Sylvia Plath, 1913-1962: Theatres of Identity." Diss. University of York, 1995. Print.

Sully, James. *Essay on Laughter*. London: Longmans, Green and Co., 1902. Print.

Wilkinson, Anne Yanko. "A Principle of Unity in *Between the Acts*." *Criticism*, 8 (1966): 53-63. Print.

Woolf, Virginia. *Between the Acts*. San Diego: Harvest/Harcourt Brace Jovanovich, Inc., 1969. Print.

——. *The Diary of Virginia Woolf*. Ed. Anne Olivier Bell and Andrew McNeillie. 5 vols. London: Hogarth Press, 1977-1984. Print.

——. *Collected Essays*. Ed. Leonard Woolf. 4 vols. New York: Harcourt, Brace & World, Inc., 1966-1967. Print.

——. *Freshwater: A Comedy*. Ed. Lucio P. Ruotolo. New York: Harcourt Brace Jovanovich, 1976. Print.

——. *The Hyde Park Gate News*. Ed. Gill Lowe. London: Hesperus, 2005. Print.

——. *The Letters of Virginia Woolf*. Ed. Nigel Nicolson and Joanne Trautmann. 6 vols. London: Hogarth Press, 1975-1980. Print.

——. *Moments of Being*. Ed. Jeanne Schulkind. San Diego: Harvest/Harcourt Brace Jovanovich, 1985. Print.

——. *Orlando: A Biography*. London: Penguin, 1993. Print.

——. *A Passionate Apprentice: The Early Journals* 1897-1909. Ed. Mitchell A. Leaska. London: Hogarth Press, 1990. Print.

Grateful acknowledgment is made to the copyright holders as follows:

For Clive Bell: extract from unpublished play, LOVE AND LIBERTY, The Society of Authors as the Literary Representative of the Estate of Clive Bell; The Master and Fellows of Trinity College Cambridge.

For Julian Bell: extracts from EPILOGUE, The Society of Authors as the Literary Representative of the Estate of Julian Bell; untitled fragment MHP/A18, Monks House Papers, University of Sussex Library, The Society of Authors as the Literary Representative of the Estate of Julian Bell.

For Quentin Bell: extracts from THE CONSPIRATORS © The British Library Board (BL4016C/ADD 83331.1), and ink sketch of Lydia Lopokova from *The New Bulletin* (BL 4016B/ADD83320); The Society of Authors as the Literary Representative of the Estate of Quentin Bell.

For extracts from unpublished letters of Vanessa Bell, grateful acknowledgment is made to Henrietta Garnett.

"So They Fidgeted": The Modernist Twitch of *Between the Acts*

David Wanczyk[1]

Virginia Woolf's 1941 novel *Between the Acts* depicts the restlessness of post-Victorian, pre-World War II Britons and suggests, as much of Woolf's work does, that people are both individual fragments and electrically united to one another. In a diary entry from the period of the novel's composition, Woolf encapsulated this idea of frayed unity, writing that we are "all waifs & strays—a rambling capricious but somehow unified whole" (*D5* 135). Set against the backdrop of encroaching fascism, though, fascism represented by ominous bombers overhead, this novel's treatment of that wholeness takes on a new dimension, as Miss La Trobe—both militaristic and marginal—stages an historical pageant for the gathered village crowd. This pageant forces the audience, especially Isa Oliver and Lucy Swithin, to consider their individuality and their commonality, their relationship to (and split from) English history. In bringing her anxious characters together so that they share an experience of a sometimes-alienating, sometimes-unifying piece of theater, Woolf addresses, in her own strange piece of art, the dangers and opportunities of group identification on the eve of war.

Before the pageant begins, Woolf lets us know that communion between people, and the difficulty of that communion, will be stage-center in her novel. She describes the setting of the pageant as "a church without a roof [. . . ,] an open-air cathedral [. . .]" (45), suggesting that the celebration could be a new kind of liturgy, a chance for the audience to become one body without having to endure the dusty trappings of the Church of England. The members of the audience—Isa and her dominating husband Giles; Giles's father, Bart; Bart's sister Lucy Swithin; and friends of the family, Mrs. Manresa and William Dodge, among others—sense that they've become a sort of congregation, too. A hush comes over them. Mrs. Manresa declares humorously, "We must possess our souls in patience" (45), and the characters feel linked, though uneasily so, as Woolf gives us their collective review of the pre-scene beat: "Their minds and bodies were too close, yet not close enough" (45). While the characters want to feel private unity with one another, then,

[1] I express my great thanks to Carey Snyder for her tireless help on this and other projects. Thanks also to Jim Cahill, Robert Cording, Marsha Dutton, Barb Grueser, Mark Halliday, David Kaufmann, J. Zachary Kessler, Joseph McLaughlin, Dinty W. Moore, Robert Strong, Joseph Plicka, Steve Vineberg, and my anonymous reviewers at *WSA*; to Robert and J.E. Miller Wanczyk, and to Megan T.S. Wanczyk for her sparkling editorial eye. I presented a previous version of this essay at The Louisville Conference on Literature and Culture since 1900, and I wish to acknowledge the organizers of that event, Danielle Day and Sylvia M. Berger.

want to be "close enough," the notion of being publicly yoked to their neighbors causes anxiety in them. They hope to be conscious of themselves as part of a group, but they would prefer isolation to any relinquishing of personal identity. In other words, they have conflicting feelings about being an audience at all. In "Virginia Woolf and the Concept of Community," Brenda Silver explains how Woolf may have thought of this audience-as-character:

> There are, according to Virginia Woolf, two types of audience: the audience present at the medieval pageant or at the Elizabethan play, composed of all classes of society, participating in a communal experience; and the reader, who almost by definition is solitary, separate, alone with her book. (292)

The particular crowd in *Between the Acts*, waiting for the beginning of the pageant, seems to embody both types; they want to participate together, and yet they seem separated: "Old Mr. Oliver sighed profoundly," "Isabella felt prisoned," and "Mrs. Manresa longed to relax and curl in a corner [. . .]" (46). They are ambivalent about one another—"too close, yet not close enough"—and seem to want to be alone.

Later in the novel, Woolf characterizes this individualist instinct with a bit of narration from the point-of-view of the audience that shows their unified reaction to the play:

> But what could [Miss La Trobe] know about ourselves? The Elizabethans, yes; the Victorians, perhaps; but ourselves; sitting here on a June day in 1939—it was ridiculous. "Myself"—it was impossible. Other people, perhaps. . .Cobbet of Cobbs Corner; the Major; old Bartholomew; Mrs. Swithin—them, perhaps. But she won't get me—no, not me. The audience fidgeted. (121)

This passage comes during the section of the pageant Miss La Trobe has dubbed, "Present Time: Ourselves." In response to that presumptuous title, the anonymous narrator—the collective narrator—ironically insists on individuality. Rachel Blau DuPlessis calls this kind of point-of-view "a transpersonal 'new combination,'" but argues that even while Woolf experimented with collective voice, "she held to a sense of individual rights and liberties. The 'anonymous' self she evokes is, then, probably a resolution of the contradiction between individualism [. . .] and the mass that must be rejected" (171).[2] As Woolf's characters duplicate their own

[2] In this line, Blau DuPlessis draws on Woolf's essay, "Anon," and Brenda R. Silver's influential article "'Anon' and 'The Reader': Virginia Woolf's Last Essays." *Twentieth Century*

thoughts of individualism they find themselves in a curious in-between space—together and separate. Eileen Barrett suggests that Woolf creates these "levels of 'betweenness' [. . .] to grant her characters consciousness of themselves in life and art" (18), and in this section of the novel that consciousness is represented by a particular act: fidgeting. The people collectively fidget *against* collectivism, against identification; they fidget against being known, being placed, being timed.

In fact, fidgeting in Woolf's conception becomes a productive reaction against order and definition. The novel doesn't merely champion the anti-authoritarian, though, doesn't merely point out the group, or the tradition, that must be rejected. As Christopher Ames writes, "*Between the Acts* seems [. . .] to place in sympathetic (and irresolvable) tension the impulse to order and the impulse to chaos or anarchy" (400). Fidgeting, then—the symptom of modernist anxiety that appears in Woolf's diary and in four key sections of *Between the Acts*[3]—represents the characters' productive suspicion of both rabid individualism and collective consciousness, of both being yoked to history and split from it.

It is well-documented in Quentin Bell's biography that Virginia Woolf suffered from a nervous condition, often serious, that she and others referred to as "The Fidgets" (Bell I 57; Bell II 193). She felt that fidgets were one of "all the horrors of the dark cupboard of illness once more displayed for my diversion" (*D*2 125). But her diary also attests to the importance of the word for her writing. In the entry for Saturday, September 14th, 1940, during the composition of *Between the Acts*, she writes, "The great advantage of this page is that it gives me fidget ground. Fidgets: caused by losing at bowls and invasion: caused by another howling banshee, by having no book I must read: and so on" (*D*5 320). We can see here that the condition resulted from domestic trifles, world crises, voices in Woolf's head, and inactivity, but also that the nervous energy spurred her on. Earlier in her life, Woolf understood her physical and mental ailments to be a kind of spurring of invention, too:

> These, this morning, the first words I have written—to call writing—for 60 days; and those days spent in wearisome headache, jumping pulse, aching back, frets, *fidgets*, lying awake, sleeping draughts, sedatives, digitalis, going for a little walk, & plunging back into bed again [. . .] Let me make a vow that this shall never, never, happen again; *& then confess that there are some compensations* [. . .] *I feel that I can take stock of things in a leisurely way. Then the dark underworld has its fascinations as well as its terrors* [emphases mine]. (*D*2 125-126)

Literature 25. 3/4 (Fall/Winter 1979). 356-441.

[3] The word appears in the novel on pages 45, 57, and twice on page 121.

Writing didn't relieve Woolf's symptoms, but rather made them work for her. Fidgeting, as she sees it in her diary, is both a malady to overcome and an incitement to artistic output. Woolf's fidgeting—what we can imagine were slight tremors of some kind—actually affected the mode of production for *Between the Acts*, too: "My hand staggers," she noted in her diary; "I will type" (*D*5 155). It is perhaps no surprise, then, that fidgeting plays a part in *Between the Acts*, since Woolf was herself suffering from the condition so acutely during its writing.

The page, the fidget ground, became an "escape" for Woolf (*D*5 245). During the early stages of the war, she had written that "all creative power is cut off" (*D*5 235); eventually, though, the "complete nullity" of war gave in to "such a pressure of ideas and work" (*D*5 241), and in the process of writing she came to be

> like an invalid who can look up and take a cup of tea. Suddenly one can take to the pen with relief [. . .] [A]ny idea is more real than any amount of war misery. And what one's made for. And the only contribution one can make—this little pitter patter of ideas is my whiff of shot in the cause of freedom. (*D*5 235)

While the fidget ground allows Woolf this feeling, fidgeting in *Between the Acts* is also a whiff of shot in the cause of personal freedom for the characters, their near-futile twitch against tyranny.

The tyranny most at issue in the novel is not primarily a German one, but a social and artistic one. The first episode has Isa, the unhappy, poetic wife, encountering Mr. Haines, the handsome gentleman farmer. She quotes Byron, but the narrator—a presence often connected in the novel to the thoughts of one or more characters—tells us that they were lifted only for a moment by the poetry. He was "circled with a tangle of dirty duckweed; and she too, in her webbed feet was entangled, by her husband" (5). Mrs. Haines, we're told, will "destroy" their emotion "as a thrush pecks the wings off a butterfly" (5). Immediately, then, we're presented with characters trapped in unhappy relationships. As the novel progresses, we'll see Giles Oliver and his father angry and overbearing; most of the female characters feeling, as Isa does, "pegged down on a chair arm, like a captive balloon, by a myriad of hair-thin ties into domesticity" (13); and we'll see William Dodge, the closeted homosexual, believing himself to be "half a man [. . .] a flickering, mind-divided little snake in the grass" (51). These are, in many ways, "damnably unhappy" people (120), and systematic patriarchy, the social tyranny Woolf also identifies in *Three Guineas*, causes their unhappiness.

Beset by this overwhelming patriarchy, the characters get together on a nice summer day to celebrate the triumphant, virile history of Grand Old England. Woolf introduces us to the idea of the pageant—this year to be directed by the outsider

Miss La Trobe—from Isa's perspective: "Every summer, for seven summers now, Isa had heard the same words; about the hammer and the nails; the pageant and the weather. Every year they said, would it be wet or fine; and every year it was—one or the other" (16). Isa's distaste for the pageant seems more than boredom. The show is a monotonously recurring celebration of a status quo that's made her a captive. In a contemporary review, Malcolm Cowley wrote that the subject of the novel was "England under glass, this England where people of breeding were sometimes not quite sure whether they were themselves or their family portraits" (448), and we can sense Isa bound by that tradition, a tradition that usually celebrates the military, country, and church. Though it's easy and academic to criticize such institutions, Woolf, I think, intends us to see this kind of pageant as an extension of their patriarchal authorities, part of a domestic authoritarianism. In *The Interrupted Moment*, Lucio Ruotolo writes, "By setting *Between the Acts* on a pageant day [. . .], Woolf suggests that it is neither Luftwaffe nor Wehrmacht that constitutes the immediate threat to life and language, but rather good English folk, of all classes and professions, bound intransigently to old ideas" (206).

While Miss La Trobe's avant-garde production upends most of those old ideas, it creates a dual anxiety: on one hand, the instability of the production, its parodies of old literary styles and older manners, and its unclear messages shock the villagers; on the other, the pageant's labeling of audience members—recall "Present Time: Ourselves"—maintains what Ruotolo calls "the absolutism of authoritarian leadership" (205). In some sense, though, the pageant represents what Melba Cuddy-Keane calls "a pluralism of style and vision antithetical to the concentrated obsessions of power and aggression at the roots of war" (xliv). But in another sense, we're invited to see Woolf's suspicion of the aggressively communal as she characterizes Miss La Trobe issuing "her rapid decisions barked out in guttural accents" (44) and moving about like "a commander pacing his deck" (43).

Even an expression of a pluralistic community, anti-fascist as it is, seems too definitive for the audience, as if that expression is a proclamation from a balcony. Again, what disturbs the crowd most is when the experience of the play compels them, as good art and good propaganda do, to consider their places in history, in the nation, and in relation to one another. They sense that they are being initiated into a group, as members of the twentieth century, of England, of each other, and they also fear they're being excluded. Woolf presents characters suspicious of identification and lack of identification, caught in a puzzle in which "self" means both *alone and powerful* and "group" means both *unified and powerless*. Of that social puzzle, Jed Esty writes, "Several times in the novel, Woolf reverses course between collective and recuperative ideas of Englishness and her fundamental wariness (as both artist and woman) about any kind of national or collective participation" (87). The author's ambivalence, then, Miss La Trobe's and the audience's ambivalence, speak to the anxiety of late-modernist identity—they yearn for connection and are repulsed by it as well.

Like in *To the Lighthouse* and *Mrs. Dalloway*, the conundrum of transcendent human connection drives *Between the Acts*, and in four passages that deepen that conundrum Woolf uses the word "fidget," as though the very complexity of human interaction compels a physical response. Again, that interaction is somehow both unavoidable and unattainable in this novel. Woolf gives us characters who seem to understand each other without speaking; at the same time, they often share only in their separation, hate each other as much as they love. Putting them all in one spot at the pageant allows Woolf to dramatize their connection and disconnection all the more pointedly. Before art provides a collective focal point, though, they're terribly uncomfortable both in their own skins and their collective skin. Woolf writes,

> They stared at the view as if something might happen in one of those fields to relieve them of the intolerable burden of sitting silent, doing nothing, in company. Their minds and bodies were too close, yet not close enough. We aren't free, each one of them felt separately, to feel or think separately, nor yet to fall asleep. We're too close; but not close enough. So they fidgeted. (45)

While this passage specifically describes the rapt attention before a show, it also exhibits a general anxiety the characters have about being wrapped up in each other so that they lose individuality without truly being collective. While Isa feels "suppressed by a leaden duty she owed to others" (47), she doesn't feel unity with those others, just an insatiable thirst (46). She and the rest of the audience fidget out of self-consciousness. They, and we, aren't sure what this moment amounts to, and Woolf suggests that each of them has the same feeling: we aren't free to think separately. And yet, they all feel that separately. Even in the moment of connection, then, there's a breakdown of empathy.

The fidgeting, though, is a collective recognition of both isolation and interdependency. With this first instance of the word Woolf suggests that fidgeting is actually a *result*, too, the characters' response to social confusion. "So they fidgeted," she writes, as if the movement is their partial answer to an impossible paradox—"We're too close; but not close enough." In fact, fidgeting here is the sort of Woolfian utterance that, as Mark Hussey reminds us, "makes itself heard in between people, in the gaps and interruptions of their dialogue" (143). He continues, "Woolf was always concerned with [. . .] the minute transactions of social intercourse" (143), and though fidgeting in response to a moment of awkwardness might be the minutest transaction of all, it's fruitful to analyze it as a kind of language, as an indication of repeated discomfort with either/ors, with the status quo.

After this moment of loneliness-in-the-crowd, Woolf gives us a private conversation between William Dodge and Lucy Swithin. Having made their escape from the waiting to tour Pointz Hall, Mr. Dodge and Mrs. Swithin approach a tenuous connection themselves, though Lucy can't remember William's name. Seemingly out of the blue, she says, "But we have other lives, I think, I hope [. . .] we live in others, Mr. . . .We live in things" (49). Mr. Dodge appreciates that this elderly woman has reached out to him, the consummate outsider. The narration connected to him suggests that "[s]he had guessed his trouble" (49). He longs to tell her about the abuse he has suffered as a homosexual, longs to tell her "you've healed me" (51). He says nothing except his name, and at that reminder Mrs. Swithin "smiled a ravishing girl's smile, as if the wind had warmed the wintry blue in her eyes to amber" (50). In a way, William declares himself to her and feels that she understands him, though this feeling is dubious; the small kindnesses, however, seem to mark this meeting as a true moment of human connection, whereas the episode immediately preceding had been a moment of disconnection even as the characters had the exact same thoughts. In fact, though, the passages seem to inform each other.

Perhaps connection relies on its opposite, deep disconnection, just as "moments of being" in Woolf's memoir "A Sketch of the Past" rely on "a kind of nondescript cotton wool," on moments of "non-being" (70).[4] Of different generations and different thought processes, Mr. Dodge and Mrs. Swithin commune by recognizing each other's yearnings, by recognizing what they individually need, not what a group or a nation needs. They feel a private unity that Woolf puts in direct comparison to the public alienation the audience feels and fidgets through. On Woolf's comparisons, Natania Rosenfeld writes, "*Between the Acts* is a work that insists on its own fragmentedness, its disruptions and disjunctions, as inseparable from its moments of harmony" (129); it's possible to see that in this quiet conversation between Lucy and William, though, a moment of disjunctive understanding outweighs those public moments of imposed harmony. Thus, when Mrs. Swithin, the most ardent proponent of the provincial pageant and its gestures toward unity, suggests that she and William return to the crowd "to go and join—" (51), she cuts off her sentence, seemingly unable to remember the purpose of the gathering. She's already had her communion.

From moments of thought-reading disconnection and the unlikely connection of Swithin and Dodge, Woolf moves us to the action of the pageant and the bizarre communiqués that the members of the audience seem to share with one

[4] "Every day includes much more non-being than being [. . .]." Woolf writes. "[T]he goodness was embedded in a kind of nondescript cotton wool. This is always so. A great part of every day is not lived consciously" (70).

another. Once again, Woolf presents us with a scene in which individual thought and troubling groupthink butt heads. "Could they talk?" she writes. "Could they move? No, for the play was going on [. . .] only the tick of the gramophone needle was heard. The tick, tick, tick seemed to hold them together, tranced" (57). While technology and art bind them, though, this scene is an instance of what Woolf called "party consciousness" (*D*3 12). She became, in her later novels, more and more intrigued with the "we" replacing the "I" in fiction (*D*5 135), and, according to Rosenfeld, that does not constitute "an erasure of individuality. Instead, it denotes an authorial stance intended to be anti-authoritarian and communicative" (135). The pageant, then, focuses the characters' thoughts, but not always didactically. It inspires a many-voiced chorus, a collaboration in which each individual has a chance to revise what the group thinks. We might say Woolf anticipated a user-generated, wiki-consciousness—consciousness 2.0—in which her characters share thoughts without squelching individual voices.

And so even while they're stuck in an art-induced trance, linked to each others' thoughts, the characters can disagree and escape over-definition. But in some cases, they do not. The following passage—which includes the second instance of "fidgeting" in the novel—deserves quoting at length because it shows how Woolf's characters argue intuitively, how they consider time, how they share consciousness, and how they sometimes protest against that sharing:

> Tick, tick, tick the machine continued.
>
> "Marking time," said old Oliver beneath his breath.
>
> "Which don't exist for us," Lucy murmured. "We've only the present."
>
> "Isn't that enough?" William asked himself. Beauty—isn't that enough? *But here Isa fidgeted.* Her bare brown arms went nervously to her head. She half turned in her seat. "No, not for us, who've the future," she seemed to say. The future disturbing our present. Who was she looking for? William, turning, following her eyes, saw only a man in grey. (57; emphasis mine)

Oliver hears the gramophone parceling out time, keeping them all bound to the moment. Mrs. Swithin, who has been reading something she calls "an Outline of History" (6), seems to have forgotten the book's lessons when she asserts that only the present exists. She believes that we are not yoked to history even as her cross dangles around her neck. Later, she'll say, "The Victorians [. . .] I don't believe [. . .] that there ever were such people. Only you and me and William dressed differently" (118). This attempt to break from the past from a woman who relies on tradition seems curious. But is it the same kind of break that a modernist might champion? Or is it an insistence on the consistency of culture through time,

Mrs. Swithin's idea of a simplified duration? A person who believes "we've only the present" *and* that the Victorians were the same as she is cannot grasp the kind of social breakage Woolf suggested in "Mr. Bennett and Mrs. Brown" when she wrote, "[I]n or about December 1910 human character changed" (*CE* 1, 320). Instead, Mrs. Swithin, in this moment, espouses an understanding of culture as static, and William and Isa react against that.

Whether the characters can hear each other up until this point is unclear, but William responds to Mrs. Swithin. He asks, "Isn't that enough?" meaning isn't the present enough. (We should remember that the narrator tells us William "asked himself" this question about the present, so it's indeterminable whether he speaks it aloud.) Then someone (William? The narrator? Isa? All of them?) conflates the concept of the present with the concept of beauty: "'Isn't that enough?' William asked himself. Beauty—isn't that enough?" There are no quotation marks around the second question, but again the characters seem to intuit each others' meanings and Isa fidgets, as if responding to Mrs. Swithin's mumbled simplification of time and to the collective hope for a cure-all, beauty. We're told that she "seemed to say" the present and beauty are not enough, "[n]o, not for us, who've the future." But it's with her fidgeting that Isa "seemed to say" this, and once again the slightest bit of movement can stand as a moment of speech in Woolf's multi-voiced passages.[5] "There are," Hussey writes, "many instances in *Between the Acts* of felt influences that pass between people without words [. . .] ; silence makes an 'unmistakable contribution' to talk" (147).[6] Swithin's and Dodge's ideas have drawn that restless, muted talk from Isa, who fidgets for the cause of ambiguity, fidgets for a qualification, fidgets because she knows easy answers won't cut it. For her, the present and beauty constrict. As she looks longingly at the man in grey, Mr. Haines, she realizes that the future—which consists of her continued unhappy marriage and the impending war—will probably render any present beauty useless.

Later, though, when Isa actually talks to William, the narrator tells us that "[t]he future shadowed their present, like the sun coming through the many-veined transparent vine leaf; a criss-cross of lines making no pattern" (79). Writing about

[5] In *To The Lighthouse*, fidgeting plays a part in the Ramsays' response to the news that Paul and Minta are engaged, too. Mrs. Ramsay teases Paul and Mr. Ramsay snorts, but their unspoken ideas about the marriage seem to have influenced each other, and Woolf writes that "[Mr. Ramsay] was beginning now that her thoughts took a turn he disliked [. . .] to fidget, though he said nothing [. . .]" (184). Mr. Ramsay rightly believes his wife is being pessimistic about the marriage, even though she's said very little out loud about that subject. Meanwhile, Mrs. Ramsay seems to know that her husband's body language is a direct repudiation of a particular unspoken thought of hers. Woolf writes, "If he says it's wrong to be pessimistic, probably it is wrong, she thought." Of course, Mr. Ramsay has only *said* that by fidgeting

[6] Here, Hussey refers to a passage on page 27 of the novel.

how what-is-to-come affects Woolf's characters, Amanda Grant argues that, for them, "[t]he future balances on a thin line between nostalgia [. . .] and nightmare" (199), and we can see in the two passages about time that Isa, our ambivalent fidgeter, contemplates the future as both a frightening limitation and an opportunity, a continuation of and a break from oppressive pattern.

Modernism, of course, continues the patterns of the past while breaking from them. In his modernist manifesto, "Tradition and the Individual Talent," T.S. Eliot writes, "No poet, no artist of any art, has his complete meaning alone. His significance, his appreciation is the appreciation of his relation to the dead poets and artists" (91). Eliot continues, arguing that the goal of new work should be that "the whole existing order [. . .] be, if ever so slightly, altered" (91). Others were less reverent to tradition. Woolf saw Joyce's *Ulysses*, for instance, as "the conscious and calculated indecency of a desperate man who feels that in order to breathe he must break the windows" ("Mr. Bennett and Mrs. Brown," 334). And yet *Ulysses*, like *Between the Acts*, radically depends on the literary tradition it revises, those broken windows of the past. The pageant scenes in the latter novel pay homage to the Elizabethan, Restoration, and Victorian traditions and, in fact, the characters of *Between the Acts* know that they are the leftover tatters of a crumbling tradition; they, too, try to figure how they fit into history and break from it. It can be said, then, that the characters' anxieties in *Between the Acts*—about the past and its influence—mirror the modernist artist's anxiety. Christopher Ames goes further still, writing, "We should recognize that Woolf's treatment of the English literary tradition here is of a piece with the typically modernist anxiety about the disabling and paralyzing potential of authoritative tradition" (396). The characters, especially Isa, are suspicious of just such an authoritarian tradition; confronted with a possibly dogmatic, definitely labeling pageant—albeit a carnivalesque pageant—they fidget or otherwise resist whenever they're pigeonholed or placed on a timeline. And yet they recognize that they must fit somehow into the past, even if they are only the fragments that remain of its ruins, even if their present is, as Hussey notes, "pre-history to catastrophic conflict" (150).

As the pageant continues, Miss La Trobe looses her theatrical minions on the crowd with all manner of reflective surfaces in order to show the gathered what she refers to as "Present Time: Ourselves"; during this episode, she asks a question through her loudspeaker that certainly applies to the modernist project in general: "*How's this wall, the great wall, which we call, perhaps miscall, civilization, to be built by* (here the mirrors flicked and flashed) *orts, scraps and fragments like ourselves?*" (127). Being told that they are fragments has two effects on the audience. They're unmoored and, conversely, labeled. They feel annoyed to be placed in a definite time and some get up to leave. Upending the traditional pageant structure, though, Miss La Trobe *wants* to make the audience feel unified in their discomfort.

She, like Woolf, wants an audience to consider their fragmentation and their unity, their flaws and redemptive traits alike. "*Let's break the rhythm and forget the rhyme*," says Miss La Trobe. "*And calmly consider ourselves. Ourselves*" (127). But the pageant's attempt to define past periods and to place contemporary people within that continuum amounts to what the narrator calls an "insulting eye" (126). La Trobe *orders* the audience to consider themselves in a certain way; they resist:

> And the audience saw themselves, not whole by any means, but at any rate sitting still.
>
> The hands of the clock had stopped at the present moment. It was now. Ourselves.
>
> So that was her little game! To show us up, as we are, here and how. All shifted, preened, minced; hands were raised, legs shifted. Even Bart, even Lucy, turned away. All evaded or shaded themselves [. . .] Each tried to shift an inch or two beyond the inquisitive insulting eye. (126)

The physicality in this passage shows us the extent to which Miss La Trobe has startled the audience, as they shift three times, not just in their chairs, but into a new kind of self-consciousness. Having caricatured the Victorians and English history critically without offering a comforting vision of a new mode, Miss La Trobe has freed the audience from cultural identification and set them adrift. They have no tradition to hide behind. "As an artist, Miss La Trobe wants to control her audience and at the same time to release them," writes Marjorie Hellerstein (59), and we wonder if Woolf had a similar desire. Did she want to turn the mirror on us so that we could clearly see the influences she identifies in "A Sketch of the Past," "all those magnets which attract us this way to be like that, or repel us the other and make us different from that" (80)?

Controlled and released, the audience feels vulnerable, and Woolf depicts this feeling most succinctly at the beginning of the "Present Time: Ourselves" episode in a passage that includes the novel's third instance of "fidgeting":

> They were neither one thing nor the other; neither Victorians nor themselves.
>
> They were suspended, without being, in limbo. Tick, tick, tick went the machine.
>
> *Isa fidgeted*; glancing to right and to left over her shoulder. (121; emphasis mine)

In the first two passages in which "fidgeted" appears (45, 57), the characters wrestle with paradoxes: we are both connected *and* separate; we are both of the present *and* somehow achronological. This third instance concerns societal identification. Again, Woolf dramatizes the restlessness of the unfixed. Isa, a character of many paradoxical both/ands, takes the broad, Brechtian message of the village play to an extreme, realizing she's neither/nor: not a Victorian and not sure what now. Here, fidgeting isn't a reaction against definition, but an anxiety about lack of any group identification at all. (Modernist fragmentation and art giveth individuality and taketh away unity.)

But doesn't fidgeting allow Isa some agency in responding to the onrush of material from the play, to the opinions of her family and neighbors? Doesn't it represent a language with which she can respond to the discomfort of her moment and her social place? Patricia Moran writes that Woolf's women often "censor [their] physicality, a censorship that typically results [. . .] in female silence" (16), but in this passage at least, Isa seems to be speaking up with her body, rebelling in the smallest way as she fidgets and looks over her shoulders for the support of someone else who feels the way she does about the historical, patriarchal limbo. Perhaps, though, fidgeting is the ultimate in ineffectuality. Couldn't it represent what Woolf calls Isa's "abortive" (11) personality? Rachel Blau DuPlessis' reading of *Between the Acts* can help with these questions. She writes that "[. . .] the novel becomes a story of missing stories. [. . .] [T]he unsaid because repressed and the unsaid because incipient vie in the same narrative space, creating oscillation between dominant presence and muted potential" (167). So while fidgeting could be seen as the symptom of female silence, of repression, we can read it as a sign of action, too, as a beginning. Being neither one thing nor the other frightens Isa, but the possibility of a fluid identity awakens something in her as well. With the help of the pageant, she recognizes her role in history, as a woman; and her physical reaction seems to suggest that she has the potential to move beyond that role.

Just a few sentences later, Woolf uses the word "fidget" for a fourth and final time. In the first passage—which comes before the beginning of the pageant—the audience fidgeted because they felt they were "too close, yet not close enough" (45). The opposing experiences of unity and alienation disconcerted them. In the next two instances of the word, Isa alone fidgets. Both times, she feels herself somehow dislodged from history. She fidgets because the present moment and beauty aren't enough to assuage her pain, and she fidgets when she realizes that she's disconnected from the past, "suspended, without being, in limbo" (121). Yet in these uncomfortable moments, Isa seems to wriggle away from traditions that limit her: away from a patriarchal community that has betrayed her and from a Victorian heritage that has bound her. In the final passage in which "fidget" appears, Woolf again uses collective narration in which all of the voices insist on individuality, but we can read it as a continuation of Isa's mental journey through the day. I revisit this passage—which comes near the end of the pageant—to show that what the characters collectively think actually seems most connected to Isa's consciousness, to her cadence:

> How long was she going to keep them waiting? "The Present Time. Ourselves." They read it on the programme [. . .].
>
> "Ourselves. . . ." They returned to the programme. But what could [Miss La Trobe] know about ourselves? The Elizabethans, yes; the Victorians, perhaps; but ourselves; sitting here on a June day in 1939—it was ridiculous. "Myself"—it was impossible. Other people, perhaps. . . Cobbet of Cobbs Corner; the Major; old Bartholomew; Mrs. Swithin—them, perhaps. But she won't get me—no, not me. The audience fidgeted. (121)

Throughout the novel, Woolf's narration is connected to the mind of one character, and then, quickly, to the collective mind of an audience-character, as private reactions become public consensus. In this passage, she seems to transition from a many-voiced perspective back to the individual one; many separate people insist at the same time that they can't be interpreted, can't be conjoined. This declaration of autonomy—"But she won't get me"—sounds most like Isa, though. She has resisted definition and unification throughout the proceedings, earlier wanting "[t]o fly away, from night and day, and issue where—no partings are—but eye meets eye [. . .]" (57). Uninterested in an imposed definition of who she is, suspicious of unity and dogma, Isa fidgets with the audience because she wants a different kind of connection, one in which individuals remain untethered, in which "eye meets eye."

In depicting Isa's personal struggle and the ambivalent reactions of the audience-character, Woolf, I think, wants to re-imagine unity for a world in which the old kind is limiting and increasingly dangerous. Hers is a new unity, not Victorian or patriarchal, and certainly not fascist. Consider, for instance, how she sets conflicting visions of "Present Time: Ourselves" against each other in the following passages, the narration of which seems inspired by jolting music from the pageant. Offering two different definitions of what British society is and what it might become, Woolf creates visions of unity and fragmentation, but doesn't help her reader choose between those visions. In the first, "Homes will be built. Each flat with its refrigerator, in the crannied wall. Each of us a free man; plates washed by machinery; not an aeroplane to vex us; all liberated; made whole. . ." (124). The narrator, with increasingly jaunty syntax, posits a traditional society, peaceful, consumerist, united. We're reminded of Ames's idea that Woolf has an impulse toward order. But then the music changes, and the music of the writing kicks up with full force:

> What a jangle and a jingle! Well, with the means at her disposal, you can't ask too much. What a cackle, a cacophony! Nothing ended. So abrupt. And corrupt. Such an outrage; such an insult; And not plain. Very up to date, all the same. What is her game? To disrupt? Jog and trot? Jerk and smirk? Put the finger to the nose? Squint and pry? Peak and spy. O, the irreverence of the generation which is only momentarily—thanks be—"the young." The young, who can't make, but only break; shiver into splinters the old vision; smash to atoms what was whole. What a cackle, what a rattle, what a yaffle [. . .]. (124)

This virtuoso performance—which seems to describe Miss La Trobe—has wider applications for the modernist project in general. We could ask, What is Woolf's game, what is the modernist's game? Is it to "shiver into splinters the old vision," Victorian art, Victorian society? We're reminded of Ames's idea that Woolf has an impulse toward chaos. Or is the game to break *and* maintain, to liberate *and* make whole?

With these two passages, Woolf imagines a future in which things can either cohere or explode or both. And as we might expect from this novel, we're not sure what vision wins out. As the pageant continues, Miss La Trobe shows the audience as they are, "And only, too, in parts. . .That's what's so distorting," they say, "and upsetting and utterly unfair" (125). There's no resolution about what "Present Time: Ourselves" is, only another level of ambiguity. The characters are both/and, in between, fidgety. Of this ambiguity, Cuddy-Keane writes,

> Caught between two worlds, the liminal space is unstable [. . .] In a positive way, the pageant breaks down barriers of isolation, creating what we might call a participatory community, united not by shared ideologies but in a collaborative act. But the shift—and the audience feels it—is also threatening, for in breaking down barriers of self-protection, the mirrors compel the audience to examine and judge themselves. (lxi)

Earlier, when the audience collectively thought, "What could [Miss La Trobe] know about ourselves? [. . .] She won't get me—no, not me," there'd been a reaction against definition, a defense of individuality and personal inscrutability. There'd been fidgeting. When confronted with the fragmenting mirrors, though, the people are upset not to be presented as whole and upset to have to consider themselves at all. Then, the villagers argue about the meaning of the play, and there's no agreement. "Woolf will not let the confusing fragmentation of the modern era be covered over by the reproduction of an old sense of continuity" (121), writes Michael Tratner, but yet again the narrator tells us that the characters are unified in their difference: "On different levels they diverged. On different levels ourselves went forward; flower gathering some on the surface; others descending to wrestle with the meaning; but all comprehending; all enlisted" (128). Woolf undercuts the militaristic unity implied by the word "enlisted" with what comes before it; each member goes a solitary way, cohering and exploding, carrying the communal experience differently, but understanding that they have shared something.

Of course, Woolf qualifies the triumph of that communal experience when the collective narrator, jumbling the order of the words, asks, "Scraps, orts, and fragments, are we, also, that?" (128). Among the characters, there's still a feeling of alienation, but Tratner writes that "[. . .] one of the goals of the pageant is to fragment everyday reality so it can be assembled in some new way" (117). Perhaps the pageant and modernist art rearrange fragments of the past into a cohesive, edifying whole. Merry Pawlowski, though, argues that "Woolf's desire for unity among the 'common mass' [. . .] is problematic, and her works indicate a failure of vision as much as a vision achieved" (53). Certainly, Woolf presents us with both compelling scenes of transcendent human connection and awful moments of disconnection. The most challenging sections, though, ask us to consider characters bonding over their isolation, their unhappiness, their delusions. They ask us to consider the extent to which groups can act communally, and whether we should value the individual thought or the group consciousness. They ask us to be split up, together. And they make us fidget. *Between the Acts*, as Ruotolo writes, puts us in "a world demanding incessant readjustment, a world [. . .] in which 'nothing remained stable long'" (4).[7]

The final, frantic word on the play comes from Isa, who responds to Mrs. Swithin's sweetly reductive understanding of the production. Mrs. Swithin, the impressionable, repeats Reverend Streatfield's interpretation, asking, "Did you feel [. . .] what he said: we act different parts but are the same?":

> "Yes," Isa answered. "No," she added. It was Yes, No. Yes, yes, yes, the tide rushed out embracing. No, no, no, it contracted. The old boot appeared on the shingle.
>
> "Orts, scraps and fragments," she quoted what she remembered of the vanishing play. (146)

Isa doesn't fidget here, but she might as well. Trapped in Woolf's everlasting impasse—are we connected or separate—she responds with hopeful despair or despairing hope. We are and we're not. The artist's connection to the audience endures as it fades.

[7] Ruotolo quotes from page 79 of "A Sketch of the Past" here.

In *Between the Acts*, the last novel she worked on before her suicide,[8] Virginia Woolf stakes a fictitious audience against a fictitious experience of art. That audience wrestles, as we do, with the overarching meaning of a fragmented, funny, finger-pointing, frustrating work. They seem to want it to ask them questions about themselves and give them answers, as long as the questions aren't too penetrating or the answers too precise. When they are, they fidget, as Woolf herself often did. The play, both invasion and art, causes the characters' self-consciousness, but provides a space for them to work out their anxiety. It acts as a "fidget-ground" for them, as writing did for Woolf, and on that ground the characters, especially Isa, resist total definition and total nihilism. Their nervous tics, and Woolf's, are productive reactions, small but powerful utterances against conclusion, against stasis, against feeling the old ways about things.

In *A Room of One's Own*, Woolf's speaker encounters a fictitious artist, Mary Carmichael, who shocks her out of complacency. In that work, those shocks, her fidgets, are grounds for the expansion of complex ideas. Woolf writes, "For whenever I was about to feel the usual things in the usual places, about love, about death, the annoying creature twitched me away, as if the important point were just a little further on" (91). That annoying creature—the artist, art itself—actively causes the restless response we know was common for Woolf, the same fidgeting response the characters experience so often in *Between the Acts*. For both author and characters, the twitch represents a necessary skepticism about canned ideas, about over-simplification. It's a quiet, physical cry for complexity caused by a challenging piece of art. *Between the Acts* twitches us toward that important point further on, too, but gives us a deepening of paradox and a sense that the usual things, the either/ors, need to be broken down. "Yes, no," says Isa, but she can't decide: whether we can be a constructive part of each other's lives or not, a part of the past or not. And when she fidgets, she seems to be operating from an ambivalent space in between, a space in which a shaky reconciliation of opposites might allow for a new way, a re-imagined blend of individuality and harmony.

[8] Mark Hussey has argued compellingly that because of the substantial changes made by Leonard Woolf to the manuscript after Woolf's death, we should not refer to *Between the Acts* as her last novel. Instead, "[it] remains in process, permanently deferred" (Hussey's edition is forthcoming, and he has graciously shared a typescript of his introduction with me).

Works Cited

Ames, Christopher. "Carnivalesque Comedy in *Between the Acts*." *Twentieth Century Literature* 44 (1998): 394-408. Print.

Barrett, Eileen. "Matriarchal Myth on a Patriarchal Stage: Virginia Woolf's *Between the Acts*." *Twentieth Century Literature* 33:1 (1987): 18-37. Print.

Bell, Quentin. *Virginia Woolf: A Biography*. 2 vols. London: Hogarth, 1972. Print.

Blau DuPlessis, Rachel. *Writing Beyond the Ending: Narrative Strategies of Twentieth-Century Women Writers*. Bloomington: Indiana UP, 1985. Print.

Cowley, Malcolm. "Review." *The New Republic*. 6 Oct. 1941. *Virginia Woolf: The Critical Heritage*. Eds: Robin Majumdar and Allen McLaurin. London: Routledge, 1975. 447-450. Print.

Cuddy-Keane, Melba. "Introduction." *Between the Acts*. 1941. By Virginia Woolf. London: Harcourt, 2008. xxxv-lxvi. Print.

Eliot, T.S. "Tradition and the Individual Talent." *The Best American Essays of the Twentieth Century*. Ed. Joyce Carol Oates. Boston: Houghton, 2000. 90-97. Print.

Esty, Jed. *A Shrinking Island: Modernism and National Culture in England*. Princeton: Princeton UP, 2004. Print.

Grant, Amanda. "Life Without Boundaries." *Virginia Woolf Miscellanies*. Eds. Mark Hussey and Vara Neverow-Turk. New York: Pace UP, 1992. 199-201.

Hussey, Mark. "Introduction." *Between the Acts* 1941. By Virginia Woolf. Cambridge: Cambridge UP, 2011. Print.

——. "'"I" Rejected; "We" Substituted': Self and Society in *Between the Acts*." *Reading and Writing Women's Lives: A Study of the Novel of Manners*. Eds. Bege K. Bowers and Barbara Brothers. Ann Arbor: UMI Research P, 1990. 141-152. Print.

Hellerstein, Marjorie H. *Virginia Woolf's Experiments with Consciousness, Time, and Social Values*. Lewiston: Mellon, 2001. Print.

Moran, Patricia. *Virginia Woolf, Jean Rhys, and The Aesthetics of Trauma*. New York: Palgrave, 2007. Print.

Pawlowski, Merry M. "Towards a Feminist Theory of the State: Virginia Woolf and Wyndham Lewis on Art, Gender, and Politics." *Virginia Woolf and Fascism: Resisting the Dictators' Seduction*. Ed. Merry M. Pawlowski. New York: Palgrave, 2001. 39-55. Print.

Rosenfeld, Natania. "Monstrous Conjugations: Images of Dictatorship in the Anti-Fascist Writings of Virginia and Leonard Woolf." *Virginia Woolf and Fascism: Resisting the Dictators' Seduction*. Ed. Merry M. Pawlowski. New York: Palgrave, 2001. 122-136. Print.

Ruotolo, Lucio P. *The Interrupted Moment: A View of Virginia Woolf's Novels.* Stanford: Stanford UP, 1986. Print.

Silver, Brenda R. "Virginia Woolf and the Concept of Community: The Elizabethan Playhouse." *Women's Studies* 4 (1977): 291-298. Print.

Tratner, Michael. "Why Isn't *Between the Acts* a Movie?" *Virginia Woolf in the Age of Mechanical Reproduction.* Ed. Pamela L. Caughie. London: Garland, 2000. 115-134. Print.

Woolf, Virginia. *Between the Acts.* 1941. Ed. Melba Cuddy-Keane. London: Harcourt, 2008. Print.

——. *The Diary of Virginia Woolf.* Eds. Anne Olivier Bell and Andrew McNeillie. 5 vols. London: Harvest, 1978-84. Print.

——. "Mr. Bennett and Mrs. Brown." *Collected Essays.* Volume 1. New York: Harcourt, 1967. 319-337. Print.

——. *A Room of One's Own.* 1929. London: Harcourt, 1989. Print.

——. "A Sketch of the Past." *Moments of Being.* Ed. Jeanne Schulkind. New York: Harvest, 1985. 61-159. Print.

——. *To The Lighthouse.* 1927. New York: Harcourt, 1955. Print.

The Voyage Out as Voyage In: Exotic Realism, Romance and Modernism

Julia Kuehn[1]

Three characteristics featured in the contemporary reviews of Woolf's first novel: its feminine character, its disjointedness and, arguably, failed aesthetic execution, and the fact that *The Voyage Out* was, in fact, a voyage in. "[N]ever was a book more feminine, more recklessly feminine," wrote the *Times Literary Supplement* on 1 April 1915, tracing its femininity through its emotional and artistic diversity in particular (Majumdar 49-50). Its move from cleverness to sentimentality, cynicism to wit, frivolity to tragedy is in the end considered by the reviewer a "failure of design," a verdict many other reviews directed at the novel. The *Morning Post* called the novel "bewildering" and its incidents "disconnected" (Majumdar 51); the latter assessment was picked up by the *Athenaeum*, which considered incidents "too loosely put together, and [with] a great deal of superfluous material" (Majumdar 59). "[T]he framework is so clumsily constructed," wrote author W. H. Hudson to Edward Garnett, a reader for Gerald Duckworth who had published the novel (Majumdar 61), and the *Nation* came to the conclusion that "[i]t is hardly a work of art, partly because of its form" (Majumdar 60).[2]

If problems concerning plot execution were the most obvious to reviewers, characters fared no better as these did apparently not create novelistic cohesion either. Poet and journalist Gerald Gould called the novel's people "unreal" and "none of [their depictions] knit[ting] into the narrative with the others" (Majumdar 53). E. M. Forster also lamented that Woolf's "chief characters are not vivid," but he did applaud the author's attempts at an interiorizing narrative mode, the aspect that established the third theme in contemporary reviews (Majumdar 53).

Allan Monkhouse, novelist and playwright, suggested in his *Manchester Guardian* review that "the interest and success of this book is the penetration into certain modes of consciousness": characters "are not content with facts and habits and exteriors" (Majumdar 57). The *Athenaeum*, too, praised how characters "explore each other's natures" while in South America (Majumdar 59), and the *Nation* reviewer pushed this line of thought further by asking:

[1] I want to thank the three anonymous readers for *Woolf Studies Annual* whose comments and suggestions have greatly enriched this essay.

[2] See also the unsigned Review of *The Voyage Out*, "Here are Books – and Books," *The Independent* (10 July 1920), 53, which concludes with the sentence: "The story is strangely lacking in construction: It has neither beginning nor end nor single point of view, but it is thoroughly [sic] interesting, a distinctly unusual book."

> Why is it that people will read about anything rather than about themselves? Is it sheer modesty, or moral cowardice, or a method of escape, or a pathetic confidence in something they believe beyond their escape or what? If they would only realize that their own psychology is far more romantic, mysterious, unknown, exciting, and potentially emotional than the adventures, heroisms and melodramas with which they are fed! *The Voyage Out*, for instance, is an analysis and, in parts, a powerful and significant one, of the personalities of some English visitors in a South American hotel. (Majumdar 60)

This essay takes its point of departure from the above quotation: what interests me is how the reviewers' observations on the novel's mode of interiority are linked with the exotic South American setting. In this context E. M. Forster also wrote that "[i]t is for a voyage into solitude that man was created," and that the main characters in *The Voyage Out* "learn this lesson, which is exquisitely reinforced by the setting of tropical scenery" (Majumdar 54). There are, as I will suggest, two modes of exoticism in the novel: the external description of otherness in the portrayal of the fictitious colony, Santa Marina, and an internal exoticism which realizes, through the voyage into consciousness, that the stranger lies often within. In this understanding of, and distinction between two modes of, exoticism I follow Victor Segalen's explications in his unfinished fragment *Essay on Exoticism*, written between 1904 and 1918. Here, Segalen endeavors to replace the "cheap finery" of an external exoticism with a more refined epistemological understanding. Among the limited notions of exoticism he counts both the conceptualization of the exotic as solely within a tropical setting ("palm tree and camel; tropical helmet; black skins and yellow sun"[18]) but also as a strictly unilateral relationship in a "colonial exoticism" in which diversity only exists for the subject "in so far as it provides him [the colonialist] with the means of duping others" (35).[3] Exploring this more complex, "inner" exoticism a subject experiences when confronted with an other through the simultaneous and paradoxical occurrence of desire, fear, curiosity and anxiety, Segalen concludes that the most productive manifestation of the exotic encounter leaves the experiencing subject deeply affected. The cognitive recognition of diversity is unsettling for the subject—the other may be both desired and suspicious, both intriguing and eventually incomprehensible—but Segalen considers this revelation of difference *and* relation in the conception

[3] A lot of work has been done on Segalen and, in the context of postcolonial studies, on exoticism. I just want to mention in this context two representative studies: Charles Forsdick, *Victor Segalen and the Aesthetics of Diversity: Journeys between Cultures* (Oxford: Oxford University Press, 2000); *"New" Exoticisms: Changing Patterns in the Construction of Otherness*. Ed. Isabel Santaolalla (Amsterdam and Atlanta, GA: Rodopi, 2000).

of foreignness as essential to a forever shifting, relative twentieth-century subjecthood.

This essay thus falls into two parts: the first analyzes the novel's description of an external colonial other in South America. It looks at Woolf's representation of the colonizer, the colonized and the colonial setting in *The Voyage Out*, the imperialist reading list imposed upon Rachel Vinrace, and the way the female protagonist navigates the seas in her quest for knowledge of self and other. The second part analyzes how Woolf internalizes the exotic other. Reviewer Ruth Murray Underhill saw the problem of *The Voyage Out* in its use of two diverging narrative modalities, realism and modernism: "the curious fabric of minute-by-minute daily life," she argues, is opposed to "the approach to truth" and an "understanding of the nature of human beings and of love" (Underhill 685). To show how exoticism in *The Voyage Out* is progressively more internalized, I draw upon *Melymbrosia*, the earlier complete draft of the novel, to suggest Woolf's mixed, conflicting, and experimental modes of representation. Specifically, the essay will analyze the Europeans' journey up the Amazon into the interior and to the native jungle village in both versions, to show how Woolf experimented with an external and an internalized exoticism.

Britain's South American and Colonial Other

Most characters in the novel have a stake in the colonial enterprise, a background in colonial administration, or benefit from colonial wealth in one way or another.[4] Willoughby Vinrace and the Flushings make, most obviously, money from the fictitious South American colony: Willoughby, it is said, "love[s] his business and buil[ds] his Empire" (*TVO* 19). He owns ten ships that "regularly [ply] between London and Buenos Aires" (20), carrying livestock and other goods between the metropolitan center and the colony. As in the case when he travels into the Amazon jungle to secure cargo, Willoughby happily and proudly "triumphs over wretched little natives who [go] on strike and refus[e] to load his ships [by] roar[ing] English oaths at them [...] The beggars had the sense to scatter" (221). With a clear insight into colonial and entrepreneurial dynamics but "robbing a whole continent of mystery" (220), he explains to his daughter that her leisurely lifestyle solely depends upon him trading what she refers to as "[p]oor little goats" (18).

Wilfrid Flushing buys native jewelry and accessories and as "they [the natives] don't know what they're worth, [...] we get 'em cheap. And we [...] sell 'em to smart women in London" (272). His plan—supported by his artist wife—is to trace more native artifacts "where none but natives had ever trod," and to enter the profitable native art scene on a larger scale: "He thought there might be giant gods hewn out of stone in the mountain-side; and colossal figures standing by themselves

[4] See Phillips's excellent work in *Virginia Woolf Against Empire*, 67-71.

in the middle of vast green pasture lands [...]. There might be prehistoric towns, like those in Greece and Asia, [...] filled with the works of this early race" (275).

If Willoughby and the Flushings thus participate willingly and directly in the historical early-twentieth century commercial exploitation of the colonies, by responding to trade opportunities and Europe's fascination with "primitive" art,[5] the relationship of other characters with the colonies is more tentative and reluctant. Mr. Pepper, Miss Allan, Helen Ambrose's brother and even Rachel's Aunt Clara, who had a "very old cockatoo that came from India" (242), seem to have been dragged into colonial reality by their more ambitious families. Mr. Pepper has been "condemned to pass the susceptible years of youth in a railway station in Bombay," and while he believes himself to have "done good work in India," the items he lists as his other achievements—including never buying "a ticket without noting the number, [devoting] January to Petronius, February to Catullus, March to Etruscan vases perhaps" (22)—suggest that his interest in and contributions to Britannia's imperial endeavors have been negligible at best. School teacher Miss Allan, too, benefits indirectly from the colonies: her only brother, Hubert, makes his living on a fruit farm in New Zealand and with another crop failed, Miss Allan's holiday in South America could now easily become financial recklessness and extravagance. It seems that Hubert, like Mr. Pepper, has been sent abroad by his determined family—"what were they to do with him this time [if he failed to make money]?" (200)—and that Miss Allan and her sister depend to some extent on him financially, at least for extras like the South American holiday. Helen's brother was also "sent out" rather unwillingly to Santa Marina "years before to make a fortune, [or] at any rate to keep clear of race-horses" (98). And given his dilapidated, insubstantial and ramshackle house and him being only "at length" able to afford a holiday, one may assume that both his interest and success in the colony have been insignificant on the whole. While all these characters may be relatively unwilling participants in Empire, they still do not condemn it. Neither do Ridley Ambrose, Terence Hewet or Evelyn Murgatroyd whom Woolf may not link directly to Empire, but who are described as characters very much in favor of an imperial and militaristic spirit: the first description of Ridley is as "a Viking or a stricken Nelson" (6); Hewet compares his own organizational talent in assembling a picnic party to Wellington's generalship (140); and suffragette and new woman Evelyn considers the idea of an armed revolution and conquered territory not only "true life" and an escape from boredom, but also a feminist's aspiration:

[5] See, on this point, Gilmore. I have no space to go into Virginia Stephen and Vanessa Bell's appearance at the ball in celebration of the Post-Impressionist exhibition of 1910. See Phillips xiii; Cummins 204-10; Lewis 106-19.

> Oh, if she had been [Garibaldi's] bride![6] If [...] this was a party of patriots, and she, red-shirted like the rest, had lain among grim men, flat on the turf, aiming her gun at the white turrets beneath them, screening her eyes to pierce through the smoke! (144)
>
> "How it makes one long to be a man! [...] I'd raise a troop and conquer some great territory and make it splendid. You'd want women for that. I'd love to start life from the very beginning as it ought to be—nothing squalid—but great halls and gardens and splendid men and women. [...] Why are there no men like Garibaldi now?" (151)[7]

Richard Dalloway is both more outspoken and ideological than these pragmatists. Accompanying the *Euphrosyne*, this former MP both bedazzles and confuses Rachel. While he preaches about Britannia's colonial significance he also translates its masculine spirit of domination into his relationship with women—be this Rachel or his wife Clarissa. It is no coincidence that the books he recommends to Rachel are Burke's *Speech on the French Revolution* and his *American Rebellion*, but also Austen's conservative gender portrayal in *Persuasion*.[8] Critic Chene Heady contextualizes Dalloway as a "self-deluded Conservative who cannot see that the height of empire is over and that a Liberal devolution of power must follow" (100). And, indeed, his sermon to Rachel about Britain's imperial achievements, responsibility and mechanisms sounds well-rehearsed but strangely anachronistic and flawed in the second decade of the twentieth century. His ideal is "Unity. Unity of aim, of dominion, of progress. The dispersion of the best ideas over the greatest areas. [...] Imagination, Miss Vinrace; use your imagination. [...] Conceive the world as a whole. [...] I can conceive no more exalted aim—to be the citizen of the Empire" (67, 69). And he explains the mechanisms of Empire as a

> complicated machine; we citizens are parts of that machine; some fulfil more important duties; others (perhaps I am one of them) serve only to

[6] Giuseppe Garibaldi (1807-82) was an Italian military and political figure. He has been dubbed the "Hero of the Two Worlds" in tribute to his military expeditions in both South America and Europe. He is considered an Italian national hero.

[7] Her suitor Mr Perrot's reply to Evelyn's aspirations reveals another interesting colonial critique: "conquer a territory? They're all conquered already, aren't they?" (152).

[8] And he detests Shelley's "Adonais" (see 43), probably both for its version of unity (with a world spirit, rather than in the more mechanistic and mundane sense) and his ambiguous gendering. See Vlasopolos on Woolf's references to Shelley in *The Voyage Out* and especially in relationship to the Richard-Rachel encounter (130-53). See also for Rachel's reading list, and particularly the books the men in Rachel's life impose upon the young woman, Friedman 101-24. See Schlack for Woolf's revisions of literary allusions in *The Voyage Out* (317-27).

> connect some obscure parts of the mechanism, concealed from the public eye. Yet if the meanest screw fails in its task, the proper working of the whole is imperilled. (69)

Rachel's attempt to understand Richard's broken metaphor which combines the mechanistic of industrial production with the organic—people are the organisms that hold the state machine together—ends in failure: when she tries to construe from Richard's argument that it is human communication and cooperation that bring social unity and progress, he calls her a "woman" and a "young Liberal" who understands nothing. Dalloway's rhetoric is superficially coherent and progressive through its two keywords of unity and imagination, but his faith in Empire and his attitude toward women are the product of the Victorian Age. His notion that "the English seem, on the whole, whiter than most men, their records cleaner" (67) is picked up by his acquiescent wife Clarissa, who feels for her husband and his teachings the same way that her "mother and women of her generation felt for Christ" (53). Clarissa's main desire is to have a son who could, like his father, become "a leader of men":

> "I can't help thinking of England. [...] Being on this ship seems to make it so much more vivid—what it really means to be English. One thinks of all we've done, and our navies, and the people in India and Africa, and how we've gone on century after century, sending out boys from little country villages—and of men like you, Dick, and it makes one feel as if one couldn't bear not to be English!" (51)

At the end of her brief sojourn with the Vinraces and unaware that her husband Richard has by the time groped and kissed Rachel, Clarissa exclaims upon seeing the Mediterranean Fleet: "Warships, Dick! Over there! Look! [...] Aren't you glad to be English!" (72). In haunting anticipation, the catachresis of Richard's image of a mechanistic state machine which relies on human organisms for its operation is brought into the context of an impending First World War, which historians have labeled "the first industrial war, a war of cavalry and machine guns."[9]

If almost all of the novel's characters have therefore an explicit colonial agenda or indirect connections, the description of Santa Marina's setting, colonial history and its locals is equally indicative. The place and its environment are described in rather non-specific and stereotypical southern hemispheric terms, with the interplay of primarily "blues and greens" (95)—mountains, the ocean, cypresses, forests—and white houses with brown roofs. What is striking, however, is the vastness of the colony ("bigger than Italy" [97]), which verges on the

[9] See Montgomery's excellent analysis of Richard Dalloway's colonial rhetoric (43).

sublime ("The effect of so much space was at first rather chilling" [146]), and its unspoilt, uninhabited, uncivilized nature ("the vast expanse of the land gave them a sensation which is given by no view, however extended, in England; the villages and hills there having names" [237]). If Woolf taps, rather stereotypically, into the myth of the empty land, the description of the natives is just as indistinct: Santa Marina locals are described by the British visitors, who have turned the colony into a twentieth-century hot spot for tourism, as "strangely beautiful, very big in stature, dark, passionate, and quick to seize the knife" (97). Such clichéd, and what Edward Said would call Orientalist, description is not transcended in the rest of the book: the Spanish servant girl Maria, the British housekeeper Mrs. Chailey says, "hardly look[s] like a human being" when she comes out of the villa to welcome the newly arrived, surrounded by pigs and hens (100); the donkey boys who accompany the British picnic party on the mountain show the joyous life of the "simple folk," merely singing and joking (145). And in a further attempt to fill the exotic place with local color, Woolf offers non-descript indigenous people on Rachel and Helen's evening walk (107), musicians at the dance (169), waiters and (nature-bound, chicken-killing) kitchen staff in the hotel (293). And, to complete this list of Orientalist examples, there is the local doctor, Rodriguez, who, with his "insignificance, his dirty appearance, his shiftiness, and his unintelligent, hairy face" (393) plays down Rachel's final illness—as does, in fact and fairness, the French doctor Lesage who is brought in for a second opinion.

It may be the reader's responsibility to distinguish the narrator's, character's and author's voice in these examples of Orientalism: some clichéd descriptions may be the result of Woolf's factual ignorance about South America which she had never visited; others, like Mr. Bax's sermon on how the British visitors to Santa Marina "owed a duty to the natives" and not only politeness but also small acts of kindness are more clearly demarcated as one bigoted character's opinion, who discriminates and hierarchizes under the cloak of Christian benevolence (267f). Arguably, Woolf's own attitude towards colonialism and the colony of Santa Marina become clearer in her delineation of an imperial genealogy.

Santa Marina's (fictitious) history is one of failed colonization in Elizabethan/ Commonwealth times but of a successful re-appropriation in the early twentieth century through trade and tourism. "[H]ardy Englishmen, tawny with sea-voyaging, hairy for lack of razors, with muscles like wire, fangs greedy for flesh, and fingers itching for gold" allegedly arrived in Elizabethan barques at the South American coast, overcame the Spaniards who were already there but who had become "bloated with fine living upon the fruits of the miraculous land" and bore away "bars of silver, bales of linen, timbers of cedar woods, golden crucifixes knobbed with emeralds" (96). A British settlement was established (women were "imported" [96]) but due to what the narrator—echoing Richard Dalloway—calls a lack of imagination the colony was disbanded less than a hundred years later. Natives came from the interior, "with subtle poisons, naked bodies, and painted idols," and "vengeful Spaniards and rapacious Portuguese" came from the sea, forcing the English to leave Santa Marina (96). Because of this unsuccessful, shameful colonization, "English history denies all knowledge of the place" (96). Only in the early twentieth century and for obscure reasons—"which will never perhaps be recorded in history books"—was Santa Marina rediscovered by the British as a trade and holiday destination (97).

The tone of this passage mocks the Renaissance explorers and Elizabethan mercantilism: the Europeans are barbaric in their greed, absurd in their rivalry ("churning up the sand, and driving each other into the surf" [96]), and incapable of proper administration. If the Elizabethans are one (here, ridiculous) stage in the genealogy of British colonialism, a benchmark further back in history is Roman imperialism. Gibbon's *History of the Decline and Fall of the Roman Empire* is a constant point of reference in *The Voyage Out*, and this is no coincidence as specifically Victorian imperialists regularly and proudly modeled themselves after their Roman predecessors. Hirst, when he is first introduced, reads Gibbon and he lends Rachel a volume to teach her—as he hopes—an appreciation of the historian's style but also to test whether a woman's brain can take in such facts and aesthetics. Her reading experience is short-lived and a failure, according to Hirst's criteria: in the passage Rachel happens upon, Roman generals who attempt the reduction of Aethiopia and Arabia Felix find themselves overwhelmed by the tropical climate which favors and protects "the unwarlike natives of those sequestered regions" (196), and they give up their northern expansion into Europe as particularly Germany is "filled with a hardy race of barbarians, who despised life when it was separated from freedom" (196). This passage invokes a desire in Rachel to know more about other, exotic places—Arabia Felix, Aethiopia—and these names also appeal to her musical ear. However, the content of the passage suggests unambiguously the failure of Roman imperial expansion and criticizes, by extension to the reality of the early twentieth century, Britain's colonial endeavors in the same regions.[10] Gibbon is closed again before Rachel has absorbed anything but a longing to learn about the foreign and other beyond the process of colonial domination as the latter, as Gibbon has shown, is bound to end in failure.

Woolf's references to contemporary British colonialism, its willing and unwilling supporters, its ideology, its places and people reveal her critique of empire which she sees as clichéd and outdated.[11] Essentially, however, the question of what

[10] See Phillips on, specifically, the two Morocco crises in 1905-06 and 1911, in which Britain was heavily involved (62-63).

[11] There is no space in this article to comment on the Dreadnought hoax and the Post-Impressionism Exhibition, which I mentioned earlier, and which suggest Woolf's personal rejection of empire. For a description of these events see Lee 278-87. See also the relevant passages in Bell, Vol. 1, especially his Appendix E and the photograph of the Abyssinian

constitutes the author's own attitude toward colonialism fades in view of the larger question of whether the description (and critique) of the *external* exotic in *The Voyage Out* actually matter at all. As W. H. Hudson wrote in his 1915 review: "Somewhere in S. America it is supposed to be and once or twice 'natives' are mentioned. [But the] scene might just as well have been in some hotel on the south coast of England" (Majumdar 61). When read against Victorian texts, issues of colonialism, empire, and the exotic are different in *The Voyage Out* where, in fact, the external exotic pales in light of the exploration of an inner exoticism and the understanding of the self's relation to an other, an epistemology that becomes manifest in Rachel's quest for knowledge.

Rachel's education and desire to know the self are not only the bridge between the external and the internal exotic in this novel, but also between the imperial romance and *bildungsroman* sides of *The Voyage Out*. It is important that Rachel comes to realize in this context—while she is formally but inadequately educated by Richmond tutors, by Richard Dalloway, Ridley Ambrose or St. John Hirst—that "knowledge" may be acquired by reading Cowper, Austen, Gibbon, Burke or Balzac, but that an "understanding" of self and world can only be gained through the contact with actual people. The distinction between knowledge (factual, rational and sober) and understanding (emotional, tortuous, philosophical and messy) occurs in the novel early on when Rachel's efforts "to come to an understanding" about her aunts' love for each other and for their ward are frustrated (34). However, it is the encounter with Richard Dalloway that best illustrates Rachel's dilemma.

The girl admits to "know[ing] nothing" (67). Richard—while he concedes that she must have gained *some* knowledge from books—thinks it overall better for a woman not to know anything, to which Rachel indignantly replies that it should be his responsibility to make her "understand" (70): "tell me—everything," she pleads (57). Understanding, this exchange suggests, goes deeper than knowledge and is only achieved in conversation and contact with real life and real people. Bookish knowledge about gender relations (proclaimed by the Dalloways to be found in Austen) or English conservatism and national character (proclaimed by Richard to be found in Burke) will only be fully understood by Rachel in her real-life encounters with, first, men like Richard and Hewet and, second, the colony of Santa Marina. What is more, the acceptance and internalization of book knowledge can even be disastrous as becomes clear when Richard's very un-Austenesque groping of Rachel leaves the young woman stunned and bewildered. (Hewet's attitude toward women may be much less aggressive than Richard's but it is in many ways equally Austenesque. It is built upon propriety, an established social status quo and the idea that a woman's ultimate happiness can only be found in marriage; notions that become increasingly strange to Rachel.) Similarly, Rachel's "knowledge" about English nationalism and

---

convoy between pp. 140 and 141.

colonialism will only be transformed to "understanding" when she meets the English tourists in Santa Marina and the South American natives, which show her that her compatriots can be as foreign to her as the "actual" foreigners. The girl's desire to "know" is increasingly interiorized and turned into a quest for understanding or, as she increasingly calls it, "truth" (136) and self-knowledge. Critics Harvena Richter, Carey Snyder, Erica Johnson, and June Cummins have offered various approaches to how Rachel's search for self-knowledge and an understanding of the world are intimately bound up with her encounter of South America's exoticism: Richter suggests that the foreign location causes the distortion of Rachel's "angle of vision" (vii), while Snyder argues that Rachel's self-nativizing reveals Woolf's critique of the English (81-108). Johnson sees Rachel's perpetual homelessness and exile, meaning her inability to identify with either England, British tourists abroad or the South Americans, as the eventual cause of her death (65-86), while Cummins suggests that the novel portrays the contact with the natives as the cause of "white" woman Rachel's sickness and death (204-10). Responding to these critics, I want to link Rachel's quest for an understanding of self and world with issues of narrative modality, and especially Woolf's simultaneous use of realist, modernist and romance elements. I will, in this context, return specifically to Mark Wollaeger's analyses of *The Voyage Out*, which link issues of selfhood with issues of colonialism, albeit not in the context of genre and aesthetics.[12]

Exotic Realism, Romance and Modernism

The previous section looked at exoticism as an external representation of the other and the self's desire to understand alterity in opposition to the self. However,

[12] Wollaeger sees Woolf's negotiation of aesthetic form in *The Voyage Out* as a response to both Conrad's *Heart of Darkness* and Leonard Woolf's *The Village in the Jungle*: Rachel's arrival at self-knowledge and knowledge about the world while in the jungle, he argues, can be seen as an echo of Marlowe's path, and Woolf's ideas of sex and gender could be seen as Virginia's reaction to Leonard's heteronormative gender vision in his novel ("The Woolfs in the Jungle"). Any invocation of, especially, *Heart of Darkness* in the context of desire, the self-other dynamic and modernism is complicated and cannot be done justice to in this essay. Critics, most notably Chinua Achebe, have criticized that a reading of the European voyage "out" as a voyage "in" renders the other as a mere signifier of European identity, thus preserving the notion of the dehumanizing colonial binary of self and other. While I understand and support this criticism I still maintain that both Wollaeger and I want to highlight especially those moments in the narrative when the self-other binary collapses and their "relation" is brought out: Rachel realizes she is the *same* as the other, native woman. Another point I would add to Wollaeger's linking of Conrad's and the Woolfs' novels is that they all present a fragmented self embedded in an ambiguous (colonial) morality and active in an equally ambiguous (because apparently primitive) setting—a fragmentation and ambiguity which renders these works modernist and post-nineteenth-century in the first place. I will turn to both these issues above.

Rachel's attempts to arrive at the "truth" about herself and about the other indicate a shift toward interiority. Woolf transcends external exotic description in *The Voyage Out* which proposes that the exotic other is not necessarily at a distance from the self—desired and suspicious at the same time—but can be inside the self, as an internal stranger. We therefore have to proceed to *The Voyage*'s internal exotic vision, the center of which is Rachel's mental development which combines contemplations on alterity with ideas of gender, and which finds a climax in the chapters that relate the Europeans' journey up the Amazon into the interior and to the native jungle village. *Melymbrosia*—begun in 1907/08 and reworked several times until it became *The Voyage Out*—serves as a comparative text to analyze the aesthetic negotiations a new author undertook in those critical years in the early twentieth century when writers saw progressively the limits and limitations of nineteenth-century forms of (exotic) representation. The central argument of this section is that Woolf moves, in her depiction of exoticism and between the texts *Melymbrosia* and *The Voyage Out*, from the external to the internal, from the worldly to the introspective and creative, from materialism to spirit, from a descriptive to a poetic mode, from "fact" to "vision," or, as Woolf herself called it (albeit in a different context), from Granite to Rainbow.[13] The early and the later draft of Rachel's story enact what Woolf called for in her essays "Modern Fiction," "An Unwritten Novel" and "Mr. Bennett and Mrs. Brown," namely the artist's necessity to move the novel from a nineteenth-century to a twentieth-century mentality. Rather than retain an external Victorian moralism or Edwardian materialism, Woolf claimed that the modern novel had to find narrative ways to portray a character's interiority, "the meaning of existence itself," and "[w]hether we call it life or spirit, truth or reality, *this, the essential thing*."[14] The fateful river excursion to the native village

[13] Zwerdling's study analyzes Woolf's revision of realism (although he surprisingly disregards the importance of *The Voyage Out* and its previous draft), and her combining "fact" with "vision," as she herself elaborated in her essay on "The Novels of Turgenev." Here, Woolf argues that the novelist "has to observe facts impartially, yet he must also interpret them. Many novelists do the one; many do the other—we have the photograph and the poem. But few combine the fact and the vision [...]." Woolf, "The Novels of Turgenev," 56. Dick, unfortunately also disregarding *The Voyage Out* but analyzing *Mrs Dalloway*, *To the Lighthouse*, *Orlando* and *The Waves*, shows how Woolf revised realism to give her characters more and more glimpses into a reality beneath reality, without, however, ever completely abandoning material reality. The reference from the worldly to the introspective and creative is to Vlasopolos (133), who analyzes the Dalloway episode as a negotiation between these two modalities.

[14] Quotations are from "Mr. Bennett and Mrs. Brown" (387); "Modern Fiction" (188, emphasis added). "An Unwritten Novel" speaks, more generally, about the need to reform the realist novel. Woolf talks about the distinction between "granite" and "rainbow" in her essay on "The New Autobiography" (149) which discusses the need to combine truth and personality in autobiography; this binary could be translated into an empiricism/fact/realism and interpretation/vision/modernism distinction.

debates this agenda especially well in three exotic scenes: the description of the jungle, Rachel and Hewet's declaration of love (including Helen's reaction to the union), and the encounter with the native village women.

The description of the Amazonian jungle is a first case in point of how Woolf changes her aesthetic from external to internal exoticism, from description to introspection. In *Melymbrosia*, the jungle is described as the exotic other to the western travelers who enter it. The account invokes a jungle fantasy by Henri Rousseau, with exotic flora and fauna, colors and noises. "Wild animals," "wild beasts," leopards, monkeys, "crying" and "shrieking" birds, alligators, deer and snakes live by the river in the impenetrable thicket of the trees, which barely let the sunshine touch the ground, and observe the unwelcome visitors with "glitter[ing]" eyes, mocking their arrival with their strange communicative cries (*MEL* 279, 300, 280, 284, 279, 282, 294, 300). The metaphors of a virgin territory and an empty terrain are invoked repeatedly. As the narrator says:

> To find the source of the river you must first pass through the towns, then the villages, then the solitary huts of Indians; you must become the only person in your world; you must be the first to cut through the thongs of creepers; the first who has ever trodden upon the mosses by the river side, or seen trees which have stood since the beginning of the world. (*MEL* 279, emphasis added)
>
> There was no pathway, but as the trees stood irregularly and a springy moss grew at their feet it was possible to make out a way zig zagging to the left and to the right, and sometimes leading straight like an English forest though perhaps the mosses here had never been pressed by human feet before. (*MEL* 283, emphasis added)
>
> [T]hey were passing an island in the middle of the river; two great white birds stood there on stilt like legs. It was a beautiful little island, with trees on it; but the beach was unmarked save by the prints of birds' feet. (*MEL* 294, emphasis added)

The jungle is untouched and removed from the six Europeans who make their journey through it. From the moment *Melymbrosia* describes the arrival of Rachel, Helen, Hewet, Hirst and the Flushings at the place of embarkation, they are in opposition to the natural scene and the natives who live there. The elderly Spaniard, who is part of the crew they have hired, observes the Europeans from the boat and identifies them as "six travelers," "[t]hree English men [and] three English women" (*MEL* 280), "strangers," "the passengers" (*MEL* 281). These quotations reveal both the locals' condescending attitude toward the adventure-seeking European tourists who are the reason why a "steam boat panted up the river regularly once a month" (*MEL* 280) and their perception of these tourists as unwelcome, yet necessary, disturbances. Rachel involuntarily adopts the notion of Terence being misplaced in the jungle when she sees him wearing "grey flannel," and a "shabby purple tie" and waistcoat (*MEL* 287) and the local boat crew also confirm later that the Europeans' "coats and dresses looked so strange" (*MEL* 300) against the jungle setting. On the whole, although Woolf at one point likens the travelers to the herd of deer detected in an Edenic jungle clearing (*MEL* 300-1), Rachel and her peers are portrayed as intruders into the natural scene. They have come to strip the country of its natural treasures (rubies, diamonds and other precious stones, as Mr. Flushing hopes), its natural wildness ("you'd have to cut down that bush with the yellow flowers" to make the clearing orderly [*MEL* 300]) and its cultural artifacts (as is the primary purpose of Mr. Flushing's excursion). As Erica Johnson suggests, through "their characterization of South America as a yet-unexploited, ahistorical land, the characters not only 'world' their location as a temporary, contingent place, but more importantly, they undermine its authenticity, thus reinscribing imperialist notions of travel and identity" (77).

The jungle being so unfamiliar only a sensitive person like Helen realizes that the assumed western (imperialist) superiority could quickly turn into a disempowered vulnerability. Having a premonition that this experience in the jungle will bring changes, as Rachel's relationship with Hewet becomes ever more intense, Helen begins to envision the jungle as "terrible and hostile" and even the herald of disaster: "It was just such a moment as she remembered years ago when at a polite river party the boat had suddenly capsized. In a second they were struggling in the water" (*MEL* 291). Nature is in a superior position to first mock and then destroy humanity, Helen realizes, especially when "civilised people" venture too far into the wild and unknown (*MEL* 291). Her warning to the young lovers, '"We must be careful here. It isn't like England"' (*MEL* 292), comes too late: like the famous explorer Mackenzie who, like Conrad's Kurtz, "went farther inland than any one's been yet" (*TVO* 323), Rachel has already caught the jungle fever both literally and metaphorically, having been offered a vision of her future by Terence that contradicts her own desires.

If the jungle thus remains an external other in *Melymbrosia*, the revisions in *The Voyage Out* eliminate to a great extent external exotic factors, like the animals, or give them a symbolic meaning. When Hirst advises Hewet and Rachel to watch out for snakes on their solitary jungle walk he senses that the two walk towards temptation (315).[15] When Hewet reads a Whitman poem to Rachel a bird responds

[15] See Richter on Woolf's symbolic use of nature imagery to express human nature: "The external world in Mrs. Woolf's novels is colored by the character's emotion [...]. In a parallel manner, the character's inner world is externalized through mental processes which abstract, concretize, or compress feelings into image, metaphor, and symbol, and so explore areas

by giving "a wild laugh" and "a monkey chuckle[s] a malicious question" (312): the poem says that one's whole past theory of life and all conformity would have to be abandoned if one followed the speaker's philosophical and ideological direction, just as Hewet expects of Rachel with regard to their union. As Joanne Frye has suggested, the exotic setting in *The Voyage Out* becomes, overall, "an unreal symbolic world" and a no-man's land (411). Nowhere is this more visible than in the passage when Hewet is about to declare his love for Rachel, or—in the later version of the novel—states their mutual attachment.

In *Melymbrosia*, the passage reads as follows: Rachel picks a flower when Hewet is about to speak of love, but the cries of monkeys delay Hewet's words: "Are they laughing at us—these creatures?" he asks, picking up "a cone and [throwing] it as high as he could among the trees; they heard the flapping of great wings. They heard the cone patter through leaves and fall" (*MEL* 284). In *The Voyage Out* the cone has turned into the symbolic "red fruit" of temptation and sin. But more importantly, Hewet's act of throwing the cone/fruit is now linked to his inner feelings. In the jungle forest, barred from the sun and good air both Rachel and Terence feel like walking "at the bottom of the sea" (315). They

> hardly spoke.
>
> Not only did the silence weigh upon them, but they were both unable to frame any thoughts. There was something between them which had to be spoken of. One of them had to begin, but which of them was it to be? Then Hewet picked up a red fruit and threw it as high as he could. When it dropped, he would speak. They heard the flapping of great wings; they heard the fruit go pattering through the leaves and eventually fall with a thud. The silence was again profound.
>
> "Does this frighten you?" Terence asked when the sound of the fruit falling had completely died away.
>
> "No," she answered. "I like it." (316)

Nature becomes both subject to and part of human emotions, thoughts and actions. Terence and Rachel's confusion after their mutual statement of love is visualized in their getting lost in the jungle, after they have turned back to join their fellow travelers: "At first Terence was certain of his way, but as they walked he became doubtful. They had to stop to consider, and then to return and start once more, for although he was certain of the direction of the river he was not certain of striking the point where they had left the others" (317). Is Hewet sure of the consequences

---

of submerged emotion usually glimpsed only by the dreaming mind" (viii). Unfortunately, Richter does not analyze *The Voyage Out*, an omission my close reading attempts to rectify.

of the path he has taken, by declaring their love, or is his seeming confidence accompanied by nagging doubts?

Rachel does not only follow Hewet's course through the jungle, confused and without direction as it may be ("stopping where he stopped, turning where he turned, ignorant of the way, ignorant why he stopped or why he turned" [317]), but she also follows Hewet's declaration of love. His "We love each other" is restated by her, but brimmed with the same doubts, which she vocalizes in her awareness that they are doing something wrong: "'Terrible—terrible,' she murmured after another pause, but in saying this she was thinking as much of the persistent churning of the water as of her own feeling. On and on it went in the distance, the senseless and cruel churning of the water" (317). The image of the conservative union Hewet paints is as "close" (315) and stifling ("hot steamy" [314]) as the surrounding atmosphere, and Rachel will soon find herself "at the bottom of the sea" (315). The conflict their love will encounter—being imprisoned by conventional gender roles, expectations and actions despite especially Rachel's, but also Hewet's, desire for a more rebellious and freer union—is reflected in nature. Upon the declaration of their love, the jungle wilderness turns into a broad and orderly path, like "a drive in an English forest" (315 and 318): unruliness must be disciplined. Likewise, the Flushings remind Rachel and Hewet, upon their return to the group, of the distinction between nature and civilization, wildness and convention when they chit-chat about barbaric education methods in an otherwise civilized nineteenth-century England (320), and when they liken the Amazonian jungle to a cultivated park in Arundel or Windsor (325). The jungle does not simply serve as a pastoral backdrop any longer, but an exotic nature becomes increasingly interwoven with people's emotions and actions as *Melymbrosia* turns into *The Voyage Out*: the material becomes the symbolic, the place a non-place, the external internalized as the exotic is integrated into, and becomes part of, the experiencing self.

Rachel and Hewet's declaration of love in these surreal surroundings adds a further facet to the characteristics the exotic description obtains in *The Voyage Out*. If the lovers' scene in *Melymbrosia* reads like an episode from popular romance, the scene becomes transformed in *The Voyage Out*: a wordy dialogue with stereotypical tropes and actions becomes now incorporated into a modernist aesthetic where silences and ambiguities speak louder than words and deeds.

Conventional behavior and speech abound in *Melymbrosia* as there is trembling, sighing and crying accompanied by passionate embraces and kisses. The dialogue is emotionally charged, with conventional lovers' vows: "Ever since I met you," says a quivering Hewet, "life's been different. [...] You my dearest, you, the one woman in the world—" (*MEL* 286-87). The reply Rachel gives, with dazed eyes, is equally predictable: she wants to know what attracted Hewet to her in the first place (*MEL* 288) and, having received a satisfactory answer, her admission of the mutual nature of these feelings makes use of the customary trope of inexpressible love: "'I love you better— ' but no comparisons came to her and the sentence ended in his arms" (*MEL* 289).

Having no other means than expression and description in *Melymbrosia*, Woolf also spells out Rachel's and Terence's (divergent) philosophies about life and love. The girl's fear of mortality, before having tasted life to the fullest, and her loss of a role model for gender relations finds expression in the melodramatic exclamation "O Terence [...]. The dead! My mother is dead!" (*MEL* 286). Her conflicted attitude toward a relationship within society's norms and expectations is revealed in her assertion that "it is as a full grown woman that I love you, not as a girl, not as a child. I want it to be a battle between us, you with your faults, I with mine" (*MEL* 289). Terence's answer is that Rachel indeed possesses "a free soul" (*MEL* 288), which implies that she will reject convention—just like him, he thinks, even if he does not fulfill this promise in the end. Rachel's search for meaning beneath the apparent surface of things, as well as Terence's reply, is also told, rather than shown:

> "We only know one thing about each other" she answered. "What is that thing Terence?"
>
> "The thing behind it all" he said. "The thing we both have. You feel that too? Then all my tortures have been vain! I knew they were! Nothing matters having that." (*MEL* 289)

Woolf already points to the lovers' irreconcilable differences in *Melymbrosia*, which thwart their happy union: Terence finds his insights into the meaning of life in and through his love for Rachel—"You've made me wake up [Rachel] instead of muddling on [...]. I've never been alive. I've never known what was in me. I've dreamt and wasted. I've been so lonely. No one understood till you came" (*MEL* 289-90). In contrast, Rachel's search for understanding happens beyond and outside of their relationship:

> "What is it that runs beneath Terence, why do we go on, and all those strange people so different passing each other—O Terence what is the meaning?" [...]
>
> "We shall understand everything Rachel" he cried. "There'll be nothing too difficult for us in the whole world so long as we have each other!" (*MEL* 290)

The Voyage Out turns away from this predictable romance mode and its verbosity; the modernist encounter of an/other in love, which can only happen in the jungle and away from society and so-called civilization, is internalized like the experience of the jungle itself. There is hardly any physical contact between the lovers in the parallel scene in the later draft, both being afraid to touch the other. And far from a romantic question and answer game, the lovers' dialogue in Woolf's later version reveals a disturbing pattern of compulsive repetition. Rather than tentatively expressing his feelings for the girl and awaiting her reply, the Terence of *The Voyage Out* avows their mutual attachment: "We are happy together" and "We love each other," to which she can only reply, "Very happy" and, reiterating, "We love each other" (316). His reply to her echo is yet another "We love each other" (317), as if repetition could provide the surplus meaning when words fail to express emotions.

As well as repetition, Woolf uses silence to hint at the metaphysical truth that cannot be spoken. From the beginning of the lovers' scene, "Terence and Rachel hardly spoke./ Not only did the silence weigh upon them, but they were both unable to frame any thoughts" (316); "There was another pause"; "He was silent for a moment. Silence seemed to have fallen upon the world" (316). Appropriately, it is nature that awakens especially Rachel from this stupor: the swish of the trees and some croaking beasts in "a remote world" bring her to acknowledge that her epiphany is indeed "terrible—terrible." Like Kurtz's "The horror, the horror," Rachel reaches a clarity of vision about life and love (and perhaps also colonial exoticism, as Kurtz does in Conrad's novel; a point to which I will come) when in foreign natural surroundings, away from society, and encircled by an otherness that has intruded on and impacted her sense of self. Nature reflects Rachel's growing awareness that a relationship with Terence would smother and drown her when she hears the "senseless and cruel churning of the water" in the background (317). As Alex Zwerdling suggests with regard to Woolf's aesthetic in general, "Insight—the ability to see into the inner nature of things—is [in *The Voyage Out*] contrasted with description" (16). We could map this distinction between two modalities onto the shift from *Melymbrosia* to *The Voyage Out*: formal experiment in language—repetition, silence, symbolism—marks the change from the "older" descriptive conventions of *Melymbrosia* to the modernist *Voyage Out*. Zwerdling believes Woolf's pursuit of a descriptive economy—away from verbosity—to be the result of her disagreement with her immediate predecessors about the nature of realism. *Melymbrosia* is certainly not a straightforward realist novel given the experimentation in theme, character and style Woolf already undergoes, not to mention her paradoxical borrowing from popular romance in the lovers' scene. However, the focus on telling rather than showing, the constant need to articulate things and the interest in a detailed (external) setting are indeed reminiscent of Victorian and Edwardian realist fiction. It seems no coincidence that Hewet, who considers himself an avant-garde writer, writes a novel entitled "Silence." Words, in the early twentieth century, fail to express the self's unsettling encounter with a human or natural other, and as the exotic other is increasingly internalized the stability of the self is questioned. The description of the village in the jungle—the destination of the Europeans' excursion—best illustrates the fragmentation of self in the latter novel when, indeed, the very dichotomy of self and other has been shown to collapse.

Upon contact with the native village women and witnessing their duties, which do not differ significantly from the picture Terence has painted of a modern English marriage, Rachel finally understands the impossibility of ever being happy in such a "strange" union. Her insights into the deeper truth of this world and of gender relations within both "primitive" and "cultured" societies, which seem exactly the same—"terrible, terrible"—mark the beginning of the end: by the time she returns from the jungle trip, Rachel has caught the mysterious fever that will kill her.

Discussing the village scene in *Melymbrosia* in his essay "The Woolfs in the Jungle," Wollaeger deems it "unremarkable" with regard to both length and also in comparison with the corresponding scene in the later text (61). In contrast, I believe that it is in the very comparison of the texts that something noteworthy comes to light, especially in terms of how the fragmentation of the self is developed, and how colonialism and the self's moral attitude toward it, are dealt with. In *Melymbrosia* the distinction between self and other remains intact throughout the scene:

> They stood in the native camp. The Indian women were squatting at the doors of their huts making baskets and did not stir from their triangular position when the strangers arrived [...]. Recovering from their surprise they began to use their hands again, and the English moved carefully round. They looked into the shady little huts; they saw the ashes on the floor [...]; they saw the children clasped tight by some old grandmother. (*MEL* 304)

The colonial gaze may already be reversed in *Melymbrosia* but the dichotomy of "the English" versus "the natives" is undisturbed between sentences: nowhere is the distance between the visitors and the native women bridged or are their separate, stable identities questioned. The native women fix their eyes upon the Europeans. Theirs is a "silent stare": some eyes express "surprise" or even a "sluggish wonder," while others are just "dull black eyes." Overall, however, they fall upon the strangers "silently" and "without hostility" (*MEL* 304-05). *The Voyage Out* tells a different story:

> Stepping cautiously, they observed the women, who were squatting on the ground in triangular shapes, moving their hands, either plaiting straw

> or in kneading something in bowls. But when they had looked for a moment undiscovered, they were seen [...]. The women took no notice of the strangers, except that their hands paused for a moment and their long narrow eyes slid round and fixed upon them with the motionless inexpressive gaze of those removed from each other far far beyond the plunge of speech. Their hands moved again, but the stare continued. It followed them as they walked, as they peered into the huts [...]; in the dusk the solemn eyes of babies regarded them, and old women stared out too. (331-32)

Wollaeger points out in "Woolf, Postcards, and the Elision of Race" (65ff.), that the self-other binary collapses in this scene: the "they" of the European observers becomes the "their" of the hands of the native women. In the following sentence, the first "they" still refers to the native women while the second one points again to the Europeans who have now been discovered. While "the women" and "the strangers" are engaged in an act of observation—the Europeans peering into the huts where native babies and grandmothers look back at them—gazes cross to the point that it can almost no longer be determined who gazes upon whom and when. The binary between self and other is brought down when the experience leaves both parties affected. It is the Europeans' subjecthood, however, which is the more disturbed, shaken and disoriented: after a short period of curiosity the visitors "become absorbed into" the village (332). Their subjectivity is swallowed up by the dominating gazes of the natives: not only is the native stare more prominent in *The Voyage Out* ("they were seen," "their long narrow eyes slid round and fixed upon them," "the stare continued," "old women stared out too," "the stare followed them," "the eyes of a woman never left their faces") but it is now also "not without hostility" (332). As if in a staring competition, the locals gain the upper hand, making the visitors "uneasy" and uncomfortable, to the point that the disintegration of their hitherto stable selves affects all Europeans apart from the blissfully unaware Flushings.

Especially Rachel is distressed by the collapsing boundaries of self and other. In *Melymbrosia*, the native women remain a mystery to her, incomprehensible as she cannot read their faces: "[Rachel] owned that she knew nothing about them" (*MEL* 305). Her later insight—"[the experience of seeing the native women] makes us seem small" (*MEL* 306)—could be seen as a progressive anti-imperialist statement about cultural relativity and Britannia's hubris to believe in her superiority. However, Rachel's epiphany in *The Voyage Out* goes deeper, affecting not only her newly realized attitude toward the (external) natives and colonization, but the core of her own subjectivity. She realizes that she and the native woman are no longer different but the same. Terence is the one in *The Voyage Out* who speaks of the cultural insignificance he feels after the village visit, while Rachel maps the domestic exoticism witnessed onto her own cultural background and character: "So it would go on for ever and ever, she said, those women sitting under the trees, the tree and the river." And, the collapse of self and other having caused a change in her sense of self: "[W]hy was it so painful being in love, why was there so much pain in happiness?" (332-33). As Cummins concludes, "the native women demonstrate to Rachel in harsh simplicity what marriage and domesticity will hold for her" (209). In an act which Snyder has called "self-nativizing" Rachel finally understands: gender roles are the same in this village in the Amazonian jungle—household chores, babies, cooking and all—as in London where Terence wants to live with her after their marriage: the external alien becomes the internalized other and therefore a (conflicting) part of the same. Woolf might not have thought of Rachel's inner journey when she wrote in "Modern Fiction" that the "life" of the modern novel should be portrayed with "as little mixture of the alien and external" (188), but the choice of the word "alien" is telling: in the modernist experience and novel, otherness has become internalized and the encountered collapse of self and other causes disorientation for the self, threatening and eventually ending the (nineteenth-century) notion of a stable subjectivity that is distinct from otherness.

It is, however, not just Rachel who puts together the pieces of the puzzle. Helen, aware that something significant has happened to Rachel through her love for Hewet, realizes the fragile character of her ward, "her eyes anxiously fixed upon the lovers, as if by doing so she could protect them from their fate" (333). Older and wiser, Helen, too, has seen the pattern of life in store for Rachel.[16] In the same way that her embroidery—"which was a matter for thought, the design being difficult and the colours wanting consideration" (233)—necessitates her to constantly look at the individual pieces and their effect on the whole,[17] Helen has seen the "larger picture" in terms of Rachel and Terence's union. She promised Rachel that she would show her more of life; the girl's little Richmond river would turn into a powerful waterfall, but Helen now knows that Rachel and Terence's waterfall of a marriage will cause Rachel to drown. And this epiphany comes about through the encounter with the exotic other; which is, in an uncanny and symbolical way prefigured by the motif of Helen's embroidery: "[Helen] was working at a great design of a tropical river running through a tropical forest, where spotted deer would eventually browse upon masses of fruit, bananas, oranges and giant pomegranates,

[16] I am not concerned with the lesbian nature of the *Melymbrosia* scene when Helen wrestles Rachel to the ground and tells her to worship her, which, in the revisions to *The Voyage Out*, is much less evocative and more toned down. See Wollaeger on this issue, who suggests that the revisions result from Virginia's reading of Leonard's very heteronormative *Village in the Jungle* after their marriage. Wollaeger, "The Woolfs in the Jungle," 51ff.

[17] As Schaefer writes, Helen's embroidery "involves her in the problem of ordering the parts and perceiving the whole" (39).

while a troop of naked natives whirled darts in the air" (30). The native darts have become the guns of the women's huts (332); bananas, oranges and pomegranates the red fruit Terence throws up in the air (316); but the deer were there, just as in the embroidery (326). The contact with the exotic other on the jungle excursion has left Rachel with the awareness that, whether in "nature" or "culture," all women are equally subjected to restricting gender roles.

The divergence between *Melymbrosia* and *The Voyage Out* can therefore be read in many ways as that between nineteenth-century fiction (concerned with externality and a more stable identity of the self) and modernist fiction (focused on interiority and with the nagging awareness of a fragmented self). And the same chasm opens up when we look at issues of morality, in this case the colonial project.

At the end of this analysis I can only tentatively map issues of colonial morality in *Melymbrosia* and *The Voyage Out* onto broader nineteenth-and twentieth-century ways of thought and representation. A more detailed inquiry would be the subject for another essay. However, for now one may suggest that many, or indeed most, nineteenth-century exotic representations worked under the premise of a stable moral position—either following the "duty" to bring "culture" to the more "primitive" peoples of the earth because of Britannia's general superiority, or completely rejecting colonialism as immoral. Much nineteenth-century exotic fiction thus worked within terms of a rather simplistic moralism and discussed "good" (progressive, ambitious) westerners in opposition to "bad" (backward, lazy) natives or—as the other side of the coin showed—"bad" westerners (corrupted by a leveling modernity) trying to impose disastrous principles upon "good" (untainted, pure, innocent) natives.

Yet again the case is more complex in Woolf's first novel. Her critique of empire remains intact between the drafts of *Melymbrosia* and *The Voyage Out* but encounters subtle and significant changes. The image of the Europeans in the native village remains one of ("well-nourished and formal") "soldiers in the midst of a crowd" (*MEL* 304), who have been lured onto the trip by the promise to see and buy native artifacts. They have—knowingly or unknowingly—Britannia's invisible flag, war drums and attitude behind them. In *Melymbrosia*, the elaboration of this colonial attitude takes up almost half of the chapter: Mr. and Mrs. Flushing, representatives of colonial exploitation and unequal relations, have the native women bring embroideries, food and drink, shawls, earrings and necklaces, and even the personal handkerchiefs of one woman, for which Mrs. Flushing has expressed a desire. Varying attitudes or voices by, for instance, Rachel, Hewet, Helen or Hirst are not heard in *Melymbrosia*'s monologic, one-dimensional representation—as anti-colonialist as it may have been conceived by its critical creator Woolf.

In *The Voyage Out*, however, even anti-colonialism is more multi-faceted, and morality less straightforward. In this version, the Europeans have become "tight-coated soldiers among these soft instinctive people" (332); the natives have been elevated, and the negotiating and still exploitative Flushings have been relegated to the background of the action. The overt critique of colonialism turns into something else as the prominence of the Flushings is reduced and emphasis is placed upon the reactions of the other Europeans who have met the native women and their treasures: Hirst wanders off; a bachelor feeling alone while his friend Hewet has found a potential marriage partner and threatens to start domestic life. Helen is a half-hearted and distracted participant in the women's showing of goods and the Flushings' bargaining. Standing among the native women, she realizes that it is not the natives who have been exposed to the colonial gaze and purchasing power, but indeed the Europeans who have "ventured too far and exposed themselves" (333). As it has to Rachel, the encounter with the native women has revealed to Helen the truth about gender relationships both in "primitive" as well as "advanced" societies, and only exceptionally strong, pragmatic and special women like Helen can break out of these conventional gender roles. Rachel, sadly, is no Helen: her internalization of the truth about life, revealed to her in the encounter with a seemingly inferior exotic other, becomes a moral as well as physical problem: she has caught the virus that will spread through her system. The exotic becomes the familiar and even the same, the European the alien, the external the internal. Whether and how Rachel's idea of colonialism has changed after the jungle excursion remains unsaid—the poor little goats her father ships between England and South America probably remain lamentable in her opinion. But more importantly, in the same way that the self is questioned in its relation to the other and becomes fragmented in *The Voyage Out* through the exotic encounter, colonial morality is also revealed as more complex: the moral binaries of good and evil become less pronounced and more ambiguous, and clearly more of an internal struggle, urging the self to question its held or taught beliefs. In terms of her biography, Virginia Woolf had to negotiate her great-grandfather's, grandfather's and father's nationalist fervor or critique of empire respectively, and her husband Leonard's complicated involvement in the colonial project, and she had to determine her own point of view.[18] And in a related artistic step, we move, between *Melymbrosia* and *The Voyage Out*, from moral certainty to moral ambiguity and complexity, from a more nineteenth-century to a modernist mentality and aesthetic, and overall, like explorer Mackenzie, "farther inland than anyone's been yet" (323).

[18] See Urmila Seshagiri, "Orienting Virginia Woolf: Race, Aesthetics, and Politics in *To the Lighthouse*." *Modern Fiction Studies* 50:1 (Spring 2004): 58-84, esp. 62-3. See also Phillips on Woolf's anti-colonial Bloomsbury associations, xxx-xxxv.

Works Cited

A. N. M. [Allan Monkhouse], Review of *The Voyage Out*. *Manchester Guardian* (15 April 1915), 4. In Majumdar 57-58. Print.

Bell, Quentin. *Virginia Woolf: A Biography*. London: Hogarth, 1972. Print.

Cummins, June. "*The Voyage Out* and *Between the Acts*: Readings of Empire." In *Virginia Woolf: Texts and Contexts. Selected Papers From the Fifth Annual Conference on Virginia Woolf*. Eds. Beth Rigel Daugherty and Eileen Barrett New York: Pace UP, 1995: 204-10. Print.

Dick, Susan. "Literary Realism in *Mrs Dalloway*, *To the Lighthouse*, *Orlando* and *The Waves*." *The Cambridge Companion to Virginia Woolf*. Eds. Sue Roe and Susan Sellers. Cambridge: Cambridge UP, 2000: 50-71. Print.

Forsdick, Charles. *Victor Segalen and the Aesthetics of Diversity: Journeys between Cultures*. Oxford: Oxford UP, 2000. Print.

Forster, E. M. Review of *The Voyage Out*. *Daily News and Leader* (8 April 1915), 7. Quoted in Majumdar, 52-55. Print.

Friedman, Susan Stanford. "Virginia Woolf's Pedagogical Scenes of Reading: *The Voyage Out*, *The Common Reader*, and her 'Common Readers.'" *Modern Fiction Studies* 38:1 (Spring 1992): 101-25. Print.

Frye, Joanne. "*The Voyage Out*: Thematic Tensions and Narrative Techniques." *Twentieth Century Literature* 26:4 (Winter 1980): 402-23. Print.

Gilmore, Lois J. "Virginia Woolf, Bloomsbury, and the Primitive." *Virginia Woolf and Communities: Selected Papers from the Eighth Annual Conference on Virginia Woolf*. Eds. Jeanette McVicker and Laura Davis. New York: Pace UP, 1999: 127-35. Print.

Heady, Chene. "'Accidents of Political Life': Satire and Edwardian Anti-Colonial Politics in *The Voyage Out*." *Virginia Woolf Out of Bounds*. Eds. Jessica Berman and Jane Goldman. New York: Pace UP, 2001: 97-105. Print.

Johnson, Erica L. "Contours of Travel and Exile in *The Voyage Out*." *JNT: Journal of Narrative Theory* 31.1 (Winter 2001): 65-86. Print.

Lee, Hermione. *Virginia Woolf*. New York: Knopf, 1997. Print.

Lewis, Andrea. "The Visual Politics of Empire and Gender in Virginia Woolf's *The Voyage Out*." *Woolf Studies Annual* 1 (1995): 106-19. Print.

Majumdar, Robin and Allen McLaurin, Eds. *Virginia Woolf: The Critical Heritage*. London and Boston: Routledge and Kegan Paul, 1975. Print.

Montgomery, Nick. "Colonial Rhetoric and the Maternal Voice: Deconstruction and Disengagement in Virginia Woolf's *The Voyage Out*." *Twentieth-Century Literature* 46:1 (Spring 2000): 34-55. Print.

Phillips, Kathy J. *Virginia Woolf Against Empire*. Knoxville: U of Tennessee P, 1994. Print.

Richter, Harvena. *Virginia Woolf: The Inward Voyage*. Princeton: Princeton UP, 1970. Print.

Santaolalla, Isabel, ed. *"New" Exoticisms: Changing Patterns in the Construction of Otherness*. Amsterdam and Atlanta, GA: Rodopi, 2000. Print.

Schaefer, Josephine O'Brien. *The Three-Fold Nature of Reality in the Novels of Virginia Woolf.* The Hague: Mouton, 1965. Print.

Schlack, Beverly Ann. "The Novelist's Voyage from Manuscripts to Text: Revisions of Literary Allusions in *The Voyage Out*." *Bulletin of Research in the Humanities* 82 (Autumn 1979): 317-27. Print.

Segalen, Victor. *Essay on Exoticism: An Aesthetics of Diversity*. Trans. and ed. Yaël Rachel Schlick. Foreword by Harry Harootunian. Durham and London: Duke UP, 2002. Print.

Seshagiri, Urmila. "Orienting Virginia Woolf: Race, Aesthetics, and Politics in *To the Lighthouse*." *Modern Fiction Studies* 50:1 (Spring 2004): 58-84. Print.

Snyder, Carey. "Woolf's Ethnographic Modernism: Self-Nativizing in *The Voyage Out* and Beyond." *Woolf Studies Annual* 10 (2004): 81-108. Print.

Underhill, Ruth Murray. "A Voyage Toward Reality." *The Bookman* (1920), 685-86. Print.

Unsigned Review of *The Voyage Out*. "Here are Books—and Books." *The Independent* (10 July 1920), 53. Print.

Vlasopolos, Anca. "Shelley's Triumph of Death in Virginia Woolf's *The Voyage Out*." *Modern Language Quarterly* 47 (Summer 1986): 130-53. Print.

Wollaeger, Mark A. "The Woolfs in the Jungle: Intertextuality, Sexuality, and the Emergence of Female Modernism in *The Voyage Out*, *The Village in the Jungle*, and *Heart of Darkness*." *Modern Language Quarterly* 64:1 (2003): 33-69. Print.

——. "Woolf, Postcards, and the Elision of Race: Colonizing Women in *The Voyage Out*." *Modernism/Modernity* 8:1 (January 2001): 43-75. Print.

Woolf, Virginia. *Melymbrosia*. Ed. with an Introduction by Louise DeSalvo. San Francisco: Cleis Press, 2002. Print.

——. "Mr. Bennett and Mrs. Brown." *The Essays of Virginia Woolf.* Vol. 3. Ed. Andrew McNeillie. London: Hogarth, 1988: 384-89. Print.

—— "Modern Fiction." *The Common Reader*. London: Hogarth, 1925: 184-95. Print.

——. "The New Autobiography." *Granite & Rainbow: Essays*. New York: Harvest, 1975: 149-55. Print.

——. "The Novels of Turgenev." *The Captain's Death Bed and Other Essays*. London: Hogarth, 1950: 53-60. Print.

——. *The Question of Things Happening: The Letters of Virginia Woolf.* Vol. II: 1912-1922. Ed. Nigel Nicolson. London: Hogarth, 1976. Print.

——. "An Unwritten Novel." *A Haunted House and Other Short Stories*. London: Hogarth, 1953: 14-26. Print.

——. *The Voyage Out*. Oxford: Oxford UP, 1992. Print.

Zwerdling, Alex. *Virginia Woolf and the Real World.* Berkeley: U of California P, 1986. Print.

Loving Maidens and Patriarchal Mothers: Revisions of the Homeric *Hymn to Demeter* and *Cymbeline* in *Mrs. Dalloway*

Amy C. Smith

> Lost maidenhood and the crossing of the borders of Hades are allegorical equivalents—the one can stand for the other equally well. This kind of equivalence only exists in a given sphere, in an immediately recognizable spiritual connection that can combine very different things, such as marriage and death, in one comprehensive idea. Mythological ideas are like the compact buds of such connections. They always contain more than the non-mythological mind could conceive. This is also true of the Kore [. . .]
>
> C. Kerényi, *Essays on a Science of Mythology* 109

> I have long thought about where fascism begins. It does not begin when the first bombs are dropped, nor with the terror that can be written about in every newspaper. It begins in the relations between a man and a woman, and I have tried to say [. . .] here in this society there is always war.
>
> Ingeborg Bachmann, *Gespräche und Interviews* 144
> (my translation)

Written a few years after the end of World War I, *Mrs. Dalloway* imagines the complexities of a future for Britain in the aftermath of soul-numbing destruction. As she makes clear in *A Room of One's Own* and *Three Guineas*, Woolf understood war as intimately connected to patriarchal forms of domination and envisioned a renewal of life for Britain in feminist terms. Woolf's practice of engaging with earlier literary models is well-documented by critics like Jane de Gay, and her engagement with the Greeks in particular is explored by Emily Dalgarno in *Virginia Woolf and the Visible World*.[1] Several literary texts are alluded to in *Mrs. Dalloway*, but here I would like to focus on revisions to the Homeric *Hymn to Demeter*, which, when framed by references to *Cymbeline*, open a complex feminist response to the aftermath of World War I.

Woolf knew that reading the Greeks was not an apolitical activity or cultural ideal, and she read and borrowed from the Greeks in ways that were explicitly and implicitly tied to a political agenda, as she does here with her revisions of the Homeric *Hymn to Demeter*. Proper "knowledge" of Greek was closed to women in her time, given their exclusion from institutions like Cambridge and Oxford. As

[1] Jane de Gay, *Virginia Woolf's Novels and the Literary Past* (Edinburgh: Edinburgh UP, 2007), Emily Dalgarno, *Virginia Woolf and the Visible World* (Cambridge: Cambridge UP, 2001).

Christine Kenyon Jones and Anna Snaith have recently shown, Woolf took courses in Greek, as well as many other subjects, at King's College Ladies' Department.[2] She also received years of tutoring in Greek from Clara Pater and Janet Case (who is sometimes credited with introducing Woolf to the feminist cause) and knew Greek well enough to translate the *Agamemnon*. While such a base of knowledge is likely to convince the contemporary reader that Woolf did know Greek, proper knowledge of Greek still functioned, at that time, as a mark of membership in an elite boys' club. In this context, her claim, in "On Not Knowing Greek," that no modern can "know" Greek is set as a challenge to the exclusionary identity of the "Oxbridge" elite formed through the exclusion of women. That essay, written while she was working on *Mrs. Dalloway*, exemplifies the radicalism Emily Dalgarno argues for: that Woolf conceived of studying the Greeks as a radical move, challenging patriarchal epistemology and militarism. Beyond her first-hand experience with Greek texts, much of Woolf's knowledge of the Greeks came through Jane Harrison's feminist presentation of them, and we see Harrison's radical interpretations of archaic material throughout Woolf's fiction and particularly in her revisions to the Homeric *Hymn to Demeter*.

Like reading Greek, the novel combines the mundane with the politically charged. The London of *Mrs. Dalloway*, while overflowing with grief and mourning for the dead, is also a London in which ordinary people buy flowers for parties and old friends greet one another on the street. Life continues, in all its joy and cruelty, deformity and grace, in the wake of the war that changed the modern world. The novel seems preoccupied with personal trivialities. Its main character, whose name the novel bears, spends much of the novel thinking back to a summer in her youth, musing about her isolation and fear of growing old, dwelling on petty jealousies and vanities. If this novel is a response to the destruction caused by the Great War, why does Woolf focus so tightly on the silly, vain wife of a politician? So much attention is devoted to the eponymous character that we might say the novel is not just *about* Clarissa Dalloway but is synonymous with her. In fact, the concerns of Clarissa—death, the ability to continue living in the face of decay and disillusionment, mourning a lost golden age—are to a great extent the concerns of the novel and of England at the time. If this novel is an attempt to think through what all-encompassing war does to and means for England, and if Clarissa is as central to the novel as I claim, then it is Clarissa, seemingly a domestic and interpersonal character, to whom we must look for insight into issues of social and national coherence.[3]

[2] "'Tilting at Universities': Woolf at King's College London." *Woolf Studies Annual* 16 (2010): 1-44.

[3] A. D. Moody shares this approach, describing Clarissa as "the living image of the surface of the society Virginia Woolf was concerned with. At the same time she is a criticism of

Early in the novel, Clarissa stands gazing at the pages of a book in a shop window. The narrator asks, "[b]ut what was she dreaming as she looked into Hatchards' shop window? What was she trying to recover? What image of white dawn in the country, as she read in the book spread open: *Fear no more the heat o' the sun, Nor the furious winter's rages*" (*MD* 9).[4] This line from *Cymbeline*, which acts as a kind of leitmotif, is the first line of the dirge sung at the apparent death of *Cymbeline*'s heroine Imogen, who is later revived.[5] The princess Imogen, disguised as a man, has been living with her long lost brothers, unbeknownst to any of them. The brothers sing this dirge when she (he) dies. The apparent death and later revival of Imogen parallels the structure of death and renewal in Septimus

---

that society [. . .] her society is what is seen to be in her; and her character, such as it is, is the character of her society" (49).

[4] One may wonder why Woolf chose this play, which is certainly not among Shakespeare's most critically respected. Jean Wyatt argues that the lines quoted from *Cymbeline* supply the novel's central structure, the movement between death and rebirth, and provide the symbols that link Clarissa and Septimus in this movement (445). In fact, there are several similarities between *Cymbeline* and *Mrs. Dalloway*. Both texts include a British war with a foreign power. Samuel Johnson dismissed *Cymbeline* as a failure because of its incongruity, and Arthur C. Kirsch maintains that the play was resistant to any coherent interpretation, evaluations that some critics have made of *Mrs. Dalloway*. Kirsch also notes the simultaneous condensation and dilation of time in the play, an important theme and technique in Woolf's novel (Simonds 29). In terms of form, Peggy Muñoz Simonds defines *Cymbeline* as a "Renaissance tragicomedy," a theatrical mixed form (32). This description is apt for *Mrs. Dalloway* as well, which combines incongruous elements—madness, war, and suicide with the simple joy of living; and a happy ending focused on a woman's return to sociality and the reunion of a father with his daughter. Both *Cymbeline* and *Mrs. Dalloway* can alternately be classified as romance: "While an earlier story, 'Mrs. Dalloway in Bond Street', primarily satirized the class insularity and superficiality of its protagonist [. . .] the novel complicates that image by interspersing romance elements of a remembered, recovered past for Clarissa as well as by adding a dying male double" (Henderson, 110).

[5] The dirge reads,

Fear no more the heat o' th' sun,
Nor the furious winter's rages,
Thou thy worldly task has done,
Home art gone, and ta'en thy wages.
Golden lads and girls all must,
As chimney-sweepers, come to dust.

Fear no more the frown o' th' great,
Thou art past the tyrant's stroke;
Care no more to clothe and eat,
To thee the reed is as the oak.
The scepter, learning, physic, must,
All follow this and come to dust.
(4.2.258-269)

Warren Smith and Clarissa Dalloway. Woolf stated that she intended Smith as a double of Clarissa, and when Clarissa is informed of his suicide at the end of the novel it has a strange revivifying effect on her, allowing her to return to social life from which she had been alienated.

Given the context and background of this quotation ("Fear no more the heat o' th' sun,/Nor the furious winter's rages") how should we read it in relation to the narrator's question about what Clarissa is trying to recover as she looks in the shop window, and how does it relate to World War I? The final line of *Cymbeline* provides a clue; the play ends with the word "peace": "Never was a war did cease (Ere bloody hands were wash'd) with such a peace" (Shakespeare 5.5.484-5). At the end of the play, the rightful king is a ratifier of *pax romana*, and the elements who wanted war with Rome—the Queen and her son Cloten—are dead. After a period of disorder, Britain is revived by the rebirth of the three royal children. "In the same vein, Imogen's dramatic 'revival' from death in Wales is a visual allusion to the cosmic renewal about to occur during the Augustan peace" (Simonds 246). Similarly, *Mrs. Dalloway* features war in the background and a happy ending in which rebirth is emphasized in Clarissa's return to life during her party, and as in *Cymbeline*, there is an analogy between the heroine and her nation. These parallels between *Mrs. Dalloway* and *Cymbeline* suggest that a restoration of peace and life are imagined possibilities in *Mrs. Dalloway*. I argue that it is this "cosmic renewal" that Clarissa is dreaming and this harmony she is trying to recover, not just for herself, but for the culture and country for which she stands in.[6] This renewal is imagined through Woolf's revisions to the Homeric *Hymn to Demeter*, which, I argue, should be read through the lens provided by the novel's revision of *Cymbeline*.

As Diana Henderson points out, Woolf revises *Cymbeline* by modifying its heroine's conclusion, a change that reflects Woolf's understanding that, as with the Greeks, reading Shakespeare and incorporating his work into twentieth-century feminist literature is not a value-neutral activity. While *Cymbeline* returns its heroine, Imogen, to the heterosexual romance plot, Woolf disrupts that trajectory, recognizing that in her novel such an ending, a reunion of Clarissa with Peter, would "erase her social critique of the Dalloway world too absolutely [...] It would remove the blinders and restrictions created by class and gender ideologies, [...]

[6] The relationship between Clarissa and post-war Britain is further suggested by the passage that follows the lines from *Cymbeline*, a statement of the cloud of grief and sadness hanging over Britain: "This late age of the world's experience had bred in them all, all men and women, a well of tears. Tears and sorrows; courage and endurance; a perfectly upright and stoical bearing" (*MD* 9-10). This description of the world in the decline of late age, bearing its suffering with a stiff upper lip, is an accurate description of Clarissa. Externally, Clarissa is the perfect hostess and politician's wife while inwardly she is preoccupied with her lost youth, fear of death, and isolation.

And it would also blunt Woolf's interwoven insight about nationalist ideologies: Britain's imperial projects carry an ideological force that shapes the thinking even of those who rationally would resist their logic and from which there is no escape into particular personal relationships" (Henderson, 130). This awareness that personal relationships, especially those organized around patriarchal order, can be imbued with the logic of empire runs through the novel and is expressed in Woolf's turn to the Homeric *Hymn to Demeter*, which, following Jane Harrison's interpretation, has come to be seen as an artifact of matriarchal culture and religion. However, Woolf goes further than a celebration of matriarchy, revising the Homeric material in two key ways. First, she changes the *Hymn*'s portrayal of female community and emotionally intimate relationships between women into female *spiritual* community and lesbian relationships. Woolf draws on the images of fertility and rebirth in the *Hymn* to achieve the cosmic renewal envisioned through her *Cymbeline* references, but her feminist analysis of contemporary geopolitical and domestic problems motivates her to decouple this traditional fertility symbolism (seen in Demeter, Persephone, and Artemis as well as in imagery of vegetation and human sexuality) from heterosexuality. She emphasizes the distinction between fertility as reproduction and fertility as spiritual rebirth by transforming the essentially secular, familial relation of the *Hymn* into a spiritual community of women. While this change may bring to the surface subliminal meanings in the *Hymn* and its related cults it reflects Jane Harrison's feminist understanding of archaic Greek religion and is a significant revision of the Homeric *Hymn to Demeter*. Second, while the *Hymn* portrays female community as cooperative and ethical in comparison to a violent and dominating patriarchal presence, Woolf includes women in her critique of patriarchy, which she blames for the war. She does this primarily through her use of flower imagery, which is central to the portrayal of female sexuality and the woman's life cycle in the *Hymn*, and through her exploration of Clarissa's split nature, embodying both cold death and joyous fertility, corresponding to the split natures of Persephone and Artemis.

Woolf's revisions of the Homeric *Hymn to Demeter*, framed by her revisions to *Cymbeline*, allow a multifaceted critique of the power structures and modes of thought that led to the war and a revolutionary vision of renewal and hope. Woolf transitions away from heterosexual and secular images of renewal and toward the possibilities of lesbian and spiritual community, but she does not ignore the threat of patriarchal and imperialist domination within relations between women, tentatively imagining a true post-war renewal that might resist recreating the same problems. By balancing her enthusiasm for the possibilities of female intimacy with an awareness of the darkness lurking in the hearts of some women, she constructs a critique of patriarchal modes of relation that is both more sophisticated and more powerful than if she had simply portrayed women as occupying a position outside of patriarchy.

The Homeric *Hymn to Demeter* features a network of goddesses with interlocking symbolism and relations. Woolf alludes to several of these goddesses in the novel, notably Demeter, Persephone, Artemis and Hecate, who function as doubles of each other throughout myth.[7] I will later discuss Clarissa's resemblance to Persephone, but Woolf also portrays Clarissa in strongly Artemisian imagery and introduces her revisions of the *Hymn* through a specifically Artemisian lens. Artemis is a minor figure in the *Hymn*, mentioned only once, in Persephone's recounting of her abduction to her mother, but Woolf knew from Harrison's work that Persephone and Artemis were strongly linked in the Greek imagination.

Within the narrative of the *Hymn*, Persephone chooses to include Artemis in the group of maidens who were present at her abduction and later versions of the story contain this feature. The *Hymn*'s original version of Persephone's abduction states that she was with the daughters of Okeanos when Hades took her, but when Persephone tells her mother what happened, upon her return from Hades, she changes the story. In Persephone's version of her abduction Athena and Artemis are present. Helene Foley interprets the absence of Artemis and Athena in the *Hymn*'s original version of the abduction as a sign that Persephone is ready for marriage, an interpretation that is supported by several other aspects of the abduction.[8] In focusing on Artemis, Woolf emphasizes a figure who is minor in the Homeric *Hymn*, and who features in the version of the abduction that does not suggest readiness for marriage; outside the *Hymn* Artemis is known for her preference for female companions and refusal of heterosexual relations. With the choice to focus on Artemis from among the goddesses in the *Hymn*, Woolf sets up her revision of the *Hymn*'s community of women from secular and familial to spiritual and lesbian.

[7] For discussions of Demeter and Persephone's identity or duality, see Jane Harrison, *Prolegomena to the Study of Greek Religion and Mythology*, Kerényi, *Eleusis* and *Essays on a Science of Mythology*, and Ann Suter, *The Narcissus and the Pomegranate*. In *Eleusis*, Kerényi goes further, asserting the identity not just of Demeter and Persephone, but of Demeter, Persephone, and Hecate. Hecate and Artemis are also linked. They are both goddesses associated with the moon (Harrison, *Mythology* 121) as well as being maternal cousins (Kerényi, *Gods of the Greeks* 132).

[8] In the *Hymn*'s version of the abduction, the girls are picking flowers in a "soft meadow," an image of female sexuality in Greek literature. "Meadows in Greek myth are liminal sites, associated not only with a transition to sexuality and fertility but with the underworld [...] The motif of abduction from a meadow and a group of maidens suggests the girl's readiness for marriage" (Foley, 34). Additionally, Persephone, Demeter's *thalos* (shoot), is described as *thaleron*, fertile or blooming, by Helios in line 79. The maidens she is playing with are already mature, described as "deep-breasted." The fact that Persephone reaches out to pick the narcissus flower on her own impulse is an indication to some critics that the *Hymn* should be read as primarily concerning the maturation of a daughter and her mother's reaction. As Ann Suter notes, Persephone "herself is thereby the active agent who, by this readiness, precipitates the action of the core story" (11).

The connections between Artemis and Persephone run deep. In *Mythology*, Harrison argues that Demeter, Persephone, Artemis, Athena, and several other goddesses derive from an earlier figure, the Mistress of Wild Beasts or the Earth-Mother of Cretan religion. As a vegetation deity, associated with the cycle of life, death and regeneration, the *Potnia therōn* has both a life-giving aspect and a terrifying and deathly aspect, which is seen in Demeter, Persephone, Artemis, Medusa and Hecate. When living things die they return to her and she is thus the guardian or, in the case of Persephone, the queen of the dead. Within this network of deathly mothers, Artemis and Persephone have a special link. They are both *Korai*, youthful maidens. They both address the transition from child to woman and combine fertility and death. As Persephone brings death and fertility together in the form of her own descent to the underworld and return to life, Artemis brings them together as the goddess of sudden death for women, the huntress, and the goddess of childbirth and nurturer of young children.[9] In this way they are two sides of the same coin: Persephone is the passive aspect of death while Artemis, as murderer, is the active side. Persephone is the maiden whose virginity is whole and untouched until the entrance of the masculine. Her transition from maiden to wife, queen, and mother is like Artemis' initiation of young girls into fully socialized womanhood.

Jean-Pierre Vernant, in his analysis of Artemis, argues that Artemis is the goddess of boundaries, articulating them and allowing them to be crossed. One of the functions of Artemis was to help youth, both boys and girls, to cross the threshold of adulthood and citizenship. For girls, sexuality within marriage is the decisive step; Artemis prepares the young girl to be a wife and mother, a transition that integrates femininity into culture. Artemis' function with regard to girls is dual: First, she establishes boundaries "between boys and girls, young and adult, beasts and men. As a result, it becomes possible to articulate both the chastity required of the young girl and the marriage that completes the woman in her adult state" (200-201). At the same time, she makes them pass over the boundary she articulates. Thus, the boundaries are preserved from effacement and the maiden is able to enter civilization (199-201). This Artemisian framework can be applied to Persephone also, as she is a figure of liminality that synchronistically joins two identities (virginal daughterhood with married womanhood/motherhood) while at the same time representing each discrete side. With respect to the boundaries both of life and death and of childhood and womanhood, Artemis and Persephone, in different ways, maintain the boundary while allowing its permeability.

[9] Jane Harrison connects Artemis's deathly aspect to Persephone's associations with death. Artemis "shares with Apollo the ministry of death for mortals […] Artemis may have her aspect as death-dealer to women merely as a correlative of Apollo; on the other hand it is perhaps more likely that she here reflects the darker underworld side of the Earth-Mother" (*Mythology* 119).

Despite her role in preparing girls for marriage and heterosexuality, Artemis refuses this transition herself. There is a strange tension within her regarding marriage. She enforces it upon women whose time it is to submit, punishing those, like Atalanta, who wish to remain eternal virgins. At the same time, perhaps in order to maintain it, she remains outside this system of meaning, which defines the identity of ancient Greek women, and creates a homosocial community of maidens, hunting and running through the woods. The marriage of a maiden, which marks the end of her time with Artemis, is always connected with death for Artemis. As Vernant writes, "Every virgin, attaining the state of matrimony, must die first for Artemis. She must vanish in her status of *parthenos*" (215).

One of the key links between Clarissa and Artemis is Clarissa's youthful love affair with Sally Seton. Clarissa falls in love with Sally Seton and wants to protect their emotional intimacy and friendship from what she perceives as Peter Walsh's patriarchal intrusions. Clarissa thinks of Sally like a balloon that is "all light, glowing," an image that suggests the bright full moon associated with Artemis (35). As Harrison writes in *Mythology*, "The moon has her dark and spectral side, but this is taken over by Hecate, leaving the brightness for Artemis" (121). But the most compelling connection is the Artemisian quality of this relationship. Eileen Barrett delineates several competing discourses of lesbianism and male homosexuality in the nineteenth and twentieth centuries and argues that the relationship between Clarissa and Sally exemplifies one of these types: "the romantic friendships between women that were thriving at the turn of the century" (147). This notion of romantic friendship between women is remarkably similar to the relationship between Artemis and her young companions. Clarissa describes her relationship with Sally in terms that recall the virgin goddesses, emphasizing that her feeling for Sally was "not like one's feeling for a man. It was completely disinterested" (*MD* 34). In this relation Clarissa is not dependent on Sally economically or socially and she can gain no status from her feelings for Sally; this independence and purity of emotion recall the virgin goddesses, and especially Artemis, with their emphasis on chastity, independent identity and separateness from gods and men.

Clarissa's love for Sally is further characterized by Artemisian qualities in her emphasis on the liminality of their age. She describes it as having "a quality that could only exist between women, between women just grown up" (34). The qualification of the women as "just grown up" rather than older women highlights the aspect of her relationship with Sally that resembles the virgin goddesses; it is a companionship between women who are not yet embedded in the system of heterosexuality. Artemis's maidens, the little girls she shepherds to the threshold of womanhood, are characterized by their location in this liminal zone between child and adult, maiden and wife; Woolf's emphasis on this liminality, on the status of "just grown up" as a necessary condition, thus marks Clarissa and Sally's relation as Artemisian. Like Artemisian maidens fearful of the transition awaiting them, Clarissa thinks of her feeling for Sally as "protective, on her side; [they] sprang from a sense of being in league together, a presentiment of something that was bound to part them (they spoke of marriage always as a catastrophe)" (34). This language recalls the events of the Homeric *Hymn to Demeter* as well; in both narratives, the bond between women is threatened by the catastrophe of marriage. Clarissa goes beyond thinking of marriage as a catastrophe, drawing a parallel between Sally's marriage and her death. When Sally appears unexpectedly at Clarissa's party, in a description that echoes and plays with Artemis's attitude toward the marriage of a maiden, Clarissa remembers how she used to worry that Sally's youthful ways were bound "to end in some awful tragedy; her death; her martyrdom; instead of which she married, quite unexpectedly" (182).

The friendship of Clarissa and Sally does ultimately end because they marry, move away, have children, and leave behind that magical moment of women "just grown up" and the pure feelings it made possible. But their intimacy is intruded upon much earlier by Peter in a scene that resembles the abduction of Persephone:

> Then came the most exquisite moment of her life passing a stone urn with flowers in it. Sally stopped; picked a flower; kissed her on the lips. The whole world might have turned upside down! The others disappeared; there she was alone with Sally [...] the revelation, the religious feeling!—when old Joseph and Peter faced them: 'Star-gazing?' said Peter. It was like running one's face against a granite wall in the darkness! It was shocking; it was horrible! Not for herself. She felt only how Sally was being mauled already, maltreated; she felt his hostility; his jealousy; his determination to break into their companionship. (35-6)

Female communion that is interrupted by men; the woman's experience of this intrusion as violent, shocking, and horrible; the interpretation of this intrusion as motivated by jealousy, hostility, and a determination to rupture the bond of women; the setting of this scene among flowers and the fact that one of the girls picks a flower—all of these elements parallel the events and tone of the Homeric *Hymn to Demeter*.[10] Here we have one of Woolf's most interesting revisions of the *Hymn*, which has been introduced by her portrayal of Clarissa and Sally's relationship as Artemisian: Woolf adapts the story of Persephone's abduction to express romantic friendship between women. By shifting her emphasis from the main tale to the minor, alternative version of the abduction that features Artemis,

[10] Sally has a parallel Persephone-like experience with Hugh Whitbread, whom she accuses of "kissing her in the smoking-room to punish her for saying that women should have votes" (*MD* 181).

Woolf revises the *Hymn* from what many critics consider a story of a girl's readiness for marriage to a story of male sexual violence against female intimacy, a meaning which is inherent in the *Hymn* but not explicit in the main tale.[11] In doing this, Woolf goes further than the myth and further than Artemis; she introduces lesbianism and spirituality in her version. These revisions are important for Woolf because they suggest an alternative mode of relation, a tentatively utopian space of lesbian intimacy and spiritual connection to counteract the dominant structure of patriarchy and imperialism that led to the war.

In this passage, Woolf combines a representation of female intimacy and lesbianism as religious ("the revelation, the religious feeling!") with a representation of male aggression and sexual possessiveness as a threat to women's spirituality, to create a meaning that is similar to, but not identical with, the meaning of the Homeric *Hymn*. Although the *Hymn* represents masculinity as a violent intrusion upon the peace and happiness of female companionship, it does not characterize the community of the flower-picking maidens as essentially spiritual. Nor does it overtly represent the female community as romantic or sexual. It may be the case, however, that these two elements of Woolf's revision of the myth lie in the background of the myth and the related rituals.

In her commentary on the *Hymn*, Helene Foley notes that Persephone's longing for her mother is expressed in a Greek word that connotes sexual desire (130). Lisa Tyler, in her analysis of mother-daughter romance in the fiction of Woolf and Doris Lessing, characterizes Demeter's and Persephone's "intense desire for each other's presence and physical closeness" as what we might today term "homoerotic." She goes on to say that "[a] young girl's love for her mother is, of course, not specifically lesbian, but, like the young boy's oedipal love, it encompasses the desire for physical and sexual intimacy as well as the more socially acceptable need for attention, affection, and care" (75). This analogy between daughter's and son's love for their mother sheds light on the passage quoted above. When Sally kisses Clarissa, all other people disappear and they are the only people in the world;

[11] In doing so, she participates in a tradition that goes back to the Homeric *Hymn* itself, reflecting social issues in the myth. Many critics see myths as symbolically expressing political and social issues. The most well-known such interpretation is that the marriage of Zeus and Hera reflects the conquest of the indigenous matriarchal peoples by Northern patriarchal peoples and the consequent "troubled marriage" of the two cultures and religions. Jane Harrison sees the same conflict with regard to the Eleusinian goddesses: "the Olympian Father Zeus [...] victoriously took over to himself the cult of the Earth-Mother and the Earth-Maidens" (*Prolegomena* 319). Ann Suter has suggested that the story of Persephone's abduction in its many forms, including the Homeric *Hymn* and other sources, may reflect, among other things, changing social relations between men and women, and women's sexuality (*Narcissus and Pomegranate* 21-22). Woolf's modern revision of the myth similarly addresses what she saw as the most pertinent issues of her time.

similarly, one of the characteristics of a boy's oedipal desire is to have his mother all to himself, to be alone with her away from the intrusive figure of the father.[12] Thus, the "romantic friendship" of Clarissa and Sally may bring to the surface the homoerotic subtext of the Homeric *Hymn to Demeter*.

In transforming the female community of the *Hymn*, which is not a religious community, into a spiritual community, Woolf may be drawing on the related Thesmophorian rituals. Harrison characterizes the Thesmophoria as a "primitive" pre-Olympian festival in honor of Demeter in which women participated in a sympathetic magical ritual intended to ensure a good crop and human offspring (*Prolegomena* 120-24). Implementing her ritual theory of myth interpretation, Harrison interprets the myth of Persephone's abduction told in the Homeric *Hymn to Demeter* as arising from the ritual practiced at the Thesmophoria. According to Harrison, the myth related in the Homeric *Hymn* derives from a ritual in which women form a religious community and elements of the myth are symbolic representations of the actual elements of the ritual. If we follow Harrison's line of thought, which in many instances Woolf did, the female community of the myth is *implicitly* a religious community. It may be that Harrison's interpretation of the myth, along with Woolf's knowledge of Greek and perhaps of the etymological implications of sexual desire in Persephone's longing for her mother, inform Woolf's revision of Persephone's abduction.[13]

Responding to the war requires a vision of a future rebirth, a critique of the tendencies and temptations that led to the destruction, and a sensitive treatment of the current moment in which life and death combine in a delicate web of grief and hope. Woolf's utopian vision of cosmic renewal and salvation through a spiritual and lesbian mode of relation is tentative in the novel, and while Woolf celebrates the possibilities of women's relationships she is also wary of unqualified and naïve praise. For Woolf, women, like men, are susceptible to reproducing exploitation and domination, to enacting the logic of imperialism and patriarchy. She also needs to portray the paradoxical state of the continuation of life in the midst of death after the war. Eliot's famous line from *The Waste Land*, "April is the cruelest month,"

---

[12] Woolf has represented this Oedipal relationship in *To the Lighthouse*. Compare James's desire to have his mother all to himself, and his hatred of and resentment toward his father for interrupting "the perfect simplicity and good sense of his relations with his mother" (*TTL* 40).

[13] Patricia Cramer sees another instance of Harrison's influence on the confluence of fertility and lesbianism within the novel, reading the narrative of *Mrs. Dalloway* as a form of the matriarchal fertility rites described by Jane Harrison: "These fertility rites which Harrison admired were structured on a two part rhythm of blame and praise — the exorcism of evil and the induction of good (*Prolegomena* 7-8) [...] Woolf's repetitive documentations of the evils of male domination can be viewed as a kind of ritual exorcism of evil [...] Woolf very specifically grounds the erotic and emotional bases of the induction phase of her narrative rituals in the lesbian body" (182).

suggests the figure of the dying and reborn vegetation god and the cruelty of the endless cycle of flowers growing out of rotting corpses. Woolf draws on the same mythic tradition to address the problem of post-war life but combines it with a gender-sensitive critique of class, empire and patriarchy, echoing the Homeric *Hymn*'s portrayal of flowers as sexual metaphors.[14] Like the Cretan Earth Mother and Artemis, Persephone combines two opposites: the fertility goddess who blossoms and becomes the grain, and the terrifying queen of the underworld who rules over the dead. Woolf draws on this coexistence of life and death in Persephone and Artemis to portray a city recovering from destruction and haunted by ghosts, life continuing in the midst of despair, and a main character who combines youthful joy with cold isolation and death. Through Eleusinian flower imagery she revises the Homeric portrayal of intimacy between women to highlight the power relations within women's relationships.

Flowers play a significant role in the *Hymn* as well as in appearances of Demeter and Persephone outside the *Hymn*. In the *Hymn*, Persephone is picking them when she is abducted; both she and her mother are vegetation goddesses, and as the daughter she is the less mature flower while Demeter is the grain and fruit. Persephone's story is analogous to the life cycle of the flower which starts as a tightly closed bud that blossoms into the flower, is fertilized and bears fruit. While the blossoming is the fulfillment of the bud's potential, it is also the end of the bud phase since the static completeness of the bud's self-contained form of life is destroyed. Through marriage, symbolized in the myth as death, Persephone's potential is actualized and she is transformed from maiden to powerful queen of the underworld. Seen from the perspective of the maiden-bud, the actualization and realization of the maiden's potential is mourned as the loss of that potential, and the loss of the fullness and wholeness that constitutes the maiden's mode of existence. Once the bud blossoms into the flower and bears fruit, the flower shrivels and dies. This process of transformation is portrayed in violent terms in the Homeric *Hymn to Demeter*, in which marriage and sexuality are not chosen, but only forced on a girl. Seen from the perspective of the matriarchate, all marriage is an act of violence because it breaks in upon the closed circle of female unity, represented in the myth as the mother-daughter relationship and the all-female society of the girls picking flowers. However, while her abduction ruptures the unity of mother and daughter, it is a necessary and fruitful moment in her development into adult-

[14] For a detailed discussion of flower imagery as sexual metaphor, see Paula Bennett. Bennett analyzes clitoral symbolism (such as buds, berries and seeds) in a wide selection of nineteenth-century American women's poetry. Bennett argues that this "language of flowers" has long been "Western culture's language of women. More specifically, it has been the language through which women's bodies, and more particularly for this article, women's genitals have been represented and inscribed" (242).

hood. Since Demeter and Persephone are two aspects of the same figure, reflecting a woman's life cycle and the different identities she will have during her life, the unity of mother and daughter and the untouched wholeness of virginity must both be broken for Persephone to mature out of the daughter phase and become a woman and mother herself. Though the introduction of the masculine element breaks the static circle of mother and daughter, this same event establishes the dynamic aspect of the circle in which daughter becomes mother.[15]

Mrs. Dalloway is full of actual flowers and flower metaphors used to describe people, including Septimus, and they are often connected to female sexuality. Flowers figure in the first sentence of *Mrs. Dalloway*, a clue to the importance of flowers as a symbol in the novel. As Clarissa starts her day, concerned with buying the flowers for her party that evening, she remembers a similar morning at Bourton when she was eighteen; on that morning too she looked out at the flowers (*MD* 3). Clarissa has a moment of perfection in the flower shop in which all the negative and horrible aspects of herself, her hatred, jealousy and insecurities, are overcome by the flowers and Miss Pym, who is herself compared to a flower. In this scene the connection between flowers and young women is made clear, and Clarissa is drawn into the fullness of this realm, the realm of beauty, life, softness and purity. Her reverie continues when she returns home, where she feels grateful to her servants, her husband, even to dogs and canaries, for giving her "exquisite moments," which she describes as "buds on the tree of life, flowers of darkness [...] as if some lovely rose had blossomed for her eyes only" (29). This "exquisite moment" is described in religious imagery ("she felt like a nun [...] felt blessed and purified") as well as in flower imagery, just like Clarissa's later memory of the most exquisite moment of her life—Sally's kiss.[16] However, the joy and peace of the moment is shattered when Clarissa reads the telephone message inviting Richard, but not her, to lunch at Lady Bruton's.

The description of Clarissa's crisis when she is not invited to luncheon at Lady Bruton's house includes flower imagery also, but here it is employed to show her alienation from the world. In this scene, the first time in the novel that her husband, Richard, enters Clarissa's thoughts, Clarissa's connection to the fullness of life is severed by her exclusion from the social event and what she perceives as her husband's abandonment of her. Now, instead of being part of the scene, transported and blessed by the fullness and flowering of the day around her, Clarissa feels

[15] Freud theorized a similar violence in the boy's usurpation of his father's role, but in his theory the violence originates within the father-son unit, whereas in the Homeric *Hymn to Demeter* the violence originates outside the community in the form of the foreign masculine element.

[16] The shift to the house in which the hall is described as "cool as a vault" also suggests death, in an ambiguous network of death, the sacred and fertility, in keeping with Woolf's Eleusinian allusions.

herself "a single figure against [...] the stare of this matter-of-fact June morning; soft with the glow of rose petals for some, she knew" (30). While the "flowering of the day" continues, it does so outside of her body and brain, which now failed, since she had not been asked to Lady Bruton's lunch party (31).

The transition Clarissa undergoes in this scene from vibrance and relationality to isolation from the world can be understood in terms of Persephone and Artemis, who are reflected in sometimes contradictory aspects of Clarissa's character. Both Clarissa and Persephone experience transformations from figures of youthful beauty to figures of coldness and isolation from loved ones. Clarissa's shift from joyful integration with the world to feelings of isolation and spiritual emptiness, at the moment Richard is first mentioned in the novel, correlates to Persephone's isolation from her family and friends when she enters marriage. Although Richard does not physically appear at this point, Clarissa re-enters her role as wife, leaving behind the freedom of being simply Clarissa. In the flower shop, Clarissa is alone with a friendly woman involved in an archetypally feminine task, choosing flowers. Not only are there no men in the shop, there is no mention of them. As it is for Persephone, Clarissa's transition from a homogeneously female community to her identity as wife is characterized by isolation rather than relation. Clarissa's growing isolation is described in images of being sliced away at and her bed growing narrower and narrower, separating her from both other people and existence itself. She states that "she feared time itself [...] how year by year her share was sliced; how little the margin that remained was capable any longer of stretching, of absorbing, as in the youthful years, the colours, salts, tones of existence" (29). Clarissa experiences these changes as being passively ravaged by outside forces, just as Persephone's movement into death and isolation is represented as an abduction in the *Hymn*.

While Clarissa often locates the causes of her isolation outside her own agency, suggesting the victimization of Persephone, she is also tied to Artemis and the active form of death she represents. Her bed may be narrowing and her share being sliced, but Clarissa attributes her lack of intimacy with others, both her husband and other women, to her "cold spirit": "[...] through some contraction of this cold spirit, she had failed him. [...] She could see what she lacked. It was not beauty; it was not mind. It was something central which permeated; something warm which broke up the surfaces and rippled the cold contact of men and women, or of women together" (31). This conviction of Clarissa, which she expresses shortly after feeling ravaged by external forces, that her coldness and isolation are part of her nature, connects her to Artemis who, as the huntress and cause of sudden death for women, carries death and isolation within herself. The moment of Clarissa's transformation from relational to isolated, while attended by the introduction of Richard Dalloway, is also described in images of a separateness characteristic of virgin goddesses like Artemis. When Clarissa feels isolated from the world, a single figure against the June day, she identifies herself as "suddenly shrivelled, aged, breastless" and "a nun withdrawing, or a child exploring a tower," both images of asexuality and virginity, the first recalling a shriveled, decaying flower (31). In one of the novel's most enigmatic lines, she describes herself as unable to dispel an existential "virginity preserved through childbirth, which clung to her like a sheet" (31). The virginity with which Clarissa defines herself is a psychological virginity, which she thinks of as due to an indescribable lack, that prevents her from experiencing intimacy with others, most notably her husband. There is an essential solitude to Clarissa, much like the virginity of Artemis, which she expresses when she explains why she could not marry Peter Walsh—he demanded too much intimacy from her, wanting to know all her thoughts, whereas she believes that "there is a dignity in people; a solitude; even between husband and wife a gulf; and that one must respect [...] for one would not part with it oneself, or take it, against his will, from one's husband, without losing one's independence, one's self-respect—something, after all, priceless" (120).

Like Persephone, Clarissa crosses the threshold from maidenhood to the status of wife, mother, and queen.[17] Like Artemis, she remains an eternal virgin, characterized by solitude and psychological independence, never completely giving herself to another person. Both Artemis and Persephone express within themselves the same opposition that Clarissa does; all three figures combine eternal virginity with marriage and childbirth: Persephone in her synchronistic combination of wife and maiden; Artemis in eternally retaining her virginity while devoting herself to helping other women cross the threshold of marriage and childbirth, and punishing those who, like Atalanta, do not do so; and Clarissa in retaining her virginity through marriage and childbirth. There are also many combinations of fertility and youthful joy with cold death and isolation: Persephone is often read as an allegory of seasonal death and renewal and alternates between the chthonic realm and the Olympian realm of light; she transitions from stasis to dynamism, and the event that seems to bring 'death' (her abduction) causes her to bring forth life by giving birth to a child; Artemis is the maiden who kills yet brings forth life; and Clarissa embodies both a cold spirit and a joyous connection and life-giving function. She combines these two facets of her

[17] While Clarissa is not a queen, Woolf draws a parallel between Clarissa and the Queen of England. Both give parties on the same night, and Clarissa feels it her duty to organize and manage the experience of her guests, in a sense ruling over them. At the beginning of the novel, when Clarissa buys the flowers for her party, a motorcar appears on Bond Street; Clarissa is certain the Queen is inside. In her inner dialogue Clarissa exclaims that, "the Queen herself [was] held up; the Queen herself unable to pass" due to the crowds gathering on the street and the traffic (17). In the next sentence, Clarissa herself is held up, unable to pass, "suspended on one side of Brook Street" (17). Later, when she feels reduced by Peter, Clarissa likens herself to "a Queen whose guards have fallen asleep and left her unprotected" (44).

character in a way that parallels Persephone's and Artemis's synchronistic combinations. Her ebullient states of connection and intimacy are tinged with darkness and subliminal exploitation, an embodiment of what A. D. Moody called "the soul that is dead and yet in life, that lives to be the agent of death" (51). As with Persephone, this paradoxical combination of opposites is expressed through flower symbolism.

Clarissa's joyous state, prior to her isolated withdrawal in her home, begins in the flower shop with Miss Pym. That scene contains some of the most beautiful flower imagery in the novel and when coupled with the novel's most famous description of flowers reveals a significant revision of the Homeric *Hymn to Demeter* and a critical analysis of the dangers of patriarchal and imperial logic within women's relationships and sexuality. As Woolf uses Artemis and the Homeric *Hymn* to suggest the ethical possibilities of lesbian and spiritual relationships in her portrayal of a romantic friendship between Clarissa and Sally, she uses flowers as images of female sexuality and of Eleusinian community to suggest that women's relationships are not immune to exploitation and domination. The most striking elements of Clarissa's description of the flowers in the flower shop scene are her anthropomorphization of them and their association with femininity. The roses look "fresh like frilled linen clean from a laundry laid in wicker trays"; the red carnations "dark and prim, holding their heads up" (*MD* 13). When Clarissa looks at the flowers, she imagines that girls are picking flowers and it is "the moment between six and seven when every flower—roses, carnations, irises, lilac—*glows*; white, violet, red, deep orange; *every flower seems to burn by itself, softly, purely in the misty beds*" (emphasis mine, 13). In this scene, as in the Homeric *Hymn to Demeter*, a group of girls picks flowers but there are more important points of comparison that become clear in comparison to another description of flowers.

After Clarissa describes her inability to have emotionally intimate relationships with men or women, she presents one exception to this situation. At some moments with other women Clarissa does experience intimacy. Her description of her feelings at these moments is one of the most celebrated images of sensuality in *Mrs. Dalloway*, that of a match burning in a crocus. Clarissa explains that while she is cold in relation to her husband, she experiences moments of yielding to the charm of a woman confessing a folly, a woman who has been foolish and is thus beneath Clarissa. She confesses that "she did undoubtedly then feel what men felt. Only for a moment; but it was enough" (32). Clarissa explicitly identifies with patriarchal power in this passage, she takes up what she understands to be the position of a man in relation to a woman (which she has earlier been on the other end of when Hugh Whitbread makes her feel "a girl of eighteen [...] a little skimpy besides Hugh; schoolgirlish" [6]) and she describes this male position as satisfying and compensatory ("but it was enough"). It is in this position of patriarchal superiority that Clarissa experiences her most intense sensual feeling:

> It was a sudden revelation, a tinge like a blush which one tried to check and then, as it spread, one yielded to its expansion, and rushed to the farthest verge and then quivered and felt the world come closer, swollen with some astonishing significance, some pressure of rapture, which split its thin skin and gushed and poured with an extraordinary alleviation over the cracks and sores! Then, for that moment, she had an illumination; a match burning in a crocus; an inner meaning almost expressed. But the close withdrew; the hard softened. It was over—the moment. (32)

While this experience happens with a woman, and thus might seem to indicate an Artemisian community of women before the entrance of the male, and therefore before heterosexuality, the imagery in this second passage suggests a heterosexual form of relation between women. It is notable that Clarissa specifies that she only yields to the charm of "a woman, not a girl, of a woman confessing" (32). This qualification is significant when contrasted to her qualification of her Artemisian relationship with Sally as one that "could only exist between women, between women just grown up," women who have not yet entered the heterosexual marriage system and are still capable of "disinterested" love.

The heterosexuality of the second image is clear if we compare the source of the flowers' light here to the source of the flowers' light in the flower shop passage. The most significant difference between these two images is that in the description of flowers when Clarissa is with Miss Pym, the illumination of the flowers comes from within themselves ("every flower seems to burn by itself, softly, purely in the misty beds" [13]), whereas in the second, the flower is illuminated by an external and phallic element (a match burning in a crocus). The softness and purity of the self-generated fire of the flowers, like "the purity, the integrity of [Clarissa's] feeling for Sally" (34), contrasts with the hardness of the illumination of the crocus and the description of the accompanying revelation as sudden and swollen with a pressure of rapture that gushed and poured out. The second description is both passionate and heterosexual, perhaps even phallic, in its imagery, while the first description evokes virginal, polymorphous sensuality prior to the introduction of the masculine order. More than this, the distinction between a collective of female flowers and a single crocus corresponds to the distinction in the Homeric *Hymn to Demeter* between the all-female collective of the matriarchate, the state of affairs prior to Persephone's abduction, and the separation, due to marriage, of a single woman from this female collective, a state in which Persephone withdraws into solitude.[18]

[18] Several commentators, including Foley, Kerényi, and Ann Suter, have associated the *Hymn*'s interpretation of marriage with matriarchal cultures. Harrison finds an emphasis on the group rather than the individual to be characteristic of matriarchal cultures. She writes that patriarchal religion "emphasized rather the individual than the group, it resulted from

We should not overlook the fact that Clarissa confesses to being able to have a passionately sexual (as opposed to sensual), hierarchical, one-on-one relationship *only* with women. The *Hymn* portrays relationships between women as the "soft and pure" non-sexual type; not so with Woolf. She portrays relationships between women in terms associated with heterosexuality in Western culture.[19] We have here another instance of Woolf's creative revision of the *Hymn* (as well as a revision of traditional heterosexual romance plots[20]), in that in Woolf's version, some of the characteristics that the *Hymn* associates with heterosexual marriage, such as exclusivity, passionate sexuality, isolation from community, and hierarchy, are associated with relationships between women. While one of the consequences of Woolf's revision of the *Hymn* is that it allows her to portray lesbian sexuality, which this passage clearly seems to be about and which many critics have noted, her characterization of these relationships as shaped by hierarchical structures also allows her to explore other questions—notably, women's complicity in patriarchy. In contrast to her portrayal of the relationship between Clarissa and Sally, here Woolf does not characterize women's relationships as immune to patriarchy; rather, she portrays Clarissa as embodying and reproducing hierarchical power structures that are associated, in both the Homeric *Hymn* and modern feminist theory, with patriarchy. Whereas the *Hymn* may be said to portray female relationships as ethical and cooperative, and heterosexual relationships as marked by the ownership and transfer of women as property (as when Zeus grants Persephone to his brother as a gift) and the coercion of women (as when Hades abducts Persephone), the ethical situation that Woolf illustrates in Clarissa's description of her feelings for women does not conform to this pattern. Here, as in *Three Guineas*, Woolf implicates women in unethical power structures in which both women and men may be subjugated.

Woolf's use of flower imagery in these scenes suggests Clarissa's preoccupation with power and position. In the flower shop with Miss Pym, she feels accepted, liked, trusted by Miss Pym, "who owed her help, and thought her kind" (13). The wave that flows over her, lifting her above her hatred and pettiness, is a combination of the sensual beauty of the flowers and feeling liked and trusted by Miss Pym who is socially subordinate to Clarissa, and in a helping relation to her.[21]

---

warlike and migratory conditions. On the other hand the worship of the Mother emphasizes the group" (*Mythology*, 63).

[19] See, for one example, Freud's distinction between infantile sexuality and adult sexuality in *Three Essays on the Theory of Sexuality* (New York: Basic Books, revised edition 2000).

[20] On the revision of the heterosexual romance plot into the mother-daughter romance, see Marianne Hirsch's *The Mother / Daughter Plot: Narrative, Psychoanalysis, Feminism* (Bloomington: Indiana UP, 1989) and Tyler.

[21] Similarly, Clarissa feels uplifted by her servants: "thank you, thank you, she went on saying in gratitude to her servants generally for helping her be like this, to be what she

If flowers function as a symbol of female sexuality in the novel, as they do in the *Hymn*, then the novel presents this symbol as embedded in a capitalist network of commodification, objectification and exploitation. As women and their sexuality are traded between men in the *Hymn*, women's lives and sexuality are for sale in the novel. Clarissa's "moment of perfection" in the flower shop is partly due to her position as the customer with the means to purchase flowers in relation to Miss Pym, whose body is associated with the flowers she sells and who must sell her flowers for a living. Mrs. Dempster's thoughts about Maisie Johnson, who appear as archetypal crone and maiden, make explicit the commodification of female sexuality and women's lives as symbolized in flowers: "That girl [...] don't know a thing yet [...] Get married [...] and then you'll know [...] For it had been a hard life [...] What hadn't she given to it? Roses; figure; her feet too [...] Roses, she thought sardonically. All trash, m'dear. For really, what with eating, drinking, and mating, the bad days and good, life had been no mere matter of roses [...] But, she implored, pity. Pity for the loss of roses. Pity she asked of Maisie Johnson, standing by the hyacinth beds" (27). Carrie Dempster and Maisie Johnson represent two negative ends of the Persephone story, the maiden, Maisie Johnson, who has recently "left her people" and aches to go home, and the crone, Mrs. Dempster, who grieves over the disappointments of marriage and the loss of roses. In contrast to Clarissa's relatively happy version of the Persephone story, these women suggest a working-class version of female sexuality and a woman's lifecycle, a life in which a woman may leave home for a frightening city to seek her fortune or marry a man who drinks too much and runs around, working every day of her life and sacrificing her figure, feet and roses, seeking only pity from young girls. While the lifecycle of a woman, the transition from youthful maiden to crone, and the conflicts over sexuality, intimacy and independence, may be universal, Woolf demonstrates that these realities are refracted through varying social positions and varying levels of agency within patriarchal and imperial power.

Clarissa's relationship with women, described through the structure and imagery of the Homeric *Hymn to Demeter* is part of a critique of the hierarchy-obsessed, power-hungry ruling class of Britain; the class that led into war the young men who were, in Richard Dalloway's words, "thousands of poor chaps, with all their lives before them, shoveled together, already half forgotten" (115). Woolf's critique of fascism, which she developed in the 1930s and 40s, is already evident here in her portrayal of Clarissa's patriarchal relation to women as well as of Lady Bruton's imperial efforts.[22] At the same time, Woolf maintains a sustained portrayal

wanted, gentle, generous-hearted. Her servants liked her" (39).

[22] Still, the relationship between gender and fascism is more complicated, as Jane Marcus shows in her discussion of Helen Zenna Smith's war narrative *Not So Quiet*. In Smith's novel, the young women driving ambulances on the French frontlines during World War

of women's exploitation under patriarchy, through more explicit characters like Lady Bradshaw and Rezia Warren Smith, but also through Clarissa's experiences.[23] Women who are complicit with and embody patriarchal power are not the ultimate beneficiaries of the spoils of war, fascism or any other forms it might take; at the end of the day they are still only women. Woolf gestures toward this in her description of Clarissa's experience of "feeling what men felt" that only lasts "a moment; but it was enough" (32). This language suggests a desperate desire for release from her usual position at the other end of the stick. She seeks compensation for her life as a woman, to feel what she believes men feel with a beautiful and subordinate woman. Whereas women like Mrs. Dempster can only resort to pleas for pity for the loss of their roses, Clarissa is in a position to temporarily recast herself in the patriarchal drama, purchasing her moments of perfection from other women and finding moments of intimacy that are modeled on heterosexuality.

Woolf's revisions of the Homeric *Hymn to Demeter* are motivated by the problem of recovering from the war and her sophisticated feminist, Marxist and anti-imperial analysis of the factors that led to the war. As her references to *Cymbeline* suggest, she envisions a cosmic renewal for Britain through the traditional matriarchal fertility symbolism of the Homeric *Hymn to Demeter*, but shifts the focus away from heterosexuality and towards spiritual, lesbian community. At the same time, her commitments to the radical possibilities of women's community and sexuality do not blind her to the ways in which women are embedded in patriarchal power structures, both as victims and as perpetrators, and the effects of this situation on their ethics. While the space of lesbianism and spirituality that Woolf opens up with these revisions is fragile in the novel and seems to be subsumed into heterosexuality, class domination and conservative politics, Woolf's revision of the *Cymbeline* plot at the novel's conclusion counters this trajectory, unsettling the heterosexual plot. By bringing Sally back as a kind of *deus ex machina*, that lost moment remains a sliver of hope, and by effecting a spiritual rebirth for Clarissa through the homosexual and mystical Septimus, Woolf returns to the decoupling of fertility and heterosexuality suggested by Artemis, the virgin goddess who assists in childbirth. The vast network of power relations, gender and class creates vari-

I are supervised by a female Commandant nicknamed "Mrs. Bitch," whom Marcus terms the "Phallic Mother." It is she who is the object of the protagonist's hatred: "When Helen figures war as an invasion of her ears, the phallic mother is the rapist. She is the one who is 'not so quiet'[…]. She is War" (274). But, while this phallic mother embodies War and represents nationalist, fascist interests, she is a dupe of sorts, "a convenient disguise for the male voice of nationalist authority, the patriarchs in whose interest the war is fought" (274).

[23] As a foreigner and wife of an ill veteran, Rezia Warren Smith is another woman on the wrong side of this power structure, a victim of the war and of British imperialism and patriarchy. Even Lady Bradshaw, the wife of the wealthy and powerful Dr. Bradshaw, is described as having "gone under […] the slow sinking, water-logged, of her will into his" (100).

ous relations of domination and exploitation as well as eddies of revolutionary and healing spiritual connection and intimacy. In seeking a truly revolutionary renewal that is not simply a reproduction of the power structure that led to the war, Woolf's relation to feminism becomes subtle and complex, celebrating the renewing qualities of matriarchal myth and feminine sensuality and spirituality while remaining sober about the multiple effects of women's place in hierarchical structures.

Works Cited

Bachmann, Ingeborg. *Wir müssen wahre Sätze finden. Gespräche und Interviews*. Ed. Christine Koschel and Inge von Weidenbaum. Munich: Piper, 1983. Print.

Barrett, Eileen. "Unmasking Lesbian Passion: The Inverted World of *Mrs. Dalloway*." *Virginia Woolf: Lesbian Readings*. Eds. Eileen Barrett and Patricia Cramer. New York: NYU P, 1997. 146-164. Print.

Bennett, Paula. "Critical Clitoridectomy: Female Sexual Imagery and Feminist Psychoanalytic Theory." *Signs* 18.2 (Winter 1993): 235-259. Print.

Cramer, Patricia. "Notes From Underground: Lesbian Ritual in the Writings of Virginia Woolf" *Virginia Woolf Miscellanies: Proceedings of the First Annual Conference on Virginia Woolf*. Eds. Mark Hussey and Vara Neverow-Turk. New York: Pace UP, 1992. 177-188. Print.

Foley, Helene P. *The Homeric* Hymn to Demeter: *Translation, Commentary, and Interpretive Essays*. Princeton: Princeton UP, 1994. Print.

Harrison, Jane E. *Mythology*. New York: Cooper Square, 1963. Print. Our Debt to Greece and Rome.

——. *Prolegomena to the Study of Greek Religion*. New York: Meridian Books, 1955. Print.

Henderson, Diana E. *Collaborations with the Past: Reshaping Shakespeare across Time and Media*. Ithaca, NY: Cornell UP, 2006. Print.

Jung, C. G. and C. Kerényi. *Essays on a Science of Mythology*. Trans. R. F. C. Hull. Rev. ed. Princeton: Princeton UP, 1969. Print. Bollingen Series 22.

Kerényi, C. *Eleusis: Archetypal Image of Mother and Daughter*. Trans. Ralph Manheim. New York: Pantheon-Random House, 1967. Print. Bollingen Series 65: 4.

——. *The Gods of the Greeks*. Trans. Norman Cameron. London: Thames and Hudson, 1951. Print.

Marcus, Jane. "Corpus/Corps/Corpse: Writing the Body in/at War." Afterword. *Not So Quiet... Stepdaughters of War*. By Helen Zenna Smith. 1930. NY: Feminist P, 1989. 241-300. Print.

Moody, A. D. "*Mrs. Dalloway* as Comedy." *Critics on Virginia Woolf.* Ed. Jacqueline E. M. Latham. Florida: U. of Miami, 1970. 48-51. Print. Readings in Literary Criticism Ser. 8. Excerpt from *Virginia Woolf.* Edinburgh: Oliver and Boyd, 1963.

Shakespeare, William. *Cymbeline. The Riverside Shakespeare: The Complete Works*. Ed. G. B. Evans and J. J. M. Tobin. 2nd ed. Boston: Houghton Mifflin, 1997. 1569-1608. Print.

Simonds, Peggy Muñoz. *Myth, Emblem, and Music in Shakespeare's* Cymbeline*: An Iconographic Reconstruction.* London: Associated University Presses, 1992. Print.

Suter, Ann. *The Narcissus and the Pomegranate: An Archaeology of the Homeric* Hymn to Demeter. Ann Arbor: Univ. of Michigan Press, 2002. Print.

Tyler, Lisa. "Mother-Daughter Passion and Rapture: the Demeter Myth in the Fiction of Virginia Woolf and Doris Lessing." *Woolf and Lessing: Breaking the Mold.* Eds. Ruth Saxton and Jean Tobin. New York: St. Martin's, 1994. 73-91. Print.

Vernant, Jean-Pierre. *Mortals and Immortals: Collected Essays*. Ed. Froma I. Zeitlin. Princeton: Princeton UP, 1991.

Woolf, Virginia. *Mrs. Dalloway*. 1925. San Diego: Harcourt, 1981. Print.

——. "On Not Knowing Greek." *The Common Reader*. 1925. Orlando: Harcourt, 1984. 23-38. Print.

——. *To the Lighthouse*. 1927. Orlando: Harcourt, 2005. Print.

Wyatt, Jean M. "*Mrs. Dalloway*: Literary Allusion as Structural Metaphor." *PMLA* 88.3 (1973): 440-451. *JSTOR*. Web. 23 March 2010.

The Meat of the Movement: Food and Feminism in Woolf

Lisa Angelella

> It is a curious fact that novelists have a way of making us believe that luncheon parties are invariably memorable for something very witty that was said, or for something very wise that was done. But they seldom spare a word for what was eaten. It is part of the novelist's convention not to mention soup and salmon and ducklings, as if soup and salmon and ducklings were of no importance whatsoever, as if nobody ever smoked a cigar or drank a glass of wine. Here, however, I shall take the liberty to defy that convention [...] (*AROO* 10)

Woolf followed her own dictum; her novels are replete with food. While she does not articulate this defense of the alimentary in terms of a feminist imperative, she does place it within her feminist manifesto. Several scholars have argued that Woolf's focus on food elevates the status of women. Diane McGee argues that food scenes allow Woolf to showcase traditional women's work and that she is one of the first writers to present the traditionally invisible work of the hostess in literature (108). Similarly, we can note her presentation of female cooks: Susan in *The Waves*, Mrs. Walker in *Mrs. Dalloway*, and Mrs. Sands in *Between the Acts*. Approaching the issue from another angle, Allie Glenny suggests that Woolf's attention to food celebrates a female sensual epistemology. Glenny writes, "this dwelling on food was, as Woolf saw it, an act of female liberation. It was part of the process both of seeing the world through our own, female, lenses and, more actively, of righting a skewed world which had purged the sensual and elevated the rational" (xii). In addition to foregrounding women's work and material orientation, I propose that Woolf's food dictum is also feminist for a third reason. While women were accepted as producers and servers of food, and while western tradition long categorized them as the bodily other of man's transcendence, the upper-and middle-class Victorian norms in which Woolf was raised did not acknowledge women to be consumers of food.[1] As has been well-documented by Helena Michie and Joan

[1] The juvenilia of the Woolf children, *Hyde Park Gate News*, reveal a young Virginia who is quite appetitive, as editor Gill Lowe notes. Among the materials of their daily lives Virginia and the children see fit to mention are "luscious" oranges (45), pie and strawberry ice (69) and cherries (70). The audience of the newsletter are Woolf's parents, whose approval she was eager to attain, so this open avowal of alimentary pleasures suggests that her appetite was not censured by her parents during childhood (as was that of Woolf's contemporaries, such as Katherine Mansfield, who records how her mother criticized her childhood heaviness). However, one account of Woolf's appetite at a tea at her brother's school shows the strictures she encountered elsewhere: "They partook of very slight refreshment though Mrs.

Brumberg, middle and upper-class Victorian culture taught women to perform their femininity by denying their appetites. Popular rhetoric and iconography equated the feminine woman with weakness and dependency: hungry women, like fainting or wasting women, were models of delicacy. And so the narrator of *A Room of One's Own* who presents herself as a hungry and demanding consumer, grousing that the nourishment is unsatisfactory, is notably indecorous. She complains of the "transparent liquid" passed off as soup, of the plain hunk of beef and of stringy prunes for dessert, bemoaning the conventional and unimaginative food. This appetite transgresses the Victorian norms within which Woolf grew up that dictated women not take an interest in food.

Women's expression of female hunger is important because Woolf saw appetite as bound up with all aspects of personhood, physical, mental and emotional: "The human frame being what it is, heart, body and brain all mixed together, and not contained in separate compartments [. . .] a good dinner is of great importance to good talk. One cannot think well, love well, sleep well, if one has not dined well" (*AROO* 18). This comment not only lays bare Woolf's modernist aesthetic bias toward the mundane and the sensual; from a feminist viewpoint, it should also suggest that restricting women's appetites curtails their manifestation of selfhood. In this article, I propose that Woolf's work engages a concept of alimentary subjectivity. By this I mean that, in eating, her characters take a desiring, interactive position toward their worlds and manifest themselves as subjects. Employing this concept, I specifically argue that it is fundamentally through depictions of meat-eating that Woolf empowers her New Women characters Mary Datchet of *Night and Day* and Sara Pargiter of *The Years*.

Women Eating

Abundant scholarship on women and food in the humanities and social sciences has shown that what and how a woman eats is not merely a personal choice but culturally and socially determined. Sociologists Nickie Charles and Marion Kerr, for instance, write, "Food practices can be regarded as one of the ways in which important social relations and divisions are symbolized, reinforced and reproduced on a daily basis" (2). Depictions of food or eating in a text, which may be passed over quickly or form the background of larger events or conversations,

---

Worsley [the headmistress] on passing by remarked that Miss Virginia had taken in a good supply. But apparently Miss Virginia did not think so for she took another piece of cake as soon as she got home" (67). Lowe suggests that Vanessa may have included this story as retaliation for an earlier criticism Woolf made of her. If that is the case, it would suggest to us that at least one Stephen daughter was internalizing the restrictions on female appetite expressed by the headmistress.

may nevertheless help explain why events and relations play out the way they do or else help to undermine those events and relations. Even appetite must be considered as not just physiological and psychological but social as well. Cixous has suggested that the rebuking of woman's appetite in the Garden of Eden is foundational for Western culture. In Heller and Moran's words, it begins the "subjugation of female oral pleasure to patriarchal law" (1). Susan Bordo makes a similar argument in *Unbearable Weight*: through Foucaltian "micropractices" of appetite denial, women perform their subordinate identity. An embodied woman may be thought to take up too much space, appropriate too many resources for herself, privilege her desires over her attractiveness and refuse the Western hierarchy of mind over body.[2]

Eating mobilizes desires, pleasures and physiological processes which exist outside of the regulation of social etiquette. As Adolph puts it, "as a process that defines a body as active, and therefore as a site of other potential activities, eating signifies a body's potential for conscious agency beyond a social network" (29). The eating body is active not only in the sense that it is moving but in that it is constituting itself and reconstructing its world. It is active in making decisions in a realm of biology outside of culture. Such a means of activity is particularly important for allowing subjectivity to women denied action and choices in other areas of their lives. Bakhtin, in *Rabelais and His World*, describes eating as such: "the body transgresses [...] its own limits: it swallows, devours, rends the world apart, is enriched and grows at the world's expense. [...] Herein man tastes the world, introduces it into his body, makes it part of himself" (281). That women should engage in activities of devouring and rending, of destruction and incorporation of the world and of transgression of former limits, poses an obvious threat in a patriarchal culture.

Within this threat lies the rationale for an ideology according to which women's attention should be devoted to serving others' appetites, rather than their own. The most famous food scene in Woolf's corpus is Mrs. Ramsay's serving of the *Boeuf en Daube* in *To the Lighthouse*, a scene in which, as Dodd notes, Mrs. Ramsay takes full pride in serving a dish but does not eat it. A closer look at this

[2] In the introduction to their anthology of articles on women and food, *Scenes of the Apple*, Heller and Moran trouble this generalization and maintain the complexity of eating norms for women. It is not just embodied but also ethereal women who pose a threat: they may be too ill and weak to take on the central role expected of them, motherhood (25). Within that volume, also, Adrienne Munich shows the limitation of any overarching claim about the mandate for Victorian women to be thin. The eponymous Victorian brazenly defied restrictions on feminine appetite and size by being publically gluttonous and corpulent, incorporating much into herself in order to embody the empire. It is important to note, though, as Munich does, that, as a woman, Victoria's eating and her fat were viewed as not just self-serving but as an image of motherly nurturing.

figure is informative as it shows the opposite of alimentary subjectivity—a servile subjectivity, in which the woman is alienated from her own bodily needs and desires and does not incorporate her external world, but rather serves it.

Mrs. Ramsay caters throughout the day to the needs of her large brood and her husband's friends. The dinner constitutes the stage upon which she performs her submissive role for everyone at once. She is expected to both feed the guests (and lavishly: the entrée has been in preparation for three days) and to facilitate their interaction. She had earlier opined that she would like to transcend her domestic life and become an investigator of social problems. Instead, she stands in her private universe, despondently ladling out the soup and catering to the guests in her conversation. Bored and servile, Mrs. Ramsay engages with the world around her only as a machine ministering to others: "But what have I done with my life? thought Mrs. Ramsay, taking her place at the head of the table, and looking at all the plates making white circles on it" (*TTL* 125). Rather than feel herself part of her sensual context or human community, "She had a sense of being past everything, through everything, out of everything, as she helped the soup" (125). The routine instruments of dinner here do not arouse Mrs. Ramsay's desires. The plates and ladle hold her body in place while her mind travels elsewhere. Her laboring hands are engaged, but her senses are not. Such selflessness certainly underlies Woolf's famous claim that feminists needed to "kill" the angel-in-the-house figure before they could act with desires and minds of their own ("Professions" 238).

Many women in literature, like Mrs. Ramsay, do not eat; those who do eat vigorously are often dismissed in one of two ways. They may be innocuous fat women, shown to be slow, socially less prestigious and perhaps comic. They may also be vampiric or monstrous women, who have abandoned all their femininity and social ties through their unethical behavior. In *Word of Mouth*, Patricia Moran argues that Woolf's writing, though staunchly feminist in many ways, is also "symptomatic" of patriarchal revulsion over women's bodies and appetites. Moran argues that often when female characters eat in Woolf's work, they surrender themselves to crude sensuality, their bodies out of control. Certainly, such logic is suggested by Woolf's anorexia and by ethereal characters like Mrs. Ramsay as well as by *Mrs. Dalloway*'s gluttonous Miss Kilman.

The last is in fact so notorious a vilified female eater of Woolf's that she deserves further examination. Woolf says of her that "food was all she lived for" (*MD* 127), showing her stewing over the fact that a child has taken the pink cake she wanted in a tea room and having her offer advice about moral restraint while devouring an éclair. Woolf connects Miss Kilman's eating with her unattractiveness and her self-absorbed moroseness: it constitutes self-medication, rather than self-fortification. In this vein, the sweet food she eats is non-nutritious and insubstantial. Sweets were often associated with women in the early twentieth century and thought appropriate to their delicate appetites (Shapiro 6); hence they did little to challenge, and perhaps even confirmed, women's ethereality. In Woolf's works, sweets tend to be associated with female characters who are portrayed as superficial, or who submit to a wholly traditional feminine role. Rezia in *Mrs. Dalloway* "liked ices, chocolates, sweet things" (116). Of the fatuous sensualist Mrs. Manresa in *Between the Acts*, Woolf writes, "She took the little silver cream jug and let the smooth fluid curl luxuriously into her coffee, to which she added a shovel full of brown sugar candy. Sensuously, rhythmically, she stirred the mixture round and round" (*BTA* 55). A female American visitor to England in *The Years* opts for ices over a tour of the Bodleian (*TY* 59). That Woolf sees sweet eating as a lazy indulgence is made explicit by Rachel in *The Voyage Out*. She connects women's predilection for sweets with their tendency to grovel in emotion: "She liked women. But where emotion was concerned, they were like flies on a lump of sugar" (*TVO* 321). Miss Kilman is such a fly to her pink cakes, but not all of Woolf's female characters demean themselves in their consumption; key to the empowerment of Woolf's female eaters is the nature of their fare.

This essay will show that the New Women Mary Datchet and Sara Pargiter trouble Moran's overarching claim that all women who eat in Woolf's works are out of control. Unlike Mrs. Ramsay, Mary and Sara are New Women eating outside of a family structure; unlike Miss Kilman, they eat iron- and protein-rich food that offers them fortification, rather than means of groveling or short-term stimulation. Other diners resist Mary and Sara's consumption, but it is this resistance Woolf vilifies, rather than the eating itself. She shows these women, in defying alimentary norms, to not be out of control, but independent and powerful.

Unladylike Fare

Woolf shows her New Women to have a substantial appetite and formidable bodily needs by having them desire the more substantial fare of meat (mostly red meat). Meat was the most expensive, prestigious food in England, and the one most associated with the public sphere, insofar as beef, especially roast, has served since Anglo-Saxon culture as Britain's national fare. Meat-eating constitutes an important practice of participating in the British state. Food historian Colin Spenser traces the English love of meat to Anglo-Saxon culture, in which carcasses were placed whole on the table (23). The same identification held into the period of Woolf's maturity, of which Spenser says, "The joint reigned supreme in the British house" in the 1930s (307). Jeremy Rifkin, in *Beyond Beef*, defines the British as "the great beef eaters of Europe" (52), and he notes that they identified with beef as a symbol: "roast beef" signified the well-fed British upper and middle classes (55). Woolf mobilizes this nationalist dimension of meat in several scenes in her work. In *Flush*, for instance, Elizabeth Barrett Browning's eponymous dog, returning from a trip to Italy (which Woolf characterized with wines and fruits), knows he has arrived back in England when he smells, "Odours of stew, odours of beef, odours of basting, odours of beef and cabbage rose from a thousand basements" (*F* 145). In that novel as well, Woolf mentions the butcher's work as central to the maintenance of civilization in Wimpole Street, London:

> a prayer rises in the heart and bursts from the lips that not a brick from Wimpole Street may be re-painted, not a curtain washed, not a butcher fail to tender or a cook to receive the sirloin, the haunch, the breast, the ribs of mutton and beef forever and ever, for as long as Wimpole Street remains, civilization is secure. (24)

By convention, women were denied access to this fundamental fare of "civilization," of British nationhood. The reason behind this is ostensibly economic: meat, the most expensive food, should be given to the bread-winner of the house. In *Three Guineas*, Woolf observes to fellow women, "If you prefer ice creams and peanuts to roast beef and beer the reason would seem to be economic rather than gustatory" (90). Women's access to meat was restricted not only in accordance with their lack of personal income, however, but also for ideological reasons. The British believed that meat's muscle and blood would stimulate indecorous passions:

> Meat, the "roast beef of Old England," was not only the traditional food of warriors and aggressors but also believed to be the fuel of anger and lust. Disgust with meat was a common phenomenon among Victorian girls; a carnivorous diet was associated with sexual precocity, especially with an abundant menstrual flow, and even with nymphomania. (Showalter 129)

Hence, as Helena Michie notes, "the portrait of the appropriately sexed woman [...] emerges as one who eats little and delicately. She is as sickened by meat as by sexual desire" (17).[3] At stake then, in Woolf's decision to focus on Mrs. Ramsay's serving of beef rather than her eating of it, is not just Mrs. Ramsay's figure but her ethereal, virginal, angel-in-the-house status.[4] Meat, in being thought to arouse

[3] In *The Waves*, Rhoda shows a marked feeling of abhorrence toward food, and meat especially. As a child, she expresses a horror of meal times, saying: "everything runs like streaks of fire when [the housekeeper] carves the beef" (*TW* 45). As an adult, dining with friends likewise repulses her: she feels that, after eating, they are all "hung with other people like a joint of meat among other joints of meat" (162). She, who is emotionally unstable and seems to have a pathological relationship to food throughout the novel, thus exhibits the opposite attitude toward meat than that of the strong female protagonists I will discuss.

[4] That Mrs. Ramsay never eats the meat is suggested by the fact that she engages rapturously

not only appetite for food but for sex, functioned as a principle creator of bodily subjects in Woolf's Britain. This cultural logic suggests that restricting women's access to meat would significantly compromise their existence as desiring subjects. The alternatives to red meat—white meat and plants—were considered insipid. Julia Twigg notes that nineteenth-century health manual recommendations for pregnant and lactating women included "delicate" and "light" meats echoing women's "feminine" nature—dishes like chicken, fish or eggs (24).

So, in eating meat, Woolf's New Women characters disrupt not only an alimentary practice but an alimentary ideology by which they were light, delicate and passive. By eating a food that is not soft and light-colored but of a tough texture and dark red hue, food which constitutes more of an affront to the eye and teeth and carving hands, women assert themselves as desiring bodies. And by eating the paradigmatic, invigorating British food, they assert themselves as Britons.

Eating Alone

In *Night and Day*, the New Woman Mary Datchet not only eats meat, but she does so unapologetically in restaurants. Thereby, Mary registers herself as a desiring subject within a public sphere. The public nature of her eating suggests Mary symbolically participates in a national community. Mary clearly transgresses the alimentary decorum that prohibited *To the Lighthouse*'s Mrs. Ramsay from eating the *Boeuf*. That her alimentary self-assertion is resisted by the public, however, is shown in the fact that she nearly always eats without companions.

Though Mary lives a generation after Mrs. Ramsay, the serving norm for women persisted, and Woolf presents it through Mary's foil in the book, Katharine Hilbery. Throughout the book, Katharine is still expected to perform Mrs. Ramsay's role of angel-in-the-house hostess, pourer of tea and server of food. Though she resists the role inwardly, being secretly a mathematician, she nevertheless upholds it. Framing the novel in the alimentary, Woolf begins the book by depicting Katharine, "in common with many other young ladies of her class [...] pouring out tea" (*ND* 3). Accustomed to the domestic task, she mindlessly carries out the "business of teacups and bread and butter" (3). This tea is only one of many in the book; Susan Fox has summed it up as a "tea party" novel (259). Throughout the novel, Woolf

---

with every sensual dimension of it but the gustatory: the haptic, olfactory and visual. Woolf describes her very active engagement with this non-feminine food, noting Mrs. Ramsay went "diving into that soft mass" (151) and "peered into the dish, with its shiny walls and its confusion of savoury brown and yellow meats and its bay leaves and its wine, and thought" (151). These and like passages suggest Mrs. Ramsay was far from being "repulsed" by the meat, displaying instead a desire that reveals her enduring corporeality. Nevertheless, these thoughts are all internal, and she never acts on that desire publically.

depicts Katharine bearing the "frail burden of silver trays and china teacups" (148). When the central conflict in the book (Katharine's father's resistance to her choice of suitor) reaches its peak, the kettle in the other room is heard boiling over: "To Katharine's mind it appeared this kettle was an enormous kettle, capable of deluging the house in its incessant showers of steam, the enraged representative of all those household duties she had neglected" (522). Through the theme of tea, Woolf suggests that the fluidity of society is surprisingly dependent upon women's complicity in administering its alimentary rituals. So, for instance, when Katharine's father feels that Katharine has behaved without propriety in becoming betrothed, he thinks that "civilization had been very profoundly and unpleasantly overthrown that evening [...] his meals would be poisoned for days to come" (502). When a peaceful resolution is ultimately secured, this too is expressed through dinner: "The lamps were lit; their lustre reflected itself in the polished wood; good wine was passed round the dinner-table; before the meal was far advanced civilization had triumphed" (528). Katharine is not a subject who actively makes the choice to serve the tea; in serving it, she occupies a prescribed role. She represents the alimentary servile position that Mrs. Ramsay occupied, devoting herself to others' needs and remaining ethereal. It is in this context that Woolf presents the New Woman. Mary, living independently, has no one to serve. By rejecting the norm of alimentary service, Mary becomes an alimentary subject.

The subjectivity that Mary gains through her positioning as a consumer is especially important since she is denied self-expression in other areas of her life. Though Mary escapes the domestic servitude that Katharine has under her father, Mary's colleague at the suffrage office, Mr. Clacton, attempts to position her within a similar patriarchal social system. Since he and Mary work for egalitarianism, this domination is ironic and underscores the limits of feminism's gains. At a meeting Woolf describes, Mr. Clacton proudly takes his seat "at the head of the table" (169). He finds Mary "a little too much inclined to order him about" (87). By disparaging her self-assertion, he is able to dismiss it. Secondly, Mary's manifestation as a desiring *body* is resisted by the man she desires, Ralph. While he does engage Mary's intellect, he cannot bring himself to entertain intimacy with her: ultimately, he can feel appreciation but not passion for this intellectual and proactive woman. His feelings are rather extended to the more traditionally feminine Katharine Hilbery. So, while Mary is constantly endeavoring to assert her subjectivity in the world around her, she retains some of Mrs. Ramsay's isolation. The novel's conclusion suggests Mary will remain single and thus sexually virginal and thus share some of Mrs. Ramsay's ethereality. Mary will similarly remain professionally unfulfilled, as the suffrage office is inefficient and racked by the aforementioned self-destructive hierarchies. Manifesting herself as a bodily subject, a desiring subject and a progressive subject remains a formidable endeavor.

By depicting Mary eating, Woolf shows her to be assertively engaging her world. In the first place, she regularly eats at restaurants. During the nineteenth century, convention forced women when eating alone away from home to stay in and have food delivered to their private hotel rooms (Warde and Martens 23). At the turn of the century, it was only the New Woman who ventured out to eat (Freeman 287), and often to her disgrace.[5] In the Edwardian feminist journal *Freewoman*, Dora Marsden impugns readers who "regard it as an indecent exhibition, if they saw a woman looking as though she were very obviously enjoying food, or obviously gratifying any of her senses" (Green 227). Mary's eating in public, like Marsden's invective, amounts to a public announcement that she is a desiring being and is willing to act on her desires. Eating alone in a restaurant signifies additional public avowals of her transgressive status: her refusal of confinement to the private sphere, her economic independence and ability to nourish herself outside a patriarchal household and her refusal of a life of domestic art that leads her to eat others' cooking. In eating out, she is moreover stimulating herself intellectually by reading the paper and engaging in her public community by playing the role of *flâneur*, observing passers-by over her paper (80).

Eating "unfeminine" meat publically, Mary invites the resistance Marsden describes. Notably, the censure comes not from straightforward traditionalists but from Mr. Clacton. Vegetarian himself, he critiques the restaurant at which Mary regularly eats lunch for its meat-centered fare. In raising this objection, Mr. Clacton joins the long tradition of men who have controlled women's consumption and have in particular vilified their meat-eating. Though his disapproval operates from a different ideological basis, it still works to control a woman's bodily engagement with the sensual world. Mr. Clacton's disapprobation may constitute Woolf's subtle critique of nineteenth-and early twentieth-century feminism's advocacy of vegetarianism. Elaine Showalter and Carol Adams document how nineteenth-century feminist literature connected oppression of women with that of animals raised for meat (Showalter 129; Adams 121). Meat was the food often force-fed to suffragette hunger-strikers, which associates it moreso with control of women's eating. Melanie Phillips describes the "ghastly procedure, which involved women being held down by several prison wardens while tubes were inserted through their nasal passages and down their throats" (226). In such force-feeding, meat is an instrument of male power used to control women's bodies.[6] Given this political

[5] In an article on food in four contemporary travel narratives by recently divorced American women (Elizabeth Gilbert, Alice Steinbach, Rita Golden Gelman and Ruth Reichl), Jane Wood notes that all the writers "are middle-aged women and have money of their own, but initially they hesitate to dine alone" (56). These women attempting to live outside the family structure, initially hesitate to nourish themselves rather than others publically. This suggests that Mary's eating alone, even for contemporary American readers, has a transgressive edge.

[6] We might note as well that Woolf composed the novel in a period of convalescence, during

context, Woolf's choice to make Mary, her advocate of suffrage, an eager meat-eater is striking. Perhaps this is because, as Linda Schlossberg argues, by hunger-striking suffragettes continued to perform the Victorian model of femininity: in their most extreme, visible belligerence, they were ironically furthering the image of women as delicate, weak and wasting. In Mary, Woolf creates a suffragist who participates in the public sphere not by this traditional alimentary sacrifice of the suffragettes but by alimentary manifestation. Eating alone at a restaurant, she displays her body and bodily needs as the hunger strikers did. She, too, shows she controls her body. But the image she leaves to those who see her is one of virility and strength. She publically exhibits that activeness Adolph says eating involves. The plodding inefficiency of Mary's suffragist office throughout the novel suggests that universal suffrage—participation in national decisions—remains elusive, but in the immediate moment, Mary participates bodily in the national community by eating the food associated with national identity.

Like her descriptions of Mrs. Ramsay, Woolf's depiction of Mary's eating the meat is rife with physical details that foreground Mary as a body. Woolf describes the sanguineous, ample meat Mary eats for lunch: "Mary generally went to a gaudy establishment, upholstered in red plush, near by, where, much to the vegetarian's disapproval, you could buy steak, two inches thick, or a roast section of fowl, swimming in a pewter dish" (80). The disapproval of the vegetarian (here Mr. Clacton) frames Mary's meal, as does the gauche establishment, which situates Mary's meat-eating outside of tasteful, middle-class norms. The large steak implies an appetitive consumer, and it metonymically encroaches upon the restaurant's upholstery: "red plush" reflects the texture of meat. This imagery of dissipation similarly underscores the threat of Mary's transgression. Moreover, the chicken is defined by its sauciness: it is "swimming" and thus uncontained. In accordance with the offensiveness of her fare, Mary eats alone, outside society, as it were; nevertheless, ostracized as it may be, her vigorous eating manifests hers as a sensual, desiring, active body in a way the ethereal server Katharine never is.

Through the clear juxtaposition of Katharine and Mary, Woolf suggests that heterosexual marriage requires the woman to be a server and that this serving role is incommensurate with woman's engagement as consumer. This alimentary economics of subjectivity is further made clear in a scene in which Mary receives a marriage proposal and must consider adopting a life like Katharine's. Notably, Woolf sets this in a restaurant. While Ralph is visiting Mary over Christmas, the two lunch together at a country inn. Ralph decides he will no longer devote himself to

---

part of which she herself was force-fed, albeit less brutally. Woolf wrote to Lytton Strachey of the treatment she was receiving during the composition of *Night and Day*: "I begin to despair of finishing a book on this method—I write one sentence—the clock strikes—Leonard appears with a glass of milk" (qtd. in Briggs 44).

youthful passions but instead propose to Mary that they settle down together. The threat this would pose to Mary's social engagement is clear, even to Ralph. While he admires Mary's interest in public issues and would not ask that she put them aside for marriage, he does assume an attitude of authority with her: he admits to himself that he has had "exacting and dictatorial ways with her" (232) and calls himself a "selfish beast" (238). Concomitantly, he has never, in his design of the plan, taken Mary's own desires into consideration. This becomes clear when, before he can make his offer, she reveals that she "cares" for him. Upon hearing this, Ralph immediately reverses his plan to propose: Mary's existence as a desiring subject threatens him. He wants her to be a wife for his own convenience; he is not interested in her passions. By having Mary eat meat during this scene, Woolf preserves Mary as desiring subject when Ralph refuses her as such. In a restaurant setting rather than a home, wherein Mary would administer to Ralph's needs and perform the subordinate status Mrs. Ramsay performs, Ralph and Mary occupy equal footing. Appropriately, their entrees are not gendered. In this traditional country inn, they both eat the national dish, red meat. Woolf writes, "For over a hundred and fifty years hot joints, potatoes, greens, and apple puddings had been served to generations of country gentlemen, and now, sitting at a table in the hollow of the bow window, Ralph and Mary took their share of this perennial feast" (235). Unlike the gaudy establishment where she eats alone in the city, Mary here eats at a respectable inn of the English countryside, a community of which she is in fact more part than Ralph is. Woolf underscores this positioning by having Mary judge Ralph's fitness for the scene. When he mentions he may abandon London life and move to the country, she questions his suitability to the community. Notably, she does this while looking across a piece of meat: "Looking across the joint, half-way through the meal, Mary wondered whether Ralph would ever come to look quite like the other people in the room" (235). It is a small but notable detail. From her position of power as consumer of a sizeable piece of meat, Mary makes a judgment upon Ralph, whom in the proposed traditional domestic arrangement, she would have been serving and very likely, subservient to. Once again the meat accompanies, and perhaps in part enables, Mary's independence.

Later in the novel, Ralph decides to proceed with his dispassionate proposal. Mary is fully cognizant of its cold practicality and flatly refuses. Unlike traditional sentimental heroines, however, she does not resort to tears and self-pity. Rather, she immerses herself in her work, giving herself reign to reflect on her feelings only at lunch, at the meat-heavy establishment. This thinking will be supported by a strong body: Woolf notes that Mary leaves the suffrage office for the restaurant determined "to set that other piece of mechanism, her body, into action" (270). In an image of empowered consumption that recalls her look across the joint, Mary is shown "cutting her meat firmly into small pieces" (272). Thereby, Mary's desire is not turned destructively inward but transferred onto meat. In the activity of cutting, she is positioned as powerful. Mary's fellow diners at the Strand notice her furious mincing;[7] the act publically displays her denunciation of Ralph. By turning from a man to food, Mary maintains control of her corporeal subjectivity. As she has from the beginning of the novel, she will continue to fuel her independent existence with this vitalizing, sanguineous substance. And she will, moreover, participate in the tradition of English nationhood, while the suffrage office plods along.

Resistant Commensality

The Years, in which Woolf intended to trace the progress of women born in the Victorian era but maturing in the early twentieth century, most successfully establishes women's alimentary subjectivity. Here Sara does eat, and outpaces Mary by eating repeatedly with men. In this commensality, she is acknowledged by those known to her as eating subject; it is an acknowledgement, however, that is colored with revulsion. Men's disgust and fear over Sara's meat-eating reveal a barrier to full commensality in early twentieth-century Britain. Nevertheless, such strong reactions reveal the power of Sara's eating transgressions, and they allow her an independent subjectivity.

The traditional gendered alimentary economics of subjectivity referenced in *To the Lighthouse* and *Night and Day*, wherein women observing traditional femininity do not eat, is also gestured to at the beginning of *The Years*, in the form of a matriarch of Mrs. Ramsay's generation, Mrs. Pargiter. At the beginning of the novel, however, Woolf kills off this angel-in-the-house figure. Mrs. Pargiter is missing from the opening dinner of the novel, over which she should be presiding. She, in fact, disrupts the meal by dying in the middle of it. Her nurse sends news of her rapidly plummeting state downstairs to the dinner table, which spreads a pall upon the supper: "they all held their knives suspended. Nobody liked to go on eating" (*TY* 36). The servant Crosby laments: "the dinner was spoilt [...] the meat was dried up, and the potatoes had a brown crust on top of them" (37). Mrs. Pargiter's illness and her dying, thus framed as selfish aberrations from the serving of her domestic duties, enable her to assert herself as subject in one final, if unintended gesture: she grinds to a halt one of the rituals most central to her angel-in-the-house selflessness. With this early death, Woolf kills off a whole generation of women with a serving subjectivity. Unlike *Night and Day*'s shadowing of Mary's transgression with the serving Katharine, the women in this novel unabashedly

[7] The public nature of Mary's act in the restaurant is highlighted by Woolf when she says the act of meat mincing gives her fellow diners "cause to judge her eccentric" (Woolf notes, however, that, in her composure, Mary gives them no other such cause).

manifest their subjectivity through the alimentary. They have an undiminished, public, bodily presence through eating. I will here focus on two scenes in which the character Sara Pargiter (with whom Woolf at one point associated herself) eats meat and thus stages her subjectivity as a consumer.[8]

Woolf first presents Sara at a domestic dinner with women. She and her sister Maggie form an all-female household. The position is not totally empowering; the sisters are poor and cook their own food. However, not all of their tasks are demeaning. Susan Squier points out that at this point in the novel, the patriarchal households in which the Pargiter cousins were born are beginning to break down (149). Sara and Maggie's father has just died, his house has been sold, and they have dispersed from it. So, in this present meal, they must perform the role of men and carve the meat. When their suffragette cousin Rose comes to dine, Maggie "helps the cutlets" (166). The words Woolf uses to describe her serving echo a line in the book's opening dinner in which Woolf had depicted the patriarch Mr. Pargiter "flicking cutlets onto plates" (36). The gesture is a revisiting and rewriting of the earlier one. In her book on table manners, Margaret Visser notes that "Knives, in the traditional view, are 'male' weapons. They are wielded aggressively, and they pertain to the masculine realm of fighting, war and the hunt; they are essential for carving meat. From a symbolic point of view, knives are phallic" (277). This masculine food calls forth manly, aggressive gestures, a dealing in knives. But in this all-female meal, the eating and serving of meat by women remains unremarkable to the characters themselves. It thereby contrasts with later meat-centered meals Sara shares with men, wherein the physicality of the meal appears exaggerated and invasive. The men display a disgust in each case which is topically class based but which ultimately signifies a repulsion toward women eating. Hence, while there is no character in the book to fill the traditional feminine norms in terms of food, the norms still remain in the minds of the male characters.

So when Sara comes across her cousin Martin in the city one day, and he invites her to lunch in a chophouse, the eaters seem swathed in the visceral. The restaurant itself is invasive in its heat: "The room was very hot and crowded" (229). And the warm, disseminating presence of the meat is the centerpiece of the affair. Martin describes it submerged in "fug," "a warm meaty smell" (233). As in Mr. Clacton's perception of Mary's lunch, the chophouse meat is a presence of great proportions and lacking in delineation. While it is a joint here, rather than a chicken swimming in a pewter dish, and thus maintains a delimited shape in itself, it is nevertheless on a cart which rolls across the room. The description of it from Martin's point of view underscores its diffusion: "A vast brownish-yellowish joint was being trundled from table to table on a lorry" (228). The joint's smell and heat

[8] At one point while writing *The Years*, Woolf wrote in her diary, "I hardly know who I am, or where; Virginia or [Sara]; in the Pargiters or outside" (*D5* 148).

disseminate: Martin notes how "smoke, mixed with the smell of meat, made the air heavy" (232). The sensations breech the limits of his tolerance by the meal's end: "The fug, the warm meaty smell of the city chop house had soon become intolerable" (228). Even though the restaurant is Martin's regular lunching establishment, he leaves it in disgust, calling it a "beastly hole" (233) and telling Sara he should not have brought her there.

Martin suddenly appears invaded and disgusted by sensation, I suggest, because of the social context: he is eating meat with his appetitive female cousin. Eating there with her, the democratic atmosphere of the restaurant becomes apparent to him. It allows Sara and various unknown inferiors of the restaurant to engage in a sensual experience on a level equal to him. Martin exhibits such gendered and class snobbery when, in the course of the meal, he refers to himself as "the god" of Crosby, the abovementioned domestic servant. In the course of depicting Sara as an active subject, Woolf shows her wielding a knife: "She took up her knife and fork and began to carve the admirable mutton" (228). Through the act of carving, she occupies a traditionally empowered role. Woolf calls the meat she carves "admirable," thus drawing attention to the muscular labor required by its large size. It is not just meat but a manly portion of meat, like Mary's two-inch thick steaks. The designation evokes Britain's national pride in its roasts, dating back to Anglo-Saxon dinners hacked whole upon the table. In carving and eating it, Sara engages in a new subject position and gives herself a new vitality. In the chophouse, the sensual properties of the meat itself are no longer under the patriarchal, centralized control of the family meal. The meal is not circumscribed—doors keep opening and closing, people keep walking by, the smell and the heat are invasive, the meat is riding by on wheels, rather than under the knife of the presiding male, and that epitome of civilization—intelligent conversation—is impossible above the general din.[9] Sara's character resonates with this disorder. She heartily partakes of the messy meat, she loosens her tongue in alcohol, and in the course of conversation, she undermines the state and the church, laughing as if to deride all order. Woolf pairs Sara's character with the chaotic restaurant: in the breakdown of hierarchy and control, she gains an opportunity to manifest herself.

Woolf pairs Sara with this sensual chaos, I would suggest, in order to capture the impact of a body transgressing its usual decorum: it suggests chaos and is repulsive. In this very repulsiveness, however, is a self-assertion indicative of

[9] This lunch is taking place in 1914, when England is on the brink of war. Dinner is that ritual by which civilization, particularly upper and middle-class Victorian British civilization is upheld, as we saw in *Night and Day*. The novel reflects larger world happenings through their effect on the characters' personal lives. So here, the chaos of the meal reflects the broken world order. Martin, who should, as the male, preside over the event, can obtain no degree of control.

strength. In *Filth: Dirt, Disgust and Modern Life*, William Cohen suggests that the filth associated with shunned social groups can be reappropriated as a rallying point of identity:

> When people who understand themselves to be degraded, dispossessed, or abjected by a dominant order adopt and appropriate (sometimes even celebrate) what is otherwise castigated as filth, there is a possibility of revaluing its aversiveness. Not merely owning up to, but taking comfort in, one's own supposed dirtiness can serve powerful purposes of self-formation and group identification. In these senses, filth is put to important use, both psychologically and politically. (x)

Though Sara does not directly embrace or associate herself with filth, she happily engages in and seems released by sensual stimuli Martin regards as beastly. The sensual chaos engages Sara's body and stimulates her will. The senses of the meal invite her forth to commingle with the sensations around her, achieving an alimentary subjectivity and involving her in a community, a public sphere: an act of self-assertion that appears repulsive to Martin but is empowering to her.

As in *Night and Day*, meat here gives women not just symbolic tender but very real flesh-and-blood vitality. As meat gives Mary a satisfaction that empowers her after the loss of Ralph, it appears to lend Sara a daringness to have a voice in matters of politics and the patriarchal church. She still has the prayer book with her which she had at the cathedral where she met Martin. When Martin asks her about it, she taps it with the fork she has been using to eat the mutton. This act of irreverence has feminist implications: she touches an artifact of hallowed, transcendent, canonized text with food and thereby defiles scholarship, the work of men, with food, the work of women. Suddenly she is able to access sensually the emblem of a world that long excluded her ideologically. In response to Martin's inquiry as to what she makes of its contents, she picks it up and announces: "The father incomprehensible; the son incomprehensible—" (229). He quickly seeks to contain this blasphemy, telling her, "Hush! [. . .] Somebody's listening" (229), and she submits: "In deference to him she assumed the manner of a lady lunching with a gentleman in a city restaurant" (229). Sara's sudden assumption of this manner highlights its socially constructed nature, opposed to the more spontaneous, immediate, direct sensations and behavior that the meat itself invites. She proceeds to participate in national concerns by denouncing the beginnings of war (it is 1914): "'Roll up the map of Europe,' said the man to the flunkey. 'I don't believe in force'!" (232). That the rebellious speech is grounded in food is indicated by her subsequent actions: "She brought down her fork. A plumstone jumped" (232). The fork she uses to eat the meat is the fork she uses to denounce religion and politics. It is at this climax to her transgressions that Martin looks around abashedly and suggests they leave. Sara has not been ladylike in her eating, drinking or behavior.

Not all of Sara's transgression can be attributed to her meat eating. While Mary was admirably level-headed and an industrious contributor to her social world, Sara provides quite another model of a meat-eating woman. She is a highly idiosyncratic, even unstable, character in many ways. Her speech is regularly enigmatic, interspersed with personal and literary allusions and barbed with non-sequiturs, leaps to fantasy and sudden changes of emotion. Woolf's first introduction of her in the novel, through the eyes of her uncle, mentions a shoulder deformity she has from being dropped as a child, a condition which introduces her according to her difference. In her talk and in her dress she shows that she has little concern for being pleasing or acceptable to others. Her remarks are repeatedly rebuked for their rudeness or else dismissed as nonsensical. As Mary's meat-eating should be understood in the context of her life as a responsible, hardy, fortified member of the British state, Sara's must be read in the context of this instability, suggestive of the passions Victorian ideology feared meat would arouse in women. Woolf, however, while mobilizing the image of the monstrous eating woman in the passions and inebriation of Sara's conversation with Martin, and moreso in her final meat meal in the book, never marginalizes her. The very fact that Sara's male cousins/eating companions express discomfort with, shock at or repulsion from her shows they are in a position of reacting to her, responding to her lead.

This dynamic is also present in Sara's final meat-centered meal with her cousin North. The meal is in an only liminally public space, the lodging house where Sara stays. Still, however, it produces a similar social arrangement. Sara, rather than serving North, is served food along with him. The traditional arrangement whereby women perform their subordinate status by serving men's appetites and denying their own is not present; they are positioned equally as consumers. Though this new dynamic is never mentioned explicitly, it is registered in North's discomfort throughout the meal. North is flummoxed by the absence of hospitality and service. Woolf reports his thoughts when he first sits down: "And there was no sign of dinner, he observed; only a dish of fruit on the cheap lodging-house table-cloth" (314). He finds the paucity of service incomprehensible: "there seemed to be some hitch in the proceedings. The door was open; the table laid; but nothing happened" (318). The servant does her job tardily and laxly, which suggests her resistance; North notices, for instance, that "the girl made a clatter laying the table with the knives and forks she held in a bunch" (315). Clattering, bunched cutlery contrasts with the perfect white circles laid along Mrs. Ramsay's table: it is an image of the resistant female server and of a decentered, non-hierarchical meal. The sound of clatter, moreover, participates in a pervasive sensual chaos.

North is sensitive to what appears to him the chaotic nature of every aspect of Sara's apartment and meal. When he first arrives at her apartment, he finds the street it is on "dirty," and he notes the "smell" and "oily" wallpaper of the hallway (311). The tablecloth, he observes, has been permeated with "gravy stain" (314). In part, these details are there to register Sara's poverty: that of an early twentieth-century British middle-class woman who has not benefited from the education and inheritances of her male family members. However, I argue that these stains and smells do not just register lack. Repulsive rather than neutral, they brazenly resist the norms of domesticity. This sensual chaos creates freedom. Moreover, in a world of such thick sensuality, Sara appears as a body and hence an independent physical agent.

Andrea Adolph suggests that nineteenth-century British manuals which prescribed norms for maintaining a clean house were replaced by twentieth-century beauty manuals which proffered body norms for women (24). Though one concerns itself with traditional domestic work and one with a more modern sex appeal, it is interesting to view both as ultimately serving to regulate women's corporeal presence. Sara's defiance of both at once likewise suggests one ultimate operative, or at least one common result: to be her own bodily agent and maintain an independent subjectivity.[10] Her body is most present and transgressive in her meat consumption.

Sara's enjoyment of the meat is especially notable in contrast to North's timidity toward it. North is a soldier with experience in colonial projects. The hard work of soldiering and colonizing were both thought to be fueled by hearty eating and often by hearty meat consumption.[11] Jeremy Rifkin notes of meat and its blood content: "Blood conjures up notions of aggression and violence—

[10] It is also notable that lower-class status is suggested by both a messy house (because of a lack of servants and shared, tight quarters) and appetite in women, as Heller and Moran say Victorian class discourse "situates the appetitive woman as lower class, either as the stout, buxom servant, or as the fallen woman or prostitute" (23). In the combination of these factors, Sara identifies outside of the classes to which the angel-in-the-house norms apply. This fact may moreover help to explain North's repulsion at Sara's house. In addition to its visceral component, it may be rooted in a perceived loss of norms delineating civilization for the upper-middle class Pargiter family. A rejection of these norms places Sara further away from social regulation and further into the non-contingent reign of the body.

[11] In the short story "Scenes from the Life of a British Naval Officer," Woolf imagined a military officer at dinner performing a ritual of dominance: "He sat alone at his dinner table as he had sat alone at his desk. Of the servants who put plates before him he had never seen more than the white hands, putting down plates, taking plates away. When the hands were not white, they were dismissed. His eyes never raised themselves above the hands and the plates. In orderly procession meat, bread [,] pastry [,] fruit were placed before the idol. The red fluid in the wine glass slowly sank, rose, sank [,] rose and sank again. All the meat disappeared, all the pastry, all the fruit. At last, taking a piece of crumb about the size of a billiard ball the Captain swept this round the plate [,] devoured it and rose" (233).

valued emotions among warriors, sportsmen, and lovers. Soldiers have always been favored with beef before battle" (239). J. Stavick postulates, moreover, that the eating of red meat was essential to British colonial identity and power. *Dracula*, he argues, betrays British fear that another culture will rise above them on the food chain.

It is particularly striking, then, that North is shy about eating the meat; Sara is the character who consumes it heartily. Moreover, Woolf again lends Sara the carving work, creating a situation in which she, rather than the soldier and colonizer, has the knife. Sara's joint at the chophouse, the "admirable mutton," evoked a sense of the animal, and the quasi-raw state of the meat in this meal produces a similar effect. Woolf writes, "she took the carving-knife and made a long incision. A thin trickle of red juice ran out; it was underdone" (318). Images of blood abound in this scene. Sara and North watch "the red juice running down into the well of the dish" (319). While North claims his time in Africa accustomed him to underdone meat, and he declines Sara's offer to send it back, he appears imposed upon by this sensual effusion. When Sara asks him if he would like another cut off the joint, he declines, "looking at the rather stringy disagreeable object which was still bleeding into the well" (321). North registers that "the willow-pattern plate was daubed with gory streaks" (321). Over the instrument of placid domesticity flows blood, emblem of action and the warring, politically entrenched world of North that traditionally lies beyond women in their kitchens. Over ceramic dishes—the symbol to Mrs. Ramsay of pointless drudgery—flows a stream of the sensual. The blood's diffusion across the plate registers the invasive corporeality of the scene, as seen through North's eyes, and the manifestation of Sara's own transgressive subjecthood.

Within the image of blood lies a reference to menses, the female condition which often underlies the association of women with mess or contamination. Showalter records the belief that heavy menstruation was the result of meat eating. This image of women consuming blood may further have evoked for readers the drinking of blood recommended to nineteenth-century women suffering from anemia, a common ailment among middle-class women. Dijkstra says anemics were encouraged to drink the blood of strong animals like oxen and that slaughterhouses commonly served it (337). From this practice, he says, it was easy to conceive of vampires and especially female vampires (338).

The threat of Sara's consumption is highlighted not only by these vampiric images but also by depictions of her chewing. For instance, when North mentions an angry letter Sara wrote him, Woolf describes Sara's response in terms of mastication: she "lifted her lip like a horse that is going to bite" (321). Depicted as a biting horse—a strong, large, and in this case belligerent animal—Sara is far from the Victorian ideal of femininity. Sara's presence as masticator is again pronounced later in the meal: just as Mary looked at Ralph across her joint, here North "looked at [Sara], biting little bits off her banana" (323).[12] In these cases Woolf renders the very practice of biting an act of willfulness, an assertion of Sara's subject position in this communication. But this violent biting, like the eating of bloody meat, suggests not just personal empowerment but destructiveness. Woolf's attention to this act of biting draws attention to the potential violence underlying all meals. Margaret Visser argues in her history of table manners, *The Rituals of Dinner*, that meals are potentially dangerous, as they involve appetites and cutting and spearing utensils. It is manners, she says, which keep these threats in check. It is no less than the fear of cannibalism, she contends, that undergirds our dining rules:

> Somewhere at the back of our minds, carefully walled off from ordinary consideration and discourse, lies the idea of cannibalism—that human beings might become food, and eaters of each other. Violence, after all, is necessary if any organism is to ingest another [...] Behind every rule of table etiquette lurks the determination of each person present to be a diner, not a dish. It is one of the chief roles of etiquette to keep the lid on the violence which the meal being eaten presupposes. (3-4)

This eating of blood and baring of teeth abrade social norms Sara should follow as hostess. Together with the messy house, they evince Sara's refusal to contain her physicality.

Sara's blatant mastication, her erratic comments, her mess, the rawness of the mutton she serves are perhaps not in themselves offered by Woolf as a model for eating behavior. They are anti-social; they make a guest uncomfortable. But their disruptiveness is what makes readers notice them. Mrs. Ramsay occupies an objectified role as a tool of others' eating; Sara has so greatly liberated herself from these expectations of servitude that her guest watches her chew.

Conclusion

The disassociation of women and meat is enduring. Within the last thirty years, Pierre Bourdieu has discussed meat-eating as a sign of a fundamental difference between men and women. He explains the internalization of women's disassociation from meat:

[12] According to Bourdieu, the banana is the only fruit which can be eaten in a manly way; the others are "fiddly," and would feminize a man's rough grasp (190). The banana, moreover, of course suggests the phallus. Hence, the banana might join the meat in this scene in representing masculine food.

> Meat, the nourishing food par excellence, strong and strong-making, giving vigour, blood, and health, is the dish for the men, who take a second helping, whereas the women are satisfied with a small portion. It is not that they are stinting themselves; they really don't want what others might need, especially the men, the natural meat-eaters, and they derive a sort of authority from what they do not see as privation. Besides, they don't have a taste for men's food, which is reputed to be harmful, when eaten to excess (for example, a surfeit of meat can 'turn the blood,' over-excite, bring you out in spots etc.) and may even arouse a sort of disgust. (192)

According to Bourdieu, women remain ethereal, denying themselves strong, healthy bodies. They may even be alienated from their own desires, for Woolf's New Women and even her angel-in-the-house reveal that women do, in fact, crave this satisfying, invigorating fare. This view suggests Mary and Sara's early twentieth-century transgression may continue to strike even modern readers as provocative.[13]

Woolf's foregrounding of women's satisfying meat consumption shows that Woolf did not have only a loathing for the female body and its appetites, as Moran contends. She rather helped to make that body more concrete, presenting it as sensual and strong. Meat-eating scenes, moreover, reveal that Woolf did not entirely fail to render the desire of the female body, as she expressed in "Professions for Women" (*DM* 141). In that work, she imagines a scenario, familiar to her personally, in which a girl is dashing through the deep seas of the unconscious, only to smash upon something hard, "something about the body, about the passions which it was unfitting for her as a woman to say. Men, her reason told her, would be shocked" (*DM* 240). Failing to express sexual desire to her satisfaction, Woolf nevertheless presents readers with scenes of meat-eating that convey many things about female subjectivity that a sexual presentation of women would convey: it is sensually and corporeally grounded, therefore operating outside ideology, and it is desirous and expansive, capable of incorporating the outside world into itself, and therefore resistant to delineation or deprivation. Mary and Sara may remain

[13] That strictures against women's meat-eating were enduring is shown by the fact that Barbara Pym's post-World War II novels continued to engage the subject, inspiring two studies. Adolph in her reading of *Jane and Prudence*, focuses on Prudence, a figure who is similar to Woolf's New Women as a single working woman who transgresses the physical restraints expected of her by eating food, especially meat, heartily. Even in the beginning of this contemporary period, her eating is transgressive. Mary Anne Schofield discusses wives' food. Women achieve independence by resisting their nurturing roles, by refusing to cook hot meat-centered meals for men. While this shows an advance over Mrs. Ramsay, the women nevertheless define their relationships to food according to men and not their own bodily desires.

always single and celibate, but they have manifested themselves as desiring beings and as bodies through their eating. Cixous said the regulation of woman's appetite forms the foundation of patriarchal rule. By liberating women's alimentary access to the world, their rights to the hardiest and most culturally important food, Woolf defied this rule. In the New Woman, she unleashed an appetite and capacity for action resistant to social norms.

Works Cited

Adams, Carol. *The Sexual Politics of Meat*. NY: Continuum, 1990. Print.

Adolph, Andrea. *Food and Femininity in Twentieth-Century British Women's Fiction*. Burlington, VT: Ashgate, 2009. Print.

Bordo, Susan. *Unbearable Weight: Feminism, Western Culture, and the Body*. Berkeley: U of California P, 1993. Print.

Bourdieu, Pierre. *Distinction: A Social Critique of the Judgement of Taste*. Trans. Richard Nice. London: Routledge and Kegan Paul, 1979. Print.

Bram, Dijkstra. *Idols of Perversity: Fantasies of Feminine Evil in Fin-de-Siècle Culture*. NY: Oxford UP, 1986. Print.

Briggs, Julia. *Reading Virginia Woolf*. Edinburgh: Edinburgh UP, 2006. Print.

Brumberg, Joan Jacobs. *Fasting Girls: The Emergence of Anorexia Nervosa as a Modern Disease*. Cambridge, MA: Harvard UP, 1988. Print.

Burgass, Catherine. "Food for the Soul: Reading Mrs. Ramsay's Boeuf en Daube." *The Poetics of Transubstantiation: From Theology to Metaphor*. Ed. Douglas Burnham and Enrico Giaccherini. Aldershot, England: Ashgate, 2005. 95-103. Print.

Charles, Nickie and Marion Keer. *Women, Food and Families*. Manchester: Manchester UP, 1988. Print.

Cohen, Paula Marantz. "The Anorexic Syndrome and the Domestic Novel." *Disorderly Eaters: Texts in Self-Empowerment*. Ed. Lilian R. Furst and Peter W. Graham. University Park, PA: PSU Press, 1992. (125-140). Print.

Cohen, William A. "Introduction." *Filth: Dirt, Disgust and Modern Life*. Ed. William A. Cohen and Ryan Johnson. Minneapolis: University of Minnesota Press, 2005. vii-xxxvii. Print.

Dodd, Elizabeth. "'No, She Said, She Did Not Want a Pear': Women's Relation to Food in *To the Lighthouse* and *Mrs. Dalloway*." *Virginia Woolf: Themes and Variations*. Ed.Vara Neverow-Turk and Mark Hussey. NY: Pace UP, 1993. 150-157. Print.

Freeman, Sarah. *Mutton and Oysters: The Victorians and Their Food*. London: Victor Gollancz Ltd., 1989. Print.

Glenny, Allie. *Ravenous Identity: Eating and Eating Distress in the Life and Work of Virginia Woolf.* NY: St. Martin's, 1999. Print.

Green, Barbara. "The New Woman's Appetite for 'Riotous Living.'" *Women's Experience of Modernity: 1875-1945*. Ed. Ann L. Ardis and Leslie W. Lewis. Baltimore: Johns Hopkins UP, 2003. 221-236. Print.

Heller, Tamar and Patricia Moran, Eds. *Scenes of the Apple: Food and the Female Body in Nineteenth and Twentieth Century Women's Writing*. Albany: SUNY Press, 2003. P.

McGee, Diane. *Writing the Meal: Dinner in the Fiction of Early Twentieth-Century Writers*. Toronto: U of Toronto P, 2001. Print.

Michie, Helena. *The Flesh Made Word: Female Figures and Women's Bodies*. Oxford: Oxford UP, 1987. Print.

Moran, Patricia. *Word of Mouth: Body Language in Katherine Mansfield and Virginia Woolf.* Charlottesville: UP of Virginia, 1996. Print.

Munich, Adrienne. "Good and Plenty: Queen Victoria Figures the Imperial Body." Heller and Moran: 45-64.

Phillips, Melanie. *The Ascent of Woman: A History of the Suffragette Movement and the Ideas Behind It*. London: Little, Brown, 1993. Print.

Rifkin, Jeremy. *Beyond Beef: The Rise and Fall of Cattle Culture*. NY: Dutton, 1992. Print.

Schlossberg, Linda. "Consuming Images: Women, Hunger and the Vote." Heller and Moran: 87-106.

Shapiro, Laura. *Perfection Salad: Women and Cooking at the Turn of the Century*. Berkeley: U of California P, 2009. Print.

Showalter, Elaine. *The Female Malady*. NY: Pantheon, 1985. Print.

Squier, Susan M. *Virginia Woolf and London: The Sexual Politics of the City*. Chapel Hill: U of North Carolina P, 1985. Print.

Stavick, J.E.D. "Love at First Beet: Vegetarian Critical Theory Meats Dracula." *The Victorian Newsletter* 89 (Spring 1996): 23-29. Print.

Visser, Margaret. *The Rituals of Dinner: The Origins, Evolution, Eccentricities and Meaning of Table Manners*. NY: Grove Weidenfeld, 1991. Print.

Warde, Alan and Lydia Martens. *Eating Out: Social Differentiation, Consumption and Pleasure*. Cambridge: Cambridge UP, 2000. Print.

Wood, Jane. "Dining Well: Food, Identity and Women's Travel Narratives." *You Are What You Eat: Literary Probes into the Palate*. Ed. Annette M. Magid. Newcastle, UK: Cambridge Scholars Publications, 2008: 56-65. Print.

Woolf, Virginia. *Between the Acts*. NY: Harcourt, Brace and Co., 1941. Print.

——. *Flush: A Biography*. NY: Harcourt, Brace and Co., 1933. Print.

——. *Hyde Park Gate News: The Stephen Family Newspaper*. Ed. Gill Lowe. London: Hesperus, 2005. Print.

——. *Mrs. Dalloway*. 1925. NY: Harcourt, Inc., 1981. Print.
——. *Night and Day*. 1919. Oxford: Oxford UP, 1999. Print.
——. "Professions for Women." *The Death of the Moth and Other Essays*. 1942. NY: Harcourt, Brace, Jovanovich, 1974. 235-242. Print.
——. *A Room of One's Own*. 1929. NY: Harcourt, Brace, Jovanovich, 1981. Print.
——. "Scenes from the Life of a British Naval Officer." *The Complete Shorter Fiction of Virginia Woolf*. Ed. Susan Dick. San Diego: Harvest, 1989. 232-234. Print.
——. *Three Guineas*. NY: Harcourt, Brace and Co., 1938. Print.
——. *To the Lighthouse*. 1927. NY: Harcourt, Brace and World, Inc., 1955. Print.
——. *The Voyage Out*. 1925. NY: Harcourt, 2001. Print.
——. *The Years*. 1937. NY: Harcourt, 1939. Print.
——. *The Waves*. 1931. NY: Harcourt, Inc, 1959. Print.

Guide to Library Special Collections

This guide updates the information in volume 16.

Name of Collection: The Beinecke Rare Book and Manuscript Library

Contact: Kevin Repp, Curator of Modern Books and Manuscripts
Patricia Willis, Curator of American Literature

Address: Yale University Library
P.O. Box 208240
New Haven, CT 06520-8240

URL: www.library.yale.edu/beinecke/brblhome.html

Hours: Mon.–Thu. 8:30 AM–8 PM
Fri. 8:30 AM–5 PM

Access Requirements: Register at the circulation desk on each visit.

Holdings Relevant To Woolf: General Collection includes autograph manuscript of "Notes on Oliver Goldsmith." Comments on Edward Gibbon, William Beckford Collection. Letters from Virginia Woolf in the Bryher Papers, the Louise Morgan and Otto Theis Papers, and the Rebecca West Papers. Related material: 41 letters from Vita Sackville-West to Violet Trefusis; files relating to Robert Manson Myers's *From Beowulf to Virginia Woolf* in the Edmond Pauker Papers.

Yale Collection of American Literature includes typewritten manuscripts of "The Art of Walter Sickert," "Augustine Birrell," "Aurora Leigh," "How Should One Read a Book?" "Letter to a Young Poet," "The Novels of Turgenev," "Street Haunting." Dial/Scofield Thayer Papers: manuscripts of "The Lives of the Obscure," "Miss Ormerod," and "Mrs. Dalloway in Bond Street." Letters from Virginia Woolf in the William Rose Benet Papers, the Benet Family Correspondence, the Henry Seidel Canby Papers, the Seward Collins Papers, the Dial/Scofield Thayer Papers, and the *Yale Review* archive. Material relating to translations of Woolf in the Thornton Wilder papers. Related material: Clive Bell, "Virginia Woolf" (Dial/Scofield Thayer Papers); 43 letters from Leonard Woolf to Helen McAfee (*Yale Review*); 11 letters from Leonard Woolf to Gertrude Stein.

Name of Collection: The Henry W. and Albert A. Berg Collection of English and American Literature

Contact: Isaac Gewirtz, Curator

Address: New York Public Library, Room 320
Fifth Avenue & 42nd Street
New York, NY 10018

Telephone: 212-930-0802
Fax: 212-930-0079
Email: igewirtz@nypl.org

Hours: Tue.–Wed. 11 AM–7 PM
Thu.–Sat. 10 AM–6 PM
Closed Sun., Mon. and legal holidays

Access Requirements: After acquiring Library card in room 315, check outerwear and *all* containers (briefcases, computer cases, handbags, folders, etc.) in First Floor cloakroom, and proceed to the Berg Collection. Traceable and photo identification required. Undergraduates working on honors theses need letter from faculty advisor.

Restrictions: Virginia Woolf's MSS are now made available on microfilm and CD. URL for Berg finding aid: http://www.nypl.org/research/manuscripts/berg/brgwoolf.xml. N.B. *All the Berg's Woolf MSS are on microfilm and CD published by Research Publications and available at many research libraries.*

Holdings Relevant To Woolf: Manuscripts/typescripts of all of the novels except *Orlando*, including: *Between the Acts, Flush, Jacob's Room, Mrs. Dalloway* (notes and fragments), *Night and Day, To the Lighthouse, The Voyage Out, The Waves, The Years*; 12 notebooks of articles, essays, fiction and reviews, 1924–1940; 36 volumes of diaries; 26 volumes of reading notes; correspondence with Vanessa Bell, Ethel Smyth, Vita Sackville-West and others. Su Hua Ling Chen's Bloomsbury correspondence.

Recent Acquisitions: Proof copy of *A Room of One's Own* (July 1929); ALS Vanessa Bell to Vita Sackville-West, April 29, 1941 [in Marler, *Selected Letters* 478-80]; Frank Dean, *Strike While the Iron's Hot: Frank Dean's Life as a Blacksmith and Farrier in Rodmell*, ed. Susan Rowland (S. Rowland, 1994) [includes map, accounts of search for VW's body and of her funeral]

Name of Collection: The British Library Manuscript Collections

Contact: Manuscripts Enquiries

Address: 96 Euston Road
London NW1 2DB
England

Telephone: 0207-412-7513
Fax: 0207-412-7745
Email: mss@bl.uk

Hours: Mon. 10 AM–5 PM
Tue.–Sat.: 9:30 AM–5 PM

Access Requirements: British Library Reader Pass (signed I.D. required and usually proof of post-graduate academic status, or other demonstrable need to use the collections—see www.bl.uk). In addition, access to most literary autograph material only available with letter of recommendation.

Restrictions: Paper Copies, Microfilms, and Photography of selected items available upon receipt of written authorization for photo duplication from the copyright holder.

Holdings Relevant to Woolf: Diaries 1930–1931 (microfilm); Mrs. Dalloway and other writings (1923–1925) three volumes; letter from Leonard Woolf to H. G. Wells (1941); two letters from Virginia Woolf and three letters from Leonard Woolf to John Lehmann (1941); letter written on behalf of Leonard Woolf to S. S. Koteliansky (1946); notebook in Italian kept by Virginia Woolf; notebook of Virginia Stephen (1906–1909); A sketch of the past revised ts (1940); letters from Virginia Woolf in the correspondence files of Lytton and James Strachey; letter from Virginia Woolf to Mildred Massingberd; letter from Virginia Woolf to Harriet Shaw Weaver (1918); letters from Virginia Woolf to S. S. Koteliansky (1923–1927); letter from Virginia Woolf to Frances Cornford (1929); letter from Virginia Woolf to Ernest Rhys (1930); correspondence of Virginia Woolf in the Society of Authors archive (1934–1937); letter and postcard from Virginia Woolf to Bernard Shaw (1940); three letters (suicide notes) from Virginia Woolf (1941); two letters from Virginia Woolf and three from Leonard Woolf to John Lehmann (1941). "Hyde Park Gate News" 1891–1892, 1895 (add. MSS 70725, 70726). Letters of Virginia and Leonard Woolf to Lady Aberconway, 1927–1941. Letter from Virginia Woolf to Frances Cornford. Letters from Virginia Woolf to Macmillan Co. 1903, 1908. Collection of RPs ("reserved photo copies"–copies of manuscripts exported, some subject to restrictions).

Name of Collection: Harry Ransom Humanities Research Center

Contact: Research Librarian

Address: The University of Texas at Austin
P.O. Box 7219
Austin, TX 78713-7219

Telephone: 512-471-9119
Fax: 512-471-2899
Email: reference@hrc.utexas.edu
Hours: Mon.–Fri. 9 AM–5 PM
Sat. 9 AM–NOON
Closed holidays; intersession Saturdays; one week each in late May and late August.

Access Requirements: Completed manuscript reader's application; current photo identification.

Holdings Relevant To Woolf: The manuscript collection includes the typed manuscript with autograph revisions of *Kew Gardens*, and the typed manuscript and autograph revisions of "Thoughts on Peace in an Air Raid." The Center holds 571 of Woolf's letters, including correspondence to Elizabeth Bowen, Lady Ottoline Morrell, Mary Hutchinson, William Plomer, Hugh Walpole and others. Further mss. relating to Virginia Woolf include letters to her from T. S. Eliot and reviews of her work. A substantial collection of the first British and American editions of Woolf's published works, as well as 130 volumes from Leonard and Virginia Woolf's library and a collection of books published by the Hogarth Press, is also housed. An art collection holds a landscape painting of Virginia's garden and a series of Cockney cartoons in a sketch book, signed "V.W." The center also has extensive holdings of materials related to Leonard Woolf, Ottoline Morrell, Mary Hutchinson, Lytton Strachey, Dora Carrington, E. M. Forster, Clive Bell, Roger Fry, Vanessa Bell, Bertrand Russell, Elizabeth Bowen, William Plomer, Stephen Spender and Hugh Walpole.

Name of Collection: King's College Archive Centre

Contact: Patricia McGuire, Archivist
King's College

Address: Cambridge CB2 1ST
Telephone: 01223-331444
Fax: 01223-331891
Email: archivist@kings.cam.ac.uk

Hours: Mon.–Thu. 9:30 AM–12:30 PM and 1:30 PM–5:15 PM. *Closed during public holidays and the College's annual periods of closure.*

Access Requirements: Proof of ID, letter of introduction, appointment in advance.

Holdings Relevant To Woolf: Woolf MSS and letters: Minute book, written up by Clive Bell, of the meetings of a play-reading society, with cast lists and comments on performances by CB. Dec. 1907–Jan. 1909, Oct. 1914–Feb. 1915. Players included variously Clive and Vanessa Bell, Roger and Margery Fry, Duncan Grant, Walter Lamb, Molly MacCarthy, Adrian and Virginia Stephen, Saxon Sydney-Turner. *Freshwater, A Comedy*—photocopy of editorial typescript prepared from the MSS at Sussex University and Monk's House; photocopy of covering letter from the publisher to "Robert Silvers," Jan. 29, 1976. Papers relating to the Virginia Woolf Centenary Conference held at Fitzwilliam College, Cambridge, Sept. 20-22, 1982. TS with corrections of "Nurse Lugton's Curtain." Typed transcript of R. Fry's memoir of his schooldays. Correspondence with Clive Bell, Julian Bell, Vanessa Bell, Richard Braithwaite, Rupert Brooke, Mrs. Brooke, Katharine Cox, Julian Fry, Roger Fry, John Davy Hayward, J. M. Keynes, Lydia Keynes, Rosamond Lehmann, Charles Mauron, Raymond Mortimer, Frances and Ralph Partridge, G. H. W. Rylands, J. T. Sheppard, W. J. H. Sprott, Thoby Stephen, Madge Vaughan. Woolf-related archival collections held: Charleston Papers; Rupert Brooke Papers; E. M. Forster Papers; Roger Fry Papers; J. M. Keynes Papers; Frances Partridge Papers; George Humphrey Wolferstan ('Dadie') Rylands Papers; J. T. Sheppard Papers; W. J. H. Sprott Papers. Various works of art by Vanessa Bell, Duncan Grant, and Roger Fry, held in various locations around King's College. Access via Second Bursar's secretary.

Name of Collection: The Lilly Library

Contact: Breon Mitchell, Director
Cherry Williams, Curator of Manuscripts
Address: The Lilly Library, Indiana University
1200 East Seventh Street
Bloomington, IN 47405-5500

Telephone: 812-855-2452
Fax: 812-855-3143
Email: liblilly@indiana.edu, mitchell@indiana.edu
chedwill@indiana.edu

Hours: Mon.–Fri. 9 AM–6 PM; Sat. 9 AM–1 PM;
Closed Sundays and Major Holidays

Access Requirements: Valid photo-identification; brief registration procedure.

Restrictions: Closed stacks; material use confined to reading room; wheelchair-accessible reading room and exhibitions (but no wheelchair-accessible restroom).

Holdings Relevant To Woolf: Corrected page proofs for the American edition of *Mrs. Dalloway*; letters to Woolf from Desmond and Mary (Molly) MacCarthy; 77 letters (published in *Letters*) from Woolf to correspondents including Donald Clifford Brace, Robert Gathorne-Hardy, Barbara (Strachey) Halpern, Richard Arthur Warren Hughes, Desmond MacCarthy and Molly MacCarthy; "Preliminary Scheme for the formation of a Partnership between Mr Leonard Sidney Woolf and Mr John Lehmann to take over The Hogarth Press" (includes contract signed by Lehmann, Leonard Woolf, and Virginia Woolf and receipt for Lehmann's payment to Virginia Woolf to purchase Virginia Woolf's share in the Hogarth Press); photographs of Virginia Woolf, Leonard Woolf, Lytton Strachey, Strachey family, Roger Fry, and Vanessa Bell (Hannah Whitall Smith mss.); (Richard) Kennedy mss. (four hand-colored lithographs of Virginia Woolf: artist's proofs for RK's portfolio, VIRGINIA WOOLF: "AS I KNEW HER"; Sackville-West, V. mss. (10,529 items: includes the correspondence of Vita Sackville-West, and Harold Nicolson); MacCarthy mss. (ca. 10,000 items: papers of Desmond and Molly MacCarthy); correspondence between LW and Mary Gaither regarding publication of *A Checklist of the Hogarth Press* (1976, repr. 1986); Todd Avery, *Close and Affectionate Friends: Desmond and Molly MacCarthy and the Bloomsbury Group* (The Lilly Library / Indiana University Libraries, 1999).

Name of Collection: Archives and Manuscripts, University of Maryland, College Park, Libraries

Contact: Beth Alvarez, Curator of Literary Manuscripts

Address: University of Maryland Libraries
College Park, MD 20742

Telephone:
Fax: 310-405-9298
Email: 301-314-2709
alvarez@umd.edu

Hours:
Dates and hours of operation subject to change. Contact Beth Alvarez before planning a research visit.

Access Requirements: Photo ID.

Holdings Relevant To Woolf: Papers of Hope Mirrlees contain five autograph letters and postcards (1919–1928) from Virginia Woolf to Mirrlees. Also in the collection are 113 letters from T. S. Eliot to Mirrlees, and three letters from Lady Ottoline Morrell to Mirrlees. A finding aid is available at http://hdl.handle.net/1903.1/1536.

Name of Collection: Monks House Papers/Leonard Woolf Papers/Charleston Papers/Nicolson Papers

Contact: Fiona Courage, Special Collections Manager

Address: University of Sussex Library
Brighton
Sussex BN1 9QL
England

Telephone: 01273-678157
Fax: 01273-678441

Email: Library.Specialcoll@sussex.ac.uk
URL: www.sussex.ac.uk/library/speccoll

Access Requirements: By appointment. Identification to be presented on arrival. Application for access (including contact details of referee) to be completed on arrival.

Restrictions: Photocopying strictly controlled.

Holdings Relevant To Woolf: The University of Sussex holds two large archives relating to Leonard and Virginia Woolf: The Monks House Papers, primarily correspondence and MSS of Virginia Woolf, including the three scrapbooks relating to *Three Guineas*; and The Leonard Woolf Papers, primarily correspondence and other papers of Leonard Woolf. (Monks House Papers are available on microfilm in many research libraries.) The Charleston Papers consist in the main of letters written to or by Clive and Vanessa Bell and Duncan Grant which had accumulated in their home; the library houses Quentin Bell's photocopied set; letters from Roger Fry, Maynard Keynes, Lytton Stachey, Virginia Woolf, Vita Sackville-West, E. M. Forster, T. S. Eliot, Frances Partridge and others. The Maria Jackson letters comprise some 900 letters from Maria Jackson to Julia and Leslie Stephen. The Nicolson Papers complement these three Sussex archives relating to the Bloomsbury Group, and consist of Nigel Nicolson's correspondence relating to his editorial work as principal editor of the six-volume *Letters of Virginia Woolf*, published between 1975 and 1980.

The Bell Papers. A. O. Bell's correspondence relating to her editorial work on Virginia Woolf's diaries, a parallel collection to the Nicolson Papers. Collection level description may be accessed at www.archiveshub.ac.uk

Name of Collection: The Morgan Library & Museum

Contact: Reading Room

Address: 225 Madison Ave.
New York, NY 10016

Telephone: 212-590-0315
Email: readingroom@themorgan.org
URL: www.themorgan.org

Access Requirements: Admission to the Reading Room is by application and by appointment.

Holdings Relevant To Woolf: Virginia Woolf. Autograph manuscript notebook, 1931 Sept. 24. 1 item (52 p.) ; 265 x 208 mm. Contains drafts of "A Letter to a Young Poet," a brief letter to the press entitled "The Villa Jones" [ff. 3–5] and a monologue by a working-class woman [ff. 44–46]. MA 3333. Purchased on the Fellows Fund with the special assistance of Anne S. Dayton, Enid A. Haupt, Mrs. James H. Ripley, Mr. and Mrs. August H. Schilling, and John S. Thacher, 1979.

Virginia Woolf. Autograph letters signed (2) and typed letter signed, dated London [etc.], to E. McKnight Kauffer, 1931 Apr. 4–23, and undated.

3 items (4 p.). Concerning a drawing of her and a bibliography of her works. MA 1679. Purchased in 1959.

Vanessa Bell. 84 autograph letters, 3 typed letters, 7 postcards, and 3 telegrams. Most, but not all, are written by Vanessa Bell to John Maynard Keynes. Concerning Duncan Grant, Roger Fry, Clive Bell, the Bell children, Leonard and Virginia Woolf, Lytton Strachey, John Maynard and Lydia Lopokova Keynes, David Garnett, Ottoline Morrell, and others. MA 3448. Items in this collection are described in 97 individual records (MA 3448.1-97). Purchased on the Fellows Fund, special gift of the Gramercy Park Foundation (Mrs. Michael Tucker), 1980.

Name of Collection: University Museums and Special Collections Service

Contact: University Archivist

Address: University of Reading
Redlands Road
Berkshire RG1 5EX
England

Telephone: 0118-378-8660
Fax: 0118-378-5632
Email: specialcollections@reading.ac.uk

Access Requirements: Appointment needed to consult material.
Permission required to consult or copy material in the Hogarth Press and Chatto & Windus collections from Random House, 20 Vauxhall Bridge Road, London SW1V 2SA, UK. (Jean Rose, Library Mgr. JRose@Randomhouse.co.uk)

Holdings Relevant To Woolf: Hogarth Press (MS2750): editorial and production correspondence relating to publications of the Press including Woolf's own titles. Production ledgers 1920s–1950s. Correspondence between Leonard Woolf and Stanley Unwin about progress with his collected edition of the works of Freud. Order books – e.g. lists of booksellers, book clubs and how many books they have ordered for a particular title. Newscuttings – press clippings of advertisements for Hogarth Press books including Virginia Woolf publications.
Chatto & Windus (MS2444): small number of

letters 1915–1925; 1929–1931. Various letters and notes by Leonard Woolf; outgoing letters to Leonard Woolf: 22 November 1927 (Letter Book 119); outgoing letters to Virginia Woolf: 29 January 1936 (Letter Book 171), 22 December 1931 (Letter Book 135), 31 December 1931 (Letter Book 135), 15 December 1920 (Letter Book 100), 20 December 1920 (Letter Book 100).

George Bell & Sons (MS1640): 5 letters from Leonard Woolf 1930–1966.

Routledge (MS1489): Reader's report by Leonard Woolf on George Padmore's "Britannia rules the blacks" (1935); "How Britain rules Africa." 1 letter from Leonard Woolf (June 1941) from Miscellaneous publishing correspondence 1941-1942 Wi-Wy RKP 174/15. Draft introduction by Leonard Woolf to *Letters on India* by Mulk Raj (1942) and 1 letter to Leonard Woolf from Mulk Raj Anand 1942-1943 RKP 178/3. Correspondence concerning the publication of *The War for Peace* by Leonard Woolf, 1939-1940 RKP 160/5. 1 letter from Virginia Woolf declining an invitation from Routledge to write a biography of Margaret Bondfield, 25 May 1940 RKP 160/5.

Megroz (MS1979/68): 2 letters from Leonard Woolf, 1926.

Allen & Unwin (MS3282): Correspondence with Leonard Woolf c.1914-1918 (re. his book *International Government*), 1923-1924; 1939-1940; 1943; 1946; 1950-1951; 1953; 1965 (concerning ill-founded rumors about the Hogarth Press); 1967 (concerning a reprint of *Empire and Commerce in Africa*).

Jonathan Cape (MS 2446): All correspondence from file JC A43. Correspondence between Jonathan Cape and Virginia Woolf and Cape and A.C. Gissing concerning Virginia Woolf's introduction to George Gissing's *Ionian Sea* to which A.C. Gissing objects. 1 postcard (1935), 1 letter (1933), 2 letters (1932) from Virginia Woolf. 1 letter (1932) from Virginia Woolf declining to write an introduction to Jane Austen's *Northanger Abbey*. 4 letters (1931) from Virginia Woolf declining to write an introduction to one of Miss Thackeray's books. Letters from Vanessa Bell:1 letter from Bell CW 152/2;1 letter from Bell CW 171/10; 2 letters from Bell CW 578/1; 1 letter from Bell CW 59/9; 1 letter from Bell (1936) CW 61/10. Artwork by Vanessa Bell for various Virginia Woolf titles

Artwork by Angelica Garnett, Philippa Bramson and others for various books.

Name of Collection: Frances Hooper Collection of Virginia Woolf Books and Manuscripts/Elizabeth Power Richardson Bloomsbury Iconography Collection.

Contact: Karen V. Kukil, Associate Curator of Special Collections
Mortimer Rare Book Room

Address: William Allan Neilson Library
Smith College
Northampton, MA 01063

Telephone: 413-585-2906
Fax: 413-585-4486
Email: kkukil@email.smith.edu
URL: www.smith.edu/libraries/libs/rarebook

Hours: Mon.–Fri. 9 AM–5 PM

Access Requirements: Appointment to be made with the Curator.

Holdings Relevant To Woolf: The Hooper Collection emphasizes Woolf as an essayist but also includes many Hogarth Press first editions, limited editions of Woolf's works, and translations. The collection includes page proofs of *Orlando*, *To the Lighthouse,* and T*he Common Reader,* corrected by Woolf for the first American editions, a proof copy of *The Waves* that Woolf inscribed to Hugh Walpole, and the proof copies of *The Years* and of *Flush*. The Collection also has one of the deluxe editions of *Orlando* that was printed on green paper. Other items include twenty-two pages of reading notes from 1926, three pages of notes on D. H. Lawrence's *Sons and Lovers*, thirty-three pages of notes for *Roger Fry*, a six-page ms. "As to criticism," a five-page ms. of "The Searchlight," and a fourteen-page ms. of "The Patron and The Crocus." The Hooper Collection also owns 140 letters between Woolf and Lytton Strachey as well as other correspondence, including a 13 February [1921] letter to Katherine Mansfield and ten letters to Mela and Robert Spira.

The Richardson Collection is a working collection of books and materials used by Richardson in preparing her *Bloomsbury Iconography*. It includes Leslie Stephen's photograph album, ninety-eight original exhibition catalogs dating back to 1929, clippings and photcopies of such items as reviews of early Woolf works, and Bloomsbury material from British *Vogue* of the 1920s. The Collection also has three preliminary pencil drawings by Vanessa Bell for *Flush*.

The Mortimer Rare Book Room also owns Woolf's 1916 Italian ms. notebook and her corrected typescripts of "Reviewing" and "The Searchlight." In addition, there is a 1923 photograph of Woolf at Garsington. Original cover designs for Hogarth

Press publications include *The Common Reader, On Being Ill,* and *Duncan Grant.* The Mortimer Rare Book Room also has a Sylvia Plath collection that includes eight of Woolf's books from Plath's library, several of which are underlined and annotated, as well as Plath's notes from her undergraduate English 211 class at Smith (1951–1952) in which she studied *To the Lighthouse.* The collection also includes Woolf's 26 February 1939 letter to Vita Sackville-West, a 1931 bronze bust of Virginia Woolf by Stephen Tomlin, a 1923 Hogarth Press edition of T.S. Eliot's *The Waste Land,* a 1919 Hogarth Press edition of *Paris* by Hope Mirrlees and first editions of Vita Sackville-West publications. Online exhibitions are available on the Mortimer Rare Book Room's web site.

Name of Collection: Woolf/Hogarth Press/Bloomsbury

Contact: Robert C. Brandeis

Address: Victoria University Library
71 Queens Park Crescent E.
Toronto M5S 1K7
Ontario Canada

Email: victoria.library@utoronto.ca

URL: http://library.vicu.utoronto.ca/special/bloomsbury.htm

Hours: Mon.–Fri. 9 AM–5 PM

Access Requirements: Prior notification; identification.

Restrictions: Limited photocopying.

Holdings Relevant To Woolf: This collection, the most comprehensive of its kind with more than 4,200 items, contains all the work of Virginia and Leonard Woolf in various editions, issues, variants and translations; all the books hand-printed by Leonard and Virginia Woolf at the Hogarth Press, including many variant issues and bindings, association copies and page proofs; a nearly comprehensive collection of Hogarth Press machine printed books to 1946 (the year Leonard Woolf and the Press joined Chatto & Windus) including presentation copies, signed limited editions, page proofs, variants as well as substantial amounts of ephemera, such as the *Catalogue of Publications to 1939* with annotations by Leonard Woolf. The collection is also very strong in Bloomsbury Art and Artists, especially the decorative arts, including important examples of Omega Workshops publications and exhibition catalogues. Materials include the catalogue of the second post-impressionist exhibition, 1912; catalogues relating to Vanessa Bell and Duncan Grant exhibitions; bronze medal of Virginia Woolf by Marta Firlet; oil on canvas portrait of Amaryllis Garnett by Vanessa Bell (c.1958); Portrait sketch of Leonard Woolf by Vanessa Bell; Duncan Grant and Vanessa Bell designed Clarice Cliff dinner plates; original Vanessa Bell and Duncan Grant sketches and designs for dust jackets and novels; bronze busts of Lytton Strachey and Virginia Woolf by Stephen Tomlin (1901–1937); as well as the Marcel Gimond bust of Vanessa Bell and the Tomlin bust of Henrietta Bingham. Original correspondence and mss material includes that by Vanessa Bell; Leonard Woolf; Ritchie family re: Anne Thackeray Ritchie/Stephen family; Duncan Grant; Quentin Bell; S. P. Rosenbaum mss. Large Ephemera Collection including items revealing Virginia Woolf's effect on popular culture.

Name of Collection:	Library of Leonard and Virginia Woolf (Washington S U)
Contact:	Trevor James Bond Special Collections Librarian
Address:	Washington State University Libraries Pullman, WA 99164-5610
Email:	tjbond@wsu.edu
URL:	www.wsulibs.wsu.edu/holland/masc/masc.htm
Hours:	Mon.–Fri. 8:30 AM–5 PM
Access Requirements:	Letter stating nature of research preferred; student or other identification.
Restrictions:	Materials must be used in the MASC area under supervision. Photocopying or photographing is permitted only when it will not harm the materials and is permitted by copyright.
Holdings Relevant To Woolf:	WSU has the Woolfs' basic working library including many works which belonged to Woolf's father, Sir Leslie Stephen, and other family members. Over 800 titles came from their Sussex home, Monks House, including some works bought at auction soon after Leonard Woolf died in 1969. Later additions include: 1,875 titles from his house in Victoria Square, London; 400 titles from his nephew Cecil Woolf; and over 60 titles from Quentin and Anne Olivier Bell. WSU has been actively collecting: all works in all editions by Virginia Woolf; all titles by Leonard Woolf; works published by the Woolfs at the Hogarth Press through 1946; books by their friends and associates, especially those by Bloomsbury authors and about Bloomsbury artists; relevant correspondence and original works of art. Original artwork by Vanessa Bell; scattered letters by Vanessa Bell, E. M. Forster, Roger Fry, Leslie Stephen, Lytton

Strachey, and Leonard Woolf. Original artwork by Richard Kennedy for illustrations in his book *A Boy at the Hogarth Press*; scattered letters by Roger Fry, Leslie Stephen, Ethel Smyth, and Leonard Woolf. Virginia Woolf's initialed copy of *Cornishiana*; Leonard Woolf's annotated copy of *An Anatomy of Poetry* by A. William-Ellis; Leslie Stephen's copy of *Lapsus Calami and Other Verses*, inscribed by James Kenneth Stephen. Several letters from Virginia Woolf, including two written in 1939 to Ronald Heffer, and a letter to Edward McKnight Kauffer. New in the Hogarth Press Collection are a copy of E. M. Forster's *Anonymity, an Enquiry*,
bound in cream paper boards, and what Woolmer calls the third label state of Forster's *The Story of the Siren*.

Name of Collection: Yale Center for British Art

Contact: Elisabeth Fairman, Senior Curator of Rare Books and Manuscripts

Address: 1080 Chapel Street
P.O. Box 208280
New Haven, CT 06520-8280

Telephone: 203-432-2814
Fax: 203-432-9613
E-mail: elisabeth.fairman@yale.edu

Hours: Tue.-Fri. 10 AM-4:30 PM

Access Requirements: Permission needed in order to reproduce.

Holdings Relevant To Woolf: Rare Books & Mss Department: 94 letters from Vanessa Bell and Duncan Grant to Sir Kenneth Clark; Prints & Drawings Department: 4 drawings by Vanessa Bell; 4 drawings by Duncan Grant; 6

drawings by Wyndham Lewis; 1 drawing by Frederick Etchells; Paintings Department: 1 painting by Vanessa Bell, 4 paintings by Duncan Grant (including portrait of Vanessa Bell); 3 paintings by Roger Fry.

Recent Acquisitions: 6 letters from Lytton Strachey (to Clive Bell, Siegfried Sassoon, et al.).

Reviews

Virginia Woolf and the Nineteenth-Century Domestic Novel. Emily Blair (Albany: SUNY P, 2007) xii + 287 pp.

The Marriage Paradox: Modernist Novels and the Cultural Imperative to Marry. Davida Pines (Gainesville, FL: UP of Florida, 2006) x + 157 pp.

From her earliest writing in the Stephen family newspaper *Hyde Park Gate News*, Virginia Woolf is preoccupied with the domestic, its space and relations; even the naming of the newspaper after the family home speaks simultaneously to its insularity and its desire to reveal what goes on behind closed doors. The ambivalence evinced in her essays and novels towards the domestic is one of the qualities that makes Woolf perennially interesting. Even as she argues for a room of one's own, she is herself difficult to pin down in any one particular personal or intellectual space. In an essay in the recent *Edinburgh Companion to Virginia Woolf and the Arts*, Victoria Rosner describes Woolf's peripatetic relationship to her own living and working space. Writing of Monk's House and its importance to Woolf's writing, Rosner says, "[She] frequently shifted the spaces where she worked [...] Her writerly wanderlust is noteworthy since many writers prefer to settle into a single space and stay [...] Woolf's numerous changes in location suggest that her quest for that room of her own sprang from a desire that could never be fully satisfied. It also suggests a refusal to become too comfortable or settled, to insist, as it were, on shifting her perspective with frequency" (188). Woolf found a fruitful discomfort in the domestic. She regarded the home and its private worlds as distinctly feminine, and was troubled by the essentially gendered association; like Lily Briscoe, she wanders out into the open in search of a vision. Yet at the same time, those close and intimate spaces are also a source of artistic power: the vision might be found in the sitting room or the kitchen, brought forward by and through a distinctly female presence.

The *Edinburgh Companion* with its substantial section on the domestic arts is just one instance of the ongoing (even increased) interest in Bloomsbury home life and housekeeping particularly, and modernist spaces more broadly. A recent traveling exhibition examining the intersections among the visual and domestic arts of Bloomsbury shows how this distinctly modernist movement placed great value on the objects, artifacts, and aesthetics of private home life; Bloomsbury domesticates modernism, and renders the domestic thoroughly modernist, in surprising but apt ways. In "A Room of Their Own: The Bloomsbury Artists in American Collections," paintings by Carrington and Duncan Grant hang alongside shutters and wallpaper; books produced by the Hogarth Press with covers by Vanessa Bell sit in cases next to plates from the Omega Workshop. Rosner in her monograph *Modernism and the Architecture of Private Life* argues that the re-imagining of private space was just as crucial to the post-Victorians of Bloomsbury as it would have been to Julia and Leslie Stephen. Rosner conceptualizes the modernist vision of private space thus, thinking through Woolf: "Woolf felt that the organization and customs of daily life were changing, if not in a fashion readily ascribed to any given individual then certainly in one measurable in its impact on the home. The peace and stability of the Victorian household deteriorated, deformed by the pressure of changing social, sexual, and cultural mores. What took its place was a far more provisional, more embodied, more unstructured kind of private life—the kind of life we still call 'modern'" (3). The dialogue among the paintings and decorative arts of Bloomsbury speaks to this rethinking of interiority, a destabilization of the representation of subjectivity and the spaces in which that subjectivity plays out.

We are in danger, however, of overstating the "peace and stability" of the Victorian household, of finding the deformed only in the modernist. One need not go to the late modernist novels of Ivy Compton-Burnett to find some darkness in the Victorian household; one can go to recent studies on eating disorders and incest in Victorian literature (by Anna Silver and Mary Jean Corbett, respectively). Might the rupture that has become so much a part of the modernist teleology generally, and Woolfian readings particularly, be a bit overdetermined? Not to rehash a much-asked question, but *did* human nature really change forever in December 1910? We might hearken to Gillian Beer's point: "One of the tropes of modernism is its insistence on its own novelty, its disconnection from the past [...] Woolf did not simply reject the Victorians and their concerns, or renounce them. Instead, she persistingly rewrote them" (qtd. in Holton 51). The dis-ease around the domestic so noteworthy in Woolf's writing has its roots in her immediate biographical and historical past, an instant she never entirely left and which remains inscribed in her writing. Alison Light's *Mrs. Woolf and the Servants* has illuminated the role domestic service played in shaping Woolf's work and her anxieties about home life. Readers of Woolf have long been aware of the deep extent to which the personal is political, and the ways in which the boundaries between private and public are most fluid. Light's work, however, shows just how uncomfortable Woolf was with the permeability between higher and lower orders, embodied (literally) by the smells and sounds of the profound intimacy made inevitable by the mistress/servant relationship. No matter how hard a family might have tried to pull curtains and keep some doors closed, the feminine and bodily nature of domestic life seeped in. The research done by Light grounds Woolf in her Victorian past, and readers of *Woolf Studies Annual* are no doubt aware of other writing in the last few years which (re)envisions Woolf in imaginative and intellectual dialogue with the Victorians. Steve Ellis's *Virginia Woolf and the Victorians*, for instance, makes a compelling case for Woolf's ongoing and concomitant "affiliation" and "dissent" with the Victorians (2); in his reading of *To the Lighthouse*, he notes how Woolf's feminism resides uneasily, and productively, alongside her re-imagining of the Victorian past—although his claim for Woolf's nostalgia may go too far (79).

Domestic space and private life, with their particularly gendered valences, similarly emerge as sites of tension and continuity between the Victorian and modernist periods in two recent monographs: Davida Pines' *The Marriage Paradox: Modernist Novels and the Cultural Imperative to Marry* and Emily Blair's *Virginia Woolf and the Nineteenth-Century Domestic Novel*. The argument that modernism arises from a mighty rupture in literary and cultural modes is less convincing than the recognition that many modernist writers—perhaps Woolf especially—engaged with continuities and conversations among their immediate predecessors; this is one reason Pines' book is less strong than Blair's. While the two books would seem to be situated in different places and employing different foci and methodologies—Pines' book concentrates very narrowly (in a mere 157 pages) on marriage in a select group of unsurprising (and slightly uninspiring) modernist novels, while Blair grounds her study more broadly in nineteenth-century domestic culture, examining not only novels but etiquette and conduct books and contemporary commentary on interior decorating—they are worth considering together for several reasons. The first has already been alluded to: they address the bigger methodological and literary-historical question of how we read modernism in relation to/in counterpoint against/in dialogue with the Victorians. Another salient reason would be that both monographs demonstrate, Blair more successfully than Pines, the ways we might understand domestic spaces and relationships in Woolf's reading and writing. Finally, both studies offer an opportunity to reflect on the place of feminism and feminist criticism in long nineteenth century and modernist studies today: Pines' work in its relative neglect of the issue, and Blair's work more explicitly in that the latter is deliberately and provocatively interrogating Woolf's foundational contribution to feminist literary criticism and canonization and the ways we as critics have followed Woolf's lead.

Through readings of *The Portrait of a Lady, The Good Soldier* and *Parade's End, Women in Love, Quicksand* and *Passing, Their Eyes Were Watching God*, and *Between the Acts*, Pines claims that modernist novels subvert the institution of marriage while ultimately reaffirming it. Positioning modernist novels of marriage within the context of "radical cultural change," namely movements towards marriage reform, the rise of sexology, and the legalization and growing incidence of divorce, Pines argues that these texts "offer a relentless critique of the marriage relationship and the social imperative to marry" while "paradoxically reinforc[ing] the marital norm" (3). If one looks at both the list of novels under study and the catalog of "radical cultural change," one might want to begin by questioning a major assumption Pines makes, a *donné* upon which the entire study rests: modernism is radical. Citing the usual suspects—Bradbury and McFarlane, Eysteinsson, Levenson—Pines makes the expected generalization that modernism "explodes tradition" (3). This manifests itself in the dual move to bring down socially sanctioned institutions like marriage, and to subvert culturally reified narratives like the marriage plot. This is not wrong or inaccurate, but it does seem to oversimplify the erotic and narrative impulses of the late nineteenth and early twentieth centuries into something resembling a *grand récit*. People's love lives, and the ways they tell their love stories, are always more complicated. For instance, Pines cites the marriage of Vita Sackville-West and Harold Nicolson as an example of modern(ist) marriage, a rejection of Victorian marriage mores: "For Sackville-West and Nicolson, then, marriage is a social, rather than a sexual, phenomenon" (94). It seems that this would be the case for thousands of couples over hundreds of years, and it does not necessarily indicate a subversion of the eminent Victorians.

More convincing and interesting is Blair's argument that Woolf's modernity was perpetually in dialogue/dialectic with the Victorians, especially around the fields of domestic space and relationships. This very sophisticated and elegant study (more so than its title would indicate) considers Woolf from numerous angles; one is reminded of Maria DiBattista's *Imagining Virginia Woolf* as Woolf's multiple writerly selves come into focus through the lens of private life and the demands placed on women in their various roles: writer, reader, mother, hostess, angel, spinster. Blair focalizes her consideration of her primary subject through teasing out a web of connections among Woolf, Elizabeth Gaskell, and Margaret Oliphant. The textual network includes Woolf's writing, notably *A Room of One's Own*, "Modern Fiction," "Mr. Bennett and Mrs. Brown," *Mrs. Dalloway* and *To the Lighthouse*, as well as her reviews; Gaskell's *Wives and Daughters*; Oliphant's *Miss Marjoribanks*; and numerous references to etiquette books, writings on hostessing, guides to interior decorating and entertaining, including the work of Mrs. Beeton, Sarah Stickney Ellis, not to mention Coventry Patmore and John Ruskin.

All of these intertexts contribute to a much deeper understanding of Woolf's ideas of nineteenth-century femininity and the women she was writing against. Blair takes as her starting point the idea that women write through their mothers, and then shows that Woolf had a very particular vision of that genealogy that did *not* include Gaskell and Oliphant, writers we have come to view as minor or marginal in contrast to those women writers Woolf elevates: Brontë, Austen, Eliot. Blair writes, "Woolf devalues the productive publishing career of Gaskell and Oliphant because of their apparent adherence to nineteenth-century models of womanly attainment by combining their domestic lives with their careers as writers" (15). Again and again, Blair shows how Woolf sought to construct a particular vision of domestic space and writing life that thwarted the prescriptions and professions of Beeton and Ellis, as manifested in Gaskell and Oliphant's fiction. Not only that, Woolf rejected the relationships that characterized such space as particularly feminine, namely motherhood. In thinking back through her mothers, these were not the mothers she had in mind, not bodily, but literary: not the fecundity of the mother Mrs. Oliphant but the creativity of the spinster Austen.

Because Pines does not take as broad a view of either Woolf's career or the forces at work in modernism, her reading of domestic life and relationships lacks the nuance or complexity of Blair's consideration; although, to be fair, because Blair only looks at *Mrs. Dalloway* and *To the Lighthouse* in any great depth as far as the novels go, we might miss how Woolf's ideas about domesticity and femininity changed over the course of her career: what would a Blairean reading of *The Years* look like? That work remains to be done, but Blair has certainly provided a model and a starting point. Pines only examines *Between the Acts*; this points to a weakness of the book overall, which is the selection of the novels under consideration. In order to make the point that modernist novels ultimately reaffirm the impulse to marry, Pines only chose modernist novels that have people getting married at the end. So, for instance, she argues that because at the end of *The Good Soldier* Leonora Ashburnham winds up remarrying after the adultery and suicide of her husband Edward, becoming the "happy wife of a perfectly normal, virtuous, and slightly-deceitful husband," the novel upholds the institution of marriage—as long as one approaches the endeavor with a level of irony which provides equipment for survival in the modern world. This would seem to miss the forest for the trees. Yes, the novel compromises the marriage plot, but one must overlook a great deal of what goes on in the novel, including its conclusion, to decide that *The Good Soldier* upholds marriage as an institution.

Similarly, one must overlook a great deal of Virginia Woolf's writing if one wants to argue that she is emblematic as a modernist writer validating and substantiating the impulse to marry. Blair actually provides an excellent counterreading to this in her analysis of Mrs. Ramsay in *To the Lighthouse*, focusing on that character's attempts to bring Paul Rayley and Minta Doyle together. Mrs. Ramsay becomes the ideal hostess, an embodiment of the etiquette that Woolf is calling into question as placing strictures on feminine life and space. Like Liesl Olson's recent *Modernism and the Ordinary*, which alludes to Woolf's comment from "A Sketch of the Past" that we require the "cotton wool of everyday life," Blair uncovers the tensions inherent in cultural change within the ordinary world of manners, clothes, and parties. The hostess is transformed into both mother and artist, conflating the roles Woolf is constantly negotiating in her own writing. Woolf draws upon the discourse of the domestic and transforms it in order to re-envision the woman writer.

Finally, Blair's study has serious implications for our understanding of Woolf's feminism, and for feminist literary criticism. A 2009 collection of essays edited by Annette Federico assessing the groundbreaking work of Sandra Gilbert and Susan Gubar, *Gilbert and Gubar's* The Madwoman in the Attic *after Thirty Years*, points to movements in the field around questions of canon and influence. The essay on Elizabeth Gaskell by Thomas Fair exemplifies some of the revisionist thinking of the collection—as well as the revisionist readings put forth by Blair of Woolf's matrilineal canon of writers. Fair argues that Gaskell was left out of Gilbert and Gubar's original reading because she wasn't angry enough (234). Blair similarly reclaims Gaskell for Woolf's canon by focusing on how both writers use the domestic as a "disruptive force" (73). The reconsideration of Woolf as reader and feminist in the context of a new way of understanding anxiety of influence—who made it into her genealogy and why, and what this says about a canon of women writers that is still evolving—could open new doors to new rooms.

— Janine Utell, *Widener University*

Works Cited

Corbett, Mary Jean. *Family Likeness: Sex, Marriage, and Incest from Jane Austen to Virginia Woolf*. Ithaca: Cornell UP, 2008. Print.

DiBattista, Maria. *Imagining Virginia Woolf: An Experiment in Critical Biography*. Princeton: Princeton UP, 2008. Print.

Ellis, Steve. *Virginia Woolf and the Victorians*. New York: Cambridge UP, 2007. Print.

Fair, Thomas P. "Elizabeth Gaskell: A Well-Tempered Madness." *Gilbert and Gubar's* The Madwoman in the Attic *after Thirty Years*. Ed. Annette R. Federico. Columbia: U of Missouri P, 2009. 217-236. Print.

Holton, Amanda. "Resistance, Regard, and Rewriting: Virginia Woolf and Anne Thackeray Ritchie." *English* 57 (2008): 42-64. Print.

Light, Alison. *Mrs. Woolf and the Servants: An Intimate History of Domestic Life in Bloomsbury*. New York: Bloomsbury, 2008. Print.

Olson, Liesl. *Modernism and the Ordinary*. New York: Oxford UP, 2009. Print.

Rosner, Victoria. *Modernism and the Architecture of Private Life*. New York: Columbia UP, 2005. Print.

———. "Virginia Woolf and Monk's House." *The Edinburgh Companion to Virginia Woolf and the Arts*. Ed. Maggie Humm. Edinburgh: Edinburgh UP, 2010. 181-194. Print.

Silver, Anna. *Victorian Literature and the Anorexic Body*. New York: Cambridge UP, 2002. Print.

A Room of Their Own: The Bloomsbury Artists in American Collections. Ed. Nancy E. Green and Christopher Reed (Ithaca: Herbert F. Johnson Museum of Art, Cornell U, 2008) 272 pp.

Beyond Bloomsbury: Designs of the Omega Workshops 1913-19. Ed. Alexandra Gerstein (London: Fontanka, 2009) 183 pp.

Two exhibitions in 2008-2009 on opposite sides of the Atlantic have produced two catalogues of particular interest to those exploring Woolf and the visual arts. *A Room of Their Own: The Bloomsbury Artists in American Collections* is the catalogue of a travelling exhibition of work by Bloomsbury artists now owned by American collectors, showcasing some well-known pieces held by museums and universities but also many hitherto unpublished works owned by private individuals not normally accessible to the general public. The exhibit focuses on Bloomsbury artists—Vanessa Bell, Dora Carrington, Roger Fry, and Duncan Grant are the chief figures represented—but ranges widely over a variety of media, including not only many paintings but also drawings and sketches, painted furniture, fabric designs, ceramics, small decorative objects, embroidery, and rugs, as well as woodcuts, book covers, actual books, and a selection of calendars, all accompanied by an apt selection of relevant photographs. *Beyond Bloomsbury: Designs of the Omega Workshops 1913-19* documents an impressive range of design drawings and Omega artifacts belonging to the Courtauld Gallery, the Victoria and Albert Museum, and other, mostly British, collections. Highlighting Vanessa Bell's work with Omega fashion and Duncan Grant's creation of theatrical designs as well as the contributions of under-acknowledged members of the Omega collaborative such as Winifred Gill, and non-Bloomsbury artists such as Henri Gaudier-Brzeska, the catalogue publishes designs for rugs, printed linens, tableware, vases, marquetry, lampstands, painted furniture, embroideries, painted screens, and theater backdrops; an appendix provides a complete pictorial inventory of Omega designs held by the Courtauld, including some fascinating sketches for full interiors, lamp shades, and toys.

Both catalogues are part of what Christopher Reed in his introduction to *Beyond Bloomsbury* calls the "broadening of 'art history'[. . .] into something often called 'visual culture'" (Gerstein 14), inaugurated by Reed in his *Bloomsbury Rooms: Modernism, Subculture, and Domesticity* (New Haven: Yale UP, 2004). Indeed Reed, who edited and wrote an important essay for one volume and the Introduction for the other, is frequently cited by contributors in both books. The two catalogues have similar formats: both present a series of short but highly informative essays on topics suggested by the collection of works in the exhibition, followed by a complete catalogue of the individual works in each show. The essays in the American volume are written by both art historians and literary specialists; those in the British are exclusively by highly specialized experts in the relevant media. Both volumes offer important and substantial contributions to the field, but the essays and works in *A Room of Their Own* will probably find a wider audience, especially in America, while *Beyond Bloomsbury* will appeal more to specialists in the history of British arts and crafts but is full of suggestive connections which might be mined by Bloomsbury scholars.

After the genial but general Introduction by Carrington biographer Gretchen Holbrook Gerzina, *A Room of Their Own* presents essays on Bloomsbury's Victorian inheritance by curator Nancy E. Green, a revision of an earlier essay on Woolf in America by Mark Hussey, an account of American collectors of Bloomsbury art by Christopher Reed, and an appreciation of Bloombsury's books and woodblocks by Benjamin Harvey. Refreshing for its integration of the visual arts into its overview of Bloomsbury's relation to its British past, Nancy Green's essay on Bloomsbury and the Victorians is a helpful supplement to more literary accounts of Woolf's inheritance such as those by S. P. Rosenbaum (1987) and Steve Ellis (2007). Green's discussions of the legacy of Julia Margaret Cameron, the wide range of influences on Roger Fry, the Stephen family's connections to the Victorian art world, as well as Duncan Grant's little-known pre-Raphaelite roots restore a sense of continuity with the immediate past often de-emphasized by studies which insist on Bloomsbury's Modernism.

Mark Hussey and Christopher Reed's essays offer complementary perspectives on Bloomsbury's American reception. Hussey's piece examines why Woolf has been so much more popular in America, showing how Leslie Stephen's "democratic sympathies" (48), aroused when he visited America, extended to his daughter and come full circle in American recognition of her feminist and political positions. The heart of the book is Reed's meticulously researched and carefully illustrated essay which explores how collectors of Bloomsbury art have influenced American critical perspectives on the group. This comprehensive history of Bloomsbury's reception in the U.S. begins by showing how attraction to the writings of Strachey, Woolf, Keynes, and Fry by American academics sparked the initial collections of Bloomsbury art, which was at first largely ignored by art museums and galleries. Pride of place justly goes to Duke University where English professor Charles Richard Saunders, who wrote two books on the Stracheys, became acquainted with Duncan Grant and purchased more than a dozen pieces by Grant and Vanessa Bell. When Saunders' daughter Nancy married Duke economics professor Crauford Goodwin, his encouragement that the young couple begin buying Bloomsbury art led to the accumulation of what Reed calls "the most comprehensive" collection of Bloomsbury art in America (80), a primary inspiration and source for the entire exhibition. (At the Duke Alumni weekend where the travelling show was premiered, it was announced that plans were afoot eventually to turn the Goodwins' home near the Duke campus into a museum, so sometime in the future this major private collection can be made available to the public.)

Reed's recounting of the further phases of Bloomsbury collecting in America is full of fascinating tidbits and insights. In the late sixties, partially incited by the revelations in Michael Holroyd's biography of Lytton Strachey, Bloomsbury began to appeal as an exemplar of a more liberal political and sexual ethos, arousing interest among both feminist academics (Carolyn Heilbrun's PhD dissertation was on the Garnett family), and gay men who took Duncan Grant as a model for healthy self-acceptance. Reed also uncovers a little known corner of Bloomsbury history completely at odds with the liberal fascination by recording the contributions of Lila Acheson Wallace to the development of a Bloomsbury heritage. (Who knew that the largest collection of Bloomsbury paintings in America in 1987 was owned by *Reader's Digest*?) Charting the ways in which Americans' personal identification with the iconoclasm and self-invention of the Bloomsbury group was facilitated by an academic openness to interdisciplinary scholarship, Reed is able to further explicate some of the foundational reasons for fascination with Bloomsbury and with Virginia Woolf in the United States.

An essay about visual design by a literary critic, the last essay in the book complements the opening one by an art historian. After some helpful notes as to the importance of Woolf's books as a means of exposing American audiences to Bloomsbury arts through the dust jackets designed by Vanessa Bell, Benjamin Harvey spends the bulk of his essay in detailed readings of the early illustrated works of Virginia Woolf as visual objects. Beginning by locating Bloomsbury interest in woodcuts in the contemporary context of Post-Impressionism, Harvey interprets Fry's aesthetics of illustration to provide a theoretical context for balancing semantic, visual, and physical elements. He then builds on the germinal work of Diane Gillespie in *The Sisters' Arts* (which he scrupulously footnotes) to provide careful analyses of the various visual versions of "Kew Gardens," "The Mark on the Wall," and *Monday or Tuesday*. The richly suggestive observations on the sequencing of stories and illustrations for *Monday or Tuesday* in particular make one long for a facsimile edition (the inexpensive Dover edition does preserve the original order in which the stories were printed).

Like many scholars before him, Harvey speaks of the illustrations to the 1927 edition of *Kew Gardens* vaguely as woodcuts. And while his analysis of what these visual designs can contribute to our reading/experiencing of Woolf's story is enlightening and useful, I would like to raise a technical question as to the exact medium of the decorations. My fifteen years' experience as a maker of woodcuts suggests that the forms are exceedingly inappropriate for woodcut—about the hardest thing in the world to do in woodcut is simple circular lines; the grain of the wood is always pulling against the curve. In addition, having done some incorporation of woodcut into offset printing, I believe the designs of the pages would be quite difficult if not impossible to pull off with woodcut. Everything has to be exactly "type-high" for the printing to work, so it would have been impossible to set the type inside the woodcuts. I've always thought that the illustrations looked like they'd been done in ink, in a manner that at times suggests woodcuts but is similar to Bell's cover designs. Jeremy Greenwood says, in *Omega Cuts* (1998), which is pretty definitive on wood and linoleum cuts, that after the five blocks Vanessa cut for the Hogarth Press in 1921 (the cover plus illustrations for *Monday or Tuesday*), "all her decorations and dustwrappers for [the press] were drawings reproduced by commercial line blocks" (25n2). He shows a lino cut from some time in the 1950s (35), but does not show any of the covers or illustrations for the 1927 edition as being woodcuts. I would also add that the fineness of line in the 1927 edition is quite different from the relatively primitive carving done in the earlier woodcuts and later lino, and would only have been achievable with *lots* more practice and a bunch of new, much finer and sharper tools.

Comprising more than half the volume, the Catalogue of Works is a treasure trove of hitherto unpublished items, many from private collections. The sheer effort required to gather together all these works—surely the largest and most varied collection of Bloomsbury art ever exhibited together at one time—is astonishing. There are well-known pieces from public collections such as the Metropolitan, MOMA, and New York Public Library's Berg Collection, and academic institutions such as Yale, Cornell, and Smith College, but many of the creations, such as Duncan Grant's magnificent decorative panel designs for the Queen Mary (1936), have never been published before. I counted about a half-dozen pieces which had previously been included in Tony Bradshaw's *A Bloomsbury Canvas*, another three from his *The Bloomsbury Artists: Prints and Book Designs*, and three more well-known paintings included in Shone's *The Art of Bloomsbury*, as well as twenty or so book-related designs that have been frequently published; but considering that there are 200 items in all, more than half the collection will be new to most viewers. The catalogue is organized, as is so much about this volume, with a genial practicality, being divided into approximately three sections—paintings and drawing, decorative arts, and book arts—each of which is organized alphabetically, with each artist's work being displayed in chronological order. Since every item of the 200 is pictured, photos are necessarily rather small. But the quality of reproduction throughout is quite good—given the caveat that no print reproduction is ever capable of capturing the variety of tones in an actual work. I carried my copy of the catalogue around the exhibition, making notes on color corrections and found only an occasional slight darkness, but hardly any of the usual tendency to over-yellow or over-blue tints.

As a collection of drawings for objects to be produced by the Omega Workshop, *Beyond Bloomsbury* has a far more specialized subject-matter and is typical of British responses to Bloomsbury in its primarily art historical focus and in its interest in placing Omega in the history of British arts and crafts. Virginia Woolf is mentioned only in passing, particularly as a purchaser of Omega clothing. The volume has more but shorter essays than its American counterpart, the first four being authored by specialists in art history: freelance author of eighteen books on textile and wallpaper means of production and reproduction Mary Schoeser on Omega textiles; Research Fellow in Ceramics and Theory at Camberwell College of the Arts in London, the Royal College of Art, Julian Stair on pottery; Research Coordinator of the Henry Moore Institute and author of *The Sculpture Reader* Jon Wood on sculpture and Henri Gaudier-Brzeska; co-editor of the forthcoming *Cultures of Femininity in Modern Fashion* Elizabeth Sheehan on dressmaking; and French art and theater historian Claudette Joannis on theatrical textiles. The final two essays are more general discussions of Roger Fry's pacifism and its connections to publishing and performance arts in World War I by Grace Brockington, author of *Above the Battlefield: British Modernism and the Peace Movement, 1900–1918* (New Haven: Yale University Press, 2010), and Roger Fry's efforts to form artistic communities during and beyond the organizing of the Omega group by Akiko Kato.

While those interested in Woolf and her immediate circle will find the articles on theater textiles and dressmaking at the Omega most relevant to their concerns, the catalogue as a whole is fascinating for the dense web of interconnections it reveals between Bloomsbury and other avant garde organizations in the UK and abroad such as the Deutsche Werkbund, the Wiener Werkstatte, and the Atelier of Paul Pioret. There is a good deal of attention to the specific techniques used in getting Omega objects made—a subject on which Roger Fry tended to be rather vague—and a thoroughgoing explication of the Omega style, the preference for artistic expression over fine finish. Especially rewarding are the lengthy entries on particular items in the catalogue itself, where design drawings are grouped whenever possible with the actual manufactured objects. Long and informative summaries head the sections on rug designs, printed linens, and tableware. Aside from the eighty-nine objects featured in the actual exhibition, there is a comprehensive appendix with color thumbnails of seventy-two other drawings held by the Courtauld Institute, making this the definitive collection of Omega design.

— Elisa Kay Sparks, *Clemson University*

Food and Femininity in Twentieth-Century British Women's Fiction. Andrea Adolph (Burlington, VT: Ashgate, 2009) viii + 183 pp.

Some pity, please, for *Mrs. Dalloway*'s Miss Kilman, a creature of the intellect ("her knowledge of modern history was thorough in the extreme") betrayed by "her unlovable body." Although Miss Kilman does "a little Extension lecturing and so on," her academic profession has been largely derailed by her high-minded German sympathies, now channeled into religious fervor. But try as she might to "control" the flesh in favor of the spirit, Miss Kilman's relationship with food gives her away: "Miss Kilman opened her mouth, projected her chin, and swallowed down the last inches of the chocolate éclair." The intensity and jealousy with which Doris Kilman devours her tea tells us everything we need to know about this character: how hungry she is to wrest Elizabeth Dalloway from her mother Clarissa, how bitterly she feels her social marginalization, and how "split asunder" she is by the duality of mind and matter. Try as she might to deny the body in favor of the eternal soul, Miss Kilman is quite literally hemmed in by matter, tripping over "all the commodities of the world" in the Army and Navy stores.

There's something coded as unattractive, even suspect, about a woman eating so greedily in public, an internalized cultural taboo that novelists call upon to signify a less than sympathetic character, as Andrea Adolph suggests in *Food and Femininity in Twentieth Century British Women's Fiction*, using Mrs. Manresa from *Between the Acts* as a primary Woolfian example: Mrs. Manresa's vigorous appetite for food—and by extension sex—parallels an upwardly mobile class status at odds with the more ethereal, and to the manor born, Isa Oliver. Andrea Adolph's work on the negative representation of eating and "consuming women" in Woolf has been published elsewhere, playing a small (or "thin," to use Adolph's term) yet significant role in this full-length monograph. The post-war British writers she examines here (Lorna Sage, Barbara Pym, Helen Dunmore,

Angela Carter, Rachel Cusk, and Helen Fielding) are all women writers who must inevitably think back through Virginia Woolf in their own fictional representations of women's domestic lives. And so Woolf's presence, and her own ambivalent relationship with food, haunts this study, with its broader focus on the mind-body binary as filtered through food preparation and consumption.

The ultimate mission of *Food and Femininity* is no less than a reconciliation of mind and body; the internalized, psychological violence that Miss Kilman suffers is representative of how this split hurts us. If western philosophy has traditionally denigrated the body, treating it as a mere vehicle for the mind, then the ongoing project to reintegrate the two is a critical step towards re-evaluating the human system as a *gestalt*. Adolph's project thus takes its place as a part of the broader, interdisciplinary field of post-human studies: what does it mean to be "human" in the twenty-first century? While I'm not convinced that this book arrives at any definitive metaphysical answers, this inconclusiveness is appropriate given Adolph's literary focus: while the writers analyzed here each wrestle with the mind-body problem, none comes close to resolving it. Nonetheless, *Food and Femininity* offers lucid and often brilliant readings of these novels generated by Woolf's "daughters," novels that track the struggle, ambivalence, and noble failures of women writers to merge body and mind. From the standpoint of feminism and literary criticism, Adolph's book is a useful and intriguing contribution to an ongoing struggle.

One of Adolph's key analytic terms to describe the problem that mind/body dualism presents us is "auto-objectification," which refers to the way that women objectify their own bodies through internalizing cultural prescriptions for female subjects: the mind, in a sense, objectifies the body, viewing it as "an object to shape and bend at will" (19). Beauty magazines and housekeeping manuals are examples of the "maintenance literature" that codifies this regimentation of the unruly body, and Adolph devotes a full chapter to the rhetoric of control and conformity that a century's worth of these texts have prescribed to an audience of (primarily) women readers. Adolph makes an important connection between housekeeping and bodily maintenance when she suggests that both types of manuals locate "matter out of place" (Mary Douglas's term) as the thing to be controlled: whether the matter is dirt, fat, or unsightly facial hairs, an excess of matter is seen as a moral failing. Maintaining a house is therefore like maintaining a body; the preparation and consumption of food is central to both and both are seen as the especial province of women. Such safeguarding and control of bodies and households was particularly important during World War II, on the so-called "Kitchen Front," where the duty of maintaining the health of the home, the family, and by extension the nation itself, fell to women. Adolph's wonderful discussion of food rationing in Britain in the 1940s shows how wartime actually re-prioritizes material life, once the state intervenes in the private sphere of the kitchen: "Refuse second helpings of other foods until you've had more potatoes" (70), as the Ministry of Food instructs housewives. Eating greedily in wartime is something more than a moral failing: it is an act of treason.

Adolph adopts Michel de Certeau's notion of "tactical acts" to show how social regimentation can be subverted through small acts of consumption; a World War Two era housewife who "makes do" with potatoes and fish paste exhibits a kind of creative agency that challenges the governmental regimentation of her kitchen. While this point wasn't convincing to me in this context (the cooking ingredients are still rationed by the state), Adolph's argument strengthens once it turns towards fiction. In her reading of Barbara Pym's 1953 *Jane and Prudence*, Adolph shows how Pym challenges the austerity culture of post-war Britain (rationing didn't end until 1954) by creating two female characters, who despite very different attitudes towards food, challenge the prescriptive dualism of mind and body. Prudence, the single career woman, accentuates her glamor by putting garlic on her salad and eating soft cheese; yet despite the sophistication and romance such ingredients are seen to imply, Prudence steadfastly remains single. Meanwhile Jane, the vicar's wife, doesn't cook at all; she opens tins, refusing the role of caretaker in a subtle act of subversion. Through their friendship, both characters offer more complex amalgamations of embodied mind and mindful body than appear on the surface.

Adolph's dual reading of Helen Dunmore's *Talking to the Dead* (1996) and Angela Carter's *The Magic Toyshop* (1967) is a virtuoso performance of literary criticism. Proposing a model of reading we might call "two texts, fat and thin," Adolph locates in both novels an interchange between a more obvious manifest narrative (the "fat") and a latent, transgressive ("thin") narrative, each of which is associated with a female character defined in part by her relationship with food and/or embodiment. In *The Magic Toyshop* this works by pairing the ripening adolescent Melanie against her etherealized and mute Aunt Margaret: the reader inevitably focuses on the gothic threats to Melanie's virginity sustained in her Uncle Philip's puppet shop, while ignoring or missing Margaret's covert incest narrative. Similarly, in *Talking to the Dead*, the very embodied Nina—who eats croissants and butter with the same passion with which she beds her sister Isabel's husband—distracts the reader from Isabel's buried crime, legible to us (if only we knew how to read it) through her anorexic and failing body. It wouldn't be possible to do justice to Adolph's reading here, but suffice it to say that Adolph effectively structures built-in suspense into her argument, making this chapter a page-turner of sorts—even for readers who haven't read Dunmore's novel.

Nonetheless, this chapter was also where I found myself disagreeing the most with Adolph. Seeking scientific evidence for a more holistic model of body/mind integration, Adolph imports the term "body image" from Paul Schilder, an Austrian neuropsychologist who used the term in his 1935 *The Image and Appearance of the Human Body*. For Schilder, body image means something like an "intellectual projection of the physical body" (3), a third term that functions as a synthesis of body and mind. Adolph uses this concept as the foundation for a model of embodied reading by arguing that "represented embodiment within the text is itself a referent for the body of the reader" (134); for Adolph, it seems that the text and the reader merge most successfully together when a character eats, providing "the means for readerly immersion in familiar perspective" (135). Adolph's reader is apparently some universal human subject, who must eat to live. But not everyone eats the same way, or eats the same foods, or has enough to eat, and so I found this generalized, universal notion of a consuming reader problematic in the extreme, which was particularly evident in Adolph's analysis of a sex scene between greedy, sensual Nina and her sister's husband Richard. Will every reader "whose physical bodies have engaged in similar activities [. . .] have the ability to comprehend the scene through their body-based knowledge" (143)? Would a male reader, a lesbian reader, a disabled reader, or a virginal reader identify with Nina's motility and body image in the same way? If readerly identification is based on shared experience, then it would seem that many readers would be entirely shut out of Nina's narrative experience.

While I am not convinced by Adolph's embodied reader (given the bodily stasis of most reading experiences, I kept thinking that Samuel Beckett might have invented the best reader-character analogue in *The Unnamable*), I am sure that Adolph would have an answer to this objection in discussion, and so I raise it primarily to demonstrate the generative potential of her argument as a part of a larger debate about "being human." As an act of literary criticism, *Food and Femininity* is "a whiff of shot in the cause of freedom," a solid and engaging approach towards locating a more holistic union of mind and body in British women's fiction.

— Catherine W. Hollis, *UC Berkeley Extension*

Approaches to Teaching Woolf's Mrs. Dalloway. Eds. Eileen Barrett and Ruth Saxton (New York: Modern Language Association, 2009) vii + 167pp.

Those with much experience teaching Woolf's work will join those thinking of teaching it for the first time in welcoming the MLA's publication of *Approaches to Teaching Woolf's* Mrs. Dalloway. Editors Eileen Barrett and Ruth Saxton have done an exemplary job of providing Woolfians and non-Woolfians alike with a pedagogical sourcebook for this novel we teach with love and sometimes with difficulty.

Much excellent scholarship has been written on *Mrs. Dalloway*, so the task of directing teachers to the best sources cannot have been an easy one. In her Introduction, Eileen Barrett recommends those works on *Mrs. Dalloway* and on Woolf generally that are widely recognized by Woolf scholars, then also notes the main argument of lesser-known works that might prove useful to some. The subsections on "Editions," "London Maps and Walks," and "Reference Works" will prove particularly welcome to those not heavily steeped in Woolf scholarship.

Based on the responses to surveys of teachers and students, Saxton and Barrett chose to divide the book into four sections: "Approaching a Modernist Text," "Using the Context of War," "Reading Intertextually," and "Teaching in Multiple Settings." Ruth Saxton's short explanation of the reasons for those choices and her short summaries of the essays contained in each section provide an excellent thumbnail sketch of the volume as a whole.

The volume contains twenty essays, but reviews demand brevity, so in what follows I briefly gloss the main thrust of each of the four sections and then discuss at a bit more length a favorite essay or two in each section. Others will find their own favorites based on their own interests. If my favorites share a common thread, it is a thoughtful attention to the needs and experience of students.

The most frequently cited concern in the volume as a whole is how to help students approach the *difficulty* of *Mrs. Dalloway*: It is a difficult novel to teach because it is difficult for students to understand for so many reasons. That concern is central to the essays in the "Approaching a Modernist Text" section. These authors all take quite different approaches, and so I have two favorites, with two very different approaches.

My favorite essay in the volume, Victoria Rosner's "'Life Struck Straight through the Streets': *Mrs. Dalloway* as City Novel," combines practical pedagogy with a truly insightful multi-layered reading of the structure of the novel through Woolf's structuring of city (and other) spaces. Rosner explains that "the city threads through the novel on many levels; [. . .] all its major themes are articulated in relation to its metropolitan context. Further, many of the experimental modernist techniques of the novel that students can find difficult to grasp, such as its narrative organization, snap into clarity when examined in terms of the novel's urban milieu" (39). Rosner explains that she teaches the novel in three seventy-five minute class periods which focus on "urban time and temporal structures, comparative discourses of modernist urbanism, and the experience of space in the city" (39). Her third-day discussion ends, intriguingly, with a comparison of the novel's interest in the metropolis with its engagement with two other spaces: the "distant world of the British Empire and the pastoral world of Bourton, Clarissa's childhood home" (42). An intellectually sophisticated and theoretically complex understanding of the novel emerges for students via Rosner's carefully constructed and clearly explained interpretive strategies. Class discussions are initiated or enriched by students' having read "early-twentieth-century essays about urban life," by researched student oral presentations, and by a stroll through David Dowling's maps of the characters' perambulations through London. Rosner's descriptions of her praxis enliven her discussion of the ways her students come to create meaning themselves, and her map for meaning-making will help others keep their own students on track to construct something comprehensible to them.

More heavily weighted towards the pedagogical, Nick Smart's "On Not Knowing Woolf" describes a pedagogy of "unknowing" for teaching *Mrs. Dalloway*—one which enlists Woolf herself (in her essay "On Not Knowing Greek") as a practitioner. Recognizing the challenge students face when first encountering this difficult text—how little they feel they know as they try to make sense of it—Smart decenters his authority as professor and enlists students self-consciously in the production of their own knowledge of the novel. On a practical level, this means everything from introducing them to the work of Pater and Joyce to taking them on a field trip in nearby Manhattan where they practice flânerie as modernist aesthetic. What individual students learn about the novel depends on exactly how "they have participated in the creation of its unexpected beauty" (48). Smart contends that his pedagogy "helps [students] develop a learning strategy they will be able to use [. . .] whenever the knowing gets rough" (48). And that is my favorite *line* in the volume.

Those who would like to teach *Mrs. Dalloway* as a war novel will find the essays in the section "Using the Context of War" most helpful. Among these, two stand out: Meg Albrinck's "'Are *YOU* in This?': Using British Recruiting Posters to Teach *Mrs. Dalloway*" does just that. Albrinck carefully describes not only how she uses World War I British recruiting posters to teach the novel, but also exactly where to find these posters and what to do with them pedagogically on a step-by-step basis. Students in her class surely enjoy a rich experience imagining a time when these posters would have compelled young men to join the military and women to shame men who did not. Such a course decenters *Mrs. Dalloway* itself in favor of that understanding of wartime nationalist ideology, but that might be exactly the way some would prefer to use the novel.

In "Women and War in *Mrs. Dalloway*," Anne Fernald provides the reader with useful textual source material—fictional and nonfictional, primary and secondary sources—for teaching women's experience of World War I through the lens of the novel. Fernald explains that "[a]pproaching *Mrs. Dalloway* as a war novel decenters some common assumptions: that war is mainly about battles, that women do not write on war, and that war is more important than its aftermath. I want students to think deeply about how war reverberates beyond the battlefield and to appreciate a novel even when it depicts a world alien to their own" (71). And indeed, the essay testifies to Fernald's concern for her students, whose specific needs and generational difficulties (hers are undergraduates at the Lincoln Center campus of Fordham University) she seems well in touch with and addresses specifically throughout the essay.

In the "Reading Intertextually" section, Mary Beth Pringle's essay "Reading at the Intersections: Teaching *Mrs. Dalloway* in a Class on Retellings" is exemplary for the way it walks the reader class by class through a six-week summer course that asks students to read Joyce's *Ulysses* as (Harold) Bloomian "misprisioning" or misreading of Homer's *Odyssey*, then *Mrs. Dalloway* as a retelling of Joyce's *Ulysses*, then Cunningham's *The Hours* as misprisioning of *Mrs. Dalloway*, and finally Kitchen's *The House on Eccles Road* as misreading of *Ulysses*. Pringle's care for and engagement with her students and the obvious value she places on their personal insights make the essay especially valuable and pleasurable to read. In spite of not being much of a fan of Harold Bloom, after reading this essay I felt a strong urge to try teaching *Mrs. Dalloway* contextualized exactly this way myself; with Pringle's carefully laid out guide, a person could in fact teach *exactly* this course.

The essays collected in the "Teaching in Multiple Settings" section are more difficult to choose favorites among, since they each focus on quite specific student demographics: students at a two-year liberal arts college in the Midwest, students at a women's prison, students at a historically black women's college, students in a Literary Masterworks general elective course, students in an Integrative Studies composition and literature course at a private liberal arts college, and—perhaps most intriguingly—physicians and their partners at a weekend Literature and Medicine Reading Retreat. It seems likely to me that those teaching the novel would find these essays useful if their own students happen to meet the demographic of these professors' students. However, many teach general education or integrative studies type courses, so might find

Hoberman's or Daugherty's essays useful. The problem of approaching students' aversion to the stylistic difficulty of the novel is far from limited to two-year college students, so McLeer's essay might be useful to many. Homophobic reactions to the novel are not at all limited to young African-American women; Sizemore's method for dealing with that problem might spark similar ideas for others. Finally, Eads' and Childress's essays are just plain fun to read due to the unusual pedagogical situation, in which most of us will never find ourselves.

What Barrett and Saxton have chosen to include in this volume seems to me admirable and pedagogically useful. The single fault I find with the volume as a whole is one of omission. Because issues revolving around gender, sexuality, and same-sex desires are so central to the novel, so complex, and, for some teachers, so difficult to address in the classroom, a section titled something like "Foregrounding Gender and Sexuality" was warranted and would have been useful. It is surprising and unfortunate not to find one. Further, in the "Feminist, Lesbian, and Queer" subsection of her otherwise comprehensive and inclusive Introduction, Barrett all but omits queer studies of Woolf, so those wanting to teach the novel as a queer work (rather than a lesbian one) will have to look elsewhere for help. Here Barrett mentions only two queer studies of the novel, one of which is an extremely short essay published only in the ninth annual Woolf conference proceedings, which Barrett tellingly pairs with a lesbian-feminist rebuttal of its argument (published in those same proceedings). By contrast, she lists three lesbian-feminist books and four lesbian-feminist essays. A very simple MLA International Bibliography search turns up several queer studies of the novel, including four published in the Fall 2006 *Virginia Woolf Miscellany*, a special issue on deviancy in Woolf's work which many Woolf scholars have on their shelves. The only essay in the *Approaches* to address the novel's themes of homoeroticism in a sustained manner is Christine Sizemore's fascinating "Overcoming Resistance to Lesbian Readings of *Mrs. Dalloway*," which discusses the ways she teaches *Mrs. Dalloway* as a lesbian novel to students whose homophobia is based in a particular racial identification. The rich possibilities for teaching the novel's queer explorations of the same-sex desires of what Woolf in "Modern Fiction" called "an ordinary mind on an ordinary day" (*CR* 149)—the most cited phrase in this volume—and/or teaching students who might resist a lesbian-feminist interpretation for non-homophobic reasons are omitted from the book. The omission of extant queer scholarship appears as a political choice, one that seems at odds with the purpose of the MLA Approaches to Teaching series.

In conclusion, for those who read book reviews to determine whether to read or buy the book, the simple answer is "yes." Reading *Approaches to Teaching Woolf's* Mrs. Dalloway felt like sitting at home in a comfy chair bandying about ideas for teaching the novel with others who love teaching it as much as I do. I feel I now have considerably more tools in my pedagogical toolbox for doing that.

— Brenda S. Helt, *Metropolitan State University*

Works Cited

Dowling, David. Mrs. Dalloway: *Mapping Streams of Consciousness*. Boston: Twayne, 1991. Print.

Woolf, Virginia. "Modern Fiction." *The Common Reader: First Series*. Ed. Andrew McNeillie. San Diego: Harcourt, 1984. 146-54. Print.

Virginia Woolf's Mrs. Dalloway*: Invisible Presences*. Molly Hoff (Clemson, SC: Clemson U Digital P, 2009) x + 286 pp.

Molly Hoff's *Virginia Woolf's* Mrs. Dalloway: *Invisible Presences*, purports to do for *Mrs. Dalloway* what Don Gifford's Ulysses *Annotated* does for Joyce's *Ulysses*. Like Gifford's indispensable volume, Hoff's book of annotations offers lengthy glosses on all the proper names, allusions, and historical references within the novel. But where Gifford's book remains a reliable and useful aid for anyone reading Joyce, Hoff's deeply flawed volume seems destined to remain little more than a curiosity.

There are so many serious flaws with this work that it is difficult to know how it came to be published. Typographic and spelling errors abound. Many sentences have a random period printed between words in lieu of a space. One annotation refers to a diagram that is not in the book. Equally disconcerting are problems that suggest the book thoroughly fails to understand either its project or its audience. The back cover promises "a useful introduction" to *Mrs. Dalloway*, but books of annotations are not useful introductions in the way that an excellent plot summary can be; books of annotations are guides for students and avid readers. Furthermore, the claim that *Mrs. Dalloway* is "an often misunderstood novel," while likely true enough, is, without supporting evidence of rampant critical folly, merely an occasion for the author to put herself forward as possessing a better understanding than most. Such judgments are not for authors to make about themselves.

The "Note on the Text" (x) further indicates some of the difficulties that will face any reader of Hoff's book. Annotations are keyed to the American editions of

1925 and 1990. Hoff gives no reason for preferring the 1925 American edition to the British edition by Hogarth and, in fact, both G. Patton Wright and Morris Beja, each of whom did textual editions of *Mrs. Dalloway*, argue that the first English edition is generally to be preferred. The Harcourt paperback of 1990 was the most widely available version of *Mrs. Dalloway* in the U.S. for many years, but Hoff should have supplanted the 1990 page numbers with those of Bonnie Kime Scott's 2005 annotated edition, which is now the standard text for American students.

In spite of organizing the book to emphasize its section breaks, this study ultimately treats them in a cursory way. Woolf divided the novel not into numbered chapters but into sections, indicated by a single blank line (or, as Hoff somewhat perplexingly explains, sections "set off with vertical spacing" [x]). Less widely known is that the first British edition has twelve sections while the first American edition has only eight (Wright 248). More recent American editions have corrected this problem, but for Hoff's book to assume the mantle of authoritative guide to *Mrs. Dalloway*, it needs to account for significant variants in the textual history such as these. Moreover, as readers, we deserve more. A critic wishing to call our attention more directly to the sections as sections might offer, as Hoff does not, an argument for their significance. For example, the fact of twelve sections in itself seems a significant number for a novel that, in draft, was called *The Hours*, especially as section nine begins with the phrase "It was precisely twelve o'clock," on page 142, just about half way through the 293-page book.

What does it mean to undertake this project of annotating *Mrs. Dalloway*? For whom might such a book be useful? The project of annotating Woolf differs from that of annotating other highly allusive modernists. Whereas a casual reader of *The Waste Land* will immediately see that she has before her a collage of quotations, allusions in *Mrs. Dalloway* are often buried so deeply that the reader can read on, unaware that she has missed an intertextual echo. In this way, *Mrs. Dalloway* may be more like a Balzac novella than Joyce's *Ulysses*. Which is to say that the audience for a book of annotations may be small. But Hoff's book never seems quite sure of which audience it imagines. Geographic referents are glossed informatively, as if to a student, but literary references are swift, and a reference to a long text will seldom quote the resonant passage, as if we might remember, offhand, a specific moment in *Major Barbara* or one of Horace's odes.

Perhaps Roland Barthes' 1970 masterpiece *S/Z* might have served Hoff as a model for the kind of annotation that most interests her. *S/Z* reprints Balzac's *Sarrasine* as the appendix to a book of annotations many times the novella's length. Barthes' starred text divides the novella of thirty-four pages into 561 fragments, and annotates them according to "the five notorious codes (hermeneutic, semantic, proairetic, cultural, and symbolic)" (x). Amidst the annotations are dozens of brief essays on topics such as voice, the braiding of meaning amongst the codes, and interpretation itself. While few of us could hope to approach Barthes's genius, *S/Z* does exist as another possible model for Hoff's text, and, had she followed it and grouped her observations together more intentionally, some of her genuinely exciting and provocative insights might have emerged more persuasively.

Take, for example, Hoff's sense that the story of *Mrs. Dalloway* rewrites the story of Alcestis. At different moments, Hoff refers to versions of Alcestis' story by Euripides, Chaucer, Gower, and Molière; there are over forty references to Alcestis in the index. However, the first annotation to mention it is oblique, linking Mrs. Foxcroft and Lady Bexborough's stoicism to classical Stoics and Alcestis herself to Christ (18-19). While both of these pairings may have merit, juxtaposing them does not prove a link between Alcestis and *Mrs. Dalloway*. However stoically Alcestis may behave in our common usage of the term, she is not a Stoic in the Classical sense, nor are Woolf's aristocratic women. Moreover, without a reminder of the story, how can we begin to see the deep structural similarities between the texts?

However, to read Euripides' version of the story, as I did, is to see why Hoff perceives a connection. *Alcestis* tells the story of Alcestis, the wife of Admetus, a feckless *bon vivant*. Admetus has, long before the play begins, gotten the Fates drunk and persuaded them to spare his life; they impose the condition that he must find another to take his place when the time of death comes. Where many others refuse Admetus' request, his wife Alcestis agrees to sacrifice herself. On the day of her death, the demigod Heracles visits Admetus, and Admetus, in spite of his dawning grief at what he has done, hosts Heracles with grace. In thanks for his hospitality and in recognition of Alcestis' extraordinary merit, Heracles goes to the underworld and brings Alcestis back.

As an intertext for *Mrs. Dalloway*, this story of a worthy young person, willingly dying early for the benefit of a good but shallow host has some promise. Is not Septimus, in his soldiering and his suicide, like the worthy Alcestis? And might not Clarissa resemble the sweet but shallow Admetus? And is it not like Woolf to switch the sexes of the old story? Woolf must have known the play; Gilbert Murray's 1915 translation includes an introduction that emphasizes the unusual strength of the heroine as well as Euripides' apparent sympathy with Admetus, both elements of the play that would have appealed to Woolf. But did Woolf read or comment on *Alcestis*? Hoff does not tell us. Furthermore, confusingly, she writes, "Clarissa takes the role of the beneficiary, her husband the famous host" (247). In *Alcestis*, host and beneficiary are one; in *Mrs. Dalloway*, Clarissa—not Richard—is the famous host. To add to the tangle, after learning of Septimus's death, Clarissa thinks about her contentment in marriage, which Hoff glosses thus: "it seems that Richard gets the credit for what Heracles had done" (232). Thus, Richard is linked to both Admetus and Heracles. But, as an uninvited guest, Sally would be the more likely Heraclean figure. However, it is death itself that has come uninvited to a scheduled party, a very different situation from the one in *Alcestis*. None of this makes good sense nor is it good scholarship. And yet, there may be merit in the juxtaposition. Gilbert Murray's judgment of Admetus as "a man who blinded himself with words and beautiful sentiments" and Heracles' comment "'Tis great turmoil when a guest comes to a mourning house" both resonate in rich ways with Clarissa's character and her distress at learning of Septimus's death. Considering *Alcestis* and subsequent versions as possible intertexts holds promise. Still, for all the thematic resonances, this reader did not hear any direct allusions to Euripides within Woolf's novel.

The flaws with the annotations themselves (the bulk of the book), the brief introduction, the afterword, and appendices are no less grave. This is in part because the annotations at one and the same time identify textual allusions and offer eccentric but illuminating insights. Hoff comes to *Mrs. Dalloway*, as we all must, with her own canon and the allusions she detects within the novel, while occasionally brilliant, continually display the lack of congruence between Hoff's reading and what we know Woolf to have read. Vast as Woolf's reading was, a scholar needs to work to document the textual echoes—through letters and diaries, notebook entries, and lists of books owned—to the actual books that we know Woolf to have read. For example, Hoff detects multiple allusions to Ovid, a writer Woolf almost certainly read, but one seldom mentioned by her. This is not to say that there are not allusions to Ovid in *Mrs. Dalloway*, only that it seems unlikely that there are dozens of them.

Many annotations also direct our attention to a small set of techniques and motifs that matter to the author, if not to Woolf. Hoff identifies dozens of instances of free indirect discourse in the text (which she—to this reader's great confusion—abbreviates as FID) without fully explaining the technique's significance, either in 1925 or today. She also finds multiple examples of the *Lebenstreppe*, or staircase of life, motif as well as that of the Ship of Fools. I know of no instances of Woolf mentioning either, nor am I persuaded that either offers significant new insight into the novel.

Other annotations seem to have confusing logical priorities. Hoff annotates "Her heart, affected, they said by influenza" starting with "'Influenza' is Italian for 'influence'" (16), a *non sequitur*. Only half way through the paragraph does she mention the 1918 influenza epidemic, but without clarifying that Clarissa seems to have been afflicted during this time, or that Peter, having left for India in 1918, had missed the epidemic and its aging affects on Clarissa. Elsewhere, she is inspired. To link "the leaden circles dissolved in the air" to "Milton's 'On Time': 'the leaden-stepping hours'" (16) and to show that Septimus's being "unable to pass" echoes the "Verdun motto in the Great War, 'Ils ne passeront pas'" (43) is to deepen our sense of those moments.

In the Afterword, Hoff claims that the novel's characters "are ironically endowed with the immortals of Greek myths who [in turn] mirror human moral character" (245); it is confusing to then be rocketed into Hoff's own rapid fire allusions to Shakespeare and the Wizard of Oz as we are here: "like the god of the creation ('what fools these mortals be'), is the sententious narrator who is clearly the scrupulously anonymous wizard behind the curtain" (245). Likening a narrator, in one sentence, to Zeus, Puck, and the Wizard of Oz is too much. The narrator of *Mrs. Dalloway*, far less obtrusive than that of *Jacob's Room* or *Orlando*, gives no indication of a god-like, or even magical and mischievous interest in controlling the plot. All the indications of a fierce, poet-like control over every word and sentence—such as Woolf's changing the flowers Rezia arranges to the more specific roses at the proof stage so as to keep the association of the word "flowers" with Clarissa alone (Woolf 141)—lie not with an internal narrator but with the author. Nor is the narrator an Oz-like bumbler, pretending to control what is beyond his power. The very attribute "sententious" requires some gloss to demonstrate where Hoff hears such an obtrusion. Is the narrator of *Mrs. Dalloway* really sententious?

I kept reading Hoff's book because, as I work on an edition of *Mrs. Dalloway*, I am seeking every possible lead for allusions. The notion of *Alcestis* as a possible intertext, as well as the insistence on the strong presence of references to Demeter and Persephone, are but two of many promising references here. Many obvious allusions go almost unnoticed here; there is little discussion of the direct allusions either to *Cymbeline* or *Othello*. Amidst the promising leads are many more false ones. Septimus does not have a "horror of being fellated in bed by Sir William Bradshaw" (180) Nor does the backfiring car in the novel's opening episode "suggest an Aristophanic fart" (41). When Clarissa teases Peter that she is having a party "Which I shan't ask you to," it is not "an allusion to a very obscure Greek fragment, Theognis' little elegy 1207-8" (83). However, Hoff's ensuing list of other such equivocal invitations makes clear that Woolf participates in a trope here and a better-written annotation might explain that participation without making it sound as though Hoff has identified Woolf to be making a traceable allusion to an obscure fragment.

No summary can adequately account for my perplexity about this book. It represents an extraordinary amount of labor and erudition, but its form, its poor execution, and its staggering unevenness mean that it will be read by only a very few.

—Anne Fernald, *Fordham University*

Works Cited

Barthes, Roland. *S/Z*. (1970) Trans. Richard Miller. Preface by Richard Howard. New York: Noonday, 1974.

Euripides. *Alcestis*. Trans. Gilbert Murray. 1915. Kindle edition.

Woolf, Virginia. *Mrs. Dalloway*. 1925. Corrected page proofs. Lilly Library, Indiana University.

Wright, G. Patton. "The Raverat Proofs of Mrs. Dalloway." *Studies in Bibliography*. 39 (1986) 241-61.

Virginia Woolf, Modernity and History: Constellations with Walter Benjamin. Angeliki Spiropoulou (Basingstoke, England: Palgrave Macmillan, 2010) viii + 240 pp.

Walter Benjamin proposes a distinct revision of historiography in which historical events are conceived as a "numbered group of threads that represent the weft of the past as it feeds into the warp of the present" (qtd. in Spiropoulou 114). Centering on a metaphor in which disparate elements are woven together in the present, Benjamin suggests what he refers to elsewhere as "materialist history." Angeliki Spiropoulou's book, *Virginia Woolf, Modernity and History: Constellations with Walter Benjamin*, ties Benjamin's materialist history to Virginia Woolf's sense of a plural history, a "web of obscure lives interlocking with each other instead of a succession of great events and a procession of great men" (124). Spiropoulou's book asserts that Benjamin and Woolf, though unknown to each other, shared crucial insights and critiques of modernity through analogous challenges to prevalent notions of historiography and modernity. She draws together Benjamin's historical theses, especially as they are presented in his monumental, unfinished *Arcades Project*, with Woolf's novels, essays, diaries, and letters, making connections among the texts primarily by means of what Benjamin refers to as "constellations"; as Spiropoulou defines the term, a constellation is "the deliberate construction of the past in the present" (146). The *Arcades Project* is an intriguing work for the purpose of her discussion; it is an *Ur*-history of modernity fashioned out of the "different odds and ends of historical sources, literature, social theory, memoirs, social types and architecture of the period" (27). While Benjamin's historiographical project is to a large degree the theoretical model for the book, Spiropoulou uses Woolf's fictions as an interlocutor for such theories, and finds in them a "rough philosophy of history" that she reads in conjunction with Benjamin's philosophies.

The conjunction of Woolf's and Benjamin's approaches to history and modernity often yields interesting, unexpected connections between them, though Spiropoulou endeavors not to collapse the two author's views. The book's second and third chapters—"Modernity, Modernism and the Past," and "Theories of History, Models of Historiography"—offer an overview and genealogy of prior and contemporaneous treatments of modernity and history; her second chapter, which offers definitions and a narrative of historiography, establishes a theoretical backdrop against which Benjamin's and Woolf's theories are contrasted. In her third chapter, Spiropoulou demonstrates that the modernity of Woolf and Benjamin contain crucial paradigmatic shifts from prevalent views of modernity, especially in modernity's emphasis on novelty, originality, and of a past that "survives in the present" (90).

These foundational chapters are followed by topical ones that tend to hinge on a particular theme read through a work of fiction, such as the problematic relationship between the human and the inhuman as it is found in *To the Lighthouse*; here, she shows that nature is "always already entwined with human history" (103). Perhaps her most interesting chapter concerns *Orlando*, where she engages with Woolf's parodic history as a means to interrogate historical time and normative gender roles, and where she likens Orlando to Benjamin's "Angel of History" (91). In this way, *Orlando* itself, Spiropoulou argues, represents a kind of refutation of the prior historiographical methods that she outlines in her third chapter. Throughout the book, Spiropoulou places Benjamin and Woolf against notions of modernity and historiography that she identifies as problems, failures or illusions for theories of the modern. She argues that Benjamin and Woolf provide critiques of these views, in particular the myths and "phantasmagorias" of the era, especially the myth of progress, historical causality, and a "dead past," all of which, Spiropoulou claims, "perpetuate structures of oppression" (25). In addition to this critique of modernity, both authors oppose "traditional historiography," which Spiropoulou regards as a method of structuring history that bestows the power of history-making on the powerful, leaving aside art and the everyday (40). Against this kind of historiography, Benjamin's *Arcades Project*, composed of fragments of text assembled in associative constellations, demonstrates a way out of the positivism and post-Enlightenment rationalism that Spiropoulou claims were prevalent at the time. Instead of a "great men" historiography, Woolf's aim is to redeem and recapture the "ordinary day" as a reply to such traditional views.

While her reading of Woolf with Benjamin fruitfully reveals how Woolf herself engages with modernity's notions of history, Spiropoulou's reading of those views is predicated on a historical methodology that Woolf and Benjamin alike seem to critique. Her depictions of Woolf are continually fashioned against a backdrop of traditional, conventional views of historiography, but it is not always clear who is represented as holding such outmoded or illusory positions. Her argument centers on the familiar notion that Woolf and Benjamin "problematize" and "complicate" these incorrect views discussed in the early chapters of the book, but this type of argument seems to force Woolf and Benjamin into dynamic, even revolutionary, positions against an otherwise static (and, perforce, reductive) background, made up of a shifting cast of figures, particularly "male modernists" and traditional historicists. Woolf is likewise frequently referred to as a "female modernist," to whom Spiropoulou unfavorably compares male modernists like Joyce, Pound, and Eliot. Yet she seldom cites the latter group in her book, leaving critical commonplaces, such as Eliot's "Mythic Method" and the Viconian cycles in *Finnegans Wake* as stand-ins for those figures and their work. This strategy is all the more problematic, given the fact that Woolf and Benjamin, through Spiropoulou's reading, both protest against such simplifications and binaries in their own historiographical project. Spiropoulou makes a gender critique of male modernists and modernism as static, simplified figures that elides difference and undervalues the dynamism and debate within and among modernist authors, a debate in which Woolf herself participated. Another issue with such a critique of gender is Benjamin's uncertain status in relationship to the critique itself: isn't he a male modernist as well? Who, then, is a male modernist? What are the consequences for employing Benjamin as an interlocutor if a gender critique is essential to Spiropoulou's book? Furthermore, Woolf seems to stand alone in the female modernist category, as other female authors are seldom, if ever, discussed. The book would be richer if Woolf had been juxtaposed against Gertrude Stein, Katherine Mansfield or other female modernists.

These issues together result in many missed opportunities for the text to engage with modernists, male and female alike, in terms of their heterogeneous and diverse projects. In fact, these issues seem to arise from a methodology that tries to discern what is novel and original in Woolf at the expense of her contemporaries, a view that seems itself to participate in the same teleology that Spiropoulou challenges in her book.

These issues notwithstanding, Spiropoulou's book points to the many representations of time and history that Woolf employs, and there is great potential in the idea of a constellation as an organizational and theoretical principle. The book suggests that fiction can show authors like Woolf "doing" history as much as non-fiction "theorists" like Benjamin do. The merit of a "constellatory" approach is that it suggests a way out of the problems that Benjamin and Woolf seem to critique, though Spiropoulou does not always show how such an approach would apply, or how a constellation is different from a comparison between two felicitously like-minded authors. In fact, there seem to be few significant differences between Woolf's perspective and Benjamin's in the book, which makes grasping the concept of constellations as employed in her work elusive. However, the idea of Benjamin's constellations themselves, coupled with the ways that Spiropoulou shows them at work in Benjamin and Woolf, suggest an interesting (even novel) way of "doing" theory itself, one that collapses simple oppositions and sees past methods of historical linearity, like Benjamin's "beads of a rosary" (146). In this sense, the book seems to be valuable to Woolf scholars because of its proposed methodology, though it is useful as well for its focus on Woolf's relationship to history and to historians, past and present. *Virginia Woolf, Modernity and History* suggests a method of inquiry that, indeed, could inspire interesting interdisciplinary approaches among historians, philosophers, and literary theorists. Perhaps Spiropoulou points to a means of theorizing that would perform and embody Woolf's way of reconstructing the ordinary day, her desire to depict "common, obscure and outsider lives" by means of the "orts, scraps and fragments" found within her novels.

— Daniel W. Bang, *Fordham University*

Virginia Woolf and the Study of Nature. Christina Alt (Cambridge: Cambridge UP, 2010) ix + 229 pp.

As Christina Alt discusses in her introduction, critics such as Gillian Beer, Louise Westling, Elizabeth G. Lambert, Michael Whitworth, and Holly Henry have demonstrated Woolf's engagement with Victorian natural history, evolutionary theory, and early twentieth-century physics. Many other critics interpret Woolf's nature imagery in the Western symbolic tradition that can be traced back to the classical Greeks and the Bible. Alt both builds on and takes issue with these critics. She focuses on the early twentieth-century life sciences rather than physics or evolution and asserts that a "scientific frame of reference adds rigour and specificity" to analysis of nature imagery in Woolf's writing (5). Alt's central argument is that Woolf sensed a "shared outlook" between the sciences and arts of her day (2) and conceptualized the modernist creative process as analogous to the new approaches in the natural sciences of the early twentieth century while using analogies to Victorian taxonomy to represent limited and constricting modes of writing.

The first two chapters discuss the life sciences in the nineteenth and early twentieth centuries. Chapter one focuses on "the taxonomic tradition of natural history" and chapter two on the "modern life sciences" that "defined themselves against this tradition" (14). Thus, Alt writes a history of the biological sciences that mirrors the reaction of literary modernism against nineteenth-century realism; at stake in the debates concerning both science and literature were definition of the "reality" under observation, the proper goals of the artistic or scientific endeavor, and the most effective methodologies through which to pursue those goals. Alt bases her discussion on recent histories of science as well as science writing just prior to and contemporary to Woolf.

The dominant approach to the study of nature in nineteenth-century Britain was taxonomy. Collection of specimens, their identification and placement in the taxonomic system, and their preservation and arrangement in collections were the major activities of natural scientists both "serious and recreational" (19). According to Alt, the focus on inductive rather than deductive reasoning in British science, the lack of state financial support for science, the vast regions of the British empire ripe for collecting specimens, and the use of science to support religion all made Victorian natural history both slow to change and widespread in British culture. Promoted as a pious, rational, and morally uplifting pursuit for all social classes and both sexes, natural history was also seen as a moderating influence on the potentially radical interests and impulses of the working classes. Alt uses Woolf's memoirs and letters to show that the pursuit of natural history in the Stephen household followed the British mainstream: focused on specimen collection and identification, intended to educate and discipline the children, and supportive of social hierarchies as the Stephens set up a family "museum" and "entomological society."

By the beginning of the twentieth century, evolutionary theory and the rise of laboratory biology challenged the centrality of taxonomic natural history. The controversies instigated by Darwin's work, Alt explains, involved not only religion but also debates regarding inductive vs. deductive reasoning and the museum vs. the laboratory. Alt draws from recent histories of science the understanding that support for evolution "can best be viewed as part of a larger agenda of seeing secular, speculative biology centred in the laboratory triumph over the museum-based, theologically justified taxonomic cataloguing that had dominated the study of nature" (42). Concern for the preservation of endangered species and for the suffering of animals, expressed through the protection, anti-vivisection, and conservation movements, also played roles on both sides of this debate. The new biology became identified with modernity and "taxonomy and the new biology were consequently used by scientifically inclined authors such as H. G. Wells to represent the clash between the Victorian and the modern" (45).

The development of ethology and ecology also marked a change in focus and method. Rather than going into the field to kill insects, birds, animals, and plants and take them home to preserve and study, ethologists and ecologists observed living creatures in their natural environments in order to understand how they behave and how ecosystems (a new concept introduced at this time) function. This approach emphasized motion, interaction, process, and change rather than the insertion of species into a fixed, static definitional system. Alt points out that many early twentieth-century writers, such as Ezra Pound, Aldous Huxley, Wyndham Lewis, James Joyce, and even Rudyard Kipling, were interested in these new sciences. Thus Woolf is not singular in her interest in the new life sciences or her incorporation of them into her writing.

Throughout her book, Alt discusses Woolf's references to science and allusions to the work of science writers such as entomologist Jean-Henri Fabre; nature writer, amateur ethologist, and novelist W. H. Hudson; bird ethologist Julian Huxley; ecologist Charles Elton; and science popularizer J. Arthur Thomson. In the third and fourth chapters, however, Alt focuses most intently on analyzing Woolf's writing. Chapter three, "'To Pin Through the Body With a Name'," argues that Woolf uses natural history to critique the social class system, imperialism, militarism, and patriarchy and also critiques the ways that "taxonomic science was used to buttress the existing social order" (99). For example, in *Jacob's Room*, Woolf uses moth and butterfly collecting as an analogy for the civilization that "captures" and "sedates" Jacob who "emerges at last a simultaneous victim and representative of civilization" (97). That Jacob himself sugars for moths, kills specimens, and makes corrections in F.O. Morris's book (the oft-reprinted *A Natural History of British Moths* [1871] perhaps) suggests that he is both a victim and a perpetrator of a social order that promotes acquisitiveness, control, and war. Woolf also uses classification "as a metaphor for the construction of identity in society" (99), presenting naming as possessive and deadening while life itself escapes rigid classification. Finally, Woolf questions the epistemological validity of classification through consistent references throughout the novel to various characters' (as well as the narrator's) failed attempts to classify Jacob whose nature remains unresolved at the end of the novel.

In contrast, Alt argues, Woolf embraced the new methods and ideas of laboratory science, ethology, and ecology and used them to figure liberatory modes of thinking and interacting. Thus, botanist William Bankes is capable of unpossessive love and Lily Briscoe can trust him to be an impartial observer of her painting, while Mr. Ramsay, whose possessive love of his wife is destructive, is a categorical thinker (*TTL*); "Woolf suggests that while a taxonomising mind, intent only on the categorization of what it sees, might be expected to stifle creativity, a mind trained in the study of function is more inclined to seek to understand the purpose of a work of art than to judge it on the basis of pre-existing categories" (110). Similarly, Alt argues, in *A Room of One's Own* Woolf condemns taxonomy's "desire for domination through knowledge" through her characterization of

Professor von X rushing for his measuring rods to prove women's inferiority (124). Alt also offers an informative re-reading of Chloe and Olivia in *A Room* and the influence of Marie Carmichael Stopes. Not only does Chloe and Olivia's work in a laboratory connote modernity and women's advancement, Woolf rewrites (rather than references as other critics have argued) Stopes's novel *Love's Creation*. There is only one woman scientist in *Love's Creation*; Lillian Rullford eventually marries her male laboratory colleague and then dies in an accident, while the novel favors her more domestic, warm, and sensitive sister who eventually marries Lillian's widower and serves as his helpmeet and mother of his children. Stopes's novel thus does not challenge gender norms and does neutralize the revolutionary potential of the woman scientist. Woolf's imagined novel, in contrast, entertains the possibility that women could combine the roles of scientist, feminist, and mother and support each other in these roles. Yet, at the same time, *Love's Creation* critiques taxonomy as a power play and presents the new biology as full of creative potential, a contrast that Woolf echoes in *A Room*.

Alt suggests that the complex motivations of modern ecology, to understand and protect the subtle balance of nature yet also to control "pest" species (which Woolf discusses admiringly in her essay on Eleanor Ormerod's entomology research and promotion of pesticides ["Lives of the Obscure"]), raise interesting questions about possible internal contradictions in Woolf's work. Alt asserts that "*Three Guineas* is [. . .] at once pacifist in its message and combative in its tone, and the violence that it recommends takes scientific form" (144). Woolf compares militarism, patriarchy, fascism, and imperialism to insect pests and recommends their destruction through the analogy of pest control. On the other hand, Alt notes that the more sympathetic and socially progressive of her characters, such as Ralph Denham, Eleanor Pargiter, and Lucy Swithin, pursue bird watching, while the more violent or dominating characters, such as Giles Oliver and William Rodney, are interested in control and extermination of other species.

Alt concludes her book by drawing together the threads of her arguments about taxonomy and the modern life sciences to propose that Woolf uses ethology and ecology as analogies for the representation of life in fiction: "in place of a literary method focused on exhaustive description in the service of definitive classification, Woolf advocated acceptance of the fact that only fleeting glimpses of a moving subject were possible or, indeed, desirable" (168). Alt argues that in Woolf's revisions of "Mr. Bennett and Mrs. Brown" she reworked her analogies for the writing process and moved "away from a taxonomic aesthetic and towards an aesthetic of observation and protection" (180). This move is also an epistemological one in which the goal of fiction is not to capture and define reality but to record "fleeting glimpses of a life in motion" (180). This approach produces "an ecological rather than a taxonomic conception of self"

(182); Clarissa Dalloway's "self" consciousness is an example of this ecological view while Holmes and Bradshaw's classificatory approach is oppressive and destructive of life. In *The Waves*, Susan and Bernard's approaches to life and language exemplify the contrast between the collector and the observer. Yet at the same time, Bernard's alphabetized notebook of phrases shows he is tempted to collect and classify, while the real value of his creativity with words lies in his "inconclusive, provisional tales" (188). Alt ends with a discussion of Woolf's radio broadcast, "Craftsmanship," in which Woolf talks about words as living organisms. Woolf "depicts words as forming a community in an ecological sense" and as changing and evolving (189-190). The writer is "a witness to the life processes and behavior of living language" (190).

Virginia Woolf and the Study of Nature offers a clear and helpful history of early twentieth-century biological sciences in Britain and demonstrates the range and durability of Woolf's interest in science and her use of it throughout her career as an analogy for the representational process and the meaning-making of art. Alt convincingly models how knowledge of the content and discourses of the life sciences of Woolf's day leads to a fuller understanding of Woolf's imagery and frames of reference. Alt's analyses of Woolf's works, while not offering strikingly new interpretations, provide useful confirmation of and greater historical context for previous critics' feminist, socialist, ecocritical, and anti-imperialist readings. However, Alt's decision to distribute discussion of each of Woolf's works throughout the book's chapters, while enabling her to develop her narrative about science, means that the reader often is left without a clear understanding of how scientific allusions and analogies work in the structure of a particular novel or short story—how they fit in, or don't, with the rest of what is going on in the piece of fiction. In addition, greater engagement with both feminist science studies and ecocritical literary theory would, I think, have strengthened Alt's analyses as well as enabled her to develop a compelling argument for how her work has significance beyond Woolf studies and, conversely, how Woolf studies fits in the larger critical and theoretical landscape, so to speak. Nevertheless, Alt's book is a significant contribution to Woolf studies and well worth reading.

— Diana L. Swanson, *Northern Illinois University*

Virginia Woolf and the Politics of Language. Judith Allen (Edinburgh: Edinburgh UP, 2010) 133 pp. + x

> Already 'other,' hybrid, provisional and resistant to definition, the 'essayistic' both expresses and enacts the inextricable connection between its aesthetics and politics—and given its resistance to all constraints, authorities and totalizing systems, it is forever seeking freedom.
> —*Virginia Woolf and the Politics of Language*, 2

Judith Allen's *Virginia Woolf and the Politics of Language* is a thoughtful and provocative book which ranges widely across Virginia Woolf's work, paying particular attention to her essays and to her "essayistic" writings. Allen begins by arguing for the importance of Michel de Montaigne as an influence on Woolf's writing and for the centrality of essayistic thinking—and writing—to Woolf's work. At many points throughout her career, Woolf herself freely acknowledged her debt to Montaigne, and this premise alone would have been more than enough to fill the slight and eminently readable book that Allen has written. While there has been a welcome increase in attention to Woolf's essays in recent years, the hundreds of essays she wrote over the course of her career remain, with a few key exceptions (such as *A Room of One's Own*, *Three Guineas*, "Modern Fiction," and "Mr. Bennett and Mrs. Brown") largely unread in comparison with her novels, and the importance of the essayistic mode in her writing is still under-theorized and largely unrecognized by critics and common readers alike[1] Allen moves beyond a consideration of the essay form in Woolf's writing to considering the ways in which the essayistic mode permeates her writing more generally. In this regard, Allen's book is a timely and welcome addition to Woolf scholarship and to a growing body of work on the essay itself.

Yet in addition to offering incisive readings of Woolf's works, Allen pushes beyond the immediate parameters of this work to make bold and large-scale claims for the relevance of Woolf's ideas about language to post-9/11 politics and to the language in which those politics are presented to the public at large. Specifically, she is concerned with the ways in which language has been used and misused by the U.S. and British governments and the press (often in questionable collaboration with one another) over the last ten years, and she argues that Woolf's suspicion of language—and her sense of the importance of adopting an essayistic

[1] Woolf's essays have received increased attention over the last decade and a half, most notably in Elena Gualtieri's *Virginia Woolf's Essays: Sketching the Past* (New York: St. Martin's, 2000) and in Beth Carole Rosenberg and Jeanne Dubino's collection, *Virginia Woolf and the Essay* (New York: St. Martin's, 1997).

approach to both writing and reading—becomes increasingly relevant as one tries to navigate this problematic territory:

> Viewing our modern world, as the first decade of the twenty-first century comes to a close, I will focus on the relevance of Woolf's mode of writing, her ideas regarding language, and the importance of how we read that language. I will demonstrate how Woolf shows her readers the importance of critical thinking in a world where uncertainty reigns, where so-called democracies are insidiously dismantled, human rights are lost, coercive practices continue, dissent is silenced, and simply reading the 'words' placed before us has become a daunting task. (Allen 11-12)

This is a tall order, to be certain, and one that at times makes it feel as if Allen has the makings of at least two separate books here—one examining Woolf's use and understanding of the essayistic mode as formulated by Montaigne, one tracing the importance of that mode in a world where those using language are never operating on an equal playing field. Maintaining that "Montaigne's seminal question 'Que sais-je?'—expressing the rampant scepticism of the late sixteenth century, reverberates today, in the first decade of the twenty-first, at a time when we are, quite ironically, inundated with 'information'" (3), Allen proceeds to excavate the linguistic manipulations—subtle and explicit—undertaken by official providers of this "information." The book's unifying claim is that the essayistic approach to language endorsed by Woolf (and pioneered by Montaigne) offers a small but necessary stay against the kind of official "totalitarian" language that is designed to deceive or to shut down individual thought. This is plausible enough, to be certain, though I do wonder at points whether Allen hasn't misjudged the relative interest of the different aspects of her argument. In other words, while it is surely true that Woolf's understanding of the essayistic mode might be applied to contemporary misuses or abuses of language, or indeed, to many other historical and contemporary examples of such misuse, it is not nearly as interesting as Allen's own explication of that mode itself.

That Woolf's indictment of the "official," public language of her own time should remain relevant today is demoralizing, though perhaps hardly surprising. Allen—convincingly, if rather loosely—employs Woolf's suspicion of language and the manipulations it allows for to draw attention to the abuses of language that emerged and continue to emerge at every stage of post-9/11 politics. She is assuredly right to draw the connections she does, and her indictment of Bush- and post-Bush era government and media is both disturbing and regrettably well-founded. Her readings of Woolf are consistently original and engaging (and often leave one wishing that Allen did not move quite as quickly as she does from idea to idea). Her endorsement of the essayistic as the only viable tool with which to approach the vagaries of language and authority is, in my own case, preaching to the choir, but also a key assertion for those who are less familiar with the essay's history and lineage. I can only hope that other readers will not be so distracted by Allen's justifiable infuriation at the evidence she provides in her final chapters that they will miss the importance of this central claim.

Allen's book makes for a markedly slim volume—a little over a hundred pages, including notes and generous blank spaces between chapters. This is a refreshing length, to be certain, and conciseness is hardly so common in scholarly monographs that one wishes to complain of it. But here the reader often feels that Allen is leaving suggestive ideas and readings undeveloped, assuming a reader who will take her claims at face value, without extensive supporting evidence. In the case of her political claims this is assuredly the case. One has a hard time conjuring the academic reader who would dispute her argument in this regard. But in her readings, Woolf's texts are at many points given short shrift. For example, the reading of *A Room of One's Own* in Chapter 3 left me wishing fervently that Allen had spent more time unpacking claims such as the following:

> The narrator obviously over-emphasises the precision and exactitude of her fictionalising, in order to call even more attention to the problematic nature of factuality. By self-consciously calling attention to the strategy of fictionalising, Woolf is confronting her audience with the problematic nature of such dichotomising. (Allen 63)

Surely such an assertion is worth investigating at some length, yet it is followed by only two short summarizing paragraphs that close this chapter without further developing this provocative formulation.

Dividing her book into three parts, Allen focuses first on establishing the lineage from Woolf to Montaigne, next on laying out the premises of the skeptical essayistic approach to language, then, in her final section upon a foray into contemporary political discourse. Allen's foundational claim, that Woolf was influenced greatly by Montaigne and by the powers implicit in the essay, a type of writing which lends itself, notoriously, to the ability to see an issue from multiple sides and to resist totalitarian thinking—is clearly valid. Anyone who has spent time with Woolf's essays would be hard put to dispute this. Woolf herself declared Montaigne to be "the first of the moderns" and the direct lineage Allen establishes is unsurprising in this regard. One might then ask whether it is necessary to prove such a connection. Assuredly it is not (i.e., I know of no Woolf scholar who would deny the lineage); what is of value are the unexpected lines Allen draws in tracing this lineage. Because Allen's book is so brief (and both Woolf's and Montaigne's bodies of essayistic work so vast), the connections she makes may at times strike a reader who has not spent significant time with these works as slightly arbitrary, but this is ultimately insignificant. Her emphasis upon Woolf's fascination with the power of individual words—that they can assume multiple meanings, and that assertions or remarks that seem to the originator as clear as can be may not strike the reader in the same way the speaker intended—is similarly indisputable. One is reminded of a particularly resonant moment in *The Years* when, after a seemingly straightforward question is misinterpreted by her hard-of-hearing uncle, the well-meaning Peggy reflects that communication is more difficult than it appears, noting to herself that "(t)he steps from brain to brain must be cut very shallow if thought is to mount them" (*TY* 334).

In Part I "'Theorising' Reading, 'Theorising' Language," Allen examines Woolf and Montaigne, considering both as writers who are especially concerned with the powers and the slipperiness of language—and perhaps especially of particular words. The first of the two chapters that makes up this section examines Woolf's own literary relationship to Montaigne, as evidenced in both her public and her private writings. Here Allen also calls upon important scholarship on the essay by T.W. Adorno and Georg Lukács, as well as by Pater, Deleuze, and other, less well known critics such as Claire de Obaldia. The second chapter explores Woolf's essay/radio broadcast "Craftmanship," and goes on to investigate the importance of titles, and of changing titles (Woolf notoriously went through multiple titles for many of her works), to her writing.

In Part II of the book, "The Politics of Writing," Allen begins by reading *A Room of One's Own.* While her primary claim in Chapter 3, "The Rhetoric of Performance in *A Room of One's Own*," is a political one—i.e., that Woolf's formal choices in the work signal a resistance to final judgment and an endorsement of differing voices with clear political connotations, the most striking effect of her reading is to suggest that the implicit powers of individual words—and the fascinating, if often troubling and problematic, slippages that occur between writer or speaker and audience—are in and of themselves a topic worth extensive intellectual investigation. Chapter 4 examines the concept of "wildness," tracing its treatment by Montaigne in essays such as "On Cannibals" and exploring its appropriation by Woolf as a category of resistance that may be occupied by women who do not find a suitable place in the "civilized" sphere of public life.

Far the most daring claim Allen makes here—and the one about which she seems to care most—is unquestionably her assertion, in her third and final section, that Woolf's texts offer useful insight into reading today's politics and understanding (and refuting) the manipulations of language enacted by our politicians. Few English department members would argue the sentiment, and her evidence, while perhaps not as actually shocking as one feels it ought to be at points, is nonetheless disturbing and at times surprising in the sheer audacity with which misrepresentations are perpetuated. Chapter 5 focuses on Woolf's 1940 essay "Thoughts on Peace in an Air Raid," examining "the importance of dialogue, of all modes of 'conversation', as exemplified by Woolf's essayistic practices and the very process of reading" (11), while Chapter 6 turns to questions of patriotism and newspapers, in both Woolf's time and our own. At points the connections feel somewhat indirect—i.e., one wonders whether Allen might not just as easily have picked any historical or contemporary example of the misuse of language upon which to test Woolf's claims and the essayistic mode. No doubt Woolf would be suspicious of current misuses and abuses of language, as she was of those in her own time. And it is also true that the essayistic approach offers a viable alternative to such approaches. Yet what exactly Allen wishes to do with this claim, beyond underscoring the appalling nature of the misuses she cites, is unclear. Though perhaps this is sufficient.

— Randi Saloman, *Wake Forest University*

Work Cited

Woolf, Virginia. *The Years*. 1937. Orlando, FL: Harcourt, 2008.

The Passions of Modernism: Eliot, Yeats, Woolf, and Mann. Anthony Cuda (Columbia: U of South Carolina P, 2010) x + 248 pp.

Anthony Cuda's *The Passions of Modernism: Eliot, Yeats, Woolf, and Mann* gives a provocative critique of psychological and aesthetic passions in four major early twentieth-century writers while challenging the continued critical neglect of the role that the emotions and the passions play in animating the modernist project. As Cuda sees it, "the sentimental" is still so often regarded "as modernism's other" (17), while critical touchstones such as T. S. Eliot's maxim of "impersonality" and W. B. Yeats's theories of the "anti-self" are frequently mis-taken as proofs that "depersonalization" is modernism's primary emotive mode. Turning to William James, who describes the "'passivity of genius, how it is essentially instrumental and defenseless, moved, not moving'" (40), Cuda emphasizes that the *passive* "receptivity" of the writer to extrinsic passion and experience is at least as important as the passionate acts and activities of artistic production. In Cuda's view, that is, passion involves being a highly sensitive receiving agent for psychological, political, cultural, and aesthetic experience and being subject to and willing to submit to their provocative unrest.

Through the study Cuda convincingly proposes that rather than understanding "modern art" as "a compensatory response to threatening chaotic stimuli" (179), we ought to pay more heed to the fascination and *frisson* that modernists thematized in subjective, personal responses to passion's play. Eliot, Yeats, Woolf, and Mann, Cuda argues, all "deeply valued the destabilizations of passion and the intensities of affect and were frequently suspicious of the illusions of a 'stabilized,' autonomous self," while a "'closed' self is not merely an obstacle to artistic creativity but a psychological impossibility, a fantasy undercut at every step by the turbulent passions to which the self succumbs and upon which it depends for its vitality" (6).

In his Introduction Cuda usefully sets the stage for his critique by mapping the philosophical and literary histories of discourses about passion from Plato and Aristotle through eighteenth and nineteenth-century Romantic philosophers and poets to Victorian thinkers and early twentieth-century writers. Such delineations help Cuda to make some highly original arguments about the character and nature of modernist passions, where what he calls "passion scenes" involve "a sustained state of suffering or being moved" (32) while they symptomatize both internal and external pressures on the psyche, prompting the writerly subject to experience a kind of "possession" by or a "surrender" to "a motivating energy unknown" to him or her (8). Through the study, Cuda chooses emblematic "passion scenes" from each writer that illuminate and exemplify the unpredictabilities of passion in their work.

Beginning with two long chapters on T. S. Eliot, Cuda chooses the emblematic "passion scene" of the "patient etherized upon a table" from the opening lines of "The Love Song of J. Alfred Prufrock" to emphasize the recurrence in Eliot's oeuvre of half-somnolent states where there is no choice but to be prone to passion. Eliot had claimed that the etherized patient bears "'an exact nightmare correspondence to some spiritual terror,'" while Cuda notes that versions of this scene "[twist] and [turn] throughout his career, accompanied at each stage by dramatizations of possible responses to passion and the intense emotional upheavals that accompany them" (33). Continuing the work of overturning our notion of T. S. Eliot as the "impersonal" writer *par excellence*, paring his fingernails above and beyond his handiwork (to paraphrase James Joyce), Cuda stresses Eliot's "experiment with physical paralysis as a correlative to the traumatic affective states of helplessness and vulnerability" (33), observing that such passive forms of "paralysis" persist through to the early parts of *Four Quartets*, where we find a "'Hypnotised'" speaker in the "'warm haze'" and "'sultry light'"(47).

The book also contains an impressive amount of archival research which frees up Cuda to move past typically examined canonical texts to draw our attention to passionate experience articulated in letters, drafts, essays, manuscripts, lectures, and other little-discussed literary fragments. Indeed, at times Cuda even eschews debate on well-known canonical texts in favor of opening up provocative discussions on hitherto neglected materials: for instance, we find a fairly limited engagement with Eliot's most famous essays that refer to the emotions and the passions—"Tradition and the Individual Talent" and "Hamlet"—in favor of highlighting under-read pieces such as Eliot's 1941 introduction to his new selection of Kipling's poetry, *A Choice of Kipling's Verse* (56), Eliot's 1952 lecture, "Scylla and Charibdis" (58), and his 1953 lecture, *The Three Voices of Poetry* (57). In the process, Cuda exposes an Eliot who is familiar yet *familiarly strange*—an Eliot who was obsessed with approaching both the ennobling and the enfeebling passions, and alternately intrigued by the sublime and the macabre aspects of emotionality. While T. S. Eliot is "the central figure" of Cuda's study (6), Cuda also devotes two substantial chapters to Yeats, along with a chapter each on Woolf and Mann. In the process Cuda produces compelling readings of their passionate engagements while always keeping Eliot's poetics, criticism, and even personal connections to these other writers in the background of the analysis.

Cuda begins his short segment on Woolf by pointing to "her provocative meditation on illness and the human passions" in "On Being Ill" (1926), an essay she sent to T. S. Eliot—after some petitioning from him—for inclusion in the *Criterion*. "Woolf fires the first salvo of her mischievously earnest essay," Cuda remarks, "by declaring the need for a new language of sickness, one that will more adequately describe physical pain and discomfort, that will be as well suited to the raging storms of desire as to the lightning bolts of a migraine" (143). "On Being Ill" is a wonderful place to start his exploration of Woolf, and Cuda will go on to underscore that in Woolf's writing "passion cannot be confined to a single psychic sphere; it is neither temporary nor aberrant" (145). Cuda then places special emphasis on the sufferings and illuminations that Woolf explores in relation to episodes and periods of illness, focusing especially on the "passion scene" of ocular "wounding" that recurs in her work and that "thematizes passive suffering while itself seeming to be the product of an analogous imaginative passivity or compulsion" (151). Cuda convincingly argues that this motif is central to understanding the "storms" of passion that Woolf's characters sustain and that animate her creative project. Far from the disembodied, "intellectual" Woolf who still reigns in some circles, Cuda deftly exposes a Woolf who was so profoundly invested in valorizing the passions that she even "wonders whether this kind of sensuous, conscious passivity might be the only authentic mode of experiencing the self" (155). Again, Cuda's fascinating proposals do urgently needed revisionist work, breaking ground and laboring against received prejudices.

In the two long and delightful chapters devoted to Yeats, Cuda traces multiple "passion scenes" as examples of the "phantasmagorical shape-changers" that are "undoubtedly connected to the deluge of symbolic images that beset the visionary poet at the height of inspiration" (103). Cuda's principal efforts here are to show that "Contrary to the prevailing scholarly consensus [. . .] Yeats was fascinated by powerlessness, by the prospect of losing control entirely" (94). Cuda points to admissions of "powerlessness" both in Yeats's personal psychology—which Cuda calls an "abnormal restlessness"—and in Yeats's persistent flirtations with Celtic legend and occult practices. Cuda's proposals here stand as significant reappraisals of Yeats's aesthetic and personal aims as Cuda nimbly reads Yeats against Yeats, pitting, in effect, Yeats's "anti-self" in conflict with his will.

In the short section on Mann Cuda changes his method slightly to focus not so much on a recurring "passion scene" as on anxieties and allegories about passions and infectious diseases that are pervasive to *Death in Venice*, *The Magic Mountain*, and *Doctor Faustus*. Yet Cuda also wants to insist on finding a redemptive interpretation of Mann's figuration of the passions in his later works, where instead of a fearful stance toward the corruption and uncontrollabilities of unhealthy passions, we discover a "gradual recognition that the passions are not merely corruptive, destructive, or disruptive but that they may create, concentrate, and build anew" (168). Taken in conjunction with his readings on illness in Woolf, Cuda's reassessment of Mann re-opens urgent questions about the relationship of disease to creative processes.

Cuda's study offers many new and singular insights that will enrich our understanding both of individual texts as well as of the larger claims of literary modernism, while his book is filled with tantalizing glimpses of a major body of unpublished and neglected work. The work here should go a long way toward pushing at the boundaries of how we read modernist renderings of passion and emotion while generously opening up exciting avenues for further discussion and research.

— Gabrielle McIntire, *Queen's University*

Race And The Modernist Imagination. Urmila Seshagiri (Ithaca: Cornell U P, 2010) xv + 251 pp.

Race has been amply studied in a wide range of American and Atlantic modernisms, and critics have of course considered racial representation within the framework of British imperialism. Yet as Urmila Seshagiri notes in *Race and the Modernist Imagination*, the "constitutive role" of race as it shapes British modernism has received far less attention (6). Seshagiri argues persuasively that race operates not only as a theme in the work of authors from Oscar Wilde to Virginia Woolf, but also as a structuring aesthetic force. Grounded in fine close readings, Seshagiri's book at the same time surpasses previous studies in its range, which encompasses fin de siècle, popular, and modernist texts. It makes the most capacious case yet that the aesthetics of Anglo-British modernism are fundamentally shaped and inspired by a racial imagination.

Seshagiri sets up broad, historical terms for thinking about the operations of race in Britain. Resituating the later nineteenth-century culture of scientific racism in Britain, she argues that a capitalist and imperialist modernity put particular pressure on kinship filiation and cultural continuity, and that race became the vocabulary through which British culture managed these pressures. That is, as Seshagiri explains in her introduction and the early section of Part One, the forces of change and migration inherent to capitalist and instrumentalist western modernity tended to break up cultural identities. For the English, those changes register, she argues, as acute discontinuities, including breaks or confusions in racial "inheritances"; and they are likewise felt as a shift from a racially homogeneous to a racially heterogeneous nation. (This point, by the way, might explain some differences between modernism in Britain and modernisms in other places, including the already deeply "discontinuous" Americas.) Seshagiri's approach allows her to consider race not only within British colonial frameworks but also as it haunts a wide range of stories of wayward or unsettled *English* identities, or the dispersion of putatively English inheritances and communities.

Within this framework, Seshagiri argues that the increasingly mixed population in London and the felt threat of racial mixtures and invasions upset long-standing assumptions of English cultural homogeneity so profoundly, and precipitated such strident racist discourses, that these disruptions gave way to alternative visions and affiliations. Among experimental artists and authors, she persuasively suggests, this new incoherence allowed a rewriting of aesthetic inheritances, and it shaped narratives of differently imagined communities—of social relations based on affiliative, elective, or "unnatural" relations rather than filial or blood inheritance. Seshagiri thus proposes that "modern authors regarded race as the key to a daring new literary horizon that privileged suddenness, autonomy, abstraction, decenteredness, rupture, flux, irresolution, and nonlinearity" (9). Race "*gives form* to experimental modernism, its immanent patterns of continuity and discontinuity perfectly suited for shaping anew the literary and cultural plots of Englishness" (9, emphasis in original). This analytical framework allows Seshagiri to read Wilde's *The Picture of Dorian Gray* next to Sax Rohmer's serial Fu Manchu stories next to Woolf's *To the Lighthouse*, just to name a few of her texts.

Seshagiri organizes this range of materials into a study with three parts. Part One turns to Wilde, Conrad, and Rohmer in order to establish the far-flung, defining coordinates of race's expression in experimental turn-of-the-century fiction. In beginning with Wilde's text and focusing in an entirely fresh way on the racialized encounters that catalyze Dorian Gray's spiral into decadence, Seshagiri is able to make full sense of this proto-modernist narrative's pre-figuration of the underlying racial logic of modernism. She closely establishes the relation between the milieu of racial mixing or racially charged encounters (for instance in London opium dens) and the disjunctive, non-essentialist, performative, and aestheticized self of modernity. Moving from Wilde to Conrad's *Heart of Darkness*, which is of course more typically read for its racial themes, Seshagiri reveals a comparable investment in racial alterity as a catalyst for modern aesthetic identities and projects. Strikingly, as Seshagiri shows, both stories trace the fall of an Anglo-British man through racialized sexual encounters and both position a painting as the central sign of this racial adventurism and ruin, indicating that race drives a modern aesthetic economy as well as a political one. Although their protagonists die ignominious, ungentlemanly (un-English) deaths, both texts also ambivalently celebrate these racial adventurers, casting those around Kurtz and Gray as naïve or blind essentialists who are unable to take the measure of the boundary-crossing and "artful" powers of these protagonists.

In the light of this pairing, it is possible to see what Seshagiri shows us next: that Sax Rohmer's wildly popular tales of a "yellow peril" (embodied in the evil Dr. Fu Manchu) dramatize an unsettlingly similar configuration wherein modernity gives rise to a "racial genius" whose boundary-crossing, however, threatens Englishness at its core. In this case, an innocent, parochial Englishman is the narrator—a far cry from Marlowe—so that the tales have a more explicitly racist thrust. Yet the underlying matrix is surprisingly similar: in all, racial trespassing raises new perspectives and thus implicitly parochializes the English self. Here the most trespassing racial figure is also the most cosmopolitan modern figure, for Fu Manchu has, for instance, mastered the urban spaces and technologies of global and British modernity. Formally, as Seshagiri also points out, the continual deferral of a triumphant (Anglo-Saxon) closure in Rohmer's serial structure also creates a kinship between Rohmer's texts and the indeterminacies of closure in

Wilde, Conrad, and other modernists. That is, all of these texts leave English readers in a state of uncertainty about who the protagonists are, racially, and who or what controls that identity. This last claim helps to justify Seshagiri's gathering of authors as different as Rohmer, Wilde, and Conrad under the rubric of modernism. Whether or not readers accept this broadening of the parameters of modernism, such a cluster productively contributes to ongoing conversations about those parameters.

Having set up this enlarged constellation of early or proto-modernists, in Part Two Seshagiri turns to the more familiar terrain of Wyndham Lewis and *BLAST*. Yet here too she draws our attention to the less avant-garde texts in the first published issue of *BLAST*—the stories of Rebecca West and Ford Madox Ford, two figures who typically appear only on the margins of discussions of modernism, perhaps because of their apparently limited or quieter experiments in form. Seshagiri uncovers the racial logic of their inclusion in this avant-garde production. Reading West's contribution to the issue ("Indissoluble Matrimony") within the frame of the racialized, transgressive performances at the ultra-modernist cabaret, the Cave of the Golden Calf, she makes fresh sense of the little-discussed mixed-race couple in the story. Some readers might wonder if inclusion in *BLAST* of the West and Ford stories automatically makes these texts "avant-garde," as Seshagiri sometimes calls them, so again this study usefully, if implicitly, raises the question of what defines modernism or the avant-garde.

Seshagiri closes Part Two with a reading of Katherine Mansfield's story "Je Ne Parle Pas Français," interpreting it as a critique of the avant-garde's practice of racial fetishization. She attributes to Mansfield a full critical distance from the racial exoticism represented through the would be avant-garde artist-narrator of the story. While this reader senses less critical distance, Seshagiri's argument is valuable insofar as it reminds us once again that "so much depends on distance," as Woolf's Lily Briscoe remarks. That is, Seshagiri's arguments call our attention back to the important if unanswerable question of an author's critical distance from (or distance-collapsing investment in) her materials, as evinced in forms and angles of narration; and this attention in turn may lead to reconsideration of modernism's characteristic turn toward narrative indeterminacy. In what ways is this narrative indeterminacy an evasion of racial critique? In what ways is it a wise undercutting of racial essences? And in what ways does it render a highly unstable mixture of contingent racial affiliations? Seshagiri's study implies that all three of these motives are in play and invites further dialogue on the question.

In Part Three, after having built her supple argument about race in the Anglo-British modernist imagination, Seshagiri shrewdly turns to Virginia Woolf, probably the most discussed author in the field of British modernism. She can now demonstrate more fully how Woolf's work shares with these others a founding concern with the troubled matrix of art, Englishness, and otherness. Critics have discussed Woolf's representations of race within the context of her attitudes toward empire, but Seshagiri's framework allows her to go further. She first of all offers a wonderfully incisive reading of *To the Lighthouse* in the context of London's avant-garde visual artists and of theorists such as Roger Fry. Revealing the degree to which Woolf's style and her creation of Lily Briscoe, the artist with Chinese eyes, reshape this avant-garde primitivism, she concludes that this novel "transforms an essentializing vision of nonwhite racial identity into an *anti-essentialist* model of English selfhood" (155, emphasis in original). With similar pointedness, Seshagiri reads Woolf's next novel, *Orlando*, against the ambivalently racialized travel narrative of Vita Sackville-West, *Passenger to Teheran*, supplementing criticism on the familiar lesbian connection between the two women with attention to the racial imaginary that Seshagiri argues they share. In *Orlando*, Seshagiri sees Woolf moving toward a more triumphal embrace of imperial Englishness. Some readers may sense more sardonic irony in Woolf's fetishization of Englishness in *Orlando* than Seshagiri allows (again there arises the question of narrative distance), yet the possible point of debate only indicates the ways in which this reading promises to catalyze productive dialogue about Woolf, race, and modernism.

Seshagiri's study thus establishes that the modernist Anglo-British imagination is indeed a racial imagination. Not simply scanning for racism or racial blind spots, she instead reveals the myriad ways that these writers "carve out abundant textual space for multiple negotiations of racial difference" even as they simultaneously, and problematically, "render the terms of art inseparable from the terms of race" (167, 192). She thus sharpens our ability to see how these modernists negotiated their ways through the charged racial fields of the early twentieth century and, with varying effects and uncertain intentions, made art within that field. Timed perfectly to crown a decade of more limited studies of race in British modernism, *Race and the Modernist Imagination* meanwhile confirms the need to retain race as a key term in ongoing studies of class, sexuality, empire, and transnationalism in modernism.

— Laura Doyle, *University of Massachusetts-Amherst*

Notes on Contributors

Lisa Angelella is a recent graduate of the University of Iowa, where her dissertation, "Alimentary Modernism," focused on the phenomenology of food and eating in transatlantic modernist novels. She is currently a Writing Fellow at the University of Houston.

Isaac Gewirtz has served as Curator of the New York Public Library's Henry W. and Albert A. Berg Collection of English and American Literature since September 2000. He received a Master's degree in Library Service and a Ph.D. in Early Modern History from Columbia University. He has curated numerous exhibitions, including, at the New York Public Library, Victorians, Moderns, and Beats; Passion's Discipline: A History of the Sonnet in the British Isles and America; "I am With You": Walt Whiman's Leaves of Grass, 1855-2005, with an accompanying volume of the same title; and Beatific Souls: Jack Kerouac's On the Road, 1957-2007, accompanied by a volume of the same title, and a volume that also emerged out of the exhibition, Kerouac At Bat: Fantasy Sports and the King of the Beats (2009). In September 2010, he co-curated an exhibition at the Morgan Museum and Library entitled Mark Twain: A Skeptic's Progress, which was accompanied a by a volume of the same title.

Julia Kuehn is Associate Professor of English at the University of Hong Kong. Her research interests lie in nineteenth and early twentieth century literature and culture, with particular focus on popular and travel writing. She is currently working on a monograph on representations of the exotic in canonical and popular women's writing published between 1880 and 1920.

Amy C. Smith is Assistant Professor of English at Lamar University where she teaches courses on world literature, Asian literature, British literature and philosophy. She is currently completing a book on Virginia Woolf's political uses of myth to be published by Northwestern University Press, and co-editing, with Isabel Mª Andrés Cuevas, the 2012 issue of *Virginia Woolf Miscellany*. She previously served as editor of *Crossings: A Counter-Disciplinary Journal,* and has published on Woolf, Iris Murdoch and the relation of art and ethics.

David Wanczyk is the Director of Special Programs and an Adjunct Professor of English at Ohio University. He has his PhD from Ohio University, where he studied creative nonfiction and nineteenth and twentieth century British Literature. He has presented conference papers on a range of British authors, including Elizabeth Inchbald, George Eliot, Amy Levy, and John Fowles. His work has been published in *Brevity*, *The Bellingham Review*, and *The New York Quarterly*. A graduate of the College of the Holy Cross, he lives in Athens, Ohio with his wife, Megan.

Elizabeth Wright is Senior Lecturer in English and European Literature at Bath Spa University. She is author of several articles and reviews on the work of Virginia Woolf and Henrik Ibsen and has recently adapted Susan Sellers' *Vanessa and Virginia* for the stage. She is currently writing a short biography of Woolf for Hesperus and a monograph connecting Woolf's life and work to theatre.

Policy

Woolf
Studies
Annual invites articles on the work and life of Virginia Woolf and her milieu. The *Annual* intends to represent the breadth and eclecticism of critical approaches to Woolf, and particularly welcomes new perspectives and contexts of inquiry. Articles discussing relations between Woolf and other writers and artists are also welcome.

Articles are sent for review anonymously to a member of the Editorial Board and at least one other reader. Manuscripts should not be under consideration elsewhere or have been previously published. It is strongly advised that those submitting work to *WSA* be familiar with the journal's content. Among criteria on which evaluation of submissions depends are whether an article demonstrates familiarity with scholarship already published in the field, whether the article is written clearly and effectively, and whether it makes a genuine contribution to Woolf studies.

Preparation of Copy

1. Articles are typically between 25 and 30 pages, and do not exceed 8000 words. Inquiries about significantly shorter or longer submissions should be sent to the Editor at woolfstudiesannual@gmail.com.

2. A separate page should include the article's title, author's name, address, telephone & fax numbers, and e-mail address. The author's name and identifying references should not appear on the manuscript to preserve anonymity for our readers.

3. All submissions must include an abstract of no more than 250 words.

4. Manuscripts should be prepared according to most recent MLA style.

5. Submissions may be sent *either* by email to woolfstudiesannual@gmail.com *or* by mail to Mark Hussey, English Dept., Pace University, One Pace Plaza, New York NY 10038. For mailed submissions, please send **three** copies of the article and abstract.

6. Authors of accepted manuscripts are responsible for any necessary permissions fees and for securing any necessary permissions.

All editorial, review, and advertising inquiries should be addressed to woolfstudiesannual@gmail.com.

Inquiries concerning orders should be addressed to PaceUP@pace.edu.

Other Woolf titles available:

"The Hours": The British Museum Manuscript of Mrs. Dalloway, transcribed and edited by Helen M. Wussow (paper 2010).

Virginia Woolf, Jacob's Room: *The Holograph Draft.* Transcribed and edited by Edward L. Bishop (paper 2010)

Women in the Milieu of Leonard and Virginia Woolf: Peace, Politics and Education Ed. Wayne K. Chapman and Janet M. Manson (1998)

Virginia Woolf and Trauma: Embodied Texts Ed. Suzette Henke & David Eberly (2007)

Woolf Across Cultures Ed. Natalya Reinhold (2004)

Woolf Studies Annual 5 (1999)

Woolf Studies Annual 6 (2000): The *Three Guineas* Correspondence, edited by Anna Snaith

Woolf Studies Annual 7 (2001)

Woolf Studies Annual 8 (2002): The Fawcett Library Correspondence, edited by Merry Pawlowski

Woolf Studies Annual 9 (2003): *Virginia Woolf and Literary History Part 1*, edited by Jane Lilienfeld, Jeffrey Oxford, and Lisa Low

Woolf Studies Annual 10 (2004): *Virginia Woolf and Literary History Part 2,* edited by Jane Lilienfeld, Jeffrey Oxford, and Lisa Low

Woolf Studies Annual 11 (2005) - *Woolf Studies Annual 16* (2010)

Virginia Woolf and Communities: Selected Papers from the Eighth Annual Conference on Virginia Woolf edited by Jeanette McVicker and Laura Davis

Virginia Woolf Turning the Centuries: Selected Papers from the Ninth

Annual Conference on Virginia Woolf edited by Ann Ardis and Bonnie Kime Scott

Virginia Woolf Out of Bounds: Selected Papers from the Tenth Annual

Conference on Virginia Woolf edited by Jessica Berman and Jane Goldman

www.ingramcontent.com/pod-product-compliance
Lightning Source LLC
Chambersburg PA
CBHW070517100726
47907CB00004B/868

9781935625056